THE PENINSULAR CAMPAIGN.

Ballantyne Press
BALLANTYNE, HANSON AND CO.
EDINBURGH AND LONDON

A NARRATIVE

OF THE

PENINSULAR CAMPAIGN

1807—1814

Its Battles and Sieges

ABRIDGED FROM "THE HISTORY OF THE WAR IN THE PENINSULA"
BY LIEUT.-GENERAL SIR W. F. P. NAPIER, K.C.B.

BY

WILLIAM T. DOBSON

WITH TEN ILLUSTRATIONS IN PERMANENT PHOTOGRAPHY

LONDON
BICKERS & SON, LEICESTER SQUARE
1889

PREFACE.

OLONEL William Francis Patrick Napier, C.B., author of the "History of the War in the Peninsula," the work which is here epitomised, was born in 1785, and entered the army at the early age of fifteen. Taking part in the expedition to Copenhagen in 1807, in the following year the young soldier was sent to Spain, where he served during the whole of the Peninsular War, in which he was several times wounded. For some years he was lieutenant-governor of Guernsey, rose to the rank of major-general in 1841, and was created K.C.B. in 1848. Colonel Napier's reputation, however, rests less on his military career than on his writings, which are all characterised by eloquence and strength of thought, while his marked enthusiasm and strong national feeling were never allowed to interfere with accurate and impartial statement of historical facts, and these features have imparted a life-like and graphic power to the descriptions in his narrative of the Peninsular War, which has ever been considered the most important of all his works, and also the most valuable and most reliable record of the events to which it refers.

vi PREFACE.

Attached to the 43rd regiment all through the war, Colonel Napier was an eye-witness to and an actor in many of the transactions which he relates regarding the struggle for independence which devastated the Peninsula for six years, and having also the advantage of a wide acquaintance with many distinguished officers who took part in these transactions, was thus enabled to correct and supplement his own personal knowledge with their recollections and opinions. Ample testimony has been borne to the accuracy of Colonel Napier's statements, and to the diligence and acuteness with which he collected his materials.

A masterpiece of detailed military history, passages from Napier's "War in the Peninsula" are said to have been recounted round the watch-fires and told in the trenches before Sebastopol, and never without warming the soldier's heart, firing his mind, and nerving his arm.

Most of the varied opinions, military observations, and statistical details are excluded from the present work, the chief object aimed at being to give only the principal events in the mighty stream of battle controlled by Wellington, which, bearing the glory of Britain in its course, burst the barriers of the Pyrenees, and left deep traces of its fury on the soil of France.

CONTENTS.

CHAP.		PAGE
I.	FIRST CAMPAIGN IN PORTUGAL—ROLICA—VIMIERO	1
II.	SIR JOHN MOORE — RETREAT TO CORUNA — BATTLE OF CORUNA	19
III.	THE FRENCH SIEGE OF ZARAGOZA	43
IV.	GRIJON—PASSAGE OF THE DOURO	59
V.	CAMPAIGN OF TALAVERA	76
VI.	CIUDAD RODRIGO—THE COA — ALMEIDA—BUSACO — TORRES VEDRAS	96
VII.	SABUGAL—FUENTES ONORO—ALMEIDA—ALBUERA—BADAJOS	116
VIII.	ELBODON—ALDEA DE PONTE—CAPTURE OF CIUDAD RODRIGO	143
IX.	SIEGE OF BADAJOZ—CAPTAIN GRANT	158
X.	ALMAREZ—THE FORTS OF SALAMANCA	185
XI.	BATTLE OF SALAMANCA—SIEGE OF BURGOS	201
XII.	BATTLE OF VITTORIA—FIRST SIEGE OF SAN SEBASTIAN	225
XIII.	BATTLES OF THE PYRENEES	246
XIV.	SAN SEBASTIAN—SAN MARCIAL—VERA	273
XV.	PASSAGE OF THE BIDASSOA—VERA—FALL OF PAMPELUNA	290
XVI.	BATTLE OF THE NIVELLE	307
XVII.	BATTLES IN FRONT OF BAYONNE	322
XVIII.	PASSAGE OF THE GAVES—GARRIS—THE ADOUR	346
XIX.	ORTHES—AIRE—BORDEAUX	365
XX.	VIC BIGORRE—TARBES—TOULOUSE—BAYONNE	383

LIST OF ILLUSTRATIONS.

LANDING OF THE BRITISH ARMY AT MONDEGO BAY *Frontispiece*

	PAGE
BATTLE OF VIMIERO	13
PASSAGE OF THE DOURO	59
BATTLE OF TALAVERA	86
BATTLE OF BUSACO	106
SIEGE OF BADAJOS	158
BATTLE OF SALAMANCA	200
BATTLE OF VITTORIA	228
PORT OF BAYONNE	323
PORT OF BORDEAUX	365
MAP OF SPAIN AND PORTUGAL	408

THE PENINSULAR CAMPAIGN.

CHAPTER I.

FIRST CAMPAIGN IN PORTUGAL.

OWING to the scandalous and degrading dissensions prevalent between rival parties in Spain about the beginning of this century, Napoleon Bonaparte hoped to find means of ultimately subjugating the whole peninsula of Spain and Portugal to his yoke, —and this was neither a recent nor a secret project—as he had already overawed the greater part of the Continent. In the earlier years of Napoleon's career, the courts of Madrid and Lisbon had joined, with apparent cordiality, in the general league of European nations against the propaganda of the doctrines of the French Revolution; but the imbecile King Charles of Spain, alarmed at the progress which the victorious troops of France were making, hastened to put an end to a desultory and disastrous war by a more disgraceful peace in a treaty at Basle in 1795, this treaty being followed soon after by a defensive and offensive league, concluded at St. Ildefonso. From this time onwards, Spain had obsequiously obeyed the commands of Napoleon, and placed her resources at his disposal; the flower of her army had fought in his Polish campaign, and many of their number had found a bloody grave amid the snows of Eylau, to serve the purposes of his selfish ambition. Britain alone, of all the European nations, continued throughout to maintain an invincible hostility against the despotism which had now overspread the rest of Europe, crushing with her fleets, wherever they met with it, the naval strength of her enemy, and the ships of Spain had recently shared with those of France in the total defeat inflicted by Nelson at Trafalgar. Rendered thus safe within her own borders from assaults by the destruction of every fleet but her own, Britain was relentless in her determination to reduce Napoleon's intolerable power; but great as her strength was, she had as yet taken little effective part in the war elsewhere than at sea. If the short campaign in Egypt, where General Abercrombie had the glory of first leading British soldiers to victory over the self-styled invincibles of Napoleon, and the brilliant affair of Maida, are excepted, the whole period from 1793 down to the beginning of the Peninsular War, presents no record of deeds adding to the military renown of Britain. Her efforts hitherto had been, as it were, merely defensive, and her armies either rested idly on her own shores, or were scattered in detachments among her colonies, being only occasionally called upon to bear a part in some petty expedition, generally as unprofitable as the means were insignificant and inadequate.

The extreme subserviency of Spain failed to conciliate the rapacious despot, and, in furtherance of his design to add the Peninsula to his dominions, Napoleon asserted that the frontier of France on the Spanish side required to be thoroughly assured, and this could only be done by placing a prince of his own choosing on the throne of Spain. In complete disregard of national rights, and without even the decency of a pretext of quarrel, he overran the country with his soldiers. The Prince-Regent of Portugal, after having temporised so far as to assume a hostile attitude towards her ancient ally and friend Britain, and having even sought to conciliate France by confiscating the property of English citizens resident in the country, retired with his court and family to his provinces in Brazil, there to wait till the advent of happier times; while the King of Spain was compelled to resign his crown, which Napoleon placed upon the head of his brother Joseph, thus rendering the Peninsula a mere appendage to France. Napoleon lived to acknowledge that the seizure of the country and the gift of its crown to his brother were fatal mistakes. An empire founded as Napoleon's had been could have no secure foundation, and one serious error in policy might easily provoke a storm which all the power and skill of its head could not repress; and such an example was now furnished by the Emperor of the French. At a time when he had the prospect of again being engaged in deadly strife with Northern Europe, Napoleon made the Spaniards his enemies, and prepared for his most persistent foe, the British Government, an advantageous field to fight out a quarrel which promised to have no termination but the ruin of one or other of the combatants.

Both Spain and Portugal offered what resistance they could by continuous insurrectionary movements, but these availed little against the hosts of French troops poured into the country. The contest, however, was soon to enter upon a new phase. The threat of invasion of England by Napoleon, followed up as it was by the assemblage of large bodies of troops and of transports along the coasts of France in preparation for a descent upon the shores of Britain, had infused a military spirit into the British people to which they had long been strangers, and this military spirit the Government of the day soon turned to account by giving every encouragement to the enrolment of volunteers, who, along with the militia, proved invaluable nurseries for the line. The hostility of Britain having hitherto been chiefly manifested at sea, and by contributions of money to the military powers opposed to France, she now at length resolved to take a more prominent share in the strife, and the Peninsula became the chosen scene of operations. Though possessing by the beginning of January 1808 a regular army under the British standard of nearly 300,000 men of all arms, exclusive of foreign mercenaries, her earliest efforts were on a moderate scale. A little army of 10,000 men was landed at Mondego Bay in Portugal, under the command of Sir Arthur Wellesley, who was destined after a few years of arduous war to banish the French from the Peninsula, and to gain a military reputation equal to, if not exceeding, that of Napoleon himself.

Without serious difficulty Portugal was wrested from the invaders, and victory almost continually followed upon the efforts of the Allies. The first successful conflict took place at Roliça, which, considering the small number actually engaged, was one of the most sanguinary conflicts in modern warfare, and this was almost immediately followed by the more decisive victory of the British arms at Vimiero. These early successes in the first Peninsular campaign proved the truth of the opinion Sir Arthur Wellesley had formed, that the thin red line of British soldiers could withstand the terrible columns by which the French troops generally cleft their way through all that ventured to oppose them; and from Vimiero onwards to Waterloo the thin line of Britain was able to throw back with great slaughter the massed columns of France.

The British army landed at Mondego Bay in Portugal in the beginning of August 1808, and Sir Arthur Wellesley at once repaired to Montemor Velho to confer with Don Bernardim Freire, the Portuguese commander-in-chief. The latter proposed that the troops of the two nations should relinquish all communication with the coast, and throwing themselves into the heart of Beira, commence an offensive campaign; he promised ample stores of provisions; but Sir Arthur having already discovered the weakness of the insurrection, placed no reliance on those promises. He supplied Freire with 5000 stand of arms and ammunition, but refused to separate from his ships; and seeing clearly that the insurgents were unable to give any real assistance, he resolved to act with reference to the probability of their deserting him in danger. The Portuguese general, disappointed at this refusal, reluctantly consented to join the British army, but he pressed Sir Arthur to hasten to Leria, lest a large magazine, filled, as he affirmed, with provisions for the use of the British army, should fall into the enemy's hands. After this the two generals separated, and the necessary preparations for a march being completed, the advanced guard of the English army quitted the banks of the Mondego on the 9th, taking the road to Leria. On the 10th Sir Arthur Wellesley followed with the main body, and thus commenced the

First Campaign in Portugal.

Sir Arthur's plan embraced these principal objects :—To hold on by the sea-coast, as well for the sake of his supplies as to avoid the drain upon his weak army; to keep his troops in a mass, that he might strike an important blow; and to strike that blow as near

Lisbon as possible, that the affairs of Portugal might be quickly brought to a crisis. He possessed very good military surveys of the ground in the immediate neighbourhood of Lisbon, and he was anxious to carry on his operations in a part of the country where he could avail himself of this resource; but the utter inexperience of his commissariat staff and the want of cavalry rendered his movements slow, and obliged him to be extremely circumspect.

Marshal Junot (Duke of Abrantes), who was at this time in Lisbon in command of the French forces in Portugal, no sooner heard of the advance of the British than he dispatched a corps under General Loison to form a junction with General De Laborde near Leria, but the British general's first movement cut the line of communication between the two French generals, and obliged Laborde to risk an action.

As the hostile troops approached each other, the Portuguese chiefs became alarmed; notwithstanding the confident language of their public manifestos and the bombastic style of their conversation, an internal conviction that a French army was invincible pervaded all ranks of the patriots. The leaders, aware of their own deficiency, and incredulous of the courage of the English soldiers, dreaded the being committed in a decisive contest, because a defeat (which they expected) would deprive them of all hope to make terms with the victors, whereas by keeping 5000 or 6000 men together, they could at any time secure themselves by a capitulation. Sir Arthur Wellesley appealed to the honour and patriotism of Freire, and warmly admonished him that he was going to forfeit all pretension to either by permitting the British army to fight without his assistance; but this argument had no effect upon Don Bernardim. He parried the imputations against his spirit and zeal by pretending that his intention was to operate independently on the line of the Tagus; and after some further discussion, Sir Arthur, as a last effort, changed his tone of rebuke to one of conciliation, and recommended to him not to risk his troops by an isolated march, but to keep in the rear of the British, and wait for the result of the first battle. This advice was so agreeable to Freire, that, at the solicitation of Colonel Trant, a military agent, he consented to leave 1400 infantry and 250 cavalry under the immediate command of the English general.

The defection of the native force was a serious evil. It shed an injurious moral influence, and deprived Sir Arthur of the aid of troops whose means of gaining intelligence and whose local knowledge might have compensated for his want of cavalry. Nevertheless, continuing his own march, his advanced guard entered Caldas the 15th, and that day also Junot reluctantly quitted Lisbon, with a reserve composed of 2000 infantry, 600 cavalry, and 10 pieces of artillery, carrying with him his grand parc of ammunition, and a military chest containing £40,000. General Travot was left at Lisbon with above 7000 men, of which number two battalions were formed of stragglers and convalescents. He occupied both sides of the Tagus, distributing 2000 men in Palmela, the Bugio fort, and on the heights of Almada, in order to protect the shipping from the insurgents of the Alemtejo, who, under the orders of the Monteiro Mor, were gathering at Setuval. A thousand French he kept on board the vessels of war, to guard the Spanish prisoners and the spare powder; with 2400 he garrisoned the citadel and supported the police. A thousand were distributed in the forts of Belem, St. Julians, Cascaes, and Ericeia (the last-named place is situated to the northward of the rock of Lisbon, and commands a small harbour a few miles west of Mafra), and a thousand were at Santarem, protecting a large depôt of stores; thus nearly one half of the French army was by Junot's combinations rendered inactive, and those in the field were divided into three parts, without any certain point of junction in advance, yet each too weak singly to sustain an action. The Duke of Abrantes seemed to forget that he was merely the chief of an advanced corps, whose safety depended upon activity and concentration.

The French reserve was transported to Villa Franca by water, from whence it was to march to Otta; but the rope ferryboat of Saccavem being removed by the natives, it cost twenty-four hours to throw a bridge across the creek at that place. On the 17th the troops were on their march, when Junot hastily recalled them to Villa Franca. This retrograde movement was occasioned by a report that the English had landed near the capital. When the falsehood of this rumour became known, the reserve resumed the road to Otta under the command of General Thiebault, Junot himself pushing forward to Alcoentre, where he found

Loison, and assumed the personal direction of that general's division.

During this time, Sir Arthur Wellesley was pressing Laborde, whose situation was becoming truly embarrassing. Loison was at Alcoentre, and the reserve was at Villa Franca; that is, one and two marches distant from Roliça. If he retired upon Torres Vedras, his communication with Loison would be lost. To fall back on Montachique was to expose the line of Torres Vedras and Mafra. To march upon Alcoentre and unite with Loison was to open the shortest road to Lisbon (that of Montachique) for the British army; and to remain at Roliça, it was necessary to fight three times his own force. Animated, however, by the danger, encouraged by the local advantages of his position, and justly confident in his own talents, Laborde resolved to abide his enemy's assault, in the feeble hope that Loison might arrive during the action.

Roliça.

Sir Arthur Wellesley attacked upon the 17th August. Early in the morning of that day, a dense mass, consisting of 13,480 infantry, 470 cavalry, and 18 guns, issued from Obidos, and soon afterwards broke into three distinct columns of battle. The left, commanded by Lieutenant-General Ferguson, was composed of his own and Major-General Bowe's brigades of infantry, reinforced by 250 riflemen, 40 cavalry, and 6 guns, forming a total of 4900 combatants. They marched by the crests of the hills adjoining the Sierra de Baragueda, being destined to turn the right flank of Laborde's position, and to oppose the efforts of Loison, if that general should appear during the action.

The column of the right, under Colonel Trant, composed of 1000 Portuguese infantry and 50 horse of the same nation, moved by the village of St. Amias, with the intention of turning the left flank of the French. The centre column, 9000 in number with 12 guns, was commanded by Sir Arthur in person, and marched straight against the enemy by the village of Mahmed. It was composed of Generals Hill's, Nightingale's, Catlin Craufurd's, and Fane's brigades of British infantry, 400 cavalry, 250 of which were Portuguese, and 400 light troops of the same nation.

As this column advanced, General Fane's brigade, extending to its left, drove back the French skirmishers, and connected the march of Ferguson's division with the centre. When the latter approached the elevated plain upon which Laborde was posted, General Hill, who moved upon the right of the main road, being supported by the cavalry and covered by the fire of his light troops, pushed forward rapidly to the attack. On his left General Nightingale displayed a line of infantry, preceded by the fire of nine guns. Craufurd's brigade and the remaining pieces of artillery formed a reserve. At this moment Fane's riflemen crowned the nearest hills on the right flank of the French; the Portuguese troops showed the head of a column beyond St. Amias upon the enemy's left, and General Ferguson was seen descending from the higher grounds in the rear of Fane. Laborde's position appeared desperate; but, with the coolness and dexterity of a practised warrior, he evaded the danger, and, covered by his excellent cavalry, fell back rapidly to the heights of Zambugeira. A fresh disposition of the English became indispensable to dislodge him from that formidable and well-chosen post.

Colonel Trant continued his march, and turned the left of the new field of battle. Ferguson and Fane being united, were directed to penetrate by the mountains, and outflank the French right. Generals Hill and Nightingale advanced against the front, which was of singular strength, and only to be approached by narrow paths winding through deep ravines. A swarm of skirmishers, starting forward, plunged into the passes, and spreading to the right and left, won their way with extreme difficulty among the rocks and tangled evergreens that overspread the steep ascent; with still greater difficulty the supporting columns followed, and their formation was soon disordered in the confined and rugged passes. The hollows echoed with a continued roll of musketry; the shouts of the advancing troops were loudly answered by the enemy, and the curling smoke that broke out from the sides of the mountain marking the progress of the assailants showed how stoutly the defence was maintained. Laborde, watching anxiously for the arrival of Loison, gradually slackened his hold on the left, but clung tenaciously to the right, in the hope of yet effecting a junction with that general. The ardour of the 9th and 29th regiments, who led the attack, favoured this skilful conduct. They pressed forward with such vigour, as to force the two strongest passes and reach the plain above, long before the flank movements of Ferguson and Trant had shaken the credit of the position; the 29th first arrived in disorder at the top; ere they could form, a French battalion came forward at a rapid pace, poured in their fire, and breaking gallantly through the midst of the English regiment, slew the colonel and many others, and made the major and fifty or sixty men prisoners. But the 29th were not to be overthrown. They rallied, and being joined by the 9th, the colonel of which also fell in this bitter fight, maintained their dangerous footing. General Laborde, who brought every arm into action at the proper time and place, made repeated efforts to destroy these regiments before they could be supported; failing in that, he yet gained time to withdraw his left wing and to rally it upon the centre and right; but the English troops were gathering thickly on the upper ground, and General Ferguson, who had at first taken an erroneous direction towards the centre, now regained the true line, and was rapidly passing the right flank of the position. The French general, seeing that the day was lost, commenced a retreat by alternate masses, protecting his movements by vigorous charges of cavalry. At the village of Zambugeira he made another desperate stand, but the English troops bore on him too heavily to be resisted, and thus disputing the ground, he fell back to the Quinta de Bugagliera; there he halted until his detachments on the side of Segura had rejoined him, and then taking to the narrow pass of Ruña, he marched all night to gain the position of Montachique, leaving three guns on the field of battle, and the road to Torres Vedras open for the victors.

The loss of the French was 600 killed and wounded; among the latter was Laborde himself. The British also suffered considerably; two lieutenant-colonels and nearly 500 men being killed, taken, or wounded; and as not more than 4000 men were actually engaged, this hard-fought action was very honourable to both sides.

The firing ceased a little after four o'clock, and Sir Arthur getting intelligence that Loison's division was only five miles

distant, took up a position for the night in an oblique line to
that which he had just forced, his left resting upon a height near
the field of battle, and his right covering the road to Lourinham.
Believing that Loison and Laborde had effected their junction,
and that both were retiring to Montachique, he resolved to march
the next morning to Torres Vedras ; but before nightfall he was
informed that General Anstruther's and General Acland's divisions, accompanied by a large fleet of store-ships, were off the
coast, the dangerous nature of which rendered it necessary to
provide for their safety by a quick disembarkation. He therefore
changed his plans, and resolved to seek for some convenient post,
that, being in advance of his present position, would likewise
enable him to cover the landing of these reinforcements. The
vigour of Laborde's defence had also an influence upon this
occasion ; before an enemy so bold and skilful no precaution
could be neglected with impunity.

Sir Arthur marched to Lourinham, and Junot at the same
time quitting Cercal with Loison's division, crossed the line of
Laborde's retreat, and pushed for Torres Vedras, which he
reached in the evening of the same day. Being joined on the
19th by Laborde, and on the 20th by his reserve, Junot reorganised his army, and prepared for a decisive battle.

The day on which the combat of Roliça was fought the insurgents attacked Abrantes, and the feeble garrison being ill commanded, gave way, and was destroyed. Sir Arthur Wellesley took
up a position on the 19th August at Vimiero, a village near
the sea-coast, and from thence sent a detachment to cover the
march of General Anstruther's brigade, which had, with great
difficulty and some loss, been that morning landed on an open
sandy beach called the Bay of Maceira. The French cavalry
scoured the neighbouring country, carried off some of the women
from the rear of the camp, and hemmed the army round so closely
that no information of Junot's position could be obtained. In
the night of the 20th, General Acland's brigade was also disembarked, and this reinforcement increased the army to 16,000
fighting men, with 18 pieces of artillery, exclusive of Trant's
Portuguese and of two British regiments under General Beresford,
which were with the fleet at the mouth of the Tagus.

Estimating Junot's whole force at 18,000 men, Sir Arthur

Wellesley judged that, after providing for the security of Lisbon, the French general could not bring more than 14,000 into the field; he designed, therefore, not only to strike the first blow, but to follow it up, so as to prevent the enemy from rallying and renewing the campaign upon the frontier. In this view he had, before quitting the Mondego, written to Sir Harry Burrard, giving an exact statement of his own proceedings and intentions, and recommending that Sir John Moore, with his division, should disembark at the Mondego, and march without delay to Santarem, by which he would protect the left of the army, block the line of the Tagus, and at the same time threaten the French communication between Lisbon and Elvas, and that without danger, because Junot would be forced to defend Lisbon against the coast army, or if, relinquishing the capital, he endeavoured to make way to Almeida by Santarem, the ground there was so strong that Sir John Moore might easily maintain it against any efforts. Moreover, the Marquis of Valladeres commanded 3000 men at Guarda, and General Freire, with 5000 men, was at Leria, and might be persuaded to support the British at Santarem.

The distance from Vimiero to Torres Vedras was about nine miles; but although the number and activity of the French cavalry completely shrouded Junot's position, it was known to be strong, and very difficult of approach, by reason of a long defile through which the army must penetrate in order to reach the crest of the mountain. There was, however, a road leading between the seacoast and Torres Vedras, which, turning Junot's position, opened a way to Mafra. Sir Arthur possessed very exact military surveys of the country through which that road led, and he projected, by a forced march on the 21st, to turn the position of Torres Vedras, and to gain Mafra with a strong advanced guard, while the main body, seizing some advantageous heights a few miles short of that town, would be in a position to intercept the French line of march to Montachique. The army was reorganised during the 20th in eight brigades of infantry and four weak squadrons of cavalry, and every preparation was made for the next day's enterprise; but at that critical period of the campaign the Ministerial arrangements, which provided three commanders-in-chief, began to work.

Sir Harry Burrard arrived in a frigate off the Bay of Maceira, and Sir Arthur was checked in the midst of his operations on the eve of a decisive battle. Having repaired on board the frigate, he made his report of the situation of affairs, and renewed his former recommendation relative to the disposal of Sir John Moore's troops; but Burrard, who had previously resolved to bring the latter down to Maceira, condemned this project, and forbade any offensive movement until the whole army should be concentrated; whereupon Sir Arthur returned to his camp. The ground occupied by the army, although very extensive, and not very clearly defined as a position, was by no means weak. The village of Vimiero, situated in a valley through which the little river of Maceira flows, contained the parc and commissariat stores. The cavalry and the Portuguese were on a small plain close behind the village, and immediately in its front a rugged isolated height with a flat top commanded all the ground to the southward and eastward for a considerable distance.

On the night of the 20th, about twelve o'clock, Sir Arthur was aroused by a German officer of dragoons, who galloped into the camp, and with some consternation reported that Junot, at the head of 20,000 men, was coming on to the attack, and distant but one hour's march. The general, doubting the accuracy of this information, merely sent out some patrols, and warned the piquets and guards to be upon the alert. Before daybreak, according to the British custom, the troops were under arms; the sun rose, and no enemy was perceived; but at seven o'clock a cloud of dust was observed beyond the nearest hills, and at eight o'clock an advanced guard of horse was seen to crown the heights to the southward, and to send forward scouts on every side. Scarcely had this body been discovered, when a force of infantry, preceded by other cavalry, was descried moving along the road from Torres Vedras to Lourinham, and threatening the left of the British position: column after column followed in order of battle, and it soon became evident that the French were coming down to fight, but that the right wing of the English was not their object. The second, third, fourth, and eighth brigades were immediately directed to cross the valley behind the village, and take post on the heights. As those brigades reached the ground, the second and third were disposed in two lines facing to the left, forming a right angle with the prolongation of Fane and Anstruther's front. The fourth and eighth brigades were to have furnished a third line; but before the latter could reach the summit the battle commenced.

The ground between the two armies was so wooded and broken, that after the French had passed the ridge where they had been first descried, no correct view of their movements could be obtained; and the British being so weak in cavalry, were forced to wait patiently until the columns of attack were close upon them. Junot had quitted Torres Vedras the evening of the 20th, intending to fall on the English army at daybreak; but the difficulty of the defile in his front retarded his march for many hours and fatigued his troops. When he first came in sight of the position of Vimiero, the British order of battle appeared to him as being on two sides of an irregular triangle, the apex of which, formed by the hill in front of the village, was well furnished with men, while the left face appeared naked, for he could only see the piquets on that side, and the passage of the four brigades across the valley was hidden from him. Concluding, then, that the principal force was in the centre, he resolved to form two connected attacks, the one against the apex, the other against the left face; for he thought that the left of the position was an accessible ridge, whereas a deep ravine, trenched along the base, rendered it utterly impervious to an attack, except at the extremity, over which the road from Torres Vedras to Lourinham passed. Junot had nearly 14,000 fighting men organised in four divisions, of which three were of infantry and one of cavalry, with twenty-three pieces of artillery. Each division was composed of two brigades, and at ten o'clock, all being prepared, he commenced the battle of

Vimiero.

Laborde marched with one brigade against the centre; General Brennier led another against the left; Loison's division followed in the same order at a short distance. Kellerman, whose division (called the reserve) was composed of grenadiers, moved in one body behind Loison, and the cavalry under Margaron, about 1300 in number, was divided, a part being on the right of Brennier, and the remainder in rear of the reserve. The artillery was distributed among the columns, and opened their fire whenever the ground was favourable for their practice.

Junot designed that Laborde's and Brennier's attacks should be simultaneous, but the latter coming unexpectedly upon the ravine before mentioned as protecting the left, got entangled among the rocks and watercourses, and Laborde alone engaged Anstruther's brigade under a heavy and destructive fire of artillery that played on its front and flank, for the eighth brigade being then in the act of mounting the heights where the left was posted, observing the advance of the columns against the centre, halted, and opened a battery on their right flank. Junot, perceiving this failure in his combinations, ordered Loison to support Laborde's attack with one brigade of his division, and directed General Solignac, with the other, to turn the ravine in which Brennier was entangled, and to fall upon the extremity of the English line.

Loison and Laborde formed one grand and two secondary columns of attack; of the latter, the one advanced against Fane's brigade, while the other endeavoured to penetrate by a road which passed on the extreme left of Anstruther; but the principal column, headed by Laborde in person, and preceded by a multitude of light troops, mounted the face of the hill with great fury and loud cries; the English skirmishers were forced in upon the lines in a moment, and the French masses arrived at the summit; but, shattered by a terrible fire of the artillery, and breathless from their exertions, and in this state, first receiving a discharge of musketry from the 15th regiment at the distance of half pistol-shot, they were vigorously charged in front and flank, and over-thrown. At the same time Fane's brigade repulsed the attack on their side, and Colonel Taylor, with the very few horsemen he commanded, passing out by the right, rode fiercely among the confused and retreating troops, and scattered them with great execution. Margaron's cavalry, seeing this, came suddenly down upon Taylor, who was there slain, and the half of his feeble squadron cut to pieces, and Kellerman, taking advantage of this check, threw one half of the reserve into a pine wood that flanked the line of retreat followed by the beaten troops, and with the other endeavoured to renew the attack by the road where the 43rd regiment were engaged in a hot skirmish among some vineyards.

The French, being wholly discomfited in the centre, and the woods and hollows filled with their wounded and straggling men, retired up the edge of the ravine in a direction almost parallel to

the British line, and left the road from Vimiero to Torres Vedras open to their opponents; but Sir Arthur Wellesley strictly forbade any pursuit at that moment, partly because the grenadiers in the pine wood flanked the line of the French retreat, and partly because Margaron's horsemen, riding stiffly between the two armies, were not to be lightly meddled with. Meanwhile (Brennier being still hampered in the ravine), General Solignac passed along the crest of the above ridge, and came upon General Ferguson's brigade, which was posted at the left of the English position. But where the French expected to find a weak flank, they encountered a front of battle on a depth of three lines protected by deep declivities on either side; a powerful artillery swept away their foremost ranks, and on their right the fifth brigade and the Portuguese were seen marching by a distant ridge towards the Lourinham road and threatening the rear. Ferguson instantly taking the lead, bore down upon the enemy; the ridge widened as the English advanced, and the regiments of the second line running up in succession, increased the front, and constantly filled the ground. The French falling fast under the fire, drew back fighting, until they reached the declivity of the ridge, and their cavalry made several efforts to check the advancing troops, but the latter were too compact to be disturbed by these attempts. Solignac himself was carried from the field severely wounded, and his retiring column, continually outflanked on the left, was cut off from the line of retreat, and thrown into the low ground about the village of Perenza. There six guns were captured, and General Ferguson, leaving the 82nd and 71st regiments to guard them, was continuing to press the disordered columns, when Brennier, having at last cleared the ravine, came suddenly in upon those two regiments and retook the artillery. His success was but momentary; the surprised troops rallied upon the higher ground, poured in a heavy fire of musketry, and with a shout returning to the charge, overthrew him and recovered the guns. Brennier himself was wounded and made prisoner, and Ferguson having completely separated the French brigades from each other, would have forced the greatest part of Solignac's to surrender, if an unexpected order had not obliged him to halt, and then the discomfited troops re-forming under the protection of their cavalry with admirable quickness and steadiness, made an orderly retreat, and were soon united to the broken brigades which were falling back from the attack on the centre.

Brennier, who, the moment he was taken, was brought to Sir Arther Wellesley, eagerly demanded if the reserve under Kellerman had yet charged, and Sir Arthur, ascertaining from other prisoners that it had, was then satisfied that all the enemy's attacks were exhausted, and that no considerable body of fresh troops could be hidden among the woods and hollows in his front. It was only twelve o'clock, the battle was already won; thirteen guns were in his possession, for seven had been taken in the centre; the fourth and eighth brigades had suffered very little; the Portuguese, the fifth, and the first brigades had not fired a shot, and the latter was two miles nearer to Torres Vedras than any part of the French army, which was, moreover, in great confusion. The relative numbers before the action were considerably in favour of the English; and the result of the action had increased that disparity. A portion of Sir Arthur's army had defeated the enemy when entire, a portion then could effectually follow up his victory, and he resolved with the five brigades on the left to press Junot closely, and driving him over the Sierra da Baragueda, force him upon the Tagus, while Hill, Anstruther, and Fane, seizing the defile of Torres Vedras, should push on to Montachique and cut him off from Lisbon.

If this able and decisive operation had been executed, Junot would probably have lost all his artillery and several thousand stragglers, and being buffeted and turned at every point, would have been glad to seek safety under the guns of Almeida or Elvas, and even that he could only have accomplished because Sir John Moore's troops were not landed at the Mondego. But Sir Harry Burrard, who was present during the action, although, partly from delicacy, and partly from approving of Sir Arthur's arrangements, he had not hitherto interfered, now assumed the chief command. From him the order which arrested Ferguson in his victorious career had emanated, by him further offensive operations were forbidden, and he resolved to wait in the position of Vimiero until the arrival of Sir John Moore. Adjutant-General Clinton and Colonel Murray, the quartermaster-general, supported Sir Harry Burrard's views, and Sir Arthur's earnest representations could not alter his determination.

Sir Harry's decision was certainly erroneous, but error is common in an art which at best is but a choice of difficulties. The circumstances of the moment were imposing enough to sway most generals; for although the French were beaten in the attacks, they rallied with surprising quickness under the protection of a strong and gallant cavalry. Sir Harry knew that his own artillery carriages were so shaken as to be scarcely fit for service; that the draft horses were few and bad, and that the commissariat parc on the plain was in the greatest confusion. The hired Portuguese carmen were making off with their carriages in all directions; the English cavalry was totally destroyed; and, finally, General Spencer had discovered a line of fresh troops on the ridge behind that occupied by the French army. Weighing all these things in his mind with the caution natural to age, Burrard was reluctant to hazard the fortune of the day upon what he deemed a perilous throw.

The Duke of Abrantes, who had displayed all that reckless courage to which he originally owed his elevation, profited by this unexpected cessation of the battle, and re-formed his broken infantry. Twelve hundred fresh men joined him at the close of the contest, and, covered by his cavalry, he retreated with order and celerity until he regained the command of the pass of Torres Vedras, so that when the day closed, the relative position of the two armies was the same as on the evening before. One general, thirteen guns, and several hundred prisoners fell into the hands of the victors, and the total loss of the French was estimated at 3000 men—an exaggeration, no doubt, but it was certainly above 2000, for their closed columns had been exposed for more than half an hour to sweeping discharges of grape and musketry, and the dead lay thickly together. A French order of battle found upon the field gave a total of 14,000 men present under arms, of which 1300 were cavalry.

The arrangements made by Sir Harry Burrard did not remain in force a long time. Early on the morning of the 22nd, Sir Hew Dalrymple disembarked and assumed the chief command. Thus in the short space of twenty-four hours, during which a battle was fought, the army fell successively into the hands of three men, who, coming from different quarters, with different views, habits, and information, had not any previous opportunity of communing even by letter, so as to arrange a common plan of operations; and they were now brought together at a critical moment, when it was more than probable they must all disagree, and that the public service must suffer from that want of vigour which is inherent to divided councils; for when Sir Hew Dalrymple was appointed to the command, Sir Arthur Wellesley was privately recommended to him by the Minister as a person who should be employed with more than usual confidence; and this unequivocal hint was backed up with too much force by the previous reputation and recent exploits of the latter, not to produce some want of cordiality; for Sir Arthur could not do otherwise than take the lead in discussing affairs of which he had more than laid the foundation, and Sir Hew would have forfeited all claims to independence in his command if he had not exercised the right of judging for himself between the conflicting opinions of his predecessors.

When General Brennier was wounded and made prisoner at Vimiero, he was at first in danger of being killed, when Corporal Mackay, of the 71st Highlanders, rescued him from those into whose hands he had fallen. Brennier offered Mackay his watch and purse in gratitude, but these the Highlander refused to accept. When Mackay delivered his prisoner up to Colonel Pack, Brennier could not help saying—"What sort of a man is this? He has done me the greatest service, and yet refuses the only reward I can offer him," when Colonel Pack replied—"We are British soldiers, sir, and not plunderers." This was conduct which the French general could not but contrast with the rapacity and cruelty of his own countrymen. Mackay was promoted serjeant on the spot. A piper named Stewart of the same regiment early in the action received a severe wound in the thigh; he would not allow himself to be carried from the field, but sitting where his comrades could hear him, continued to play warlike airs to the end of the battle. Both these men were rewarded by the Highland Society—Mackay with a gold medal, and Stewart with a handsome set of Highland pipes.—*Southey's History of the War.*

CHAPTER II.

SIR JOHN MOORE—RETREAT TO CORUNA—BATTLE OF CORUNA.

HE Convention of Cintra, concluded between Sir Hew Dalrymple and Marshal Junot after the battle of Vimiero, by which Portugal was freed from the invader and the French troops sent back to their own country, was greatly disapproved of in Britain by many who were incapable of knowing the whole circumstances. The Government ordered an inquiry, the result of which was to free Sir Arthur Wellesley, who had returned home, from all blame; but so strong and unreasoning was the public sentiment, that he did not regain employment afterwards without high influence and considerable difficulty. Portugal having been liberated, the Government proposed to carry the war into Spain, and the British forces, now raised to 30,000 men, were placed under the command of Sir John Moore—an appointment in the highest degree popular at home, where he was greatly respected. Moore was a native of Glasgow, and after having travelled some time on the Continent in the suite of the Duke of Hamilton, entered the army, where he soon attained the rank of lieutenant-colonel. He served in the West Indies, in Holland, and in Egypt, and also in Corsica and Ireland. When in Corsica he stormed the Convention Fort and the outworks of Calvi, which was followed by the conquest of the island; and in Ireland he gained the battle of Wexford, which proved the prelude to the suppression of the Rebellion. He now began his campaign by marching from Lisbon into Spain. It was a bold measure, but one of doubtful prudence, seeing that the Emperor Napoleon was

himself present in Spain, and had nearly 300,000 troops scattered over the country, which he began at once to concentrate, and rapidly marched to oppose Moore, who, warned of his peril, turned and made a disastrous retreat towards the coast.

The Emperor was informed of General Moore's advance on the 21st December 1808, and preparations were immediately made for opposing him : 10,000 men were left to control Madrid, and on the evening of the 22nd, 50,000 men were at the foot of the Guadarama. A deep snow choked the passes of the Sierra, and, after twelve hours of ineffectual toil, the advanced guards were still on the wrong side; the general commanding reported that the road was impracticable, but Napoleon, rebuking him fiercely, urged the columns to another attempt, and the passage of the mountain was effected amidst a storm of hail and drifting sleet. The cold and fatigue were so intense that many soldiers and draft animals died during the two days that the operation lasted.

Personally urging on the troops with unceasing vehemence, the Emperor arrived at Tordesillas on the 26th with the guards and the divisions of La Pisse and Dessolles. From Tordesillas Napoleon communicated with Soult, informing him of these movements, and concluded his dispatch thus: "Our cavalry scouts are already at Benevente. If the English pass to-day in their position, they are lost; if, on the contrary, they attack you with all their force, retire one day's march : the farther they proceed the better for us. If they retreat, pursue them closely;" and then, full of hope, he hastened to Valderas, but had the mortification to learn that, notwithstanding his rapid march, having scarcely rested night or day, he was twelve hours too late. The British were across the Esla !

In fact, Soult was in full pursuit when this letter was written, for Sir John Moore had begun to retreat the moment the intelligence of Napoleon's march from Madrid reached him. The heavy baggage and stores had been immediately moved to the rear; but the reserve, the light brigades, and the cavalry remained at Sahagun, the latter pushing their patrols up to the enemy's lines and skirmishing, with a view to hide the retrograde march. On the 24th, General Hope, with two divisions, fell back by the road of Mayorga, and General Baird, with another, by that of Valencia de San Juan, where there was a ferryboat, to cross the Esla river. The Marquis of Romana undertook to guard the bridge of Mansilla. The enemy's dragoons, under Lorge, arrived the same day at Frechilla, and the division of Laborde at Paredes. Next day the general-in-chief, with the reserve and light brigades, followed the route of Hope's column to Valderas; Baird passed the Esla at Valencia on the 26th, and took post on the other side, but with some difficulty, for the boat was small, the fords deep, and the river rising; while the troops under the commander-in-chief approached the bridge of Castro Gonzalo early in the morning. The stores and baggage were a long time passing, a dense fog intercepted the view, and so nicely timed was the march, that the scouts of the imperial horsemen were already infesting the flank of the column, and even carried off some of the baggage. The left bank of the river being high, and completely commanding the bridge, the second light brigade, under General Robert Crawfurd, and two guns, were posted on that side to protect the passage, for the cavalry were still on the march from Sahagun, and Soult, aware of the retreat, was pressing forward vigorously. When Lord Paget had passed Mayorga, he discovered a strong body of horse appertaining to Ney's corps embattled on a swelling mound close to the road. The soil was deep, and soaked with snow and rain. Two squadrons of the 10th riding stiffly against the enemy, mounted the hill, and, notwithstanding the superiority of numbers and position, overthrew him, killed 20 men, and took 100 prisoners. This was a bold and hardy action; but the English cavalry had been engaged more or less for twelve successive days, and with such fortune and bravery that above 500 prisoners had already fallen into their hands; and their leaders being excellent, their confidence was unbounded. From Mayorga Lord Paget proceeded to Benevente; but Marshal Soult, Duke of Dalmatia, with great judgment, directed his march towards Astorga by the road of Mancilla; and Romana, leaving 3000 men and two guns to defend the bridge at that place, fell back to Leon.

Thus by a critical march Sir John Moore had recovered his communications with Astorga, and so far baffled the Emperor; but his position was by no means safe, or even tenable. The town of Benevente, a rich open place, remarkable for a small but curious Moorish palace or castle containing a fine collection of ancient armour, is situated in a plain that, extending from the Gallician mountains to the neighbourhood of Burgos, appeared to be boundless. On the left it was skirted by the hills near the town of Leon, which was enclosed with walls, and capable of resisting a sudden assault. The river Esla wound through the plain about four miles in front of Benevente, and the bridge of Castro Gonzalos was the key to the town, but the right bank of the Esla was completely commanded from the farther side, and there were many fords. In this exposed situation Sir John Moore resolved to remain no longer than was necessary to clear out his magazines at Benevente, and to cover the march of his stores; but the road to Astorga by Leon being much shorter than that through Benevente, he wrote to Romana to request that he would maintain himself at Leon as long as he could; hearing also that the Marquis intended to retreat into Gallicia, Sir John repeated his desire to have that road left open for the English army. Romana, who assented to both these requests, had a great rabble with him, and as Leon was a walled place, and a number of citizens and volunteers were willing, and even eager, to fight, the town might have made a formidable resistance. Sir John Moore hoped that it would do so, and gave orders to break down the bridge at Castro Gonzalo in his own front, the moment the stragglers and baggage should have passed.

On the night of the 26th, the chasseurs of the imperial guard rode close up to the bridge of Castro Gonzalo, and captured some women and baggage. The following remarkable instance of courage and discipline occurred at this place. John Walton, a native of the south of Ireland, and Richard Jackson, an Englishman, were posted in a hollow road on the plain beyond the bridge, and at a distance from their piquet. If the enemy approached, one was to fire, run back to the brow of the hill, and give notice if there were many or few; the other was to maintain his ground. A party of cavalry following a hay-cart stole up close to these men, and suddenly galloped in, with a view to kill them and surprise the post. Jackson fired, but was overtaken, and received twelve or fourteen severe wounds in an instant; he came staggering on, notwithstanding his mangled state, and gave the signal. Walton, with equal resolution and more fortune, defended himself with his bayonet, and wounded several of the assailants, who retreated, leaving him unhurt; but his cap, his knapsack, his belts, and his musket were cut in above twenty places, and his bayonet was bent double, his musket covered with blood, and notched like a saw from the muzzle to the lock. Jackson escaped death during the retreat, and finally recovered of his wounds.

The cavalry and the stragglers being all over the river, General Crawfurd commenced the destruction of the bridge; torrents of rain and snow were descending, and half the troops worked, while the other half kept the enemy at bay from the heights on the left bank; for the cavalry scouts of the imperial guards were spread over the plain. At ten o'clock at night a large party following some waggons endeavoured to pass the piquets and gallop down to the bridge; but the event did not answer their expectations. This anxiety to interrupt the work induced General Crawfurd to destroy two arches of the bridge and to blow up the connecting buttress; but the masonry was so solid and difficult to pierce, that it was not until twelve o'clock in the night of the 28th that all the preparations were completed. The troops then descended the heights on the left bank, and passing with the greatest silence by single files over planks laid across the broken arches, gained the other side without loss—an instance of singular good fortune, for the night was dark and tempestuous; the river, rising rapidly with a roaring noise, was threatening to burst over the planks, and the enemy was close at hand. To have resisted an attack in such an awkward situation would have been impossible, but happily the retreat of the troops was undiscovered, and the mine being sprung with good effect, Crawfurd marched to Benevente, where the cavalry and the reserve still remained. Several thousand infantry slept in the long galleries of an immense convent built round a square; the lower corridors were filled with the horses of the cavalry and artillery, so thickly stowed that it was scarcely possible for a single man to pass them, and there was but one entrance. Two officers returning from the bridge, being desirous to find shelter for their men, entered the convent, and with horror perceived that a large window-shutter being on fire, and the flames spreading to the rafters above, in a few moments the straw under the horses would ignite, and 6000 men and animals would inevitably perish in the flames. One of the officers (Captain Lloyd of the 43rd), a man of great activity, strength, and presence of mind, made a sign to his companion to keep silence, and springing on to the nearest horse, ran along the backs of the others until he reached the flaming shutter, which he tore off its hinges and cast out of the window; then returning quietly, awakened some of the soldiers, and cleared the passage without creating any alarm, which in such a case would have been as destructive as the flames.

The army gained two days' rest at Benevente, but as very little could be done to remove the stores, the greater part of them were destroyed. On the 28th, Hope's and Fraser's divisions marched to Labaneza; and on the 29th to Astorga, where Baird's division joined them from Valencia San Juan. On the same day the reserve and Crawfurd's brigade quitted Benevente, but the cavalry remained in the town, leaving parties to watch the fords of the Esla. Soon after daybreak, General Lefebre Desnouettes, seeing only a few cavalry posts on the great plain, rather hastily concluded that there was nothing to support them, and crossing the river at a ford a little way above the bridge with 600 horsemen of the imperial guards, he advanced into the plain. The piquets at first retired fighting, but being joined by a party of the 3rd German hussars, they charged the leading French squadrons with some effect. General C. Stewart then took the command, and the ground was obstinately disputed. At this moment the plain was covered with stragglers, and baggage-mules, and followers of the army; the town was filled with tumult; the distant piquets and vedettes were seen galloping in from the right and left; the French were pressing forward boldly, and every appearance indicated that the enemy's whole army was come up and passing the river. Lord Paget ordered the 10th hussars to mount and form under the cover of some houses at the edge of the town; he desired to draw the enemy, whose real situation he had detected at once, well into the plain before he attacked. In half an hour, everything being ready, he gave the signal: the 10th hussars galloped forward, the piquets, that were already engaged, closed together, and the whole charged. In an instant the scene changed: the enemy were seen flying at full speed towards the river, and the British close at their heels; the French squadrons, without breaking their ranks, plunged into the stream, and gained the opposite heights, where, like experienced soldiers, they wheeled instantly, and seemed inclined to come forward a second time; but a battery of two guns being opened upon them, after a few rounds they retired. During the pursuit in the plain, an officer was observed separating from the main body, and making towards another part of the river; being followed, and refusing to stop when overtaken, he was cut across the head and brought in a prisoner. He proved to be General Lefebre. Although the imperial guards were outnumbered in the end, they were very superior at the commencement of this fight, which was handsomely contested on both sides. The British lost 50 men killed and wounded; the French left 55 killed and wounded on the field, and 70 prisoners, besides the general and other officers. Lord Paget maintained his posts on the Esla under an occasional cannonade until the evening, and then withdrew to La Baneza.

While these things were passing, Napoleon arrived at Valderas, Ney at Villaton, and Lapisse at Toro; the French troops were worn down with fatigue, yet the Emperor still urged them forward. The Duke of Dalmatia, he said, would intercept the retreat of the English at Astorga, and their labours would be finally rewarded; but the destruction of the bridge of Castro Gonzalo was so well accomplished, that twenty-four hours were required to repair it, and the fords were now impassable. It was the 30th before Bessieres could cross the Esla; but on that day he passed through Benevente with 9000 cavalry, and bent his course towards La Baneza. The same day, Franceschi forced the bridge of Mansilla de las Mulas by a single charge of his light horsemen, and captured the artillery and one half of the division left by Romana to protect it. The latter immediately abandoned Leon and many stores, and the Duke of Dalmatia entered that town without firing a shot.

The rear of the English army was still in Astorga, the head-quarters having arrived there on the day before. In the preceding month large stores had been gradually brought up to that town by Sir David Baird, and as there were no means of transport to remove them, orders were given, after supplying the immediate wants of the army, to destroy them; but Romana, who would neither defend Leon nor Mansilla, had, contrary to his promises, preoccupied Astorga with his fugitive army; and when the English divisions marched in, such a tumult and confusion arose, that no orders could be executed with regularity, no distribution made, nor the destruction of the stores be effected. The disorder thus unexpectedly produced was very detrimental to the discipline of the troops. The resources which he had depended on for the support of his soldiers became mischievous, and contributed to disorganise instead of nourishing them, and he had the farther vexation to hear Romana, the principal cause of this misfortune, proposing (with an army unable to resist a thousand light infantry) to commence offensive operations and plans, in comparison of which the visions of Don Quixote were wisdom.

On the 31st, the light brigades separated from the army at Bonillas, and bent their course by cross-roads towards Orense and Vigo. This detachment was made to lessen the pressure on the commissariat, and to cover the flanks of the army. Fraser's and Hope's divisions entered Villa Franca; Baird's division was at Bembibre. The reserve, with the head-quarters, halted at Cambarros, a village six miles from Astorga, but the cavalry fell back in the night to the same place, and then the reserve marched to Bembibre. The Marquis of Romana, after doing so much mischief by crossing the line of march, left his infantry to wander as they pleased, and retired with his cavalry and guns to the valley of the Mincio.

Upon the 1st of January 1809, the Emperor took possession of Astorga. On that day 70,000 French infantry, 10,000 cavalry, and 200 pieces of artillery, after many days of incessant marching, were there united. The congregation of this mighty force, while it evinced the power and energy of the French monarch, attested also the genius of the English general, who, with a handful of men, had found the means to arrest the course of the conqueror, and to draw him, with the flower of his army, to this remote and unimportant part of the Peninsula, at the moment when Portugal and the fairest provinces of Spain were prostrate beneath the strength of his hand. The stupendous march of the Emperor was rendered fruitless by the quickness of his adversary; but Napoleon, though he had failed to destroy the English army, resolved, nevertheless, to cast it forth of the Peninsula, and being himself recalled to France by tidings that the Austrian storm was ready to burst, he fixed upon the Duke of Dalmatia to continue the pursuit, adding for this purpose three divisions of cavalry and three of infantry to his former command. Thus, including Laborde, Heudelet, and Loison's division, nearly 60,000 men and 91 guns were put on the track of the English army.

The Duke of Dalmatia, a general who, if the Emperor be excepted, was nowise inferior to any of his nation, commenced his pursuit of the English army with a vigour that marked his eager desire to finish the campaign in a manner suitable to the brilliant opening at Gamonal, and thus Sir John Moore, after having twice baffled the Emperor's combinations, was still pressed in his retreat with a fury that seemed to increase every moment. The separation of his light brigades, a measure which he adopted after the advice of his quartermaster-general, weakened the army by 3000 men; but he still possessed 19,000 of all arms, good soldiers to fight and strong to march. There was no choice but to retreat. The astonishing rapidity with which the Emperor had brought up his overbearing numbers and thrust the English army into Gallicia, had rendered the natural strength of the country unavailing. The resources were few, even for an army in winter quarters, and for a campaign in that season, there were none at all. All the draft cattle that could be procured would scarcely have supplied the means to transport ammunition for two battles, but the French, sweeping the rich plains of Castile with their powerful cavalry, might have formed magazines at Astorga and Leon, and from thence have been supplied in abundance, while the English were starving.

Before he advanced from Salamanca, Sir John Moore, foreseeing that his movement must sooner or later end in a retreat, had sent officers to examine the roads of Gallicia and the harbours which offered the greatest advantages for embarkation. By the reports of those officers, which arrived from day to day, and by the state of the magazines he had directed to be formed, his measures were constantly regulated. It was now only the fifteenth day since Sir John Moore had left Salamanca, and already the torrent of war, diverted from the south, was foaming among the rocks of Gallicia. Nineteen thousand British troops, posted in strong ground, might have offered battle to very superior numbers; but where was the use of merely fighting an enemy who had 300,000 men in Spain? Nothing could be gained by such a display of courage; but the English general, by a quick retreat, might reach his ships unmolested, embark, and carrying his army from the narrow corner in which it was cooped to the southern provinces, establish there a good base of operations, and renew the war under favourable circumstances. It was by this combination of a fleet and army that the greatest assistance could be given to Spain, and the strength of England become most formidable. A few days' sailing would carry the troops to Cadiz; but six weeks' constant marching would not bring the French army from Gallicia to that neighbourhood. The northern provinces were broken, subdued in spirit, and possessed few resources. The southern provinces had scarcely seen an enemy, were rich and fertile, and there also was the seat of government. Sir John Moore reasoned thus, and resolved to fall down to the coast and embark, with as little loss or delay as might be. Vigo, Coruña, and Ferrol were the principal harbours; and their relative advantages could not be determined except by the reports of the engineers, none of which were yet received, so rapidly had the crisis of affairs come on; but as those reports could only be obtained from day to day, the line of retreat became of necessity subject to daily change.

When the Duke of Dalmatia took the command of the pursuing army, Hope's and Fraser's divisions were at Villa Franca, Sir David Baird's at Bembibre, the reserve and cavalry at Cambarros, six miles from Astorga. The reserve and the cavalry marched during the night to Bembibre: on their arrival, Baird's division proceeded to Villa Franca, but the immense wine vaults of Bembibre had such temptations, that many hundreds of his men remained behind inebriated; the followers of the army crowded the houses, and a number of Romana's disbanded men were mixed with this heterogeneous mass of marauders, drunkards, muleteers, women, and children; the weather was dreadful, and, notwithstanding the utmost exertions of the general-in-chief, when the reserve marched the next morning, the number of those unfortunate wretches was not diminished. Leaving a small guard to protect them, Sir John Moore proceeded to Calcabellos; but scarcely had the reserve marched out of the village, when some French cavalry appeared. In a moment the road was filled with the miserable stragglers, who came crowding after the troops, some with loud shrieks of distress and wild gestures, others with brutal exclamations; many, over-

RETREAT TO CORUNA.

come with fear, threw away their arms. Those who preserved theirs were too stupidly intoxicated to fire; and kept reeling to and fro, alike insensible to their danger and to their disgrace. The enemy's horsemen, perceiving this confusion, bore down at a gallop, broke through the disorderly mob, cutting to the right and left as they passed, and riding so close to the columns, that the infantry were forced to halt in order to check their audacity.

At Calcabellos the reserve took up a position, and the general-in-chief went on to Villa Franca. In that town great excesses had been committed by the preceding divisions; the magazines were plundered, the bakers driven away from the ovens, the wine-stores forced, and the commissaries prevented from making the regular distributions; the doors of the houses were broken, and the scandalous insubordination of the soldiers proved that a discreditable relaxation of discipline on the part of the officers had taken place. The general immediately arrested this disorder, caused one man taken in the act of plundering a magazine to be shot in the market-place, and issued severe orders to prevent a recurrence of such inexcusable conduct, after which he returned to the reserve at Calcabellos. The Guia, a small but at this season of the year a deep stream, ran through that town, and was crossed by a stone bridge. On the Villa Franca side, a lofty ridge, rough with vineyards and stone walls, was occupied by 2500 infantry, with a battery of six guns. Four hundred riflemen and about the same number of cavalry were posted on a hill two miles beyond the river, to watch the two roads of Bembibre and Foncevadon. The 3rd of January, a little after noon, the French General Colbert approached this hill with six or eight squadrons; but observing the ground behind Calcabellos strongly occupied, he demanded reinforcements. Marshal Soult, believing that the English did not mean to make a stand, sent orders to Colbert to charge without delay; and the latter, stung by the message, obeyed with precipitate fury. From one of those errors so frequent in war, the British cavalry, thinking a greater force was riding against them, retired at speed to Calcabellos. The riflemen, who, following their orders, had withdrawn when the French first came in sight, were just passing the bridge, when a crowd of staff officers, the cavalry, and the enemy, came in upon them in one mass; in the confusion thirty or forty men were taken, and Colbert, crossing the river, charged on the spur up the road. The remainder of the riflemen threw themselves into the vineyards, and permitting the enemy to approach within a few yards, suddenly opened such a deadly fire, that the greatest number of the French horsemen were killed on the spot, and among the rest Colbert himself. His fine martial figure, his voice, his gestures, and, above all, his daring valour, had excited the admiration of the British, and a general feeling of sorrow was predominant when the gallant soldier fell. The French voltigeurs now crossed the river; a few of the 52nd regiment descended from the upper part of the ridge to the assistance of the riflemen, and a sharp skirmish commenced, in which 200 or 300 men of both sides were killed or wounded: towards evening Merle's division of infantry appeared on the hills in front of the town, and made a demonstration of crossing the river opposite to the left of the English position; but the battery of the latter checked this movement, and night coming on, the combat ceased.

From Villa Franca to Lugo the road led through a rugged country; the cavalry were therefore sent on to the latter town at once. The reserve reached Herrerias, a distance of eighteen miles, on the morning of the 5th. Baird's division was at Nogales, Hope's and Fraser's near Lugo. At Herrerias, Sir John Moore, who constantly directed the movements of the rear-guard himself, received the first reports of the engineers relative to the harbours. It appeared that Vigo, besides its greater distance, offered no position to cover the embarkation, but Coruña and Betanzos did. This induced him to relinquish his first intention of going to Vigo, and made him regret the absence of his light brigades. The transports were now ordered round from Vigo to Coruña; and in the meantime the general sent orders to the leading division to halt at Lugo, his intention being to rally the army there, to restore discipline, and to offer battle to the enemy if he was inclined to accept it.

These orders were carried to Sir David Baird by one of the aides-de-camp of the commander-in-chief; but Sir David forwarded them by a private dragoon, who got drunk and lost the dispatch. This blamable irregularity was ruinous to General Fraser's troops; in lieu of resting two days at Lugo, that general unwittingly pursued his toilsome journey towards St. Jago de Compostella, and then returned without food or rest, losing by this pilgrimage above 400 stragglers. On the 4th, the reserve reached Nogales, having by a forced march of thirty-six miles gained twelve hours' start of the enemy. At the entrance of this village they met a large convoy, consisting of English clothing, shoes, and ammunition, intended for Romana's army but moving towards the enemy —a circumstance perfectly characteristic of the Spanish mode of conducting public affairs. There was a bridge at Nogales which the engineers failed to destroy, but this was a matter of little consequence, as the river was fordable above and below; indeed, the general was unwilling, unless for some palpable advantage, which seldom presented itself, to injure the communications of a country that he was unable to serve. At this period of the retreat the road was crowded with stragglers and baggage; the peasantry, although armed, did not molest the French, but fearing both sides alike, drove their cattle and carried off their effects into the mountains on each side of the line of march; even there the villainous marauders contrived to find them, and in some cases were by the Spaniards killed—a just punishment for quitting their colours. Under the most favourable circumstances, the tail of a retreating force exhibits terrible scenes of distress; and on the road near Nogales, the followers of the army were dying fast from cold and hunger. The soldiers, barefooted, harassed, and weakened by their excesses at Bembibre and Villa Franca, were dropping to the rear by hundreds. Broken carts, dead animals, and the piteous appearance of women with children, struggling or falling exhausted in the snow, completed a picture of war which, like Janus, has a double face.

Towards evening the French recovered their lost ground, and passed Nogales, galling the rear-guard with a continual skirmish; and here it was that dollars to the amount of £25,000 were abandoned. This small sum was kept near head-quarters to answer sudden emergencies, and the bullocks that drew it being tired, the general, who could not save the money without risking an ill-timed action, had it rolled down the side of the mountain; part of it was gathered by the enemy, part by the Gallician peasants. The same evening the reserve approached Constantino; the French were close upon the rear, and a hill within pistol-shot of the bridge offered them such an advantage, that there was little hope to effect the passage without great loss. The general caused the riflemen and artillery to take possession of the hill, under cover of which the remainder of the reserve hastily passed across the river Minho without being perceived by the enemy, who were unusually cautious, and not aware of the vicinity of the bridge; the guns then descended at a trot, the riflemen followed, and when the French, now undeceived, came up at a brisk pace, the passage was effected, and a good line of battle formed at the other side; a fight commenced, but notwithstanding that the assailants were continually reinforced as their columns of march arrived, General Paget maintained the post with two regiments until nightfall, and then retired to Lugo, in front of which the whole army was assembled.

On 7th January Sir John Moore, in a general order, gave a severe but just rebuke to the officers and soldiers for their previous want of discipline, and at the same time announced his intention to offer battle. It has been well said, that a British army may be gleaned in a retreat, but cannot be reaped. Whatever may be their misery, the soldiers will always be found clean at review and ready at a fight. Scarcely was this order issued, when the line of battle, so attenuated before, was filled with vigorous men, full of confidence and valour. Fifteen hundred had fallen in action or dropped to the rear; but as three fresh battalions left by Sir David Baird in his advance to Astorga had joined the army between Villa Franca and Lugo, 19,000 combatants were still under arms when the French columns appeared in sight. The right of the English position was in comparatively flat ground, and partially protected by the bend of the Minho. The centre was amongst vineyards, with low stone walls. The left, which was somewhat withdrawn, rested on the mountains, being supported and covered by the cavalry. It was the intention of the general to engage deeply with his right and centre before he closed with his left wing, in which he had posted the flower of his troops, hoping thus to bring on a decisive battle, and trusting to the valour of the men to handle the enemy in such sort as that he should be glad to let the army continue its retreat unmolested. Other hope than this, to re-embark the troops without loss, there was none, except by stratagem.

It was midday before the French marshal arrived in person at the head of 10,000 or 12,000 men; the remainder of his power followed in some disarray, for the marches had not been so easy but that many even of the oldest soldiers had dropped behind. As the French columns came up, they formed in order of battle along a strong mountainous ridge fronting the English. The latter were not distinctly seen, from the inequalities of the ground, and Soult, feeling doubtful if they were all before him, took four guns and some squadrons commanded by Colonel Lallemande, advanced towards the centre, and opened a fire, which was soon silenced by a reply from fifteen pieces. The Marshal being then satisfied that something more than a rear-guard was in his front, retired. About an hour after he made a feint on the right, and at the same time sent a column of infantry and five guns against the left. On that side the three regiments which had lately joined were drawn up. The French pushed the outposts hard, and were gaining the advantage, when the English general-in-chief arriving, rallied the light troops, and with a vigorous charge broke the adverse column, and treated it very roughly in the pursuit. The estimated loss of the French was between 300 and 400 men.

At daybreak on the 8th the two armies were still embattled. On the French side, 17,000 infantry, 400 cavalry, and 50 pieces of artillery were in line, but Soult deferred the attack until the 9th. On the English side, 16,000 infantry, 1800 cavalry, and 40 pieces of artillery impatiently awaited the assault, and blamed their adversary for delaying a contest which they ardently desired; but darkness fell without a shot having been fired, and with it fell the English general's hope to engage his enemy on equal terms.

What was to be done? Assail the French position? remain another day in expectation of a battle? or in secrecy gain a march, get on board without being molested, or at least obtain time to establish the army in a good situation to cover the embarkation? General Moore adopted the third plan, and prepared to decamp in the night; he ordered the fires to be kept bright, and exhorted the troops to make a great exertion, which he trusted would be the last required of them.

The country immediately in the rear of the position was intersected by stone walls and a number of intricate lanes; precautions were taken to mark the right tracks by placing bundles of straw at certain distances, and officers were appointed to guide the columns. At ten o'clock the troops silently quitted their ground, and retired in excellent order; but a moody fortune pursued Sir John Moore throughout this campaign, baffling his prudence and thwarting his views, as if resolved to prove the unyielding firmness of his mind. A terrible storm of wind and rain mixed with sleet commenced as the army broke up from the position; the marks were destroyed, and the guides lost the true direction; only one of the divisions happily gained the main road, the other two were bewildered, and when daylight broke, the rear columns were still near to Lugo. The fatigue, the depression of mind occasioned by this misfortune, and the want of shoes, broke the order of the march, and the stragglers were becoming numerous, when unfortunately, one of the generals commanding a leading division, thinking to relieve the men during a halt which took place in the night, desired them to take refuge from the weather in some houses a little way off the road. Complete disorganisation followed this imprudent act; from that moment it became impossible to make the soldiers of the division keep their ranks; plunder succeeded, the example was infectious, and what with real suffering and evil propensity encouraged by this error of inexperience, the main body of the army, which had bivouacked for six hours in the rain, arrived at Betanzos on the evening of the 9th, in a state very discreditable to its discipline.

The commander-in-chief, with the reserve and the cavalry, as usual, covered the march; in the course of it he ordered several bridges to be destroyed, but the engineers failed of success in every attempt. Fortunately, the enemy did not come up with the rear before the evening, and then only with their cavalry, otherwise many prisoners must have fallen into their hands. The number of stragglers uncovered by the passage of the reserve was so numerous, that, being pressed by the enemy's horse, they united in considerable bodies and repulsed them, a signal proof that the disorder was occasioned as much by insubordination in the regiments as by the fatigue of the march. The reserve, commanded by General Edward Paget, an officer distinguished during the retreat by his firmness, ability, and ardent zeal, remained in position during the night a few miles from Betanzos. The rest of the army was quartered in that town, and as the enemy could not gather in strength on the 10th, the commander-in-chief halted that day, and the cavalry passed from the rear-guard to the head of the column.

As the troops approached Coruña the general's looks were directed towards the harbour; an open expanse of water painfully convinced him that to Fortune at least he was no way beholden; contrary winds detained the fleet at Vigo, and the last consuming exertion made by the army was thus rendered fruitless! The men were now put into quarters, and their leader awaited the progress of events. Three divisions occupied the town and suburbs; the reserve was posted with its left at the village of El Burgo, and its right on the road of St. Jago de Compostella. For twelve days these hardy soldiers had covered the retreat, during which time they had traversed eighty miles of road in two marches, passed several nights under arms in the snow of the mountains, were seven times engaged with the enemy, and they now assembled at the outposts, having fewer men missing from the ranks (including those who had fallen in battle) than any other division in the army. The bridge of El Burgo was immediately destroyed, and an engineer was sent to blow up that of Cambria, situated a few miles up the Mero river; this officer was mortified at former failures, and so anxious to perform his duty in an effectual manner, that he remained too near the mine, and was killed by the explosion; but there was also a bridge at Celas, two leagues higher up, and at that place Franceschi's cavalry crossed on the 12th, intercepted some stores coming from St. Jago, and made a few prisoners.

The town of Coruña, although sufficiently strong to oblige an enemy to break ground before it, was weakly fortified, and to the southward commanded by some heights close to the walls. Sir John Moore caused the land front to be repaired and strengthened, and also disarmed the sea-face of the works and occupied the citadel. The inhabitants cheerfully and honourably joined in the labour, although they were fully aware that the English intended to embark, and that they compromised their own safety by aiding the operation. Three miles from the town, 4000 barrels of powder were piled in a magazine built upon a hill; a smaller quantity, collected in another storehouse, was at some distance from the first: to prevent these magazines from falling a prey to the enemy, they were both exploded on the 13th. The inferior one blew up with a terrible noise and shook the houses in the town; but when the train reached the great store, there ensued a crash like the bursting forth of a volcano, the earth trembled for miles, the rocks were torn from their bases, and the agitated waters rolled the vessels as in a storm; a vast column of smoke and dust, shooting out fiery sparks from its sides, arose perpendicularly and slowly to a great height, and then a shower of stones and fragments of all kinds bursting out of it with a roaring sound, killed several persons who remained too near the spot. A stillness, only interrupted by the lashing of the waves on the shore, succeeded, and the business of the war went on.

The ground in front of Coruña is impracticable for cavalry, and as the horses still left alive were generally foundered, and it being impossible to embark them all in the face of an enemy, a great number were reluctantly ordered to be shot. These poor animals, already worn down and feet-broken, would otherwise have been distributed among the French cavalry, or used as draft cattle, until, by procrastinated sufferings of the nature they had already endured, they should be killed.

The enemy were now collecting in force on the Mero, and it became necessary to choose a position of battle. A chain of rocky elevations commencing on the sea-coast, north-west of the place, and ending on the Mero just behind the village of El Burgo, offered an advantageous line of defence; but this ridge was too extensive for the English army, and if not wholly occupied, the French might have turned it by the right, and moved along a succession of eminences to the very gates of Coruña. There was no alternative but to take post on an inferior range, enclosed as it were within the other, and completely commanded by it within cannon-shot.

The French army had been so exhausted by continual toil, that it was not completely assembled on the Mero before the 12th. The infantry took post opposite El Burgo; the cavalry of La Houssaye lined the river as far as the ocean, and Franceschi crossed at the bridge of Celas, seven miles higher up. On the 14th, the bridges of El Burgo being rendered practicable for artillery, two divisions of infantry and one of cavalry passed the river. To cover this march some guns opened on the English posts at

El Burgo, but were soon silenced by a superior fire. The same evening the transports from Vigo hove in sight, and soon after entered the harbour of Coruña, and the dismounted cavalry, the sick, all the best horses, and fifty-two pieces of artillery were embarked during the night; eight British and four Spanish guns were, however, retained on shore ready for action.

The 15th, Laborde's division arrived, and the French occupied the great ridge enclosing the British position. Towards evening their cavalry, supported by some light troops, extended towards the left, and a slight skirmish took place in the valley below. At the same time the English piquets opposite the right of the French got engaged, and being galled by the fire of two guns, Colonel M'Kenzie of the 5th, at the head of some companies, endeavoured to seize the battery; but a line of infantry, hitherto concealed by some stone walls, arose and poured in such a fire of musketry, that the colonel was killed, and his men forced back with loss. In the course of the night, Marshal Soult with great difficulty established a battery of eleven guns (eight and twelve pounders) on the rocks which formed the left of his line of battle. Laborde's division was posted on the right; half of it occupied the high ground, the other half was placed on the descent towards the river. Merle's division was in the centre. Mermet's division formed the left. The position was covered in front of the right by the villages of Palavia Abaxo and Portosa, and in front of the centre by a wood; the left was strongly posted on the rugged heights, where a great battery was established. The distance from that battery to the right of the English line was about 1200 yards, and midway the little village of Elvina was held by the piquets of the latter nation.

All the encumbrances of the army were shipped in the night of the 15th and on the morning of the 16th, and everything was prepared to withdraw the fighting men as soon as the darkness would permit them to move without being perceived. The precautions taken would without doubt have ensured the success of this difficult operation, but a more glorious event was destined to give a melancholy but graceful termination to the campaign. About two o'clock in the afternoon a general movement along the French line gave notice of the approaching battle of—

Coruña.

The British infantry, 14,500 strong, occupied the inferior range of hills already spoken of. The right was formed by Baird's division, and, from the oblique direction of the ridge, approached the enemy, while the centre and left were of necessity withheld in such a manner that the French battery on the rocks raked the whole of the line. General Hope's division, crossing the main road, prolonged the line of the right's wing, and occupied strong ground abutting on the muddy bank of the Mero. A brigade from Baird's division remained in column behind the extremities of his line, and a brigade of Hope's was posted on different commanding points behind the left wing. The reserve was drawn up near Airis, a small village situated in the rear of the centre. This last point commanded the valley which separated the right of Baird's division from the hills occupied by the French cavalry; the latter were kept in check by a regiment detached from the reserve, and a chain of skirmishers extending across the valley connected this regiment with the right of Baird's line. General Fraser's division remaining on the heights immediately before the gates of Coruña, was prepared to advance to any point, and also watched the coast road. These dispositions were as able as the unfavourable nature of the ground would admit of, but the advantage was all on the enemy's side. His light cavalry, under Franceschi, reaching nearly to the village of St. Christopher, a mile in the rear of Baird's division, obliged Sir John Moore to weaken his front by keeping back Fraser's division until Soult's plan of attack should be completely developed. General Laborde's division being come up, the French force could not be less than 20,000 men; and the Duke of Dalmatia having made his arrangements, did not lose any time in idle evolutions, but distributing his lighter guns along the front of his position, opened a heavy fire from the battery on his left, and instantly descended with three solid masses to the assault. A cloud of skirmishers led the way, and the British piquets being driven back in disorder, the village of Elvina was carried by the first column, which afterwards dividing, one half pushed on against Baird's front, the other turned his right by the valley. The second column made for the centre. The third engaged the left by the village of Palavia

Abaxo. The weight of the French guns overmatched the English six-pounders, and their shot swept the position to the centre.

Sir John Moore observing that, according to his expectations, the enemy did not show any body of infantry beyond that which, moving up the valley, outflanked Baird's right, ordered General Paget to carry the reserve to where the detached regiment was posted, and, as he had before arranged with him, to turn the left of the French attack and menace the great battery. Then directing Fraser's division to support Paget, he threw back the 4th regiment, which formed the right of Baird's division, opened a heavy fire upon the flank of the troops penetrating up the valley, and with the 50th and 42nd regiments met those breaking through Elvina. The ground about that village was intersected by stone walls and hollow roads; a severe, scrambling fight ensued, but in half an hour the French were borne back with great loss. The 50th regiment entered the village with them, and after a second struggle drove them for some distance beyond it. Meanwhile the general bringing up a battalion of the brigade of guards to fill the space in the line left vacant by those two regiments, the 42nd mistook his intention, and retired, and at that moment the enemy, being reinforced, renewed the fight beyond the village, the officer commanding the 50th was wounded and taken prisoner, and Elvina became the scene of a second struggle; this being observed by the commander-in-chief, who directed in person the operations of Baird's division, he addressed a few animating words to the 42nd, and caused it to return to the attack. General Paget, with the reserve, now descended into the valley, and the line of skirmishers being thus supported, vigorously checked the advance of the enemy's troops in that quarter, while the 4th regiment galled their flank. At the same time the centre and left of the army also became engaged; Sir David Baird was severely wounded, and a furious action ensued along the line, in the valley, and on the hills.

Sir John Moore, while earnestly watching the result of the fight about the village of Elvina, was struck on the left breast by a cannon-shot; the shock threw him from his horse with violence; he rose again in a sitting posture, his countenance unchanged, and his steadfast eye still fixed upon the regiments engaged in his front; no sigh betrayed a sensation of pain; but in a few moments, when he was satisfied the troops were gaining ground, his countenance brightened, and he suffered himself to be taken to the rear. Then was seen the dreadful nature of his hurt; the shoulder was shattered to pieces, the arm was hanging by a piece of skin, the ribs over the heart broken and bared of flesh, and the muscles of the breast torn into long strips, which were interlaced by their recoil from the dragging of the shot. As the soldiers placed him in a blanket his sword got entangled, and the hilt entered the wound. Captain Hardinge, a staff officer, who was near, attempted to take it off, but the dying man stopped him, saying, "It is as well as it is. I had rather it should go out of the field with me." And in that manner, so becoming to a soldier, Moore was borne from the fight.

During this time the army was rapidly gaining ground. The reserve, overthrowing everything in the valley, and obliging La Houssaye's dragoons (who had dismounted) to retire, turned the enemy's left, and even approached the eminence upon which the great battery was posted. On the left, Colonel Nicholls, at the head of some companies of the 14th, carried Palavio Abaxo (which General Foy defended but feebly), and in the centre the obstinate dispute for Elvina terminated in favour of the British; so that when the night set in their line was considerable advanced beyond the original position of the morning, and the French were falling back in confusion.

If at this time General Fraser's division had been brought into action along with the reserve, the enemy could hardly have escaped a signal overthrow; for the little ammunition Soult had been able to bring up was nearly exhausted, the river Mero, with a full tide, was behind him, and the difficult communication by the bridge of El Burgo was alone open for a retreat. On the other hand, to continue the action in the dark was to tempt fortune, for the French were still the most numerous, and their ground was strong. The disorder they were in offered such a favourable opportunity to get on board the ships, that Sir John Hope, upon whom the command of the army had devolved, satisfied with having repulsed the attack, judged it more prudent to pursue the original plan of embarking during the night, and this operation was effected without delay; the arrangements being so complete that neither confusion nor difficulty occurred.

The piquets kindling a number of fires, covered the retreat of the columns, and were themselves withdrawn at daybreak, and embarked, under the protection of General Hill's brigade, which was posted near the ramparts of the town. When the morning dawned, the French, observing that the British had abandoned their position, pushed forward some battalions to the heights of St. Lucie, and about midday succeeded in establishing a battery, which playing upon the shipping in the harbour, caused a great deal of disorder among the transports. Several masters cut their cables, and four vessels went ashore; but the troops being immediately removed by the men-of-war's boats, the stranded vessels were burnt, and the whole fleet at last got out of harbour. General Hill's brigade then embarked from the citadel; but General Beresford, with a rear-guard, still kept possession of that work until the 18th, when the wounded being all put on board, his troops likewise embarked. The inhabitants faithfully maintained the town against the French, and the fleet sailed for England.

Thus ended the retreat to Coruña. From the spot where he fell the general who had conducted it was carried to the town by a party of soldiers. The blood flowed fast, and the torture of his wound increased; but such was the unshaken firmness of his mind, that those about him judging from the resolution of his countenance that his hurt was not mortal, expressed a hope of his recovery. Hearing this, he looked steadfastly at the injury for a moment, and then said, "No, I feel that to be impossible." Several times he caused his attendants to stop and turn him round, that he might behold the field of battle, and when the firing indicated the advance of the British, he discovered his satisfaction and permitted the bearers to proceed. Being brought to his lodgings, the surgeons examined his wound, but there was no hope; the pain increased, and he spoke with great difficulty. At intervals he asked if the French were beaten, and addressing his old friend Colonel Anderson, he said, "You know that I always wished to die this way." Again he asked if the enemy were defeated, and being told they were, observed, "It is a great satisfaction to me to know we have beaten the French." His countenance continued firm and his thoughts clear; once only, when he spoke of his mother, he became agitated. He inquired after the safety of his friends and the officers of his staff, and he did not even in this moment forget to recommend those whose merit had given them claims to promotion. His strength was failing fast, and life was just extinct, when, with an unsubdued spirit, he exclaimed, "I hope the people of England will be satisfied! I hope my country will do me justice!" The battle was scarcely ended when his corpse, wrapped in a military cloak, was interred by the officers of his staff in the citadel of Coruña. The guns of the enemy paid his funeral honours, and Soult, with a noble feeling of respect for his valour, raised a monument to his memory.

Thus ended the career of Sir John Moore, a man whose uncommon capacity was sustained by the purest virtue, and governed by a disinterested patriotism more in keeping with the primitive than the luxurious age of a great nation. His tall graceful person, his dark searching eyes, strongly defined forehead, and singularly expressive mouth, indicated a noble disposition and a refined understanding. The lofty sentiments of honour habitual to his mind, adorned by a subtle playful wit, gave him in conversation an ascendancy that he could well preserve by the decisive vigour of his actions. He maintained the right with a vehemence bordering upon fierceness, and every important transaction in which he was engaged increased his reputation for talent, and confirmed his character as a stern enemy to vice, a steadfast friend to merit, a just and faithful servant of his country. The honest loved him, the dishonest feared him; for while he lived, he did not shun, but scorned and spurned the base, and, with characteristic propriety, they spurned at him when he was dead.

CHAPTER III.

THE FRENCH SIEGE OF ZARAGOZA.

WHILE the campaign of Coruña was being so disastrously carried on, in another part of the country the French troops were vigorously though unsuccessfully withstood. During the months of June, July, and August 1808, an attempt had been made to capture the city of Zaragoza from the insurrectionary Spaniards, at which time the French had to retire ingloriously. A further effort was made in December, which lasted till February 21, 1809, when the town was compelled through complete exhaustion to capitulate. The houses of Zaragoza were fireproof, and generally of only two stories, and in all the quarters of the city the numerous massive convents and churches rose like castles above the low buildings; while the greater streets, running into a broad way called the Cosso, divided the town into a variety of districts, unequal in size, but each containing one or more large structures. The citizens, sacrificing all personal convenience, and resigning all idea of private property, gave up their goods, their bodies, and their houses to the war, and being promiscuously mingled with the peasantry and the regular soldiers, the whole formed one mighty garrison, well suited to the vast fortress into which Zaragoza was transformed; for the doors and windows of the houses were built up and their fronts loopholed; internal communications were broken through the party-walls; the streets were trenched and crossed by earthen ramparts mounted with cannon, and every strong building was turned into a separate fortification. There was no weak point, because there could be none in a town which was all fortress, and where the space covered by the city was the measurement for the thickness of the ramparts : nor in this emergency were the leaders unmindful of moral force.

The people were cheered by a constant reference to the former successful resistance; their confidence was raised by the contemplation of the vast works that had been executed; and it was recalled to their recollection that the wet, usual at that season of the year, would spread disease among the enemy's ranks, and would impair, if not entirely frustrate, his efforts. Neither was the aid of superstition neglected; processions imposed upon the sight, false miracles bewildered the imagination, and terrible denunciations of the divine wrath shook the minds of men whose former habits and present situation rendered them peculiarly susceptible of such impressions. Finally, the leaders were themselves so prompt and terrible in their punishments, that the greatest cowards were likely to show the boldest bearing in their wish to escape suspicion.

To avoid the danger of any great explosion, the powder was made as occasion required; this was the more easily effected because Zaragoza contained a royal depôt and refinery for saltpetre, and there were powder-mills in the neighbourhood, which furnished workmen familiar with the process of manufacturing that article. The houses and trees beyond the walls were all demolished and cut down, and the materials carried into the town. The public magazines contained six months' provisions; the convents were well stocked, and the inhabitants had likewise laid up their own stores for several months. Companies of women, enrolled to attend the hospitals and to carry provisions and ammunition to the combatants, were commanded by the Countess of Burita, a lady of heroic disposition, who is said to have displayed the greatest intelligence and the noblest character during both sieges. There was also a garrison of 30,000 men, and, with the inhabitants and peasantry, presented altogether a mass of 50,000 combatants, who, with passions excited almost to frenzy, awaited an assault amidst those mighty entrenchments, where each man's home was a fortress and his family a garrison. To besiege with only 35,000 men a city so prepared was truly a gigantic undertaking.

On the 20th of December, the two marshals, Moncey and

Mortier, having established their hospitals and magazines at Alagon on the Xalon, advanced in three columns against Zaragoza. The right and centre columns arrived in front of the town that evening. The latter, after driving back the Spanish advanced guards, halted at a distance of a league from the Capuchin convent of the Trinity; the former took post on both sides of the Huerba, and having seized the aqueduct by which the canal is carried over that river, proceeded to raise batteries and to make dispositions for an immediate assault on Monte Torrero. Meanwhile General Gazan, with the left column, reached Villa Nueva, on the Gallego river, without encountering an enemy. Monte Torrero was defended by 5000 Spaniards, under the command of General St. Marc; but at daybreak on the 21st the French opened their fire against the fort, and one column of infantry having attracted the attention of the Spaniards, a second, unseen, crossed the canal under the aqueduct, and, penetrating between the fort and the city, entered the former by the rear, and at the same time a third column stormed the works protecting the great sluices. These sudden attacks and the loss of the fort threw the Spaniards into confusion, and they hastily retired to the town, which so enraged the plebeian leaders that the life of St. Marc was with difficulty saved by Palafox, governor of the city.

It had been concerted among the French that General Gazan should assault the suburb, simultaneously with the attack on the Torrero; and that officer, having encountered a body of Spanish and Swiss troops placed somewhat in advance, drove the former back so quickly, that the Swiss, unable to make good their retreat, were, to the number of 300 or 400, killed or taken. But notwithstanding this fortunate commencement, Gazan did not attack the suburb itself until after the affair at Monte Torrero was over, and then only upon a single point, and without any previous examination of the works. The Spaniards, recovering from their first alarm, soon reinforced this point, and Gazan was forced to desist, with the loss of 400 men. This important failure more than balanced the success against the Monte Torrero. It restored the shaken confidence of the Spaniards at a most critical moment, and checking in the French at the outset that impetuous spirit, that impulse of victory, which great generals so carefully watch and improve, threw them back upon the tedious and chilling process of the engineer.

The 24th of December the investment of Zaragoza was completed on both sides of the Ebro. General La Coste, an engineer of reputation and aide-de-camp to the Emperor, directed the siege. His plan was, that one false and two real attacks should be conducted by regular approaches on the right bank of the Ebro, and he still hoped to take the suburb by a sudden assault. The trenches being opened on the night of the 29th of December, the 30th the place was summoned, and terms were offered. The example of Madrid was cited to induce a surrender. Palafox replied, that if Madrid had surrendered, Madrid had been sold: Zaragoza would neither be sold nor surrender! On the receipt of this haughty answer the attacks were commenced; the right being directed against the convent of San Joseph; the centre against the upper bridge over the Huerba; the left, which was the false one, against the castle of Aljaferia.

The 31st, Palafox made sorties against all the three attacks. From the right and centre he was beaten back with loss, and he was likewise repulsed on the left at the trenches; but some of his cavalry gliding between the French parallel and the Ebro, surprised and cut down a post of infantry stationed behind some ditches that intersected the low ground on the bank of that river. This trifling success exalted the enthusiasm of the besieged, and Palafox gratified his personal vanity by boasting proclamations and orders of the day, some of which bore the marks of genius, but the greater part were ridiculous.

Marshal Moncey being called to Madrid, Junot assumed the command of the third corps, and about the same time Marshal Mortier was directed to take post at Balatayud with Suchet's division, for the purpose of securing the communication with Madrid. The gap in the circle of investment left by this draft of 8000 men being but scantily stopped by extending General Morlot's division, a line of contravallation was constructed at that part to supply the place of numbers. The besieged, hoping and expecting each day that the usual falls of rain taking place would render the besiegers' situation intolerable, continued their fire briskly, and worked counter-approaches on to the right of the French attacks; but the season was unusually dry, and a thick fog rising each morning covered the besiegers' advances and protected their workmen both from the fire and from the sorties of the Spaniards.

On the 10th of January, thirty-two pieces of French artillery being mounted and provisioned, the convent of San Joseph and the head of the bridge over the Huerba were battered in breach and the town was bombarded. San Joseph was so much injured by this fire, that the Spaniards, resolving to evacuate it, withdrew their guns. Nevertheless 200 of their men made a vigorous sortie at midnight, and were upon the point of entering one of the French batteries, when they were taken in flank by two guns loaded with grape, and were finally driven back, with loss of half their number. On the 11th, the besiegers' batteries continued to play on San Joseph, with such success that the breach became practicable, and at four o'clock in the evening some companies of infantry, with two field-pieces, attacked by the right, and a column was kept in readiness to assail the front when this attack should have shaken the defence. Two other companies of chosen men were directed to search for an entrance by the rear, between the fort and the river. The defences of the convent were reduced to a ditch eighteen feet deep and a covered way which extended along the banks of the Huerba for some distance. A considerable number of men occupied this covered way; but, when the French field-pieces on the right raked it with a fire of grape, the Spaniards were thrown into confusion, and crossing the bed of the river, took shelter in the town. At that moment the front of the convent was assaulted; but while the depth of the ditch and the Spanish fire checked the impetuosity of the assailants at that point, the chosen companies passed round the works, and finding a small bridge over the ditch, crossed it, and entered the convent by the rear. The front was carried by escalade almost at the same moment, and the few hundred Spaniards that remained were killed or made prisoners.

The French, who suffered but little in this assault, immediately lodged themselves in the convent, raised a rampart along the edge of the Huerba, and commenced batteries against the body of the place and against the works at the head of the upper bridge, from whence, as well as from the town, they were incommoded by the fire that played into the convent. On the

15th, the bridge-head in front of Santa Engracia was carried with the loss of only three men; but the Spaniards cut the bridge itself and sprung a mine under the works. The explosion, however, occasioned no mischief, and the third parallels being soon completed, and the trenches of the two attacks united, the defences of the besieged were thus confined to the town itself. They could no longer make sallies on the right bank of the Huerba without overcoming the greatest difficulties. The passage of the Huerba was then effected by the French, and breaching and counter-batteries, mounting fifty pieces of artillery, were constructed against the body of the place. The fire of these guns played also upon the bridge over the Ebro, and interrupted the communication between the suburb and the town.

Unshaken by this aspect of affairs, the Spanish leaders, with great readiness of mind, immediately forged intelligence of the defeat of the Emperor, and, with the sound of music and amidst the shouts of the populace, proclaimed the names of the marshals who had been killed, asserting, also, that Palafox's brother, the Marquis of Lazan, was already wasting France. This intelligence, extravagant as it was, met with implicit credence, and their anticipations of victory seemed realised when the night-fires of a succouring force were discerned blazing on the hills behind Gazan's troops. The difficulties of the French were indeed fast increasing, for while enclosing Zaragoza they were themselves encircled by insurrections, and their supplies so straitened that famine was felt in their camp. Disputes amongst the generals also diminished the vigour of the operations, and the bonds of discipline being relaxed, the military ardour of the troops naturally became depressed. The soldiers reasoned openly upon the chances of success, which, in times of danger, is only one degree removed from mutiny.

The nature of the country about Zaragoza was exceedingly favourable to the Spaniards. The town, although situated in a plain, was surrounded, at the distance of some miles, by strong and high mountains, and, to the south, the fortresses of Mequinenza and Lerida afforded a double base of operations for any forces that might come from Catalonia and Valencia. The besiegers drew all their supplies from Pampeluna, and their long line of operations was difficult to defend from the insurgents, who gathered in considerable numbers. The Marquis of Lazan, anxious to assist his brother, had drafted 5000 men from the Catalonian army, and, taking post on the left of the Ebro, drew together all the armed peasantry of the valleys, hemmed in the division of Gazan, and even sent detachments to harass the French convoys coming from Pampeluna.

In this state of affairs Marshal Lannes arrived before Zaragoza, and took the supreme command of both corps on the 22nd of January. The influence of his firm and vigorous character was immediately perceptible. A few days before the arrival of Marshal Lannes, the besieged being exceedingly galled by the fire from a mortar-battery, situated at some distance behind the second parallel of the central attack, eighty volunteers, under the command of Don Mariano Galindo, endeavoured to silence it. They surprised and bayoneted the guard in the nearest trenches, and passing on briskly to the battery, entered it, and were proceeding to spike the artillery, when unfortunately the reserve of the French arrived, and the alarm being given, the guards of the first trenches also assembled in the rear of this gallant band, intercepting all retreat. Thus surrounded, Galindo, fighting bravely, was wounded and taken, and the greatest part of his comrades perished with as much honour as simple soldiers can attain.

The armed vessels in the river now made an attempt to flank the works raised against the castle of Aljaferia, but the French batteries forced them to drop down the stream again; and between the nights of the 21st and the 26th of January the besiegers' works being carried across the Huerba, the third parallels of the real attacks were completed. An oil manufactory, and some other advantageous posts on the left bank of the river, were also taken possession of and included in the works, and at the false attack a second parallel was commenced at the distance of 150 yards from the castle of Aljaferia; but these advantages were not obtained without loss. The Spaniards made sallies, in one of which they spiked two guns and burnt a French post on the right.

The besiegers' batteries had, however, broken the wall of the town in several places. Two practicable breaches were made nearly fronting the convent of San Joseph; a third was commenced in the convent of Saint Augustin, facing the oil manufactory, and on the 29th, at twelve o'clock, the whole army being under arms, four chosen columns rushed out of the trenches and burst upon the ruined works of Zaragoza. On the right, the assailants twice stormed an isolated stone house that defended the breach of Saint Augustin, and twice they were repulsed, and finally driven back with loss. In the centre the attacking column, regardless of two small mines that exploded at the foot of the walls, carried the breach fronting the oil manufactory, and then endeavoured to break into the town; but the Spaniards opened such a fire of grape and musketry, that the French were content to establish themselves on the summit of the breach, and to connect their lodgment with the trenches by new works. The third column was more successful; the breach was carried, and the neighbouring houses also, as far as the first large cross street; beyond that the assailants could not penetrate, but they were enabled to establish themselves within the walls of the town, and immediately brought forward their trenches, so as to comprehend this lodgment within their works. The assault of the fourth column, which was directed against San Engracia, was made with rapidity and vigour, and the victorious troops, unchecked by the fire from the houses, and undaunted by the simultaneous explosion of six small mines planted in their path, swept the ramparts to the left as far as the bridge over the Huerba; and, at that moment, the guards of the trenches, excited by the success of their comrades, broke forth, without orders, mounted the walls, pushed along the ramparts to the left, bayoneted the artillerymen at their guns in the Capuchin convent, and, continuing their career, endeavoured, some to reach the semicircular battery, and others to break into the town.

This wild assault was soon checked by grape from two guns planted behind a traverse on the ramparts, and by a murderous fire from the houses. As their ranks were thinned, the ardour of the French sunk, and the courage of their adversaries increased. The former were, after a little, driven back upon the Capuchins; and the Spaniards were already breaking into that convent in pursuit, when two battalions, detached by General Morlot from the trenches of the false attack, arrived, and secured possession of that point, which was, moreover, untenable by the Spaniards, inasmuch as the guns of the convent of Santa Ergracia saw it in reverse. The French took, on this day, more than 600 men. But General La Coste immediately abandoned the false attack against the castle, fortified the Capuchin convent and a house situated at an angle of the wall abutting upon the bridge over the Huerba, and then joining them by works to his trenches, the ramparts of the town became the front line of the French. The walls of Zaragoza thus went to the ground, but Zaragoza herself remained erect; and as the broken girdle fell from the heroic city, the besiegers started at the view of her naked strength. The regular defences had, indeed, crumbled before the skill of the assailants, but the popular resistance was immediately called, with all its terrors, into action; and, as if Fortune had resolved to mark the exact moment when the ordinary calculations of science should cease, the chief engineers on both sides were simultaneously slain. The French general, La Coste, a young man, intrepid, skilful, and endowed with genius, perished like a brave soldier; but the Spanish colonel, San Genis, died not only with the honour of a soldier, but the glory of a patriot; falling in the noblest cause, his blood stained the ramparts which he had himself raised for the protection of his native place.

The war being now carried into the streets of Zaragoza, the sound of the alarm-bell was heard over all the quarters of the city, and the people, assembling in crowds, filled the houses nearest to the lodgments made by the French. Additional traverses and barricades were constructed across the principal streets; mines were prepared in the more open spaces; and the communications from house to house were multiplied, until they formed a vast labyrinth, of which the intricate windings were only to be traced by the weapons and the dead bodies of the defenders. The members of the junta, become more powerful from the cessation of regular warfare, with redoubled activity and energy urged the defence, but increased the horrors of the siege by a ferocity pushed to the very verge of frenzy. Every person, without regard to rank or age, who excited the suspicions of these furious men, or of those immediately about them, was instantly put to death; and amidst the noble bulwarks of war, a horrid array of gibbets was to be seen, on which crowds of wretches were suspended each night, because their courage had sunk beneath the accumulating dangers of their situation, or because some doubtful expression or gesture of distress had been misconstrued by their barbarous chiefs.

From the heights of the walls which he had conquered, Marshal Lannes contemplated this terrific scene, and judging that men so passionate and so prepared could not be prudently encountered in open battle, he resolved to proceed by the slow but certain process of the mattock and the mine. Hence from the 29th of January to the 2nd of February, the efforts of the French were directed to the enlargement of their lodgments on the walls; and they succeeded, after much severe fighting and several explosions, in working forward through the nearest houses; but at the same time they had to sustain many counter-assaults from the Spaniards, especially one, exceedingly fierce, made by a friar on the Capuchins' convent of the Trinity. The crossing of the large streets divided the town into certain small districts or islands of houses, and to gain possession of these it was necessary not only to mine, but to fight for each house. To cross the large intersecting streets, it was indispensable to construct traverses above or to work by underground galleries; because a battery raked each street, and each house was defended by a garrison that, generally speaking, had only the option of repelling the enemy in front or dying on the gibbet erected behind. But as long as the convents and churches remained in possession of the Spaniards, the progress of the French among the islands of small houses was of little advantage to them, because the large garrisons in the greater buildings enabled the defenders not only to make continual and successful sallies, but also to countermine their enemies, whose superior skill in that kind of warfare was often frustrated by the numbers and persevering energy of the besieged. To overcome these obstacles, the breaching batteries opposite the fourth front fired upon the convents of Saint Augustine and Saint Monica, and the latter was assaulted on the 31st of January. At the same time a part of the wall in another direction being thrown down by a petard, a body of the besiegers poured in, and, taking the main breach in rear, cleared not only the convent, but several houses around it. The Spaniards, undismayed, immediately opened a gallery from Saint Augustin and worked a mine under Saint Monica, but at the moment of its being charged, the French discovered and stifled the miners.

SIEGE OF ZARAGOZA.

On the 1st of February the breach in Saint Augustin became practicable, and the attention of the besieged being drawn to that side, the French sprung a mine which they had carried under the wall from the side of Saint Monica, and immediately entered by the opening. The Spaniards, thus unexpectedly taken in the rear, were thrown into confusion, and driven out with little difficulty. They, however, rallied in a few hours after, and attempted to retake the structure, but without success, and the besiegers, animated by this advantage, broke into the neighbouring houses, and at one push carried so many as to arrive at the point where the street called the Quemada joined the Cosso, or public walk. The besieged rallied, however, at the last house of the Quemada, and renewed the combat with so much fury that the French were beaten from the greatest part of the houses they had taken, and suffered a loss of 100 men. On the side of San Engracia a contest still more severe took place; the houses in the vicinity were blown up, but the Spaniards fought so obstinately for the ruins, that the attacking force was scarcely able to make good a lodgment, although two successive and powerful explosions had, with the buildings, destroyed a number of the defenders.

The experience of these attacks induced a change in the mode of fighting on both sides. Hitherto the play of the French mines had reduced the houses to ruins, and thus the soldiers were exposed completely to the fire from the next Spanish posts. The engineers, therefore, diminished the quantity of powder, that the interior only might fall and the outward walls stand, and this method was found successful. Hereupon the Spaniards, with ready ingenuity, saturated the timbers and planks of the houses with rosin and pitch, and setting fire to those which could no longer be maintained, interposing a burning barrier which often delayed the assailants for two days, and always prevented them from pushing their successes during the confusion that necessarily followed the bursting of the mines. The fighting was, however, incessant; a constant bombardment, the explosion of mines, the crash of falling buildings, clamorous shouts, and the continued echo of musketry deafened the ear, while volumes of smoke and dust clouded the atmosphere, and lowered continually over the heads of the combatants, as hour by hour the French, with a terrible perseverance, pushed forward their approaches to the heart of the miserable but glorious city.

Their efforts were chiefly directed against two points, namely, that of San Engracia, which may be denominated the left attack, and that of Saint Augustin and Saint Monica, which constituted the right attack. At San Engracia they laboured on a line perpendicular to the Cosso, from which they were only separated by the large convent of the Daughters of Jerusalem, and by the hospital for madmen, which was entrenched, although in ruins since the first siege. The line of this attack was protected on the left by the convent of the Capuchins, which La Coste had fortified to repel the counter-assaults of the Spaniards. The right attack was more diffused, because the localities presented less prominent features to determine the direction of the approaches; and the French having mounted a number of light six-inch mortars on peculiar carriages, drew them from street to street and house to house, as occasion offered. On the other hand, the Spaniards continually plied their enemies with hand-grenades, which seem to have produced a surprising effect, and in this manner the never-ceasing combat was prolonged until the 7th of February, when the besiegers, by dint of alternate mines and assaults, had worked their perilous way at either attack to the Cosso, but not without several changes of fortune and considerable loss. They were, however, unable to obtain a footing on that public walk, for the Spaniards still disputed every house with undiminished resolution.

Meanwhile, Lannes having caused trenches to be opened on the left bank of the Ebro, a battery of twenty guns played against an isolated structure called the Convent of Jesus, which covered the right of the suburb line. On the 7th of February this convent was carried by storm, and with so little difficulty, that the French, supposing the Spaniards to be panic-stricken, assailed the suburb itself, but were quickly driven back with loss; they, however, made good their lodgment in the convent. On the town side three days were wasted by the besiegers in vain attempts to pass the Cosso; they then extended their flanks—on the right with a view to reach the quay, and so connect this attack with that against the suburb, and on the left to obtain possession of the large and strongly-built convent of Saint Francisco, in which, after exploding an immense mine and making two assaults, they finally established themselves. On the 11th and 12th, mines were worked under the university, a large building on the Spanish side of the Cosso, in the line of the right attack; but their play was insufficient to open the walls, and the storming party was beaten, with the loss of fifty men. Nevertheless, the besiegers, continuing their labours, passed the Cosso by means of traverses, and prepared fresh mines under the university, but deferred their explosion until a simultaneous effort could be combined on the side of the suburb.

At the left attack also, a number of houses bordering on the Cosso being gained, a battery was established that raked that great thoroughfare above ground, while under it six galleries were carried, and six mines loaded to explode at the same moment. But the spirit of the French army was now exhausted; they had laboured and fought without intermission for fifty days; they had crumbled the walls with their bullets, burst the convents with their mines, and carried the breaches with their bayonets,— fighting above and beneath the surface of the earth, they had spared neither fire nor the sword, their bravest men were falling in the obscurity of a subterranean warfare; famine pinched them, and Zaragoza was still unconquered! "Before this siege," they exclaimed, "was it ever heard of that 20,000 men should besiege 50,000?" Scarcely a fourth of the town was won, and they themselves were already exhausted. "We must wait," they said, "for reinforcements, or we shall all perish among their cursed ruins, which will become our own tombs, before we can force the last of these fanatics from the last of their dens."

Marshal Lannes, unshaken by these murmurs and obstinate to conquer, endeavoured to raise the soldiers' hopes. He pointed out to them that the losses of the besieged so far exceeded their own, that the Spaniards' strength would soon be wasted and their courage must sink, and that the fierceness of their defence was already abated; their utter destruction must quickly ensue from the united effects of battle, misery, and pestilence. These exhortations succeeded, and on the 18th February, all the combinations being complete, a general assault took place. The French at the right attack, having opened a party-wall by the explosion of a petard, made a sudden rush through some burning ruins, and carried, without a check, the island of houses leading down to the quay, with the exception of two buildings. The Spaniards were thus forced to abandon all the external fortifications between Saint Augustin and the Ebro, which they had preserved until that day. And while this assault was in progress, the mines under the university, containing 3000 lbs. of powder, were sprung, and the walls tumbling with a terrific crash, a column of the besiegers entered the place, and after one repulse secured a lodgment. During this time fifty pieces of artillery thundered upon the suburb and ploughed up the bridge over the Ebro, and by mid-day opened a practicable breach in the great convent of Saint Lazar, which was the principal defence on that side. Lannes, observing that the Spaniards seemed to be shaken by this overwhelming fire, immediately ordered an assault, and Saint Lazar being carried forthwith, all retreat to the bridge was thus intercepted, and the besieged falling into confusion, and their commander, Baron Versage, being killed, were all destroyed or taken, with the exception of 300 men, who, braving the terrible fire to which they were exposed, got back into the town. General Gazan immediately occupied the abandoned works, and having thus cut off above 2000 men that were stationed on the Ebro above the suburb, forced them also to surrender.

This important success being followed on the 19th by another fortunate attack on the right bank of the Ebro, and by the devastating explosion of 1600 lbs. of powder, the constancy of the besieged was at last shaken. An aide-de-camp of Palafox came forth to demand certain terms, before offered by the Marshal, adding thereto that the garrison should be allowed to join the Spanish armies, and that a certain number of covered carriages should follow them. Lannes rejected these proposals, and the fire continued, but the hour of surrender was come. Fifty pieces of artillery on the left bank of the Ebro laid the houses on the quay in ruins. The church of Our Lady of the Pillar, under whose especial protection the city was supposed to exist, was nearly effaced by the bombardment, and the six mines under the Cosso, loaded with many thousand pounds of powder, were ready for a simultaneous explosion, which would have laid a quarter of the remaining houses in the dust. In fine, war had done its work, and the misery of Zaragoza could no longer be endured.

The bombardment, which had never ceased since the 10th of January, had forced the women and children to take refuge in the vaults, with which the city abounded. There the constant combustion of oil, the closeness of the atmosphere, unusual diet, and fear and restlessness of mind, had combined to produce a pestilence which soon spread to the garrison. The strong and the weak, the daring soldier and the shrinking child, fell before it alike, and such was the state of the atmosphere and the predisposition to disease, that the slightest wound gangrened and became incurable. In the beginning of February the deaths were from 400 to 500 daily; the living were unable to bury the dead, and thousands of carcasses, scattered about the streets and courtyards, or piled in heaps at the doors of the churches, were left to dissolve in their own corruption, or to be licked up by the flames of the burning houses as the defence became contracted.

The suburb, the greatest part of the walls, and one-fourth of the houses were in the hands of the French; 16,000 shells thrown during the bombardment, and the explosion of 45,000 lbs. of powder in the mines, had shaken the city to its foundations; and the bones of more than 40,000 persons, of every age and sex, bore dreadful testimony to the constancy of the besieged.

Palafox was sick, and many of the plebeian chiefs having been slain in battle or swept away by the pestilence, the obdurate violence of the remaining leaders was so abated that a fresh junta was formed, and after a stormy consultation, the majority being for a surrender, a deputation waited upon Marshal Lannes on the 20th of February to negotiate a capitulation.

They proposed that the garrison should march out with the honours of war; that the peasantry should not be considered as prisoners; and at the particular request of the clergy, they also demanded that the latter should have their full revenues guaranteed to them and punctually paid. This article was rejected with indignation, and, according to the French writers, the place surrendered at discretion; but the Spanish writers assert that Lannes granted certain terms, drawn up by the deputation at the moment. With this the deputies returned to the city; but fresh commotions had arisen during their absence. The party for protracting the defence, although the least numerous, were the most energetic; they had before seized all the boats on the Ebro,

THE PENINSULAR CAMPAIGN.

fearing that Palafox and others, of whom they entertained suspicions, would endeavour to quit the town; and they were still so menacing and so powerful, that the deputies durst not pass through the streets, but retired outside the walls to the castle of Aljaferia, and from thence sent notice to the junta of their proceedings. The dissentient party would, however, have fallen upon the others the next day, if the junta had not taken prompt measures to enforce the surrender. The officer in command of the walls near the castle, by their orders, gave up his post to the French during the night, and on the 21st of February from 12,000 to 15,000 sickly beings laid down those arms which they were scarcely able to support, and this cruel and memorable siege was finished.

Reference has been made, in the preceding chapter, to the exertions of the companies of women commanded by the Countess of Burita, in attendance at the hospitals and carrying provisions and ammunition to the defenders of Zaragoza. A singular instance of female heroism in the previous siege of June 1808 deserves to be recorded here. Augustina, a handsome woman of about twenty-two years of age, arrived at a battery near one of the gates with refreshments for her lover, at a time when not one of the defenders was left alive, so tremendous had been the fire the French had kept up against this post. For a short time the Zaragozans hesitated to re-man the guns. Augustina sprang forward over the dead and dying, snatched the match from the hand of a dead artilleryman, and fired off a 26-pounder; then, jumping upon the gun, vowed never to quit it alive during the siege. This sight animated with fresh courage all who saw it. The Zaragozans rushed into the battery, renewed their fire with greater vigour than ever, and the French were repulsed with great slaughter. At the later siege the Maid of Zaragoza again greatly distinguished herself, serving at the same gun as formerly. When the final capture of the city took place, she was too well known to escape notice, and was made prisoner. Being removed to an hospital, where, as she was supposed to be dying, little care was taken, she availed herself of this to effect her escape to Seville.—*Southey's History of the War.*

CHAPTER IV.

GRIJON—PASSAGE OF THE DOURO.

HERE was absolute dismay when the shattered remnants of Moore's expedition were seen by the English people, and the opinion at first was loudly urged that resistance to Napoleon except by sea was only a vain sacrifice of men's lives; but this opinion soon gave place to an earnest determination to prosecute the war with renewed vigour. After some months of vacillation, the Government decided to act again in Portugal, and sent out Sir Arthur Wellesley in April 1809 to take the supreme command. His appointment gave unity of action and purpose to the British and allied forces, putting a stop to the petty jealousies and dissensions which had been but too prevalent among the various leaders of the different bodies of troops. It was a gigantic undertaking to expel from the Peninsula the invading force of 300,000 of the best troops in the world, ably led and amply supplied, to oppose whom Britain at no time during the campaigns had more than 50,000 men in the field, aided by a somewhat unreliable force of Spanish and Portuguese; but the genius of their chief gave these apparently insufficient means an efficacy not entirely their own.

The forces of the enemy against whom Wellesley was to operate were at this time greatly divided. Napoleon himself had been compelled to return to France, owing to the renewed outbreak of hostilities by Austria, and had left the command of his forces in Spain to Marshal Soult, who now concerted with General Victor a combined attack on certain provinces of Portugal. The former

THE PENINSULAR CAMPAIGN.

was to advance through Coimbra upon Lisbon, while Victor was to co-operate by marching from Alcantara to Abrantes, and, after securing that fortress, was to continue his progress towards the capital. Many delays, however, occurred in the execution of this project, which, had it been promptly carried out, would have caused the embarkation of the British army and given a new aspect to the war. But Soult remained inactive at Oporto, influenced by dread of risking his army by an unsupported operation and the increasing embarrassments of his position. The bridge of Amarante was in possession of the Portuguese, and his only line of communication with Spain was thus cut off. A body of 6000 troops under General Laborde were sent to gain this bridge at any sacrifice, but so firm was the resistance, and so strong were the works by which it was defended, that the French were repeatedly repulsed. On a further attempt, by the explosion of a mine a breach was effected, and the French cavalry having crossed the river, the Portuguese were at length driven back.

Sir Arthur Wellesley soon perceived that the numerical superiority of the enemy was neutralised by the separation of their various corps, and he determined by a prompt and rapid advance to attack Soult and drive him from Oporto. This resolution he communicated to General Cuesta, the commander-in-chief of the Spanish forces, who was requested to content himself meanwhile with keeping Victor in check until the return of the British from Oporto, when the allies might act in combination on the south of the Tagus.

These projects of Wellesley did not escape the penetration of Soult, who, seeing the danger of being enclosed in the north of Portugal, determined to extricate himself from the perils of his situation by evacuating the country. Soult's difficulties at this time were not a little added to by the fact that serious discontent prevailed among the ranks of the French army. A secret society called the Philadelphes existed, the members of which had bound themselves to overthrow, whenever a favourable opportunity might occur, the imperial dynasty and to revive democracy in France. The head of this conspiracy in Soult's army was D'Argenton, an adjutant-major, who was in constant communication with the British head-quarters through one of the field-officers, to whom he proposed a scheme for seducing the French soldiers from their

DISPOSITION OF SOULT'S FORCES.

duty and arresting Soult. But his advances had been received with caution, and treated with the reserve which prudence required. This much, however, Sir Arthur Wellesley learned, that a mutinous spirit was at work in Oporto and that there were large numbers of sick in the hospitals.

Preparations were immediately made by Soult for the evacuation by removing his sick and baggage, he then destroyed the bridge across the Douro, and gave orders that all boats should be brought to his side of the river. Imagining that Wellesley would avail himself of his maritime resources to effect a landing near the mouth of the Douro, which would give Soult time for a leisurely retreat, he dispatched orders to prevent the allies crossing at other points. Had Soult been right in his calculations as to Wellesley's intentions, no hindrance would have existed to his retreat, but the English general had bolder measures in view, his purpose being to force the passage of the Douro and drive the enemy from the country.

After the capture of the bridge at Amarante, Laborde was recalled to Oporto, but a brigade of cavalry and a regiment of infantry were left to keep up the communication with Loison; and as the insurgent General Bonthielo had appeared on the Lima, General Lorge's dragoons were directed on that side. Mermet's division was pushed towards the Vouga, and thus the French army was extended by detachments from that river to the Tamega; and the wings, separated by the Douro and occupying two sides of a triangle, were without communication, except by the boat-bridge of Oporto. It required three days, therefore, to unite the army on its centre, and five days to concentrate it on either extremity. The situation of the allies was very different. Sir Arthur Wellesley having, unknown to Soult, assembled the bulk of the troops at Coimbra, commanded the choice of two lines of operation; one, by which, in four or five marches, he could turn the French left and cut them off from Tras os Montes; the other, by the roads leading upon Oporto, by which, in two marches, he could throw himself unexpectedly, and in very superior numbers, upon the enemy's right, with a fair prospect of crushing it between the Vouga and the Douro.

In taking the first of these two lines, which were separated by the lofty ridges of the Sierra de Caramula, the march could be

covered by Wilson's corps at Viseu, and by Sylveira's near
Lamego. Along the second the movement could be screened by
Trant's corps on the Vouga.

The Duke of Dalmatia's dispositions were made in ignorance
of Sir Arthur Wellesley's position, numbers, and intentions. He
was not even aware of the vicinity of such an antagonist, but
sensible that to advance directly upon Lisbon was beyond his
own strength, he already meditated to cross the Tamega, and
then, covered by that river and the Douro, to follow the great
route of Bragança, and so enter the Salamanca country. In view
of this, Loison had been directed to get possession of Mezamfrio
and Pezo de Ragoa, and General Mermet was directed to support
Franceschi's retreat when the army should commence its movement towards the Tamega.

On the 9th of May, D'Argenton was arrested; the film fell
from Soult's eyes, and all the perils of his position broke at once
upon his view. Treason in his camp, which he could not prove,
a powerful enemy close in his front, the insurgents again active in
his rear, and the French troops scattered from the Vouga to the
Tamega, and from the Douro to the Lima, and commanded by
officers whose fidelity was necessarily suspected, while the extent
of the conspiracy was unknown.

Appalling as this prospect was, the Duke of Dalmatia did not
quail at the view. The general officers assured him of the fidelity
of the troops, and Loison was immediately ordered under any
circumstances to hold Amarante fast. The greatest part of the
guns and stores at Oporto were directed upon the Tamega, and
the ammunition that could not be removed was destroyed.
General Lorge was commanded to withdraw from Viana and proceed to Amarante, and while D'Argenton was closely, although
vainly, pressed to discover the names of the conspirators, Soult
prepared to execute his intended movement through the Tras
os Montes. But the war was coming on with a full and swift
tide. Loison, upon whose vigour the success of the operation depended, was already giving way; Sir Arthur Wellesley was across
the Vouga, and Franceschi and Mermet were struggling in his
grasp.

The English general resolved to operate along both the routes
before spoken of, but the greater facility of supplying the troops

WELLESLEY'S PLAN OF ATTACK.

by the coast-line, and above all, the exposed position of the French right wing, so near the allies and so distant from succour, induced him to make the principal attack by the high-road leading to Oporto. The army was formed in one division of cavalry and three of infantry, exclusive of Beresford's separate corps.

Sir Arthur Wellesley's plan was partly arranged upon the suggestion of the field-officer who had met D'Argenton. He had observed, during his intercourse with the conspirators, that the Lake of Ovar was unguarded by the French, although it extended twenty miles behind their outposts, and that all the boats were at Aveiro, which was in possession of the allies. On his information it was decided to turn the enemy's right by the lake. Accordingly, General Hill embarked, the evening of the 9th, with one brigade, the other being to follow him as quickly as possible. The fishermen looked on at first with surprise; but soon comprehending the object, they voluntarily rushed in crowds to the boats, and worked with such a will that the whole flotilla arrived at Ovar precisely at sunrise on the 10th, and the troops immediately disembarked. That day, also, Marshal Beresford, having rallied Wilson's corps upon his own, reached Pezo de Ragoa and repulsed Loison, pursuing him to Amarante. Both flanks of the French army were now turned, and at the same moment Sir Arthur, with the main body, fell upon Franceschi; for while the flotilla was navigating the Lake of Ovar, the attempt to surprise that general at Albergaria Nova was in progress. Sherbrooke's division was still in the rear; but General Cotton with the light cavalry, crossed the Vouga a little after midnight, endeavoured to turn the enemy's left, and to get into his rear; the head of Paget's division, marching a little later, was to pass through the defiles of Vouga directly upon Albergaria, and Trant's corps was to make way between Paget's division and the Lake of Aveiro.

This enterprise, so well conceived, was baffled by petty events, such as always abound in war. Sir Arthur Wellesley did not perfectly know the ground beyond the Vouga; and late in the evening of the 9th, Colonel Trant, having ascertained that an impracticable ravine, extending from the lake to Olivera de Azemiz, would prevent him from obeying his orders, passed the bridge of Vouga, and carried his own guns beyond the defiles, in order to leave the bridge clear for the British artillery and for General Richard Stewart's brigade. Stewart was charged to conduct the guns through the defile; but the task was difficult, several carriages broke down, and Trant's corps thus took the lead of Paget's column, the march of which was impeded by the broken gun-carriages. Meanwhile the cavalry, under Cotton, were misled by the guides, and came, in broad daylight, upon Franceschi, who, with his flank resting upon a wood garnished with infantry, boldly offered a battle that Cotton durst not, under such circumstances, accept. Thus, an hour's delay, produced by a few trifling accidents, marred a combination that would have shorn Soult of a third of his infantry and all his light cavalry. When Sir Arthur Wellesley came up to Albergaria with Paget's infantry, Franceschi was still in position, skirmishing with Trant's corps, and evidently ignorant of what force was advancing against him. Being immediately attacked, and his foot dislodged from the wood, he retreated along the road to Oliveira de Azemis, being briskly pursued by the allied infantry; but extricating himself valiantly from his perilous situation, he reached Oliveira without any serious loss; and continuing his march during the night, joined Mermet the next morning at Grijon.

Franceschi, in the course of the 10th, could see the whole of the English army including the troops with Hill; and it may create surprise that he should pass so near the latter general without being attacked. But Hill was strictly obedient to his orders, which forbade him to act on the enemy's rear; and while the number of men on the left of the Douro was unknown, it would have been rash to interpose a single brigade between the advance-guard and the main body of the French. General Hill was sent to Ovar, that the line of march might be eased and the enemy's attention distracted, and so that a division of fresh soldiers might be at hand to follow the pursuit, and arrive on the bridge of Oporto pell-mell with the flying enemy. The soldier-like retreat of Franceschi prevented the last object from being attained. Next morning the pursuit was renewed, and the men, marching strongly, came up with the enemy at Grijon about eight o'clock in the morning.

Grijon.

The French were drawn up on a range of steep hills across the road. A wood, occupied with infantry, covered their right flank; their front was protected by villages and broken ground, but their left was ill placed. The British troops came on briskly in one column, and the head was instantly and sharply engaged. The 16th Portuguese regiment, then quitting the line of march, gallantly drove the enemy out of the wood covering his right, and at the same time the Germans, who were in the rear, bringing their left shoulders forward, without any halt or check, turned the other flank of the French. The latter immediately abandoned the position, and being pressed in the rear by two squadrons of cavalry, lost a few killed and about 100 prisoners. The heights of Carvalho gave them an opportunity to turn and check the pursuing squadrons; yet, when the British infantry, with an impetuous pace, drew near, they again fell back; and thus fighting and retreating, a blow and a race, wore the day away. During this combat, Hill was to have marched by the coast-road towards Oporto, to intercept the enemy's retreat; but by some error in the transmission of orders, that general, taking the route of Feria, crossed Trant's line of march, and the time lost could not be regained.

The British halted at dark, but the French, continuing their retreat, passed the Douro in the night, and at two o'clock in the morning the bridge was destroyed. All the artillery and baggage still in Oporto were immediately directed along the road to Amarante, and Mermet's division followed the same route, having instructions to secure all the boats and vigilantly to patrol the right bank of the Douro. Loison, also, whose retreat from Pezo de Ragoa was still unknown, once more received warning to hold on by the Tamega without fail, as he valued the safety of the army. Meanwhile the Duke of Dalmatia commanded all the craft in the river to be secured, and having placed guards at the most convenient points, proposed to remain at Oporto during the 12th, to give time for the different detachments of the army to concentrate at Amarante. Soult's personal attention was principally directed to the river in its course *below* the city; for the reports of his cavalry led him to believe that Hill's division had been disembarked at Ovar from the ocean, and he expected that the vessels would come round, and the passage be attempted at the mouth of the Douro. Nevertheless, thinking that Loison still held Pezo with 6000 men, and knowing that three brigades occupied intermediate posts between Amarante and Oporto, he was satisfied that his retreat was secured, and thought there was no rashness in maintaining his position for another day. The conspirators, however, were also busy; his orders were neglected, or only half obeyed, and false reports of their execution transmitted to him; and in this state of affairs the head of the British columns arrived at Villa Nova, and before eight o'clock in the morning of the 12th they were concentrated in one mass, but covered from the view of the enemy by the height on which the convent of Sarea stands.

The Douro rolled between the hostile forces. Soult had suffered nothing by the previous operations, and in two days he could take post behind the Tamega, from whence his retreat upon Bragança would be certain, and he might, in passing, defeat Beresford, for that general's force was feeble as to numbers, and in infancy as to organisation; and the utmost that Sir Arthur expected from it was that, vexing the French line of march and infesting the road of Villa Real, it would oblige Soult to retire to Gallicia instead of Leon; but this could not be, unless the main body of the allied troops followed the French closely. Now, Soult at Salamanca would be more formidable than Soult at Oporto, and hence the ultimate object of the campaign, and the immediate safety of Beresford's corps, alike demanded that the Douro should be quickly passed. But how force the passage of a river, deep, swift, and more than 300 yards wide, while 10,000 veterans guarded the opposite bank? Alexander the Great might have turned from it without shame!

The height of Sarea, round which the Douro came with a sharp elbow, prevented any view of the upper river from the town; but the Duke of Dalmatia, confident that all above the city was secure, took his station in a house westward of Oporto, whence he could discern the whole course of the lower river to its mouth. Meanwhile, from the summit of Sarea, the English general, with an eagle's glance, searched all the opposite bank and the city and country beyond it. He observed horses and baggage moving on the road to Vallonga, and the dust of columns as if in retreat, and no large body of troops was to be seen under arms near the river. The French guards were few and distant from each other, and the patrols were neither many nor vigilant; but a large unfinished building standing alone, yet with a short and easy access to it from the river, soon fixed Sir Arthur's attention. This building, called the Seminary, was surrounded by a high stone wall, which coming down to the water on either side, enclosed an area sufficient to contain at least two battalions in order of battle; the only egress being by an iron gate opening on the Vallonga road. The structure itself commanded everything in its neighbourhood, except a mound, within cannon-shot, but too pointed to hold a gun. There were no French posts near, and the direct line of passage from the height of Sarea, across the river to the building, being to the right hand, was of course hidden from the troops in the town. Here, then, with a marvellous hardihood, Sir Arthur resolved, if he could find but one boat, to make his way, in the face of a veteran army and a renowned general.

PASSAGE OF THE DOURO.

A boat was soon obtained; for a poor barber of Oporto, evading the French patrols, had during the night come over the water in a small skiff; this being discovered by Colonel Waters, a staff officer of a quick and daring temper, he and the barber, and the prior of Amarante, who gallantly offered his aid, crossed the river, and in half an hour returned unperceived with three or four large barges. Meanwhile, eighteen or twenty pieces of artillery were got up to the convent of Sarea; and Major-General John Murray, with the German brigade, some squadrons of the 14th dragoons, and two guns, reached Avintas, three miles higher up the river, his orders being to search for boats and to effect a passage there also if possible. Some of the British troops were now sent towards Avintas to support Murray; while others came cautiously forwards to the brink of the river. It was ten o'clock; the enemy were tranquil and unsuspicious; and an officer reported to Sir Arthur Wellesley that one boat was brought up to the point of passage. "Well, let the men cross," was the reply; and upon this simple order, an officer and twenty-five soldiers of the Buffs entered the vessel, and in a quarter of an hour were in the midst of the French army.

The Seminary was thus gained without any alarm being given, and everything was still quiet in Oporto: not a movement was to be seen; not a hostile sound was to be heard: a second boat followed the first, and then a third passed a little higher up the river; but scarcely had the men from the last landed, when a tumultuous noise of drums and shouts arose in the city; confused masses of the enemy were seen hurrying forth in all directions, and throwing out clouds of skirmishers, who came furiously down upon the Seminary. The citizens were descried gesticulating vehemently, and making signals from their houses; and the British troops instantly crowded to the bank of the river, Paget's and Hill's divisions at the point of embarkation, and Sherbrooke's where the old boat-bridge had been cut away from Villa Nova. Paget himself passed in the third boat, and, mounting the roof of the Seminary, was immediately struck down, severely wounded. Hill took Paget's place; the musketry was sharp, voluble, and increasing every moment as the number accumulated on both sides. The enemy's attack was fierce and constant; his fire augmented faster than that of the British, and his artillery also began to play on the building. But the English guns from the convent of Sarea commanded the whole enclosure round the Seminary, and swept the left of the wall in such a manner as to confine the French assault to the side of the iron gate. Murray, however, did not appear; and the struggle was so violent, and the moment so critical, that Sir Arthur would himself have crossed, but for the earnest representations of those about him, and the just confidence he had in General Hill.

Some of the citizens now pushed over to Villa Nova with several great boats; Sherbrooke's people began to cross in large bodies; and, at the same moment, a loud shout in the town and the waving of handkerchiefs from all the windows gave notice that the enemy had abandoned the lower part of the city: and now, also, Murray's troops were seen descending the right bank from Avintas. By this time three battalions were in the Seminary; and Hill, advancing to the enclosure wall, opened a destructive fire upon the French columns as they passed, in haste and confusion, by the Vallonga road. Five pieces of French artillery were coming out of the town on the left; but, appalled by the line of musketry to be passed, the drivers suddenly pulled up, and while thus hesitating, a volley from behind stretched most of the artillerymen on the ground; the rest, dispersing among the enclosures, left their guns on the road. This volley was given by a part of Sherbrooke's people, who, having forced their way through the streets, thus came upon the rear. In fine, the passage was won, and the allies were in considerable force on the French side of the river.

To the left, General Sherbrooke was in the town, and pressing the rear of the enemy, who were quitting it. In the centre, General Hill, holding the Seminary and the wall of the enclosure, sent a damaging fire into the masses as they passed him; and his line was prolonged on the right, although with a considerable interval, by General Murray's corps. The remainder of the army kept passing the river at different points; and the artillery from the height of Sarea still searched the enemy's columns as they hurried along the line of retreat.

If General Murray had then fallen boldly in upon the disordered crowds, their discomfiture would have been complete; but he suffered column after column to pass him without even a cannon-shot, and seemed fearful lest they should turn and push him into the river. General Charles Stuart and Major Hervey, however, impatient of this inactivity, charged with the two squadrons of dragoons, and rode over the enemy's rear-guard as it was pushing through a narrow road to gain an open space beyond. Laborde was unhorsed, Foy badly wounded; and, on the English side, Major Hervey lost an arm; and his gallant horsemen, receiving no support from Murray, were obliged to fight their way back with loss.

This finished the action; the French continued their retreat, and the British remained on the ground they had gained. The latter lost 20 killed, a general and 95 men wounded; the former had about 500 men killed and wounded, and five pieces of artillery were taken in the fight; a considerable quantity of ammunition and 50 guns (of which the carriages had been burnt) were afterwards found in the arsenal, and several hundred men were captured in the hospitals.

Napoleon's veterans were so experienced, so inured to warfare, that no troops in the world could more readily recover from such a surprise, and before they reached Vallonga their columns were again in order, with a regular rear-guard covering the retreat. A small garrison at the mouth of the Douro was cut off, but, guided by some friendly Portuguese, it rejoined the army in the night; and Soult, believing that Loison was at Amarante, thought he had happily escaped a great danger, and was still formidable to his enemies.

Sir Arthur Wellesley employed the remainder of the 12th and the next day in bringing over the rear of the army, together with the baggage, the stores, and the artillery. General Murray's Germans, however, pursued on the morning of the 13th, but not farther than about two leagues on the road of Amarante. The reasons for halting were, first, that a part of the army was still on the left bank of the Douro; secondly, that the troops had outmarched provisions, baggage, and ammunition, and having passed over above eighty miles of difficult country in four days, during three of which they were constantly fighting, both men and animals required rest; thirdly, that nothing was known of Beresford, whose contemporary operations it is time to relate. The moment of his arrival on the Douro was marked by the repulse of Loison's division, which immediately fell back to Mezamfrio, followed by the Portuguese patrols only, for Beresford halted on the left bank of the river, because the British regiments were still in the rear. This was on the 10th. Sylveira, who was at Villa Real, had orders to feel towards Mezamfrio for the enemy, and the Marshal's force was thus, with the assistance of the insurgents, in readiness to turn Soult from the route of Villa Real to Bragança.

On the 11th, Loison continued his retreat, and Beresford finding him so timid, followed, skirmishing with his rear-guard, and at the same time Sylveira advanced from Villa Real. On the 12th, the French outposts in front of Amarante were driven in, and on the 13th Loison abandoned that town, and took the route of Guimaraens. These events were unknown to Sir Arthur Wellesley on the evening of the 13th, but he heard that Soult, after destroying his artillery and ammunition near Penafiel, had passed over the mountain towards Braga; and judging this to arise from Beresford's operations on the Tamega, he reinforced Murray with some cavalry, ordering him to proceed by Penafiel and open a communication with Beresford. The latter was at the same time directed to ascend the Tamega, and intercept the enemy at Chaves.

Meanwhile the main body of the army marched in two columns upon the Minho, the one by the route of Barca de Troffa and Braga, the other by the Ponte d'Ave and Bacellos. But on the evening of the 14th, the movements of the enemy about Braga gave certain proofs that Chaves or Montalegre would be the point of his retreat. Hereupon the left column was directed upon Braga, and Beresford was instructed to move upon Villa del Rey, if Soult took the line of Montalegre.

The 15th, Sir Arthur reached Braga. Murray was at Guimaraens on his right, and Beresford, who had anticipated his orders, was near Chaves, having sent Sylveira towards Salamonde with instructions to occupy the mountain passes. But at this time Soult was fifteen miles in advance of Braga, having, by a surprising effort, extricated himself from one of the most dangerous situations that a general ever escaped from. Soult, as he advanced along the narrow pass between the mountains and the Douro, rested his hopes of safety entirely upon Loison's holding Amarante. Several days, however, had elapsed since that general had communicated, and an aide-de-camp was sent on the morning of the 12th to ascertain his exact position. Colonel Tholosé, the officer employed, found Loison at Amarante, but neither his remonstrances, nor the after-coming intelligence that Oporto was evacuated and the army in full retreat upon the Tamega, could induce that general to remain there, and he marched towards Guimaraens, abandoning the bridge of Amarante without a blow, and leaving his commander and two-thirds of the army to what must have appeared inevitable destruction.

The news of this unexpected calamity reached Soult at one o'clock on the morning of the 13th, just as he had passed the rugged banks of the Souza river. The weather was boisterous, the men were fatigued, voices were heard calling for a capitulation, and the whole army was stricken with dismay. Then it was that the Duke of Dalmatia justified by his energy that fortune which had raised him to his high rank in the world. Being by a Spanish pedlar informed of a path that, mounting the right bank of the Souza, led over the Sierra de Catalina to Guimaraens, he on the instant silenced the murmurs of the treacherous or fearful in the ranks, destroyed the artillery, abandoned the military chest and baggage, and loading the animals with sick men and musket ammunition, repassed the Souza and followed his Spanish guide with a hardy resolution.

The rain was falling in torrents, and the path was such as might be expected in those wild regions, but the troops made good their passage over the mountains, and at Guimaraens happily fell in with Loison. During the night they were joined by Lorge's dragoons from Braga, and thus, almost beyond hope, the whole army was concentrated. If Soult's energy in command was conspicuous on this occasion, his sagacity and judgment were not less remarkably displayed in what followed. Most generals would have moved by the direct route upon Guimaraens to Braga; but he, with a long reach of mind, calculated from the slackness of pursuit after he passed Vallonga, that the bulk of the English army must be on the road to Braga, and would be there before him; or that, at best, he should be obliged to retreat fighting, and must sacrifice the guns and baggage of Loison's and Lorge's corps in the face of an enemy—a circumstance that might operate fatally on the spirit of his soldiers, and would certainly give opportunities to the malcontents; and already one of the generals (apparently Loison) was recommending a convention like Cintra. But with a firmness worthy of the highest admiration, Soult destroyed all the guns and the greatest part of the baggage and ammunition of Loison's and Lorge's divisions; then leaving the high-road to Braga on his left, and once more taking to the mountain paths, he made for the heights of Carvalho d'Este, where he arrived late in the evening of the 14th, thus gaining a day's march in point of time. From Carvalho he retired to Salamonde, from whence there were two lines of retreat. The one through Ruivaens to Chaves; the other, shorter, although more impracticable, leading into the road running from Ruivaens to Montalegre. But the scouts brought intelligence that the bridge of Ruivaens, on the little river of that name, was broken, and defended by 1200 Portuguese with artillery; and that another party had been, since the morning, destroying the Ponte Nova on the Cavado river.

The destruction of the first bridge blocked the road to Chaves; the second, if completed, and the passage well defended, would have cut the French off from Montalegre. The night was setting

PASSAGE OF THE DOURO.

in, the soldiers were harassed, barefooted, and starving; the ammunition was damp with the rain, which had never ceased since the 13th, and which was now increasing in violence, accompanied with storms of wind. The British army would certainly fall upon the rear in the morning; and if the Ponte Nova, where the guard was reported to be weak, could not be secured, the hour of surrender was surely arrived. In this extremity, Soult sent for Major Dulong, an officer justly reputed for one of the most daring in the French ranks. Addressing himself to this brave man, he said, "I have chosen you from the whole army to seize the Ponte Nova, which has been cut by the enemy. Do you choose one hundred grenadiers and twenty-five horsemen; endeavour to surprise the guards and secure the passage of the bridge. If you succeed, say so, but send no other report; your silence will suffice." Thus exhorted, Dulong selected his men and departed. Favoured by the storm, he reached the bridge unperceived of the Portuguese, killed the sentinel before any alarm was given, and then, followed by twelve grenadiers, began crawling along a narrow slip of masonry, which was the only part of the bridge undestroyed. The Cavado river was in full flood, and roaring in a deep channel; one of the grenadiers fell into the gulf, but the noise of the storm and the river was louder than his cry. Dulong, with the eleven still creeping onwards, reached the other side, and falling briskly on the first posts of the peasants, killed or dispersed the whole. At that moment, the remainder of his men advanced close to the bridge; and some crossing, others mounting the heights, shouting and firing, scared the Portuguese supporting posts, who imagined the whole army was upon them; and thus the passage was gallantly won.

At four o'clock, the bridge being repaired, the advanced guards of the French commenced crossing; but as the column of march was long, and the road narrow and rugged, the troops filed over slowly; and beyond the Ponte Nova there was a second obstacle still more formidable. For the pass in which the troops were moving being cut in the side of a mountain, open on the left for several miles, at last came upon a torrent called the Misarella, which, breaking down a deep ravine, or rather gulf, was only to be crossed by a bridge, constructed with a single lofty arch, called the *Saltador*, or leaper; and so narrow that only three persons could pass abreast. Fortunately for the French, the *Saltador* was not cut, but entrenched and defended by a few hundred Portuguese peasants, who occupied the rocks on the farther side; and here the good soldier Dulong again saved the army; for, when a first and second attempt had been repulsed with loss, he carried the entrenchments by a third effort; but at the same instant fell deeply wounded himself. The head of the column now poured over, and it was full time, for the English guns were thundering in the rear, and the Ponte Nova was choked with dead.

Sir Arthur Wellesley, quitting Braga on the morning of the 16th, had come, about four o'clock, upon Soult's rear-guard, which remained at Salamonde to cover the passage of the army over the bridges. The right was strongly protected by a ravine, the left occupied a steep hill, and a stout battle might have been made; but men thus circumstanced, and momentarily expecting an order to retreat, will seldom stand firmly; and on this occasion, when some light troops turned the left, and General Sherbrooke, with the guards, mounting the steep hill, attacked the front, the French made but one discharge, and fled in confusion to the Ponte Nova. As this bridge was not on the direct line of retreat, they were for some time unperceived, and gaining ground of their pursuers, formed a rear-guard; but, after a time, being discovered, some guns were brought to bear on them; and then man and horse, crushed together, went over into the gulf; and the bridge, and the rocks, and the defile beyond were strewed with mangled bodies.

This was the last calamity inflicted by the sword upon the French army in this retreat: a retreat attended by many horrid as well as glorious events; for the peasants in their fury, with an atrocious cruelty, tortured and mutilated every sick man and straggler that fell into their power; and on the other hand, the soldiers, who held together in their turn, shot the peasants; while the track of the columns might be discovered from afar by the smoke of the burning houses.

The French reached Montalegre on the 17th; and an English staff-officer, with some cavalry, being upon their rear as far as Villella, picked up some stragglers; but Sir Arthur, with the main body of the army, halted that day at Ruivaens. On the 18th he renewed the pursuit, and a part of his cavalry passed Montalegre, followed by the guards; the enemy was, however, drawn up behind the Salas in force, and no action took place. Soult crossed the frontier on the 18th May; and on the 19th entered Orense, but without guns, ammunition, or baggage, his men exhausted with fatigue and misery, the greatest part being without shoes, many without accoutrements, and in some instances even without muskets. He had quitted Orense seventy-six days before with about 22,000 men, and 3500 had afterwards joined him from Tuy. He returned with 19,500, having lost by the sword and sickness, by assassination and capture, 6000 good soldiers; of which number above 3000 were taken in hospitals, and about 1000 were killed by the Portuguese, or had died of sickness previous to the retreat. The remainder were captured, or had perished within the last eight days. He had carried fifty-eight pieces of artillery into Portugal, and he returned without a gun; yet was his reputation as a stout and able soldier nowise diminished.

CHAPTER V.

CAMPAIGN OF TALAVERA.

HE liberation of Portugal having been effected by the operations at the Douro, Soult, after losing baggage and artillery, with his dispirited, disorganised, and fugitive army, found refuge across the frontier at Orense, near the spot from which, a few months before, he had witnessed the disastrous embarkation of the remnants of Moore's army. Here the pursuit of the British terminated, and Wellesley marched his army to Abrantes on the Tagus, from whence, thinking that Soult's forces were so shattered that they probably would be of little account in the war for several months, he purposed an effective movement against Madrid.

While the campaign at the Douro was in progress, other successes of importance to the cause were being gained by the Spanish general Romana in Gallicia, where Marshal Ney and Kellerman were in command. Romana having taken the town of Vigo from the French, and also defeated a body of troops sent to its relief, kept moving about the country in such a way as never to allow the enemy to come up with him and bring him to close action, although the opposing forces were almost daily in sight of each other. This kind of guerilla warfare was so far in favour also of the allies, that it delayed for a time the much-desired junction of the forces of Soult and Ney.

The Spanish troops under Cuesta still kept watch upon General Victor, who had retreated to Talavera, and the British troops on the banks of the Tagus were being rapidly brought into order to commence their march into Spain. No sooner had intelligence of the movements of the allies and their conjectured intentions reached Madrid, than King Joseph, accompanied by Marshal Jourdan, set out with all disposable troops and effected a junction with Victor, dispatching orders at the same time to Soult to join with Ney and advance to intercept the line of march of the allies and cut off their retreat.

On the 22nd July the allies moved in two columns to drive the French posts from Talavera; and Cuesta, marching by the high-road, came first up with the enemy's rear-guard near the village of Gamonal; but then commenced a display of ignorance, timidity, and absurdity that has seldom been equalled in war. General Latour Maubourg, with 2000 dragoons, came boldly on to the table-land of Gamonal, and sustaining a cannonade, not only checked the head of the Spanish leading column, but actually obliged General Zayas, who commanded it, to display his whole line, consisting of 15,000 infantry and 3000 cavalry; nor did the French horsemen give back at all until the appearance of the red uniforms on their right informed them that it was time to retire. Then, and not till then, Latour Maubourg, supported by some infantry, retreated behind the Alberche, and without loss, although many batteries and at least 6000 Spanish horse were close on his rear; but the latter could never be induced to make even a partial charge, however favourable the opportunity, and by two o'clock the whole French army was safely concentrated on its position. Ruffin's division on the left touched the Tagus, and protected the bridge over the Alberche, which was more immediately defended by a regiment of infantry and fourteen pieces of artillery. Villatte's and Lapisse's divisions, drawn up in successive lines on some high ground that overlooked the surrounding country, formed the right; the heavy cavalry were in second line near the bridge; and in this situation Victor rested for several days.

It was at all times difficult to obtain accurate information from the Spaniards by gentle means; hence, the French were usually better supplied with intelligence than the British, while the native generals never knew anything about the enemy until they felt the weight of his blows. Up to this period, Sir Arthur's best sources of information had been the intercepted letters of the French;

and now, although the latter had been in the same position, and without any change of numbers, since the 7th July, the inhabitants of Talavera could not, or would not, give any information of their strength or situation; nor could any reasonable calculation be formed of either, until some English officers crossed the Tagus, and, from the mountains on the left bank of that river, saw the French position in reverse.

The general outline of an attack was, however, agreed upon for the next morning, but the details were unsettled; and when the English commander came to arrange these with Cuesta, the latter was gone to bed. The British troops were under arms at three o'clock the next morning, but Cuesta's staff were not aroused from slumber until seven o'clock; and the old man finally objected to fight that day, alleging, among other absurd reasons, that it was Sunday. But there was something more than absurdity in these proceedings. Victor, who was not ignorant of the weak points of his own position, remained tranquil, being well assured that no attack would take place, for it is certain that he had a correspondence with some of the Spanish staff; and the secret discussions between Sir Arthur Wellesley and Cuesta, at which only one staff officer of each party was present, became known to the enemy in twenty-four hours after. Indeed, Cuesta was himself suspected of treachery by many, yet apparently without reason.

In the course of the 23rd, the Spanish officer commanding the advanced posts reported that the French guns were withdrawn, and that it was evident they meant to retreat. Cuesta then became willing to attack, and proposed, in concert with Sir Arthur Wellesley, to examine Victor's position; but, to the surprise of the English commander, the Spaniard arrived in a coach drawn by six horses to perform this duty; and when the inequalities of the ground obliged him to descend from his vehicle, he cast himself at the foot of a tree, and in a few moments went to sleep. Yet he was always ready to censure and to thwart every proposal of his able coadjutor. This time, however, he consented to fall upon the enemy, and the troops were in motion early in the morning of the 24th; but Victor, Duke of Belluno, was again informed of their intention; and having withdrawn his movable column from Escalona and relinquished the road to Madrid, retreated during the night to Torijos. Thus the first combination of the allies failed entirely; and each hour the troops of the enemy were accumulating round them; for Venegas, who should have been at Fuente Duenas, high up on the Tagus, had not even passed Damyel; and King Joseph was collecting his whole strength in front, between Toledo and Talavera, while Soult was fast gathering his more formidable power behind the mountains of Bejar.

The English general was indeed still ignorant of the danger which threatened him from the Salamanca country, or he would, doubtless, have withdrawn at once to Plasencia, and secured his communications with Lisbon and with Beresford's troops; but other powerful reasons were not wanting to prevent his farther advance. Before he quitted Plasencia he had completed contracts with the Alcaldes in the Vera de Plasencia for 250,000 rations of forage and provisions; and this, together with what he had before collected, would have furnished supplies for ten or twelve days, a sufficient time to beat Victor and carry the army into a fresh country; but distrustful, as he had reason to be, of the Spaniards, he gave notice to Cuesta and the junta, that beyond the Alberche he would not move unless his wants were immediately supplied; for hitherto the rations contracted for had not been delivered, and his representations to the junta and to Cuesta were by both equally disregarded. There were no means of transport provided; the troops were already on less than half allowance, and absolute famine approached; and when the general demanded food for his soldiers at the hands of those whose cause he came to defend, he was answered with false excuses and insulted by false statements. Under any circumstances this would have forced him to halt; but the advance having been made in the exercise of his own discretion, and not at the command of his Government, there could be no room for hesitation: wherefore, remonstrating warmly, but manfully, with the supreme junta, he announced his resolution to go no farther—nay, even to withdraw from Spain altogether.

The English general's resolution to halt at Talavera made little impression upon Cuesta. A French corps had retreated before him, and Madrid, nay, the Pyrenees themselves, instantly rose on the view of the sanguine Spaniard: he was resolved to be the first in the capital, and he pushed forward in pursuit, reckless alike of military discipline and of the friendly warnings of Sir Arthur, who vainly admonished him to open his communications as quickly as possible with Venegas, and to beware how he let the enemy know that the British and Spanish armies were separated. On the 26th Cuesta discovered that he had been pursuing a tiger. Meanwhile, Sir Arthur Wellesley, foreseeing the consequence of this imprudence, had sent General Sherbrooke across the Alberche, where he could support the Spaniards, and at the same time hold communication with Sir Robert Wilson.

On the 10th July, the march of the British upon Plasencia became known, and it was manifest that Sir Arthur had no design to act north of the Douro; wherefore the Duke of Dalmatia resolved to advance to Salamanca. Marshal Victor retired upon Toledo instead of Madrid, and in this showed himself an able commander. Toledo was the strategic pivot upon which every movement turned. It was the central point, by holding which the army of Venegas was separated from the allies on the Alberche. If the latter advanced, Soult's operations rendered every forward step a stride towards ruin. If, leaving Venegas to his fate, they retired, it must be rapidly, or there would be neither wisdom nor safety in the measure. The King knew that Foy would reach Soult the 24th, and as that marshal had already assembled his army about Salamanca, which was only four days' march from Plasencia, he might be in the valley of the Tagus by the 30th; hence, to ensure complete success, the royal army needed only to keep the allies in check for four or five days. This was the plan that Soult had recommended, that the King promised to follow, and that Marshal Jourdan strenuously supported. The unskilful proceedings of Cuesta and Venegas, the separation of the allies, the distressed state of the English army, actually on the verge of famine (a circumstance that could hardly be unknown to Victor), greatly facilitated the execution of this project, which did not preclude the King from punishing the folly of the Spanish general, whose army, scattered and without order, discipline, or plan, so strongly invited an attack. Cuesta had some faint perception of his danger on the 25th, and he gave orders to retreat on the 26th; but the French, suddenly passing the Guadarama, at two o'clock in the morning of that day, quickly drove the Spanish cavalry out of Torrijos, and pursued them to Alcabon. Here General Zayas had drawn up 4000 infantry, 2000 horsemen, and eight guns on a plain, and offered battle.

ALCABON.

The Spanish right rested on the road of Domingo Peres, and the left on a chapel of the same name. The French cavalry, under Latour Maubourg, advanced in a parallel line against the Spaniards, and a cannonade commenced; but at that moment the head of the French infantry appearing in sight, the Spaniards broke, and fled in disorder towards St. Ollalla, followed at full gallop by the horsemen, who pressed them so sorely that the panic would, doubtless, have spread through the whole army, but for the courage of Albuquerque, who, coming up with a division of 3000 fresh cavalry, held the enemy in play while Cuesta retreated in the greatest disorder towards the Alberche.

After reaching St. Ollalla, the French slackened their efforts; the main body halted there, and the advanced guards, save a few cavalry posts, did not pass El Bravo, and no attempt was made to profit from the unconnected position of the allies—a gross and palpable error; for either by the sword or dispersion, the Spaniards lost on that day not less than 4000 men; and such was their fear and haste, that it required but a little more perseverance in the pursuit to cause a general route. Albuquerque alone showed any front; but his efforts were unavailing, and the disorder continued to increase until General Sherbrooke placed his divisions between the scared troops and the enemy. Sir Arthur Wellesley, who, at the first alarm, had hastened to the front, seeing the confusion beyond the Alberche, knew that a battle was at hand; and being persuaded that in a strong defensive position only could the Spaniards be brought to stand a shock, earnestly endeavoured to persuade Cuesta, while Sherbrooke's people could yet cover the movement, to withdraw to Talavera, where there was ground suited for defence; but Cuesta's uncouth nature again broke forth; his people were beaten, dispirited, fatigued, bewildered; clustered on a narrow slip of low, flat land between the Alberche, the Tagus, and the heights of Salinas; and the first shot fired by the enemy must have been the signal of defeat; yet it was in vain that Sir Arthur Wellesley pointed out those things, and entreated of him to avoid

F

the fall of the rock that trembled over his head; he replied that his troops would be disheartened by any further retreat, that he would fight where he stood; and in this mood he passed the night.

On the 27th July, at daylight, the British general renewed his solicitations, at first fruitlessly; but when the enemy's cavalry came in sight, and Sherbrooke prepared to retire, Cuesta sullenly yielded, yet turning to his staff with frantic pride, observed that "he had first made the Englishman go down on his knees." Sir Arthur Wellesley now assumed the direction of both armies. General Mackenzie's division and a brigade of light cavalry were left on the Alberche to cover the retrograde movement, but the rest of the allied troops were soon in full march for the position of Talavera, which was about six miles in the rear. Sir Robert Wilson, who had opened a communication with Madrid, and who would certainly have entered that capital but for the approaching battle, was also recalled. He returned on the 28th to Escalona, and hung on the enemy's rear, but did not attempt to join the army. Between the Alberche and the town of Talavera the country was flat, and covered with olives and cork-trees; and on the north, nearly parallel to the Tagus, and at a distance of about two or three miles, a chain of round but steep hills bounded the woody plain. Beyond these hills, but separated from them by a deep and rugged valley, something less than half a mile wide, was the high mountain-ridge which divides the bed of the Alberche from that of the Tietar. Hence, a line drawn perpendicularly from the Tagus would cross the first chain of hills at the distance of two miles, and at two miles and a half would fall on the mountains.

Sir Arthur Wellesley, taking the town of Talavera, which was built close to the river, as his fixed point, placed the right of the Spaniards there, drawing their army up in two lines, with the left resting upon a mound, where a large field-redoubt was constructed, and behind which a brigade of British light cavalry was posted. The front was covered by a convent, by ditches, mud walls, breastworks, and felled trees. The cavalry was posted behind the infantry, and the rear was supported by a large house in the wood, well placed, in case of defeat, to cover a retreat on to the main roads leading from Talavera to Arzobispo and Oropesa. In this position they could not be attacked seriously, nor their disposition be even seen; and thus one half of the line necessary to be occupied by the allies was rendered nearly impregnable, and yet held by the worst troops. The front of battle was prolonged by the British infantry. General Campbell's division, formed in two lines, touched the Spanish left; General Sherbrooke's division stood next to Campbell's, but arranged on one line only, because General Mackenzie's division, destined to form the second, was then near the Alberche. It was intended that General Hill's division should close the left of the British by taking post on the highest hill in the chain before mentioned, as bounding the flat and woody country; but, by some accident, the summit of this height was not immediately occupied.

The whole line, thus displayed, was about two miles in length, the left being covered by the valley between the hill and the mountain; and from this valley a ravine or watercourse opened deeply in the front of the British left, but being gradually obliterated in the flat ground about the centre of the line. Part of the British cavalry was with General Mackenzie, and in the plain in front of the left, and part behind the great redoubt, at the junction of the allied troops. The British and Germans under arms that day were somewhat above 19,000 sabres and bayonets, with 30 guns. The Spaniards, after their previous defeat, could only produce from 33,000 to 34,000 men; but they had 70 guns. The combined army, therefore, offered battle with 44,000 infantry, nearly 10,000 cavalry, and 100 pieces of artillery; and the French were coming on with at least 80 guns, and, including the King's guards, nearly 50,000 men, of which above 7000 were cavalry. The French were all hardy veterans, while the genuine soldiers of the allied army did not exceed 19,000.

The King, having passed the night at St. Ollalla, put his troops in motion again before daylight on the 27th July. Latour Maubourg, with the cavalry, preceded the column, and the first and fourth corps, the royal guards, and reserve followed in succession. The appearance of the leading squadrons hastened, as we have seen, Cuesta's decision, and about one o'clock in the afternoon, the first corps reached the heights of Salinas, from whence the dust of the allies, as they took up their position, could be perceived; but neither their situation nor disposition could be made out on account of the forest, which, clothing the country from the Tagus nearly to the foot of the first range of hills, masked all their evolutions. Marshal Victor, however, being well acquainted with the ground, instantly guessed their true position; and, in pursuance of his advice, the King ordered the fourth corps to march against the left of the allies, the cavalry against the centre, and Victor himself with the first corps against the right; the guards and the reserve supported the fourth corps.

Two good routes, suitable to artillery, led from the Alberche to the position; the one, being the royal road to Talavera, was followed by the fourth corps and the reserve; the other, passing through a place called the Casa des Salinas, led directly upon Sir Arthur Wellesley's extreme left, and was followed by the first corps; but to reach this Casa, which was situated near the plain in front of the British left wing, it was necessary to ford the Alberche, and to march for a mile or two through the woods. A dust, which was observed to rise near the Casa itself, indicated the presence of troops at that place; and, in fact, General Mackenzie's division and a brigade of light cavalry were there posted, the infantry in the forest, the cavalry on the plain; but no patrols were sent to the front; and this negligence gave rise to the combat of

SALINAS.

About three o'clock, Lapisse and Ruffin's division, having crossed the Alberche, marched in two columns towards the Casa de Salinas, and their light infantry came so suddenly on the British outposts that the latter were surprised, and Sir Arthur Wellesley, who was in the Casa, nearly fell into the enemy's hands. The French columns followed briskly, and charged so hotly that the English brigades were separated; and being composed principally of young battalions, got into confusion; one part fired upon another, and the whole were driven into the plain. But in the midst of the disorder, the 45th, a stubborn old regiment, and some companies of the 5th battalion of the 60th, were seen in perfect array; and when Sir Arthur rode up to the spot, the fight was restored, and maintained so steadily that the enemy was checked. The infantry, supported by two brigades of cavalry, then crossed the plain, and regained the left and centre of the position, having lost about 400 men. General Mackenzie, with one brigade, immediately took post in second line behind the guards; the other, commanded by Colonel Donkin, finding the hill on the left unoccupied, drew up there, and so completed the position. The cavalry was formed in column behind the left of the line.

Victor, animated by the success of this first operation, brought up Villatte's division, together with all the artillery and light cavalry, to the Casa de Salinas; then issuing from the forest, rapidly crossed the plain, and advancing, with a fine military display, close up to the left of the position, occupied an isolated hill directly in front of Colonel Donkin's ground, and immediately opened a heavy cannonade upon that officer's brigade. Meanwhile, the fourth French corps and the reserve, approaching the right more slowly, and being unable to discover the true situation of Cuesta's troops, sent their light cavalry forward to make that general show his lines. The French horsemen rode boldly to the front, and commenced skirmishing with their pistols, and the Spaniards answered them with a general discharge of small arms; but then 10,000 infantry and all the artillery, breaking their ranks, fled to the rear; the artillerymen carried off their horses, the infantry threw away their arms, and the Adjutant-General O'Donoghue was amongst the foremost of the fugitives. Nay, Cuesta himself was in movement towards the rear. The panic spread, and the French would fain have charged; but Sir Arthur Wellesley, who was at hand, immediately flanked the main road with some English squadrons: the ditches on the other side rendered the country impracticable; and the fire of musketry being renewed by those Spaniards who remained, the enemy lost some men, and finally retreated in disorder.

The greatest part of Cuesta's runaways fled as far as Oropesa, giving out that the allies were totally defeated and the French army in hot pursuit; thus the rear became a scene of incredible disorder: the commissaries went off with their animals; the paymasters carried away their money-chests; the baggage was scattered, and the alarm spread far and wide. Cuesta, however, having recovered from his first alarm, sent many of his cavalry regiments to head the fugitives and drive them back; and a part of the artillery and some thousands of the infantry were thus recovered during the night; but in the next day's fight the Spanish army was less by 6000 men than it should have been, and the great redoubt in the centre was silent for want of guns.

Combat on the Evening of the 27th.

The hill on the left of the British army was the key of the whole position. It was steep and rugged on the side towards the French, and it was rendered more inaccessible by the ravine at the bottom ; but towards the English side it was of a smooth ascent. Victor, however, observing that the extreme summit was unoccupied, and that Donkin's brigade was feeble, conceived the design of seizing it by a sudden assault. The sun was sinking, and the twilight and the confusion among the Spaniards on the right appeared so favourable to his project, that, without communicating with the King, he immediately directed Ruffin's division to attack, Villatte to follow in support, and Lapisse to fall on the German legion, so as to create a diversion for Ruffin, but without engaging seriously himself. The assault was quick and vigorous : Colonel Donkin beat back the enemy in his front, but his force was too weak to defend every part, and many of the French turned his left, and mounted to the summit behind him. At this moment, General Hill was ordered to reinforce him ; and it was not yet dark when that officer, while giving orders to the colonel of the 48th regiment, was fired at by some troops from the highest point. Thinking they were stragglers from his own ranks firing at the enemy, he rode quickly up to them, followed by his brigade-major, Fordyce, and in a moment found himself in the midst of the French. Fordyce was killed, and Hill's own horse was wounded by a grenadier, who immediately seized the bridle; but the general, spurring the animal hard, broke the man's hold, and galloping down the descent, met the 29th regiment, and, without an instant's delay, led them up with such a fierce charge, that the enemy could not sustain the shock.

The summit was thus recovered; and the 48th regiment and the 1st battalion of detachments were immediately brought forward, and, in conjunction with the 29th and Colonel Donkin's brigade,

presented a formidable front of defence; and in good time, for the troops thus beaten back were only a part of the 9th French regiment, forming the advance of Ruffin's division; but the two other regiments of that division had lost their way in the ravine; hence the attack had not ceased, but only subsided for a time. Lapisse was in motion, and soon after opened his fire against the German legion; and the French battalions, being re-formed in one mass, again advanced up the face of the hill with redoubled vigour. The fighting then became vehement; and, in the darkness, the opposing flashes of the musketry showed with what a resolute spirit the struggle was maintained, for the combatants were scarcely twenty yards asunder, and for a time the event seemed doubtful; but soon the well-known shout of the British soldier was heard, rising above the din of arms, and the enemy's broken troops were driven once more into the ravine below. Lapisse, who had made some impression on the German legion, immediately abandoned his false attack, and the fighting of the 27th ceased. The British lost about 800 men, and the French about 1000 on that day. The bivouac-fires now blazed up on both sides, and the French and British soldiers became quiet; but, about twelve o'clock, the Spaniards on the right being alarmed at some horse in their front, opened a prodigious peal of musketry and artillery, which continued for twenty minutes without any object; and during the night, the whole line was frequently disturbed by desultory firing from both the Spanish and English troops, by which several men and officers were unfortunately slain.

Marshal Victor, who had learned from the prisoners the exact position of the Spaniards, until then unknown to the French generals, now reported his own failure to the King, and proposed that a second attempt should be made in the morning at daylight; but Marshal Jourdan opposed this, as being a partial enterprise, which could not lead to any great result. Victor, however, was earnest for a trial, and, resting his representation on his intimate knowledge of the ground, pressed the matter so home, that he won Joseph's assent, and immediately made dispositions for the attack.

88   THE PENINSULAR CAMPAIGN.

Combat on the Morning of the 28th.

About daybreak, Ruffin's troops were drawn up, two regiments abreast, supported by a third in columns of battalions; and in this order went forth against the left of the British, a part directly against the front, and a part from the valley on the right, thus embracing two sides of the hill. Their march was rapid and steady; they were followed by Villatte's division, and their assault was preceded by a burst of artillery that rattled round the height and swept away the English ranks by whole sections. The sharp chattering of the musketry succeeded, the French guns were then pointed towards the British centre and right, the grenadiers instantly closed upon General Hill's division, and the height sparkled with fire. The inequalities of the ground broke the compact formation of the troops on both sides, and small bodies were seen here and there struggling for the mastery with all the virulence of a single combat; in some places the French grenadiers were overthrown at once, in others they would not be denied, and reached the summit; but the reserves were always ready to vindicate their ground, and no permanent footing was obtained. Still the conflict was maintained with singular obstinacy; Hill himself was wounded, and his men were falling fast; but the enemy suffered more, and gave back, step by step at first, and slowly, to cover the retreat of their wounded; but finally, unable to sustain the increasing fury of the English, and having lost above 1500 men in the space of forty minutes, the whole mass broke away in disorder, and returned to their own position, covered by the renewed play of their powerful artillery.

To this destructive fire no adequate answer could be made, for the English guns were few and of small calibre; and when Sir Arthur Wellesley desired a reinforcement from Cuesta, the latter sent him only two pieces; yet even those were serviceable, and the Spanish gunners fought them gallantly. The principal line of the enemy's retreat was by the great valley, and a favourable opportunity for a charge of horse occurred; but the English cavalry, having retired during the night for water and forage, were yet too distant to be of service. However, these repeated efforts of the French against the hill, and the appearance of some of their light troops on the mountain beyond the left, taught the English general that he had committed a fault in not prolonging his flank across the valley; and he hastened to rectify it. For this purpose, he placed the principal mass of his cavalry there, with the leading squadrons looking into the valley, and having obtained from Cuesta General Bassecour's division of infantry, posted it on the mountain itself, in observation of the French light troops. Meanwhile, the Duke of Albuquerque, discontented with Cuesta's arrangements, came with his division to Sir Arthur Wellesley, who placed him behind the British, thus displaying a formidable array of horsemen, six lines in depth.

Immediately after the failure of Ruffin's attack, King Joseph, having in person examined the whole position of the allies from left to right, demanded of Jourdan and Victor if he should deliver a general battle. The former replied that the great valley and the mountain being unoccupied on the 27th, Sir Arthur Wellesley's attention should have been drawn to the right by a feint on the Spaniards; that during the night the whole army should have been silently placed in column at the entrance of the great valley, ready at daybreak to form a line of battle on the left, to a new front, and so have attacked the hill from whence Victor had been twice repulsed. Such a movement, he said, would have obliged the allies to change their front also, and during this operation they might have been assailed with hopes of success. But this project could not now be executed; the English, aware of their mistake, had secured their left flank by occupying the valley; and the mountain and their front was inattackable. Hence, the only prudent line was to take up a position on the Alberche, and await the effect of Soult's operations on the English rear. While the French generals were engaged in council, the troops on both sides took some rest, and the English wounded were carried to the rear; but the soldiers were suffering from hunger; the regular service of provisions had ceased for several days, and a few ounces of wheat in the grain formed the whole subsistence of men who had fought, and who were yet to fight, so hardly. The Spanish camp was full of confusion and distrust. Cuesta inspired terror, but no confidence; and Albuquerque, whether from conviction or instigated by momentary anger, just as the French were coming on to the final attack, sent one of his staff to inform the English commander that Cuesta was betraying him. The aide-de-camp charged with this message delivered it to Colonel Donkin, and that officer carried it to Sir Arthur Wellesley. The latter, seated on the summit of the hill which had been so gallantly contested, was intently watching the movements of the advancing enemy; he listened to this somewhat startling message without so much as turning his head, and then drily answering, "Very well, you may return to your brigade," continued his survey of the French. Donkin retired, filled with admiration of the imperturbable resolution and quick penetration of the man; and indeed Sir Arthur's conduct was, throughout that day, such as became a general upon whose vigilance and intrepidity the fate of 50,000 men depended.

Battle of Talavera.

The dispositions of the French were soon completed. From nine o'clock in the morning until mid-day the field of battle offered no appearance of hostility; the weather was intensely hot, and the troops on both sides descended and mingled, without fear or suspicion, to quench their thirst at the little brook which divided the positions; but at one o'clock in the afternoon, the French soldiers were seen to gather round their eagles, and the rolling of drums was heard along the whole line. Half-an-hour later, the King's guards, the reserve, and the fourth corps were descried, near the centre of the enemy's position, marching to join the first corps; and at two o'clock the table-land and the height on the French right, even to the valley, were covered with the dark and lowering masses. At this moment some hundreds of English soldiers, employed to carry the wounded to the rear, returned in one body, and were, by the French, supposed to be Sir Robert Wilson's corps joining the army; nevertheless, the Duke of Belluno, whose arrangements were now completed, gave the signal for battle; and eighty pieces of artillery immediately sent a tempest of bullets before the light troops, who, coming on swiftly and with the violence of a hailstorm, were closely followed by the broad, black columns in all the majesty of war.

Sir Arthur Wellesley, from the summit of the hill, had a clear view of the whole field of battle; and first he saw the fourth corps rush forwards, with the usual impetuosity of French soldiers, and clearing the intersected ground in their front, fall upon Campbell's division with infinite fury; but that general, assisted by Mackenzie's brigade and by two Spanish battalions, withstood their utmost efforts. The English regiments, putting the French skirmishers aside, met the advancing columns with loud shouts, and, breaking in on their front, lapping their flanks with fire, and giving no respite, pushed them back with a terrible carnage. Ten guns were taken; but, as General Campbell prudently forbore pursuit, the French rallied on their supports, and made a show of attacking again: vain attempt! The British artillery and musketry played too vehemently upon their masses, and a Spanish regiment of cavalry charging on their flank at the same time, the whole retired in disorder, and the victory was secured in that quarter.

But while this was passing on the right, Villatte's division, preceded by the grenadiers, and supported by two regiments of light cavalry, was seen advancing up the great valley against the left, and, beyond Villatte's, Ruffin was discovered marching towards the mountain. Sir Arthur Wellesley immediately ordered Anson's brigade of cavalry, composed of the 23rd light dragoons and the 1st German hussars, to charge the head of these columns; and this brigade, coming on at a canter, and increasing its speed as it advanced, rode headlong against the enemy, but in a few moments came upon the brink of a hollow cleft, which was not perceptible at a distance. The French, throwing themselves into squares, opened their fire; and Colonel Arenstchild, commanding the hussars, an officer whom forty years' experience had made a master in his art, promptly reined up at the brink, exclaiming, in his broken phrase, "I will not kill my young mens!"

The English blood was hotter! The 23rd, under Colonel Seymour, rode wildly down into the hollow, and men and horses fell over each other in dreadful confusion. The survivors, still untamed, mounted the opposite bank by twos and threes; Seymour was wounded, but Major Frederick Ponsonby, a hardy soldier, rallying all who came up, passed through the midst of Villatte's columns, and, reckless of the musketry from each side, fell with inexpressible violence upon a brigade of French chasseurs in the rear. The combat was fierce but short; Victor had perceived the first advance of the English, and detached his Polish lancers and Westphalian light-horse to the support of Villatte, and these fresh troops coming up when the 23rd, already overmatched, could scarcely hold up against the chasseurs, entirely broke them. Those who were not killed or taken made for Bassecour's Spanish division, and so escaped, leaving behind 207 men and officers, or about half the number that went into action.

During this time the hill, the key of the position, was again attacked, and Lapisse, crossing the ravine, pressed hard upon the English centre; his own artillery, aided by the great battery on his right, opened large gaps in Sherbrooke's ranks, and the French columns came close up to the British line in the resolution to win; but they were received with a general discharge of all arms, and so vigorously encountered, that they gave back in disorder; and, in the excitement of the moment, the brigade of English guards, quitting the line, followed up their success with inconsiderate ardour. The enemy's supporting columns and dragoons advanced, the men who had been repulsed turned again, and the French batteries pounded the flank and front of the guards.

Thus maltreated, the latter drew back, and, at the same moment, the German legion, being sorely pressed, got into confusion. Hill's and Campbell's divisions, on the extremities of the line, still held fast; but the centre of the British was absolutely broken, and the fate of the day seemed to incline in favour of the French, when suddenly Colonel Donellan, with the 48th regiment, was seen advancing through the midst of the disordered masses. At first, it seemed as if this regiment must be carried away by the retiring crowds, but, wheeling back by companies, it let them pass through the intervals, and then, resuming its proud and beautiful line, marched against the right of the pursuing columns, and plied them with such a destructive musketry, and closed upon them with such a firm and regular pace, that the forward movement of the French was checked. The guards and the Germans immediately rallied; a brigade of light cavalry came up from the second line at a trot; the artillery battered the enemy's flanks without intermission, and the French, beginning to waver, soon lost their advantage, and the battle was restored.

In all actions there is one critical and decisive moment which will give the victory to the general who knows how to seize it. When the guards first made their rash charge, Sir Arthur Wellesley, foreseeing the issue of it, had ordered the 48th down from the hill, although a rough battle was going on there; and at the same time he directed Cotton's light cavalry to advance. These dispositions gained the day. The French relaxed their efforts by degrees; the fire of the English grew hotter; and their loud and confident shouts—sure augury of success—were heard along the whole line.

In the hands of a great general, Joseph's guards and the reserve, which were yet entire, might have restored the combat; but all combination was at an end on the French side. The fourth corps, beaten back on the left with the loss of ten guns, was in confusion; the troops in the great valley on the right, amazed at the furious charge of Seymour's 23rd, and awed by the sight of four distinct lines of cavalry still in reserve, remained stationary. No impression had been made on the hill; Lapisse himself was mortally wounded, and at last his division giving way, the whole army retired to its position, from whence it had descended to the attack. This retrograde movement was covered by skirmishers and an increasing fire of artillery; and the British, reduced to less than 14,000 sabres and bayonets, and exhausted by toil and the want of food, could not pursue. The Spanish army was incapable of any evolution, and about six o'clock all hostility ceased, each army holding the position of the morning. But the battle was scarcely over when, the dry grass and shrubs taking fire, a volume of flames passed with inconceivable rapidity across a part of the field, scorching, in its course, both the dead and the wounded.

On the British side two generals (Mackenzie and Langworth), 31 officers of inferior rank, and 767 sergeants and soldiers were killed upon the spot, and three generals, 192 officers, 3718 sergeants and privates wounded. Nine officers, 643 sergeants and soldiers were missing; thus, making a total loss of 6268 in the two days' fighting, of which 5422 fell on the 28th. The French suffered more severely. Two generals and 944 killed, 6294 wounded, and 156 prisoners; furnishing a total of 7389 men and officers, of which 4000 were of the first corps. Of seventeen guns captured, ten were taken by General Campbell's division, and seven were left in the woods by the French. The Spaniards returned above 1200 men killed and wounded, but the correctness of the report was very much doubted at the time.

On the 29th, at daybreak, the French army quitted its position, and before six o'clock was in order of battle on the heights of Salinas, behind the Alberche. That day, also, General Robert Crawfurd reached the English camp, with the 43rd, 52nd, and 95th or rifle regiment, and immediately took charge of the outposts. These troops, after a march of twenty miles, were in bivouac near Malpartida de Plasencia, when the alarm caused by the fugitive Spanish spread to that part. Crawfurd allowed the men to rest for a few hours, and then withdrawing about fifty of the weakest from the ranks, commenced his march with the resolution not to halt until he reached the field of battle. As the brigade advanced, crowds of the runaways were met with; and those not all Spaniards, propagating the vilest falsehoods: "the army was defeated,"—" Sir Arthur Wellesley was killed,"—" the French were only a few miles distant;" and some, blinded by their fears, affected even to point out the enemy's advanced posts on the nearest hills. Indignant at this shameful scene, the troops hastened rather than slackened the impetuosity of their pace; and leaving only seventeen stragglers behind, in twenty-six hours they had crossed the field of battle in a close and compact body, having in that time passed over sixty-two English miles, and in the hottest season of the year, each man carrying from fifty to sixty pounds weight upon his shoulders. Had the historian Gibbon known of such a march, he would have spared his sneer about the " delicacy of modern soldiers !"

The British army had suffered so much, that the 29th and 30th were passed by Sir Arthur in establishing his hospitals at Talavera, and in fruitless endeavours to procure provisions and the necessary assistance to prevent the wounded men from perishing. Neither Cuesta nor the inhabitants of Talavera, although possessing ample means, would render the slightest aid, nor would they even assist to bury the dead. The corn secreted in Talavera was alone sufficient to support the army for a month; but the troops were starving, although the inhabitants, who had fled across the Tagus with their portable effects at the beginning of the battle, had now returned. It is not surprising that, in such circumstances, men should endeavour to save their property, especially provisions;

yet the apathy with which they beheld the wounded men dying for want of aid left an indelible impression on the minds of the English soldiers. From that period to the end of the war their contempt and dislike of the Spaniards were never effaced; and long afterwards, Badajos and St. Sebastian suffered for the churlish behaviour of the people of Talavera. The principal motive of action with the Spaniards was always personal rancour; hence, those troops who had behaved so ill in action, and the inhabitants, who withheld alike their sympathy and their aid from the English soldiers, to whose bravery they owed the existence of their town, were busily engaged after the battle in beating out the brains of the wounded French as they lay upon the field; and they were only checked by the English soldiers, who, in some instances, fired upon the perpetrators of this horrible iniquity.

Cuesta also gave proofs of his ferocious character; he, who had shown himself alike devoid of talent and real patriotism, whose indolence and ignorance of his profession had banished all order and discipline from his army, and whose stupid pride had all but caused its destruction, now assumed the Roman general, and proceeded to decimate the regiments that had fled in the panic on the 27th. Above fifty men he slew in this manner; and if his cruelty, so contrary to reason and the morals of the age, had not been mitigated by the earnest intercession of Sir Arthur Wellesley, more men would have been destroyed in cold blood by this savage old man than had fallen in the battle.

CHAPTER VI.

CIUDAD RODRIGO—THE COA—ALMEIDA—BUSACO— TORRES VEDRAS.

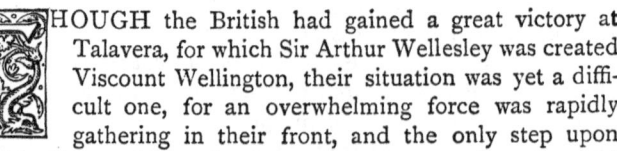HOUGH the British had gained a great victory at Talavera, for which Sir Arthur Wellesley was created Viscount Wellington, their situation was yet a difficult one, for an overwhelming force was rapidly gathering in their front, and the only step upon which the allies could prudently venture was to again retire and take up the line of the Tagus, there to assume a defensive position till stores could be collected and a favourable prospect of acting on the offensive occurred. From thence, owing to the great number of sick, a movement was afterwards made into Portugal, with the hope that, in comfortable cantonments, an improvement might be effected in the general health of the troops. Halting at Badajoz, the army remained here, notwithstanding many inconveniences, till December, during which period there was quietly preparing in the rear that stupendous line of works at Torres Vedras which afterwards baffled the efforts of the French armies and proved the salvation of the Peninsula. During this time the Spaniards, with their usual want of care and prudence, were continually coming into contact with the enemy and suffering reverses, particular instances of this being at Arzobispo and Almonacid.

The French were also vigorously strengthening their means and preparing to open the campaign with a force which might bear down all opposition on the part of Wellington and his army. Arrangements being completed by the French, Massena, who was now in chief command, dispatched Ney to invest the fortress of

Ciudad Rodrigo. This fortress had been commanded, in the beginning of the year, by a person whose conduct had been so suspicious that Lord Wellington demanded his removal. But Don Andreas Herrasti, the actual governor, was a veteran of fifty years' service, whose silver hairs, dignified countenance, and courteous manners excited respect; and whose courage, talents, and honour were worthy of his venerable appearance. His garrison amounted to 6000 fighting men, besides the citizens; and the place, built on a height overhanging the northern bank of the Agueda river, was amply supplied with artillery and stores of all kinds. The works were, however, weak, consisting of an old rampart, nearly circular, about thirty feet in height, and without other flanks than a few projections containing some light guns; a second wall, about twelve feet high, called a *fausse braie*, with a ditch and covered way, surrounded the first, but was placed so low on the hill as scarcely to offer any cover to the upper rampart. There were no bomb-proofs, even for the magazine, and Herrasti was forced to place his powder in the church, which he secured as he might. Beyond the walls, and totally severed from the town, the suburb of Francisco, defended by an earthen entrenchment and strengthened by two large convents, formed an outwork to the north-east of the place. The convent of Santa Cruz served a like purpose on the north-west; and between these posts there was a ridge called the Little Teson, which, somewhat inferior in height to the town, was only 150 yards from the body of the place. There was also a Greater Teson, which, rising behind the lesser at the distance of 600 yards from the walls, overlooked the ramparts, and saw into the bottom of the ditch. The country immediately about Ciudad Rodrigo, although wooded, was easy for troops; especially on the left bank of the Agueda, to which the garrison had access by a stone bridge within pistol-shot of the castle gate. But the Agueda itself, rising in the Sierra de Francia, and running into the Douro, is subject to great and sudden floods; and six or seven miles below the town, near San Felices, the channel deepens into one continued and frightful chasm, many hundred feet deep, and overhung with huge desolate rocks.

On the 25th of April 1810, the French pitched a camp upon a lofty ridge five miles eastward of the city; and in a few days, a second, and then a third arose; and these portentous clouds continued to gather on the hills until June, when 50,000 fighting men came down into the plain, and throwing two bridges over the Agueda, begirt the fortress. This multitude, composed of the sixth and eighth corps and a reserve of cavalry, was led by Ney, Junot, and Montbrun. The sixth corps invested the place, the eighth occupied San Felices Grande and other points, and the cavalry swarmed on both sides of the river; but the battering train and a great escort was still two days' march in the rear, for the rains inundating the flat country between the Agueda and the Tormes rendered the roads impassable. The bridges were established on the 2nd and 7th of June, the one above, the other below the town; and on the 13th ground was broken on the Greater Teson. On the 22nd the artillery arrived, and preparations were made to contract the circle of investment on the left bank of the Agueda, which had hitherto been but slightly watched. But that night, Julian Sanchez, with 200 horsemen, passed silently out of the castle gate, and crossing the river, fell upon the nearest French posts, pierced their line in a moment, and reached the English light division, then behind the Azava, six miles from Ciudad Rodrigo. This event induced Ney to reinforce his troops on the left bank, and a movement was directed against General Crawfurd on the 25th, on which day also the French batteries opened.

Ney's plan was to breach the body of the place without attending to the Spanish fire. Salvos from forty-six guns constantly directed on one point soon broke the old masonry of the ramparts; but the besieged, who could bring twenty-four guns to bear on the Teson, shot so well that three magazines blew up at once in the trenches, and killed above one hundred of the assailants. On the 27th, the Prince of Esling (Marshal Massena) arrived in the camp and summoned the governor to surrender. Herrasti answered in the manner to be expected from so good a soldier; and the fire was resumed until the 1st of July, when Massena, sensible that the mode of attack was faulty, directed the engineers to raise counter-batteries, to push their parallels to the Lesser Teson, work regularly forward, blow in the counterscap, and pass the ditch in form. Meanwhile, to facilitate the progress of the new works, the convent of Santa Cruz on the right flank was carried after a fierce resistance; and on the left the suburb was attacked, taken, and retaken by a sally, in which great loss was inflicted on the French. Howbeit, the latter remained masters of everything beyond the walls.

During the cessation of fire consequent upon the change in the French dispositions, Herrasti removed the ruins from the foot of the breach and strengthened his flank defences; but on the 9th of July, the besiegers' batteries being established on the Lesser Teson, re-opened with terrible effect. In twenty-four hours the fire of the Spanish guns was nearly silent, part of the town was in flames, a reserve magazine exploded on the walls, the counterscarp was blown in by a mine to an extent of thirty-six feet, the ditch filled by the ruins, and a broad way made into the place. At this moment, three French soldiers of heroic courage, suddenly running out of the ranks, mounted the breach, looked into the town, and having thus, in broad daylight, proved the state of affairs, discharged their muskets, and, with matchless fortune, retired unhurt to their comrades. The columns of assault immediately assembled. The troops, animated by the presence of Ney, and excited by the example of the three men who had so gallantly proved the breach, were impatient for the signal. A few moments would have sent them raging into the midst of the city, when the white flag waved on the rampart, and the venerable governor was seen standing alone on the ruins, and signifying by his gestures, that he desired to capitulate. He had striven manfully while reason warranted hope, and it was no dishonour to his silver hairs that he surrendered when resistance could only lead to massacre and devastation.

Immediately after the fall of Ciudad Rodrigo, Massena advanced to the Coa, where he was opposed by General Crawfurd, whose orders had been to cross that river, but from headstrong ambition remained on bad ground to confront the enemy's advance with a small army of 4000 infantry, 1100 cavalry, and 6 guns. His cavalry piquets were upon the plain in his front, his right on some broken ground, and his left resting on an unfinished tower, eight hundred yards from Almeida, but defended by the guns of that fortress.

THE COA.

A stormy night ushered in the 24th of July. The troops, drenched with rain, were under arms before daylight, expecting to retire, when a few pistol-shots in front, followed by an order for the cavalry reserves and the guns to advance, gave notice of the enemy's approach; and as the morning cleared, 24,000 French infantry, 5000 cavalry, and 30 pieces of artillery were observed marching beyond the Turones. The British line was immediately contracted and brought under the edge of the ravine; but meanwhile Ney, who had observed Crawfurd's false disposition, came down with the swoop of an eagle. Four thousand horsemen and a powerful artillery swept the plain. The allied cavalry gave back, and Loison's division coming up at a charging pace, made towards the centre and left of the position. While the French were thus pouring onward, several ill-judged changes were made on the English side; part of the troops were advanced, others drawn back, and the 43rd most unaccountably placed within an enclosure of solid masonry, at least ten feet high, situated on the left of the road, with but one narrow outlet about half-musket-shot down the ravine. While thus imprisoned, the firing in front redoubled, the cavalry, the artillery, and the caçadores successively passed by in retreat, and the sharp clang of the 95th rifle was heard along the edge of the plain above. A few moments later, and the 43rd would have been surrounded, but that here, as in every other part of this field, the quickness and knowledge of the battalion officers remedied the faults of the general. One minute sufficed to loosen some large stones, a powerful effort burst the enclosure, and the regiment, reformed in column of companies, was the next instant up with the riflemen. There was no room to array the line, no time for anything but battle, every captain carried off his company as an independent body, and joining as he could with the 95th or 52nd, the whole presented a mass of skirmishers, acting in small parties and under no regular command; yet each confident in the courage and discipline of those on his right and left, and all regulating their movements by a common discretion, and keeping together with surprising vigour.

It is unnecessary to describe the first burst of French soldiers. It is well known with what gallantry the officers lead, with what

THE COA.

vehemence the troops follow, and with what a storm of fire they waste a field of battle. At this moment, with the advantage of ground and numbers, they were breaking over the edge of the ravine, their guns, ranged along the summit, played hotly with grape, and their hussars, galloping over the glacis of Almeida, poured down the road, sabring everything in their way. Ney, desirous that Montbrun should follow this movement with the whole of the French cavalry, and so cut off the troops from the bridge, sent five officers in succession to urge him on; and so mixed were friends and enemies at the moment, that only a few guns of the fortress durst open, and no courage could have availed against such overwhelming numbers. But Montbrun enjoyed an independent command, and as the attack was made without Massena's knowledge, he would not stir. Then the British regiments, with singular intelligence and discipline, extricated themselves from their perilous situation. For falling back slowly, and yet stopping and fighting whenever opportunity offered, they made their way through a rugged country tangled with vineyards, in despite of their enemies, who were so fierce and eager, that even the horsemen rode in amongst the enclosures, striking at the soldiers as they mounted the walls or scrambled over the rocks.

As the retreating troops approached the river, they came upon a more open space; but the left wing being harder pressed, and having the shortest distance, arrived while the bridge was still crowded and some of the right wing distant. Major M'Leod of the 43rd, seeing this, rallied four companies on a hill just in front of the passage, and was immediately joined by a party of the 95th, and at the same time two other companies were posted by Brigade-Major Rowan on another hill flanking the road; these posts were thus maintained until the enemy, gathering in great numbers, made a second burst, when the companies fell back. At this moment the right wing of the 52nd was seen marching towards the bridge, which was still crowded with the passing troops, M'Leod, a very young man, but with a natural genius for war, immediately turned his horse round, called to the troops to follow, and, taking off his cap, rode with a shout towards the enemy. The suddenness of the thing, and the distinguished action of the man, produced the effect he designed; a mob of soldiers rushed after him, cheering and charging as if a whole army had been at their backs, and the enemy's skirmishers, astonished at this unexpected movement, stopped short. Before they could recover from their surprise, the 52nd crossed the river, and M'Leod, following at full speed, gained the other side also without a disaster.

As the regiments passed the bridge, they planted themselves in loose order on the side of the mountain. The artillery drew up on the summit, and the cavalry were disposed in parties on the roads to the right. The French skirmishers, swarming on the right bank, opening a biting fire, which was returned as bitterly; the artillery on both sides played across the ravine, the sounds were repeated by numberless echoes, and the smoke, rising slowly, resolved itself into an immense arch, spanning the whole chasm, and sparkling with the whirling fuzes of the flying shells. The enemy gathered fast and thickly; his columns were discovered forming behind the high rocks, and a dragoon was seen to try the depth of the stream above, but two shots from the 52nd killed horse and man, and the carcasses floating between the hostile bands, showed that the river was impassable. The monotonous tones of a French drum were then heard, and in another instant the head of a noble column was at the long narrow bridge. A drummer and an officer in a splendid uniform leaped forward together, and the whole rushed on with loud cries. The depth of the ravine at first deceived the soldiers' aim, and two-thirds of the passage was won ere an English shot had brought down an enemy; yet a few paces onwards the line of death was traced, and the whole of the leading French section fell as one man! Still the gallant column pressed forward, but no foot could pass that terrible line; the killed and wounded rolled together until the heap rose nearly even with the parapet, and the living mass behind melted away rather than gave back.

The shouts of the British now rose loudly, but they were confidently answered, and in half an hour a second column, more numerous than the first, again crowded the bridge. This time, however, the range was better judged, and ere half the distance was won, the multitude was again torn, shattered, dispersed, and slain; ten or twelve men only succeeded in crossing, and took shelter under the rocks at the brink of the river. The skirmishing was renewed, and a French surgeon coming down to the very foot of the bridge, waved his handkerchief and commenced dressing the wounded under the hottest fire; nor was his appeal unheeded: every musket turned from him, although his still undaunted countrymen were preparing for a third attempt. The impossibility of forcing the passage was, however, become too apparent, and this last effort, made with feebler numbers and less energy, failed almost as soon as it commenced.

Nevertheless, the combat was unnecessarily continued; by the French, as a point of honour, to cover the escape of those who had passed the bridge; by the English, from ignorance of their object. One of the enemy's guns was dismantled, a powder-magazine blew up, and many continued to fall on both sides until about four o'clock, when a heavy rain causing a momentary cessation of fire, the men amongst the rocks returned, unmolested, to their own party, the fight ceased, and Crawfurd retired. Forty-four Portuguese, 272 British, including 28 officers, were killed, wounded, or taken, and it was at first supposed that Lieutenant Dawson and half a company of the 52nd, which had been posted in the unfinished tower, were also captured; but that officer kept close until the evening, and then, with great intelligence, passed all the enemy's posts, and crossing the Coa at a ford, rejoined his regiment.

In this action the French lost above 1000 men; the slaughter at the bridge was fearful to behold; but Massena claimed to have taken two pieces of artillery, and it was true; for the guns intended to arm the unfinished tower near Almeida were lying dismounted at the foot of the building. They, however, belonged to the garrison of Almeida, and that they were not mounted and the tower garrisoned was a great negligence; the enemy's cavalry could not otherwise have fallen so dangerously on the left of the position, and the after-investment of Almeida would have been retarded.

After the combat on the Coa the French proceeded at once to Almeida, which soon fell into their hands through the treacherous conduct of some Portuguese officers.

ALMEIDA.

This fortress, although regularly constructed with six bastions, ravelins, an excellent ditch, and covered way, was extremely defective. The ramparts were too high for the glacis, and from some near ground on the side of the attack the bottom of the ditch might be seen. An old square castle, built on a mound in the centre of the town, contained three bomb-proofs, the doors of which were not secure; but with the exception of some damp casements in one bastion, there was no other magazine for the powder. Colonel Cox was governor, and his garrison, composed of one regular and two militia regiments, a body of artillery and a squadron of cavalry, amounted to about 4000 men.

On the 18th August the trenches were begun under cover of a false attack, and in the morning of the 26th, 65 pieces of artillery mounted in ten batteries opened at once. Many houses were soon in flames and the garrison was unable to extinguish them; the counter-fire was, however, briskly maintained, little military damage was sustained, and towards evening the cannonade slackened on both sides; but just after dark the ground suddenly trembled, the castle, bursting into a thousand pieces, gave vent to a column of smoke and fire, and with a prodigious noise the whole town sunk into a shapeless ruin. Treason or accident had caused the magazines to explode, and the devastation was incredible. The ramparts were breached, the greatest part of the guns thrown into the ditch, 500 people were struck dead on the instant, and only six houses left standing; the stones thrown out hurt forty of the besiegers in the trenches, and the surviving garrison, aghast at the horrid commotion, disregarded all exhortations to rally. Fearing that the enemy would take the opportunity to storm the ramparts, the governor beat to arms, and running to the walls, with the help of an artillery officer, fired off the few guns that remained; but the French shells fell thickly all the night, and in the morning of the 27th August two officers appeared at the gates with a letter from Massena offering terms.

Cox, sensible that further resistance was impossible, still hoped that the army would make a movement to relieve him, if he could impose upon the enemy for two or three days; and he was in the act of refusing the Prince of Esling's offer, when a mutiny, headed openly by the lieutenant-governor, one Bernardo Costa, and secretly by José Bareiros, the chief of artillery, who had been for some time in secret correspondence with the French, obliged him to yield. The remainder of the native officers, disturbed by fear, or swayed by the influence of those two, were more willing to follow than to oppose their dishonourable proceedings, and Costa expressed his resolution to hoist the white flag. The governor seing no remedy by force, endeavoured to procrastinate, and being ignorant of Bareiros's treason, sent him to the enemy with counter-propositions. Bareiros immediately informed Massena of the true state of the garrison, and never returned; and the final result was a surrender upon agreement that the militia should retire to their homes and the regulars remain prisoners of war. While the treaty was pending, and even after the signature of the articles, in the night of the 27th the French bombarded the place. This act, unjustifiable and strange, because Massena's aide-de-camp, Colonel Pelet, was actually within the walls when the firing commenced, was excused on the ground of an error in the transmission of orders; it, however, lasted during the whole night, and Cox also asserts that the terms of the capitulation with respect to the militia were violated.

Bareiros, having joined the enemy, escaped punishment, but De Costa, being tried, was afterwards shot as a traitor by the orders of Marshal Beresford. His cowardice and mutiny merited this chastisement, yet the principal evidence against him was an explanatory letter written by Cox while a prisoner at Verdun. The explosion, the disappearance of the steeple, and cessation of fire, proclaimed the misfortune of Almeida in the allied camp; but the surrender was first ascertained by Lord Wellington on the 29th, when, with a telescope, he observed many French officers on the glacis of the place. From the great strength of Massena's army at this time there was little chance that Lord Wellington could arrest its progress or offer any steady front, and when the fall of Almeida occurred, he began to retreat in order to place his divisions in a secure position, and in prospect of going into winter quarters, also issued a proclamation advising the native population to retire with all their property from the immediate district. The British fell back to Busaco, where, having obtained a strong post, Wellington determined to await the enemy and risk a battle.

Battle of Busaco.

Ney was averse to attack, but Massena resolved to attempt carrying the position. To facilitate the attack, the light French troops, dropping by twos and threes into the lowest parts of the valley, endeavoured in the evening to steal up the wooded dells and hollows, and to establish themselves unseen close to the piquets of the British light division. Some companies of rifle corps and caçadores checked this, but similar attempts, made with more or less success, at different points of the position, seeming to indicate a night-attack, excited all the vigilance of the troops. Yet, were it otherwise, none but veterans tired of war could have slept, for the weather was calm and fine, and the dark mountain masses, rising on either side, were crowned with innumerable fires, around which more than 100,000 brave men were gathered.

Before daybreak on the 27th September, the French formed five columns of attack; three under Ney opposite the convent, and two under Reynier at St. Antonio de Cantara, these points being about three miles asunder. Reynier's troops had comparatively easier ground before them, and were in the midst of the piquets and skirmishers of the third division almost as soon as they could be perceived to be in movement. The allies resisted vigorously, and six guns played along the ascent with grape, but in less than half an hour the French were close upon the summit, so swiftly and with such astonishing power and resolution did they scale the mountain, overthrowing everything that opposed their progress. The right of the third division was forced back; the 8th Portuguese regiment was broken to pieces, and the hostile masses gained the highest part of the crest, just between the third and the fifth divisions. The leading battalions immediately established themselves amongst the crowning rocks, and a confused mass wheeled to the right, intending to sweep the summit of the sierra; but at that moment Lord Wellington caused two guns to open with grape upon their flank, while a heavy musketry was still poured into their front, and in a little time the 45th and 88th regiments charged so furiously that even fresh men could not have withstood them. The French, quite spent with their previous efforts, opened a straggling fire, and both parties, mingling together, went down the mountain-side with a mighty

clamour and confusion; the dead and dying strewing the way even to the bottom of the valley.

Meanwhile the French who first gained the summit had reformed their ranks with the right resting upon a precipice overhanging the reverse side of the sierra, and thus the position was in fact gained, if any reserve had been at hand, for the greatest part of the third division, British and Portuguese, was fully engaged, and a misty cloud capped the summit, so that the enemy, thus ensconced amongst the rocks, could not be seen, except by General Leith. That officer had put his first brigade in motion to his own left as soon as he perceived the vigorous impression made on the third division, and he was now coming on rapidly; yet he had two miles of rugged ground to pass in a narrow column before he could mingle in the fight. Keeping the Royals in reserve, he directed the 38th to turn the right of the French; but the precipice prevented this; and meanwhile Colonel Cameron, informed by a staff officer of the critical state of affairs, formed the 9th regiment in line under a violent fire, and without returning a single shot, ran in upon and drove the grenadiers from the rocks with irresistible bravery, plying them with a destructive musketry as long as they could be reached, and yet with excellent discipline refraining from pursuit, lest the crest of the position should be again lost; for the mountain was so rugged that it was impossible to judge clearly of the general state of the action. The victory was, however, secure. Hill's corps edged in towards the scene of action; the second brigade of Leith joined the first, and a great mass of fresh troops was thus concentrated, while Reynier had neither reserves nor guns to restore the fight.

Ney's attack had as little success. From the abutment of the mountain upon which the light division was stationed the lowest parts of the valley could be discerned. The ascent was steeper and more difficult than where Reynier had attacked, and Crawfurd, in a happy mood of command, had made masterly dispositions. The table-land was sufficiently scooped to conceal the 43rd and 52nd regiments, drawn up in line; and a quarter of a mile behind them, but on higher ground, a brigade of German infantry appeared to be the only solid line of resistance on this part of the position. In front of the two British regiments, some rocks, overhanging the descent, furnished natural embrasures, in which the guns of the division were placed, and the whole face of the hill was planted with the skirmishers of the rifle corps and of the two Portuguese caçadore battalions.

While it was yet dark, a straggling musketry was heard in the deep hollows separating the armies; and when the light broke, the three divisions of the French sixth corps were observed entering the woods below and throwing forward a profusion of skirmishers; soon afterwards Marchand's division, emerging from the hollow, took the main road, as if to turn the right of the light division, Loison's made straight up the face of the mountain in front, and the third remained in reserve.

General Simon's brigade, which led Loison's attack, ascended with a wonderful alacrity, and though the light troops plied it unceasingly with musketry, and the artillery bullets swept through it from the first to the last section, its order was never disturbed, nor its speed in the least abated. Ross's guns were worked with incredible quickness, yet their range was palpably contracted every round, and the enemy's shot came singing up in a sharper key, until the skirmishers, breathless and begrimed with powder, rushed over the edge of the ascent, when the artillery suddenly drew back, and the victorious cries of the French were heard within a few yards of the summit. Crawfurd, who, standing alone on one of the rocks, had been intently watching the progress of the attack, then turned, and in a quick shrill tone desired the two regiments in reserve to charge. The next moment a horrid shout startled the French column, and 1800 British bayonets went sparkling over the brow of the hill. Yet so truly brave and hardy were the leaders of the enemy, that each man of the first section raised his musket, and two officers and ten soldiers fell before them. Not a Frenchman had missed his mark! They could do no more! The head of their column was violently overturned and driven upon the rear, both flanks were lapped over by the English wings, and three terrible discharges at five yards' distance completed the rout. In a few minutes a long trail of carcasses and broken arms indicated the line of retreat. The main body of the British stood fast; but several companies followed the pursuit down the mountain, until Ney, moving forward his reserve, and opening his guns from the opposite height, killed some men, and thus warned the rest to recover

their own ground. The German brigade then spread over the
hill, and the light division resumed its original position.

Loison showed no disposition to renew the attack, but
Marchand's people, who had followed the main road, broke into
several masses, gained a pine wood half-way up the mountain,
and sent a cloud of their skirmishers against the highest part at
the very moment that Simon was defeated. Such, however, was
the difficulty of ascending, that Pack alone held the enemy in
check, and half a mile higher up Spencer showed a line of the
royal guards which forbade any hope of success; and from the
salient point of land occupied by the light division, Crawfurd's
artillery took the main body of the French in the wood in flank.
Ney, who was there in person, after sustaining this murderous fire
for an hour, relinquished the attack. The desultory fighting of
the light troops then ceased, and before two o'clock, Crawfurd
having assented to a momentary truce, parties of both armies
were mixed amicably together searching for the wounded men.

Towards evening, however, a French company having, with
signal audacity, seized a village within half-musket-shot of the
light division, refused to retire; which so incensed Crawfurd, that
turning twelve guns on the village, he overwhelmed it with bullets for
half an hour. After paying the French captain this distinguished
honour, the English general, recovering his temper, sent a company
of the 43rd down, which cleared the village in a few minutes.
Meanwhile an affecting incident, contrasting strongly with the
savage character of the preceding events, added to the interest of
the day. A poor orphan Portuguese girl, about seventeen years of
age, and very handsome, was seen coming down the mountain,
and driving an ass, loaded with all her property, through the
midst of the French army. She had abandoned her dwelling in
obedience to the proclamation, and now passed over the field of
battle with a childish simplicity, totally unconscious of her perilous
situation, and scarcely understanding which were the hostile and
which the friendly troops, for no man on either side was so brutal
as to molest her.

In this battle of Busaco, the French, after astonishing efforts of
valour, were repulsed in the manner to be expected from the
strength of the ground and the goodness of the soldiers opposed
to them; and their loss was great. General Graind'orge and

about 800 men were slain, Generals Foy and Merle wounded, Simon made prisoner, and the sum total may be estimated at 4500 men, while that of the allies did not exceed 1300. For on the one side musketry and artillery were brought into full activity, but the French sought to gain the day by resolution and audacity rather than by fire.

Though the French had suffered so severe a defeat at Busaco, even with their numerical superiority, Lord Wellington did not choose to risk a second pitched battle at this time on the line of the Mondego, and learning that the enemy was gathering together again in great force, he gave orders that the allies should continue their retreat by way of Coimbra and Leiria to Torres Vedras. But Massena, whether stung to the quick by his unexpected defeat or urged forward by his necessities, after making a fruitless attempt to turn the flank of the British and bring on another battle on the 28th, in which he hoped for better success, now entered upon a vigorous pursuit of the allied forces. On the 1st October, the British outposts were attacked, and driven from the hills bounding the plain of Coimbra to the north. The French, on entering this plain, suffered some loss from a cannonade, and the British cavalry were drawn up in line, but with no serious intention of fighting, and were soon after withdrawn across the Mondego, yet somewhat unskilfully; for the French following briskly, cut down some men even in the middle of the river, and were only prevented from forcing the passage by a strong skirmish, in which fifty or sixty men fell.

This scrambling affair obliged the light division to march hastily through Coimbra, to gain the defiles of Condeixa, which commence at the end of the bridge, and all the inhabitants who had not before quitted the place rushed out, each with what could be caught up in the hand, and driving before them a number of animals loaded with sick people or children. At the entrance to the bridge, the press was so great that the troops halted for a few moments just under the prison; the jailor had fled with the keys, the prisoners, crowding to the windows, were endeavouring to tear down the bars with their hands, and even with their teeth, and bellowing in the most frantic manner, while the bitter lamentations of the multitude increased, and the pistol-shots of the cavalry, engaged at the ford below, were distinctly heard. Captain William Campbell, an officer of Crawfurd's staff, burst the prison doors, and released the wretched inmates, while the troops forced their way over the bridge; yet, at the other end, the uphill road, passing between high rocks, was so crowded that no effort, even of the artillery, could make way. A troop of French dragoons crossed a ford, and hovering close upon the flank, increased the confusion; and a single regiment of foot would have sufficed to destroy the division, wedged in as it was in a hollow way, and totally incapable of advancing, retreating, or breaking out on either side. At last, some of the infantry opened a passage on the right flank, and, by great exertions, the road was cleared for the guns; but it was not until after dusk that the division reached Condeixa, although the distance was less than eight miles. Head-quarters were that night at Redinha, and the next day at Leiria.

Hitherto the marches had been easy, the weather fine, and provisions abundant; nevertheless, the usual disorders of a retreat had already commenced. In Coimbra, a quantity of harness and intrenching tools were scattered in the streets; at Leiria, the magazines were plundered by the troops and camp-followers; and at Condeixa, a magazine of tents, shoes, spirits, and salt meat was destroyed or abandoned to the enemy; and while the streets were flowing ankle-deep with rum, the light division and Pack's Portuguese brigade, at the distance of a quarter of a mile, were obliged to slaughter their own bullocks, and received only half rations of liquor. Lord Wellington arrested this growing disorder with a strong hand. Three men, taken in the fact at Leiria, were hanged on the spot; and some regiments, whose discipline was more tainted than others, were forbidden to enter a village. This vigorous exercise of command, aided by the fine weather and the enemy's inactivity, restored order amongst the allies; while Massena's conduct, the reverse of the English general's, introduced the confusion of a retreat in the pursuing army. In Coimbra the French general permitted waste; and in a few days, resources were dissipated that, under good arrangements, would have supplied his troops for two months; and during this licentious delay the advantage gained by his dangerous flank march was lost.

Everywhere on the route the British were accompanied by

crowds of inhabitants—men, women, and children—the sick and the aged—crowding the fields in every direction, carrying with them everything they possibly could, in order to leave the country bare and void of supplies to the enemy following in the rear. In a few days the army reached the lines of Torres Vedras, forming three distinct series of defence, comprising fifty miles of fortification, 150 forts, and 600 pieces of artillery, and here the troops found themselves in a position in which they might securely bid defiance to the utmost efforts of the enemy.

Massena, surprised at the extent and strength of works, the existence of which had only become known to him five days before he came upon them, employed several days to examine their nature. The heights of Alhandra he judged unattackable; but the valleys of Calandrix and Aruda attracted his attention. Through the former he could turn Hill's position, and come at once upon the weakest part of the second line; yet the abattis and the redoubts erected, and hourly strengthening, gave him little encouragement to attack there; while the nature of the ground about Aruda was such that he could not ascertain what number of troops guarded it, although he made several demonstrations, and frequently skirmished with the light division, to oblige Crawfurd to show his force. That general, by making the town of Aruda an advanced post, rendered it impossible to discover his true situation without a serious affair; and in a short time his division, with prodigious labour, secured the position in a manner really worthy of admiration. Across the ravine on the left, a loose stone wall, sixteen feet thick and forty feet high, was raised; and across the great valley of Aruda a double line of abattis was drawn; not composed, as is usual, of the limbs of trees, but of full-grown oaks and chestnuts, dug up with all their roots and branches, dragged by main force for several hundred yards, and then re-set and crossed, so that no human strength could break through. Breast-works, at convenient distances, to defend this line of trees, were then cast up; and along the summits of the mountain, for a space of nearly three miles, including the salient points, other stone walls, six feet high and four in thickness, were built; so that a good defence could have been made against the attacks of 20,000 men.

The next points that drew Massena's attention were the Monte

Agraça and the vale of the Upper Zizandre, where no earthworks had been constructed; and the valley of Zibreira, and even the hills above Runa, had not been fortified. Here it was possible to join battle on more equal terms, but the position of the allies was still very formidable; the flanks and rear were protected by great forts, and not only was a powerful mass of troops permanently posted there, but six battalions, drawn from Hill's corps, and placed at Bucellas, could, in a very short time, have come into action. Massena's dispositions were not made without several skirmishes, especially near Sobral, on the morning of the 14th October, when, attempting to dislodge the 71st regiment from a fieldwork, his troops were repulsed, pursued, and driven from their own retrenchments, which were held until evening, and only evacuated because the whole of the eighth corps was advancing for the purpose of permanently establishing its position. The loss of the allies in these petty affairs amounted to 150, of which the greatest part fell at Sobral; that of the enemy was estimated higher. The English general, Harvey, was wounded, and at Villa Franca the fire of the gunboats killed the French general, St. Croix, a young man of signal ability and promise.

The war was now reduced to a species of blockade: Massena's object being to feed his army until reinforcements reached it; Lord Wellington's to starve the French before succour could arrive. The former spread his movable columns in the rear to seek for provisions, and commenced forming magazines at Santarem, where his principal depôt was established; but the latter drew down all the militia of the north on the French rear, and a movable column under Colonel Waters issuing from Torres Vedras, made incursions against the enemy's marauding detachments, capturing many prisoners, and part of a considerable convoy which was passing the Baragueda. The French were thus continually harassed, yet their detachments scoured the whole country, even beyond Leiria, and obtained provisions in considerable quantities. The increasing strength of the works, and the report of deserters from the allied forces, soon convinced Massena that it was impracticable to force the lines without great reinforcements. His army suffered from sickness, from the irregular forces in the rear, and from the vengeance of individuals, driven to despair by the excesses which many French soldiers,

H

taking advantage of the times, committed in their foraging courses. Nevertheless, with an obstinate pertinacity only to be appreciated by those who have long made war, the French general maintained his forward position until the country for many leagues behind him was a desert, and then, reluctantly yielding to necessity, he sought for a fresh camp in which to make head against the allies, while his foragers searched more distant countries for food.

Massena continued in front of Torres Vedras for above a month, the piquets of each army being close to each other, but by a kind of tacit agreement no acts of hostility between these took place; and during this time Wellington was continually receiving reinforcements and supplies both by land and sea, which Massena was powerless to prevent. The sick of the French army increasing rapidly from exposure and deficiency of provisions, Massena determined to retire from his cantonments about the beginning of November, with a view to forming an hospital and gathering supplies at a place where the surrounding country was not so wasted.

This movement was not interrupted by Lord Wellington. The morning of the 15th November proved foggy, and it was some hours after daybreak ere he perceived the void space in his front which disclosed the ability of the French general's operations. Fane had reported that boats were collecting at Santarem, and information arrived at the same time that reinforcements for Massena were on the march from Ciudad Rodrigo. The enemy's intention was not clearly developed. It might be a retreat to Spain; it might be to pass round the Monte Junta, and so push the head of his army on Torres Vedras, while the allies were following the rear. In either case, it was important to strike a blow at the rear before the reinforcements and convoy, said to be on the road from Ciudad Rodrigo, could be met with. Two divisions and a body of cavalry were at once detached in pursuit; 400 prisoners were made, principally marauders; and a remarkable exploit was performed by one Baxter, a sergeant of the 16th dragoons. This man, having only five troopers, came suddenly upon a piquet of fifty men, who were cooking. The Frenchmen ran to their arms, and killed one of the dragoons; but the rest broke in amongst them so strongly, that Baxter, with the assistance of some countrymen, made forty-two captives.

The new position of the French at Santarem was undoubtedly a strong one, and was improved by their obtaining possession of one bank of the Mondego, by which not only their flank, but all approaches from the rear, were tolerably secured. The allies again went into cantonments, and both armies remained quiet during the remainder of the year, few occurrences of any importance taking place.

Colonel Waters, mentioned above, was frequently intrusted by Wellington with important missions. On one occasion, when sent out to obtain certain information, he was captured on his return journey by some French dragoons, whose officer detached two men to carry Waters to head-quarters. On their way the men took his watch and purse, and he shortly overheard them plotting to murder him at a mill where they were to stop, and to report that they had to shoot him while attempting to escape. Dismounting at the mill the two men went into the house, leaving their prisoner outside in the hope he would attempt to escape. Waters instantly threw his cloak over an olive bush, and placed his cocked hat above it. Some empty flour-sacks lay near, while a horse laden with filled sacks stood by, and Waters contrived to enter one of the empty sacks and throw himself across the horse. When the soldiers came out they fired their carbines at the supposed prisoner and at once galloped off. Shortly after the miller came and mounted the horse, when Waters managed to rid himself of the sack and sat up to the surprise of the man, who thought he saw a ghost, for the flour had completely whitened his fellow-traveller. who now pushed the miller from the horse and rode off with it. At the British camp, Wellington was lamenting his fate, when a shout from the soldiers made his lordship turn round, and a spectral-looking figure rode up to him. Wellington, taking him by the hand, then said—"Waters, you never yet deceived me, and though you come in a most questionable shape, I must congratulate you and myself."—*Gronow's Recollections.*

CHAPTER VII.

SABUGAL—FUENTES ONORO—ALMEIDA—ALBUERA—BADAJOS.

URING the early months of 1811 the French were kept in a state of continual activity by repeated attacks not only in the rear, but almost within their very position at Santarem, and it soon became evident to Massena that the time for offensive operations in this direction for him had passed away. Knowing also that Wellington had received considerable reinforcements, the French commander made secret and skilful preparations for further retreat, and on the 5th of March put his army in motion for the frontier. After pushing the enemy back in every direction and defeating them in several minor engagements, Wellington compelled Massena to again evacuate Portugal, almost the last stand of the French here being at Sabugal. At daybreak on the 3rd of April 1811, the cavalry under General Slade was directed to cross the Upper Coa; the light division was ordered to ford a little below; the third division still lower; and the fifth division, with the artillery, to force the bridge of Sabugal; the first and seventh, with the exception of a battalion at Seceiras, were held in reserve. The English general having thus 10,000 men pivoted on the fifth division at Sabugal, designed to turn Reynier's left and surround him before he could be succoured. One of those accidents which are frequent in war marred this well-concerted plan, and brought on the—

COMBAT OF SABUGAL.

The morning was so foggy that the troops could not gain their respective posts of attack with that simultaneous regularity which is so essential to success; and in the light division no measures were taken by Sir William Erskine to put the columns in a right direction: the brigades were not even held together, and he carried off the cavalry and the 3rd caçadores without communicating with Colonel Beckwith. This officer, who commanded the first brigade, being without any instructions, halted at a ford to await further orders, and at that moment a staff officer rode up, and somewhat hastily asked why he did not attack? The thing appeared rash, but with an enemy in his front he could make no reply, and instantly passing the river, which was deep and rapid, mounted a very steep wooded hill on the other side. Four companies of the 95th led in skirmishing order, and were followed by the 43rd regiment; but the caçadores and the other brigade, being in movement to the true point, were already distant, and a dark heavy rain setting in, rendered it impossible for some time to distinguish friends or foes. The attack was thus made too soon, for, owing to the obscurity, none of the divisions of the army had reached their respective posts. It was made also in a partial and dangerous manner, and on the wrong point; for Reynier's whole corps was directly in front, and Beckwith, having only one bayonet regiment and four companies of riflemen, was advancing against more than 12,000 infantry, supported by cavalry and artillery. Scarcely had the riflemen reached the top of the hill, when a compact and strong body of French drove them back upon the 43rd. The weather cleared at that instant, and Beckwith at once saw and felt all his danger, but he met it with a heart that nothing could shake. Leading a fierce charge, he beat back the enemy, and the summit of the hill was attained, but at the same moment two French guns opened with grape at the distance of a hundred yards, a fresh body appeared in front, and considerable forces came on either flank of the regiment. Fortunately, Reynier, little expecting to be attacked, had, for the convenience of water, placed his principal masses in the low ground behind the height on which the action commenced; his renewed attack was therefore uphill; yet the musketry, heavy from the beginning, now increased to a storm; the French sprung up the acclivity with great clamour, and it was evident that nothing but the most desperate fighting could save the regiment from destruction.

Captain Hopkins, commanding a flank company of the 43rd, immediately ran out to the right, and, with admirable presence of mind, seized a small eminence close to the French guns and commanding the ascent up which the French troops turning the right flank were approaching. His first fire was so sharp, that the assailants were thrown into confusion; they rallied and were again disordered by the volleys of this company; a third time they endeavoured to form a head of attack, when Hopkins with a sudden charge increased the disorder, and at the same moment the two battalions of the 52nd regiment, which had been attracted by the fire, entered the line. Meanwhile, the centre and left of the 43rd were furiously engaged and wonderfully excited; for Beckwith, wounded in the head, and with the blood streaming down his face, rode amongst the foremost of the skirmishers, directing all with ability, and praising the men in a loud cheerful tone.

The musket-bullets flew thicker and closer every instant, but the French fell fast; a second charge cleared the hill, a howitzer was taken, and the British skirmishers were even advanced a short way down the descent, when small bodies of French cavalry came galloping in from all parts, and obliged them to take refuge with the main body of the regiment. The English line was instantly formed behind a stone wall above; yet one squadron of dragoons surmounted the ascent, and, with incredible desperation, riding up to this wall, were in the act of firing over it with their pistols, when a rolling volley laid nearly the whole of them lifeless on the ground. By this time, however, a second and stronger column of infantry had rushed up the face of the hill, endeavouring to break in and retake the howitzer, which was on the edge of the descent and only fifty yards from the wall; but no man could reach it and live, so deadly was the 43rd's fire. Meanwhile two English guns came into action, and the two battalions of the 52nd, charging upon the flank of the assailants, vindicated the right of the division to the height. A squadron of French cavalry, which had followed the columns in their last attack, then fell in amongst the 52nd men, extended as they were from the circumstances of the action, and at first created considerable confusion, but it was finally repulsed.

Reynier, convinced at last that he had acted unskilfully in sending up his troops piecemeal, put all his reserves, amounting to nearly 6000 infantry with artillery and cavalry, in motion, and outflanking the division on its left, appeared resolute to storm the contested height. But at this critical period the fifth division passed the bridge of Sabugal, the British cavalry appeared on the hills beyond the enemy's left, and General Colville with the leading brigade of the third division issuing out of the woods on Reynier's right, opened a fire on that flank, which instantly decided the fate of the day. The French general hastily retreated upon Rendo, where the sixth corps, which had been put in march when the first shots were heard, met him, and together they fell back, pursued by the English cavalry. The loss of the allies in this bloody encounter, which did not last quite an hour, was nearly 200 killed and wounded; that of the enemy was enormous; 300 dead bodies were heaped together on the hill, the greatest part round the captured howitzer, and more than 1200 were wounded; so unwisely had Reynier handled his masses and so true and constant was the English fire. Although the principal causes of this disproportion undoubtedly were, first, the heavy rain, which gave the French only a partial view of the British, and secondly, the thick wood, which ended near the top of the hill, leaving an open and exposed space upon which the enemy mounted after the first attack; yet it was no exaggeration in Lord Wellington to say, "that this was one of the most glorious actions that British troops were ever engaged in." The next day the light division took the route of Valdespina, to feel for the enemy on the side of the passes leading upon Coria; but Massena was in full retreat for Ciudad Rodrigo, and on the 5th crossed the frontier of Portugal.

While these events were passing at Sabugal, Trant, crossing the Lower Coa with 4000 militia, had taken post two miles from Almeida, when the river suddenly flooded behind him. Near Fort Conception there was a brigade of the ninth corps, which had been employed to cover the march of the battering train from Almeida to Ciudad Rodrigo; but ere those troops discovered Trant's dangerous situation, he constructed a temporary bridge and was going to retire, when he received a letter from the British head-quarters desiring him to be vigilant in cutting the communication with Almeida, and fearless, because the next day a British force would be up to his assistance. Marching then to Val de Mula, he interposed between the fortress and the brigade of the ninth corps. The latter were already within half a mile of his position, and his destruction appeared inevitable; but suddenly two cannon-shots were heard to the southward, the enemy immediately formed squares and commenced a retreat, and six squadrons of British cavalry and Bull's troop of horse-artillery came sweeping over the plain in their rear. Military order and coolness marked the French retreat, yet the cannon-shots ploughed with a fearful effect through their dense masses, and the horsemen continually flanked their line of march. They, however, gained the rough ground, and finally escaped over the Agueda, but with the loss of 300 men killed, wounded, and prisoners. The Prince of Essling had reached Ciudad Rodrigo two days before, and Lord Wellington now stood victorious on the confines of Portugal, having executed what to others appeared incredibly rash and vain even to attempt.

Massena entered Portugal with 65,000 men, his reinforcements while at Santarem were about 10,000, he repassed the frontier with 45,000; hence the invasion of Portugal cost him about 30,000 men, of which 14,000 might have fallen by the sword or been taken; and when he reached the Agueda, his cavalry detachments, heavy artillery, and convalescents again augmented his army to more than 50,000 men, but the fatigues of the retreat and the want of provisions would not suffer him to show a front to the allies; wherefore, drawing 200,000 rations from Ciudad, he fell back to Salamanca, and Lord Wellington invested Almeida.

Here Colonel Waters, who had been taken near Belmonte during the retreat, rejoined the army. Confident in his own resources, he had refused his parole, and when carried to Ciudad Rodrigo, rashly mentioned his intention of escaping to the Spaniard in whose house he was lodged. This man betrayed him; but a servant, detesting his master's treachery, secretly offered his aid, and Waters coolly desired him to get the rowels of his spurs sharpened. When the French army was near Salamanca, Waters, being in the custody of gens-d'armes, waited

ATTEMPTED RELIEF OF ALMEIDA.

until their chief, who rode the only good horse in the party, had alighted, then giving the spur to his own beast, he galloped off, —an act of incredible resolution and hardihood, for he was on a large plain, and before him, and for miles behind him, the road was covered with the French columns. His hat fell off, and, thus distinguished, he rode along the flank of the troops, some encouraging him, others firing at him, and the gens-d'armes, sword in hand, close at his heels; but suddenly breaking at full speed between two columns, he gained a wooded hollow, and having baffled his pursuers, evaded the rear of the enemy's army. The third day he reached head-quarters, where Lord Wellington had caused his baggage to be brought, observing that he would not be long absent.

Shortly after Sabugal, Wellington reconnoitred Badajos, in preparation for the capture of that important stronghold, which had been taken by the French under General Mortier on the 10th March; but while the preparatory arrangements were in progress, he was recalled northwards by the movements of Massena, and Marshal Beresford was left in charge of the siege operations. Massena was trying to effect the relief of Almeida, and to prevent this Wellington concentrated his army to give battle, adopting a position protecting the approach to Almeida.

The allies occupied a fine table-land lying between the Turones and the Dos Casas, the whole distance being five miles. The Dos Casas, flowing in a deep ravine, protected the front of this line, and the French general could not, with any prudence, venture to march against Almeida, lest the allies, crossing the ravine at the villages of Alameda and Fuentes Onoro, should fall on his flank and drive him into the Agueda. Hence, to cover the blockade maintained by Pack's brigade and an English regiment, it was sufficient to leave the fifth division near Fort Conception, and the sixth division opposite Alameda. The first and third were then concentrated on a gentle rise, about a cannon-shot behind Fuentes Onoro, where the steppe of land which the army occupied turned back, and ended on the Turones, becoming rocky and difficult as it approached that river.

FUENTES ONORO.

The French came up in great force against Alameda and Fort Conception, while General Loison fell upon Fuentes Onoro, which was occupied by five battalions of chosen troops, detached from the first and third divisions. Most of the houses of this village were quite in the bottom of the ravine, but an old chapel and some buildings on a craggy eminence overhung one end. The low parts were vigorously defended; yet the violence of the attack was so great and the cannonade so heavy, that the British abandoned the streets, and could scarcely maintain the upper ground about the chapel. Colonel Williams, the commanding officer, fell badly wounded, and the fight was becoming very dangerous, when the 24th, the 71st, and the 79th regiments, coming down from the main position, charged so roughly, that the French were forced back, and, after a severe contest, finally driven over the stream of the Dos Casas. During the night the detachments were withdrawn; but the 24th, the 71st, and 79th regiments were left in the village, where 260 of the allies and somewhat more of the French had fallen.

On the 4th May Massena arrived, and being joined by Bessieres with 1200 cavalry and a battery of the imperial guard, examined all the line, and made dispositions for the next day. His design was to hold the left of the allies in check with the second corps, but to turn the right with the remainder of the army. It was Massena's intention to have made his dispositions in the night, in such a manner as to commence the attack at daybreak on the 5th May, but a delay of two hours occurring, the whole of his movements were plainly descried. The eighth corps, withdrawn from Alameda, and supported by all the French cavalry, was seen marching above the village of Poço Velho, and at the same time the sixth corps and Drouet's division took ground to their own left, but still keeping a division in front of Fuentes. At this sight the light division and the English horse hastened to the support of General Houston, while the first and third divisions made a movement parallel to that of the sixth corps. The latter, however, drove the left wing of the seventh division, consisting of Portuguese and British, from the village of Poço Velho with loss, and was gaining ground in the wood also, when the riflemen of the light division arriving at that point, restored the fight. The French cavalry, then passing Poço Velho, commenced forming in order of battle on the plain. The guerilla chief Julian Sanchez immediately retired across the Turones, partly in fear, but more in anger at the death of his lieutenant, who, having foolishly ridden close up to the enemy, making many violent gestures, was mistaken for a French officer, and shot by a soldier of the guards before the action commenced.

Montbrun occupied himself with Sanchez for an hour; but when the guerilla chief had fallen back, the French general turned the right of the seventh division, and charged the British cavalry, which had moved up to its support. The combat was unequal, for not more than 1000 troopers were in the field. After one shock, in which the enemy were partially checked and the French colonel, Lamotte, taken fighting hand to hand by General Charles Stewart, the cavalry withdrew behind the light division. Houston's people, being thus entirely exposed, were charged strongly, and Captain Ramsay's horse-artillery was cut off and surrounded. The light division instantly threw itself into squares, but the main body of the French horsemen were upon the seventh division ere a like formation could be effected. Nevertheless, the troops stood firm, and although some were cut down, the chasseurs Britanniques, taking advantage of a loose wall, received the attack with such a fire that the enemy recoiled. Immediately after this, a great commotion was observed amongst the French squadrons; men and officers closed in confusion towards one point where a thick dust was rising, and where loud cries and the sparkling of blades and flashing of pistols indicated some extraordinary occurrence. Suddenly the multitude was violently agitated, an English shout arose, the mass was rent asunder, and Norman Ramsay burst forth at the head of his battery, his horses breathing fire and stretching like greyhounds along the plain, his guns bounding like things of no weight, and the mounted gunners in close and compact order protecting the rear. But while this brilliant action was passing in one part, the enemy were making progress in the wood, and the English divisions being separated and the right wing turned, it was abundantly evident that the battle would soon be lost, if the original position was not immediately regained.

In this posture of affairs Lord Wellington directed the seventh division to cross the Turones and move down the left bank to Frenada, the light division to retire over the plain, the cavalry to cover the rear. He also withdrew the first and third divisions, placing them and the Portuguese in line on the steppe running perpendicular to the ravine of Fuentes Onoro. General Crawfurd, who had the command of the light division, first covered the passage of the seventh division over the Turones, and then retired slowly over the plain in squares, having the British cavalry principally on his right flank. He was followed by the enemy's horse, which continually outflanked him, and near the wood surprised and sabred an advanced post of the guards, making Colonel Hill and fourteen men prisoners, but then continuing their charge against the 42nd regiment, the French were repulsed. Many times Montbrun made as if he would storm the light division squares, but the latter were too formidable to be meddled with; yet in all this war there was not a more dangerous hour for England. The whole of that vast plain as far as the Turones was covered with a confused multitude, amidst which the squares appeared but as specks, for there was a great concourse, composed of commissariat followers of the camp, servants, baggage, led horses, and peasants attracted by curiosity, and finally, the broken piquets and parties coming out of the woods. The seventh division was separated from the army by the Turones; 5000 French cavalry with 15 pieces of artillery were close at hand impatient to charge; the infantry of the eighth corps was in order of battle behind the horsemen; the wood was filled with the skirmishers of the sixth corps, and if the latter body, pivoting upon Fuentes, had issued forth, while Drouet's divisions fell on that village, while the eighth corps attacked the light division, and while the whole of the cavalry made a general charge, the loose multitude encumbering the plain would have been driven violently in upon the first division, in such a manner as to have intercepted the latter's fire and broken their ranks.

No such effort was made. Montbrun's horsemen merely hovered about Crawfurd's squares; the plain was soon cleared, the cavalry took post behind the centre, and the light division formed a reserve to the right of the first division, sending the riflemen amongst the rocks to connect it with the seventh division, which had arrived at Frenada, and was there joined by Julian Sanchez. At sight of this new front, so deeply lined with troops, the French stopped short, and commenced a heavy cannonade, which did great execution from the closeness of the allied masses; but twelve British guns replied with vigour, and the violence of the enemy's fire abated. Their cavalry then drew out of range, and a body of French infantry attempting to glide down the ravine of the Turones was repulsed by the riflemen and the light companies of the guards. But all this time a fierce battle was going on at Fuentes Onoro. Massena had directed Drouet to carry this village at the very moment when Montbrun's cavalry should turn the right wing; it was, however, two hours later ere the attack commenced. The three British regiments made a desperate resistance; but overmatched in number, and little accustomed to the desultory fighting of light troops, they were pierced and divided; two companies of the 79th were taken, Colonel Cameron was mortally wounded, and the lower part of the town was carried; the upper part was, however, stiffly held, and the rolling of the musketry was incessant. Had the attack been made earlier, and the whole of Drouet's division thrown frankly into the fight, while the sixth corps moving through the wood closely turned the village, the passage must have been forced and the left of the new position outflanked; but now Lord Wellington, having all his reserves in hand, detached considerable masses to the support of the regiments in Fuentes. The French continued also to reinforce their troops until the whole of the sixth corps and a part of Drouet's division were engaged, when several turns of fortune occurred. At one time the fighting was on the banks of the stream and amongst the lower houses; at another upon the rugged heights and round the chapel, and some of the enemy's skirmishers even penetrated completely through towards the main position; but the village was never entirely abandoned by the defenders, and in a charge of the 71st, 79th, and 88th regiments, led by Colonel M'Kinnon against a heavy mass which had gained the chapel eminence, a great number of the French fell. In this manner the fight lasted until evening, when the lower part of the town was abandoned by both parties, the British maintaining the chapel and crags, and the French retiring a cannon-shot from the stream.

When the action ceased, a brigade of the light division relieved the regiments in the village; and a slight demonstration by the second corps near Fort Conception having been repulsed, both armies remained in observation. Fifteen hundred men and officers, of whom 300 were prisoners, constituted the loss of the allies; that of the enemy was estimated at the time to be near 5000. During the battle, the French convoy for the supply of Almeida being held at Gallegos in readiness to move, Lord Wellington sent Julian Sanchez from Frenada to menace it and to disturb the communication with Ciudad Rodrigo. This produced no effect, and a more decisive battle being expected on the 6th May, the light division made breastworks amongst the crags of Fuentes Onoro, while Lord Wellington entrenched that part of the position which was immediately behind this village, so that the carrying of it would have scarcely benefited the enemy. Fuentes Onoro, strictly speaking, was not tenable; there was a wooded tongue of land on the British right that overlooked, at half-cannon-shot, all the upper as well as the lower part of the village both in flank and rear, yet was too distant from the position to be occupied by the allies.

On the 6th the enemy sent his wounded to the rear, making no demonstration of attack, and as the 7th passed in a like inaction, the British entrenchments were perfected, and next day Massena withdrew his main body across the Agueda, the sixth and eighth corps and the cavalry at Ciudad Rodrigo, the second corps by the bridge of Barba del Puerco. Bessieres also carried off the imperial guards, for Massena had been recalled to France, and Marmont assumed the command of the army of Portugal.

Both sides claimed the victory; the French, because they won the passage at Poço Velho, cleared the wood, turned our right flank, obliged the cavalry to retire, and forced Lord Wellington to relinquish three miles of ground and to change his front; the English, because the village of Fuentes, so often attacked, was successfully defended, and because the principal object (the covering the blockade of Almeida) was attained. Certain it is that Massena at first gained great advantages. Napoleon would have made them fatal; but it is also certain that, with an overwhelming cavalry, on ground particularly suitable to that arm, the Prince of Essling, having, as it were, indicated all the errors of the English general's position, stopped short at the very moment when he should have sprung forward. By some this has been attributed to negligence, by others to disgust at being superseded by Marmont; but the true reason seems to be that discord in his army had arisen to actual insubordination. In the battle of Fuentes Onoro, more errors than skill were observable on both sides, and the train of accidents did not stop there. The prize contended for presented another example of the uncertainty of war.

Evacuation of Almeida.

General Brennier, a prisoner at Vimiero, and afterwards exchanged, was governor of Almeida. During the battle of Fuentes Onoro, his garrison, consisting of 1500 men, skirmished boldly with the blockading force, and loud explosions, supposed to be signals of communication with the relieving army, were frequent in the place. When all hopes of succour vanished, a soldier named Tillet contrived, with extraordinary courage and presence of mind, to penetrate, although in uniform, through the posts of blockade, carrying Brennier orders to evacuate the fortress. The French general had, however, by crossing the Agueda, left Almeida to its fate; the British general placed the light division in its old position with cavalry posts on the Lower Agueda, and desired Sir William Erskine to send the 4th regiment to Barba del Puerco, while General Alexander Campbell continued the blockade with the sixth division and with General Pack's brigade. Campbell's dispositions were either negligently made or negligently executed. Erskine never transmitted the orders to the 4th regiment, and in the meantime, Brennier, undismayed by the retreat of the French army, was preparing to force his way through the blockading troops. An open country and a double line of posts greatly enhanced the difficulty, yet Brennier was resolute not only to cut his own passage, but to render the fortress useless to the allies. To effect this, he ruined all the principal bastions, and kept up a constant fire of his artillery in a singular manner, for always he fired several guns at one moment with very heavy charges, placing one across the muzzle of another, so that, while some shots flew towards the besiegers and a loud explosion was heard, others destroyed pieces without attracting notice.

At midnight of the 10th, all being ready, he sprung his mines, sallied forth in a compact column, broke through the piquets, and passed between the quarters of the reserves, with a nicety that proved at once his talent of observation and his coolness. General Pack following, with a few men collected on the instant, plied him with a constant fire, yet nothing could shake or retard his column, which in silence, and without returning a shot, gained the rough country leading upon Barba del Puerco. Here it halted for a moment, just as daylight broke, and Pack, who was at hand, hearing that some English dragoons were in a village a short distance to the right, sent an officer to bring them out upon the French flank, thus occasioning a slight skirmish and consequent delay. The troops of blockade had paid little attention at first to the explosion of the mines, thinking them a repetition of Brennier's previous practice; but Pack's fire having roused them, the 36th regiment was close at hand, and the 4th, also, having heard the firing, was rapidly gaining the right flank of the enemy. Brennier, having driven off the cavalry, was again in march; yet the British regiments, throwing off their knapsacks, followed at such a pace that they overtook the rear of his column in the act of descending the deep chasm of Barba del Puerco, killed and wounded many, captured about 300, and even passed the bridge in pursuit; there, however, the second corps, which was in order of battle awaiting Brennier's approach, repulsed them with a loss of 30 or 40 men. Had Sir William Erskine given the 4th regiment its orders, the French column would have been lost.

The French having retired from Almeida and retreated into Spain under the command of Marmont, Massena at this juncture having been recalled by Napoleon, Lord Wellington directed his attention to the help of Beresford at Badajos; but before he could reach that place news came to him of the obstinate and sanguinary combat of Albuera, fought by Marshal Beresford against Soult on the 16th of May.

In the morning of the 15th, the British occupied the left of the position of Albuera, which was a ridge about four miles long, having the Aroya Val de Seville in rear and the Albuera river in front. The right of the army was prolonged towards Almendral, the left towards Badajos, and the ascent from the river was easy, the ground being in all parts practicable for cavalry and artillery. Somewhat in advance of the centre were the bridge and village of

Albuera, the former commanded by a battery, the latter occupied by Alten's brigade. The second division, under General William Stewart, was drawn up in one line, the right on a commanding hill over which the Valverde road passed, the left on the road of Badajos, beyond which the order of battle was continued in two lines by the Portuguese troops under General Hamilton and Colonel Collins.

The right of the position, which was stronger and higher and broader than any other part, was left open for Blake's army, because Beresford, thinking the hill on the Valverde road to be the key of the position, as protecting his only line of retreat, was desirous to secure it with the best troops. The French had fifty guns and above 4000 veteran cavalry, but only 19,000 chosen infantry; yet being of one nation, obedient to one discipline, and animated by one spirit, their excellent composition amply compensated for the inferiority of numbers, and their general's talent was immeasurably greater than his adversary's.

Soult examined Beresford's position without hindrance on the evening of the 15th, and he resolved to attack the next morning, for he had detected all the weakness of the English general's dispositions for battle. The hill in the centre, commanding the Valverde road, was undoubtedly the key of the position if an attack was made parallel to the front; but the heights on the right presented a sort of table-land, trending backwards towards the Valverde road, and looking into the rear of the line of battle. The right of the allies and the left of the French approximated to each other, being only divided by a wooded hill, about cannon-shot distance from either, but separated from the allies by the Albuera, and from the French by a rivulet called the Feria. This height, neglected by Beresford, was ably made use of by Soult, concentrating behind it 15,000 men and forty guns within ten minutes' march of Beresford's right wing, and yet that general could neither see a man nor draw a sound conclusion as to the real plan of attack. The light cavalry, the division of the first corps under General Werlé, Godinot's brigade and ten guns still remained at the French marshal's disposal, and these he formed in the woods extending along the banks of the Feria towards its confluence with the Albuera, Godinot being ordered to attack the village and bridge.

I

ALBUERA.

During the night, Blake and Cole arrived with above 16,000 men; but so defective was the occupation of the ground, that Soult had no change to make in his plans from this circumstance, and a little before nine o'clock in the morning, Godinot's division issued from the woods in one heavy column of attack, preceded by ten guns. He was flanked by the light cavalry and followed by Werlé's division of reserve, and making straight towards the bridge, commenced a sharp cannonade, attempting to force the passage. The allies' guns on the rising ground above the village answered the fire of the French, and ploughed through their columns, which were crowding without judgment towards the bridge, although the stream was passable above and below. But Beresford, observing that Werlé's division did not follow closely, was soon convinced that the principal effort would be on the right, and therefore sent Blake orders to form a part of the first and all the second line of the Spanish army, on the broad part of the hills, at right angles to their actual front. Then drawing the Portuguese infantry of the left wing to the centre, he sent one brigade down to support Alten, and directed General Hamilton to hold the remainder in columns of battalions ready to move to any part of the field. The 13th dragoons were posted near the edge of the river, above the bridge, and meanwhile the second division marched to support Blake. The horse-artillery, the heavy dragoons, and the fourth division also took ground to the right; the cavalry and guns being posted on a small plain behind the Aroya, and the fourth division in an oblique line about half-musket-shot behind them. This done, Beresford galloped to Blake, for that general had refused to change his front, and, with great heat, told Colonel Hardinge, the bearer of the order, that the real attack was at the village and bridge. Beresford had sent again to entreat that he would obey, but this message was as fruitless as the former, and when the marshal arrived, nothing had been done. The enemy's columns were, however, now beginning to appear on the right, and Blake, yielding to this evidence, proceeded to make the evolution, yet with such pedantic slowness, that Beresford, impatient of his folly, took the direction in person.

Great was the confusion and the delay thus occasioned, and

ere the troops could be put in order the French were amongst them. For scarcely had Godinot engaged Alten's brigade, when Werlé, leaving only a battalion of grenadiers and some squadrons to watch the 13th dragoons and to connect the attacks, counter-marched with the remainder of his division, and rapidly gained the rear of the fifth corps as it was mounting the hills on the right of the allies. At the same time the mass of light cavalry suddenly quitted Godinot's column, and crossing the river Albuera above the bridge, ascended the left bank at a gallop, and sweeping round the rear of the fifth corps, joined Latour Maubourg, who was already in face of Lumley's squadrons. Thus half an hour had sufficed to render Beresford's position nearly desperate. Two-thirds of the French were in a compact order of battle on a line perpendicular to his right, and his army, disordered and composed of different nations, was still in the difficult act of changing its front. It was in vain that he endeavoured to form the Spanish line sufficiently in advance to give room for the second division to support it; the French guns opened, their infantry threw out a heavy musketry, and their cavalry, outflanking the front and charging here and there, put the Spaniards in disorder at all points; in a short time the latter gave way, and Soult, thinking the whole army was yielding, pushed forward his columns while his reserves also mounted the hill, and General Ruty placed all the batteries in position.

At this critical moment General William Stewart arrived at the foot of the height with Colonel Colborne's brigade, which formed the head of the second division. The colonel, seeing the confusion above, desired to form in order of battle previous to mounting the ascent, but Stewart, whose boiling courage overlaid his judgment, led up without any delay in column of companies, and attempted to open out his line in succession as the battalions arrived at the summit. Being under a destructive fire, the foremost charged to gain room, but a heavy rain prevented any object from being distinctly seen, and four regiments of hussars and lancers, which had passed the right flank in the obscurity, came galloping in upon the rear of the line at the instant of its development, and slew or took two-thirds of the brigade. One battalion only (the 31st), being still in column, escaped the storm and maintained its ground, while the French

THE PENINSULAR CAMPAIGN.

horsemen, riding violently over everything else, penetrated to all parts. In the tumult, a lancer fell upon Beresford, but the marshal, a man of great strength, putting his spear aside, cast him from his saddle, and a shift of wind blowing aside the mist and smoke, the mischief was perceived from the plains by General Lumley, who sent four squadrons out upon the lancers, and cut many of them off.

During this first unhappy effort of the second division, so great was the confusion, that the Spanish line continued to fire without cessation, although the British were before them; whereupon Beresford, finding his exhortations to advance fruitless, seized an ensign and bore him and his colours, by main force, to the front; yet the troops would not follow, and the man went back again on being released. In this crisis, the weather, which had ruined Colborne's brigade, also prevented Soult from seeing the whole extent of the field of battle, and he still kept his heavy columns together. His cavalry, indeed, began to hem in that of the allies, but the fire of the horse-artillery enabled Lumley, covered as he was by the bed of the Aroya and supported by the fourth division, to check them on the plain, while Colborne still maintained the heights with the 31st regiment. The British artillery, under Major Dickson, was likewise coming fast into action, and William Stewart, who had escaped the charge of the lancers, was again mounting the hill with General Houghton's brigade, which he brought on with the same vehemence, but, instructed by his previous misfortune, in a juster order of battle. The weather now cleared, and a dreadful fire poured into the thickest of the French columns convinced Soult that the day was yet to be won.

Houghton's regiments soon got footing on the summit; Dickson placed the artillery in line; the remaining brigade of the second division came up on the left, and two Spanish corps at last moved forward. The enemy's infantry then recoiled, yet soon recovering, renewed the fight with greater violence than before; the cannon on both sides discharged showers of grape at half-range, and the peals of musketry were incessant, and often within pistol-shot; but the close formation of the French embarrassed their battle, and the British line would not yield them one inch of ground nor a moment of time to open their ranks. Their fighting was, however, fierce and dangerous. Stewart was twice wounded, Colonel Duckworth of the 48th was slain, and the gallant Houghton, who had received many wounds without shrinking, fell and died in the act of cheering his men. Still the struggle continued with unabated fury. Colonel Inglis and 22 officers, and more than 400 men out of 570 that had mounted the hill, fell in the 57th alone, and the other regiments were scarcely better off; not one-third were standing in any; ammunition failed, and, as the English fire slackened, the enemy established a column in advance upon the right flank; the play of Dickson's artillery indeed checked them a moment, but again the Polish lancers charging, captured six guns. In this desperate crisis, Beresford, who had already withdrawn the 13th dragoons from the banks of the river and brought Hamilton's Portuguese into a situation to cover a retrograde movement, wavered;—destruction stared him in the face, his personal resources were exhausted, and the unhappy thought of a retreat rose in his agitated mind. Yet no order to that effect was given, and it was urged by some about him that the day might still be redeemed with the fourth division. While he hesitated, Colonel Hardinge boldly ordered General Cole to advance, and then riding to Colonel Abercrombie, who commanded the remaining brigade of the second division, directed him also to push forward into the fight. The die being thus cast, Beresford acquiesced, and this terrible battle was continued.

The fourth division had only two brigades in the field; the one Portuguese, under General Harvey, the other British, commanded by Sir W. Myers, and composed of the 7th and 23rd regiments, was called the fusilier brigade. General Cole directed the Portuguese to move between Lumley's dragoons and the hill, where they were immediately charged by some of the French horsemen, but beat them off with great loss; meanwhile he led the fusiliers in person up the height. At this time six guns were in the enemy's possession, the whole of Werlé's reserves were coming forward to reinforce the front column of the French, and the remnant of Houghton's brigade could no longer maintain its ground; the field was heaped with carcasses, the lancers were riding furiously about the captured artillery on the upper part of the hill, and on the lower slopes a Spanish and an English regiment in mutual error were exchanging volleys: behind all, General

Hamilton's Portuguese, in withdrawing from the heights above the bridge, appeared to be in retreat. The conduct of a few brave men soon changed this state of affairs. Colonel Robert Arbuthnot, pushing between the double fire of the mistaken troops, arrested that mischief, while Cole with the fusiliers, flanked by a battalion of the Lusitanian legion under Colonel Hawkshawe, mounted the hill, dispersed the lancers, recovered the captured guns, and appeared on the right of Houghton's brigade exactly as Abercrombie passed it on the left.

Such a gallant line, issuing from the midst of the smoke and rapidly separating itself from the confused and broken multitude, startled the enemy's heavy masses, which were increasing and pressing onwards as to an assured victory: they wavered, hesitated, and then vomiting forth a storm of fire, hastily endeavoured to enlarge their front, while a fearful discharge of grape from the artillery whistled through the British ranks. Cole and three colonels fell wounded, and the fusilier battalions, struck by the iron tempest, reeled and staggered like sinking ships. Suddenly and sternly recovering, they closed on their terrible enemies, and then was seen with what a strength and majesty the British soldier fights. In vain did Soult, by voice and gesture, animate his Frenchmen; in vain did the hardiest veterans, extricating themselves from the crowded columns, sacrifice their lives to gain time for the mass to open out on such a fair field; in vain did the mass itself bear up, and fiercely striving, fire indiscriminately upon friends and foes, while the horsemen hovering on the flank threatened to charge the advancing line. Nothing could stop that astonishing infantry. No sudden burst of undisciplined valour, no nervous enthusiasm, weakened the stability of their order; their flashing eyes were bent on the dark columns in their front, their measured tread shook the ground, their dreadful volleys swept away the head of every formation, their deafening shouts overpowered the dissonant cries that broke from all parts of the tumultuous crowd, as foot by foot and with a horrid carnage it was driven by the incessant vigour of the attack to the farthest edge of the hill. In vain did the French reserves, joining with the struggling multitude, endeavour to sustain the fight; their efforts only increased the irremediable confusion, and the mighty mass, giving way like a loosened cliff, went headlong down the ascent. The rain flowed after in streams discoloured with blood, and 1500 unwounded men, the remnant of 6000 unconquerable British soldiers, stood triumphant on the fatal hill!

While the fusiliers were thus striving on the upper part of the hill, the cavalry and Harvey's brigade continually advanced, and Latour Maubourg's dragoons, battered by Lefebre's guns, retired before them, yet still threatening the British with their right, and covering the flank of their own infantry from a charge of Lumley's horse. Beresford, seeing that Colonel Hardinge's decision had brought on the critical moment of the battle, then endeavoured to secure a favourable result. Blake's first line had not been at all engaged, and were ordered to move upon the village; Alten's Germans and Hamilton's and Collins's Portuguese were thus rendered disposable, forming a mass of 10,000 fresh men, with which the English general followed up the attack of the fusiliers and Abercrombie's brigade, and at the same time the Spanish divisions advanced. Nevertheless, so rapid was the execution of the fusiliers, that the enemy's infantry were never attained by these reserves, which yet suffered severely; for General Ruty got the French guns all together and worked them with prodigious activity, while the fifth corps still made head; and when the day was irrevocably lost, he regained the other side of the Albuera, and protected the passage of the broken infantry.

Beresford, being too hardly handled to pursue, formed a fresh line with his Portuguese parallel to the hill from whence Soult had advanced to the attack in the morning, and where the French troops were now rallying with their usual celerity. Meanwhile the fight continued at the village, but Godinot's division and the connecting battalion of grenadiers on that side were soon afterwards withdrawn, and the action terminated before three o'clock. The serious fighting had endured only four hours, and in that space of time nearly 7000 of the allies and above 8000 of their adversaries were struck down. Three French generals were wounded, two slain, and 800 soldiers so badly hurt as to be left on the field. On Beresford's side only 2000 Spaniards and 600 Germans and Portuguese were killed or wounded; hence it is plain with what a resolution the pure British fought, for they had only 1500 men left standing out of 6000! The trophies of the French were 500 unwounded prisoners, a howitzer, and several stand of colours; the British had nothing of that kind to boast of; but the horrid piles of carcasses within their lines told, with dreadful eloquence, who were the conquerors, and all the night the rain poured down, and the river and the hills and the woods on each side resounded with the dismal clamour and groans of dying men. Beresford, obliged to place his Portuguese in the front line, was oppressed with the number of his wounded; they far exceeded that of the sound amongst the British soldiers, and when the latter's piquets were established, few men remained to help the sufferers.

Morning came, and both sides remained in their respective situations, the wounded still covering the field of battle, the hostile lines still menacing and dangerous. The greater multitude had fallen on the French part, but the best soldiers on that of the allies; and the dark masses of Soult's powerful cavalry and artillery, as they covered all his front, seemed alone able to contend again for the victory: the right of the French also appeared to threaten the Badajos road, and Beresford, in gloom and doubt, awaited another attack. On the 17th, however, the third brigade of the fourth division came up by a forced march, and enabled the second division to retake their former ground between the Valverde and the Badajos roads. On the 18th May Soult retreated, and left to the generosity of the English general several hundred men too deeply wounded to be removed; but all that could travel he had in the night of the 17th sent towards Seville; then protecting his movements with all his horsemen and six battalions of infantry, he filed the army in the morning to its right and gained the road of Solano.

When Beresford discovered the enemy's retreat, he dispatched General Hamilton to make a show of reinvesting Badajos, which was effected at daybreak on the 19th, but on the left bank only. Meanwhile the allied cavalry, supported by Alten's Germans, followed the French line of retreat. Lord Wellington reached the field of battle on the 18th, and, after examining the state of affairs, now undertook the siege of Badajos in person, and in a few days the place was completely invested. According to the regular rules of art, Soult should have been driven over the mountains before the siege was begun, but there was no time to do this, and Marmont was equally to be dreaded on the other side; wherefore Lord Wellington could only try, as it were, to snatch away the fortress from between them.

SIEGE OF BADAJOS.

There is no operation in war so certain as a modern siege, provided the rules of art are strictly followed, but, unlike the ancient sieges in that particular, it is also different in this: that no operation is less open to irregular daring, because the course of the engineer can neither be hurried nor delayed without danger. Lord Wellington knew that a siege of Badajos in form required longer time and better means than were at his disposal, but he was forced to incur danger or adopt some compendious mode of taking that place. The time that he could command—and time is in all sieges the greatest point—was precisely that which the French required to bring up a force sufficient to disturb the operation, and more than twenty days of free action against the place were not to be calculated upon.

The carriages of the battering guns used in Beresford's siege were so much damaged, that the artillery officers asked eleven days to repair them, and the scanty means of transport for stores was much diminished by carrying the wounded from Albuera to the different hospitals. Thus more than fifteen days of open trenches and nine days of fire could not be expected. With good guns, plentiful stores, and a corps of regular sappers and miners, this time would probably have sufficed; but none of these things were in the camp, and it was a keen jest of Picton to say that "Lord Wellington sued Badajos *in forma pauperis*."

The guns, some of them cast in Philip II.'s reign, were of soft brass, and false in their bore; the shot were of different sizes, and the largest too small; the Portuguese gunners were inexperienced; there were but few British artillerymen, few engineers, no sappers or miners, and no time to teach the troops of the line how to make fascines and gabions. Regular and sure approaches against the body of the place by the Pardaleras and the Picurina outworks could not be attempted; but it was judged that Beresford's lines of attack on the castle and Fort Christoval might be successfully renewed by pushing the double attacks simultaneously, and with more powerful means. San Christoval might thus be taken, and batteries from thence could sweep the interior of the castle, which was meanwhile to be breached. Something also was hoped from the inhabitants, and something from the effect of Soult's retreat after Albuera.

This determination once taken, everything was put in motion with the greatest energy. Major Dickson, an artillery officer whose talents were very conspicuous during the whole war, had, with unexpected rapidity, prepared a battering train of thirty 24-pounders, four 16-pounders, and twelve 8 and 10-inch howitzers, made to serve as mortars by taking off the wheels and placing them on trucks. Six iron Portuguese ship-guns were forwarded from Salvatierra, making altogether fifty-two pieces, a considerable convoy of engineers' stores had already arrived, and a company of British artillery marched from Lisbon to be mixed with the Portuguese, making a total of 600 gunners. The regular engineer officers present were only twenty-one in number; but eleven volunteers from the line were joined as assistant-engineers, and a draft of 300 intelligent men from the line strengthened the force immediately under their command.

Hamilton's Portuguese division was already before the town, and on the 24th of May, at the close of evening, General Houston's division invested San Christoval. A flying bridge was then laid down on the Guadiana, and on the 27th Picton's division, arriving from Campo Mayor, crossed the river by the ford above the town, and joined Hamilton, their united force being about 10,000 men. General Hill commanded the covering army, which, including the Spaniards, was spread from Merida to Albuera. The cavalry was pushed forward in observation of Soult, and a few days after, intelligence having arrived that Drouet's division was on the point of effecting a junction with that marshal, two regiments of cavalry and two brigades of infantry, which had been quartered at Coria as posts of communication with Spencer, were called up to reinforce the covering army.

While the allies were engaged at Albuera, Phillipon, the governor of Badajos, had levelled their trenches, repaired his own damages, and obtained a small supply of wine and vegetables from the people of Estremadura, who were still awed by the presence of Soult's army; and within the place all was quiet, for the citizens did not now exceed 5000 souls. He had also mounted more guns, and when the place was invested, parties of the townsmen mixed with soldiers were observed working to improve the defences; wherefore, as any retrenchments made in the castle behind the intended points of attack would have frustrated the besiegers' object by prolonging the siege, Lord Wellington had a large telescope placed in the tower of La Lyppe, near Elvas, by which the interior of the castle could be plainly looked into, and all preparations discovered.

In the night of the 29th, ground was broken for a false attack against the Pardaleras, and the following night 1600 workmen, with a covering party of 1200, sank a parallel against the castle, on an extent of 1100 yards, without being discovered by the enemy, who did not fire until after daylight. The same night 1200 workmen, covered by 800 men under arms, opened a parallel 450 yards from San Christoval and 700 yards from the bridge-head. On this line one breaching and two counter batteries were raised against the fort and against the bridge-head, to prevent a sally from that point; and a fourth battery was also commenced to search the defences of the castle; but the workmen were discovered, and a heavy fire struck down many of them.

On the 31st the attack against the castle, the soil being very soft, was pushed forward without much interruption and rapidly; but the Christoval attack, being carried on in a rocky soil, and the earth brought up from the rear, proceeded slowly and with considerable loss. The direction of the parallel against the castle was such that the right gradually approached the point of attack, by which the heaviest fire of the place was avoided; yet, so great was the desire to save time, that before the suitable point of distance was attained, a battery of fourteen 24-pounders with six large howitzers was marked out. On the Christoval side the batteries were not finished before the night of the 1st of June, for the soil was so rocky that the miner was employed to level the ground for the platforms; and the garrison, having mortars of 16 and 18 inches diameter mounted on the castle, sent every shell amongst the workmen. These huge missiles would have ruined the batteries on that side altogether, if the latter had not been on the edge of a ridge, from whence most of the shells rolled off before bursting; yet so difficult is it to judge rightly in war, that

Phillipon stopped this fire, thinking it was thrown away. The progress of the works was also delayed by the bringing of earth from a distance, and woolpacks purchased at Elvas were found to be an excellent substitute.

In the night of the 2nd, the batteries on both sides were completed, and armed with forty-three pieces of different sizes, of which twenty were pointed against the castle; the next day the fire of the besiegers opened, but the windage caused by the smallness of the shot rendered it very ineffectual at first, and five pieces became unserviceable. However, before evening the practice was steadier, the fire of the fort was nearly silenced, and the covering of masonry fell from the castle wall, discovering a perpendicular bank of clay. During the night of the 4th, the garrison began to entrench themselves behind the castle breach; before morning their labourers were well covered, and two additional pieces from Christoval were made to plunge into the trenches with great effect. On the other hand, the fire of the besiegers had broken the clay bank, which took such a slope as to appear nearly practicable, and the stray shells and shots set fire to the houses nearest the castle, but three more guns were disabled.

On the 6th June there were two breaches in Christoval, and the principal one being found practicable, a company of grenadiers with twelve ladders was directed to assault it, while a second company turned the fort by the east to divert the enemy's attention. Three hundred men from the trenches were at the same time pushed forward by the west side to cut the communication between the fort and the bridge-head; and a detachment with a six-pounder moved into the valley of the Gebora, to prevent any passage of the Guadiana by boats.

The storming party, commanded by Major M'Intosh of the 85th regiment, was preceded by a forlorn hope under Mr. Dyas of the 51st, and this gallant gentleman, guided by the engineer, William Forster, a young man of uncommon bravery, reached the glacis about midnight, and descended the ditch without being discovered. The French had, however, cleared all the rubbish away, the breach had still seven feet of perpendicular wall, many obstacles, such as carts chained together and pointed beams of wood were placed above it, and large shells were ranged along the ramparts to roll down upon the assailants. The forlorn hope finding the opening impracticable, was retiring with little loss, when the main body, which had been exposed to a flank fire from the town as well as a direct fire from the fort, came leaping into the ditch with ladders, and another effort was made to escalade at different points; the ladders were too short, and the garrison, consisting of only seventy-five men, besides the cannoneers, made so stout a resistance, and the confusion and mischief occasioned by the bursting of the shells was so great, that the assailants again retired with the loss of more than 100 men.

Bad success always produces disputes, and the causes of this failure were attributed by some to the breach being impracticable from the first; by others to the confusion which arose after the main body had entered. During the night the iron guns were placed in battery against the castle, but two more of the brass pieces became unserviceable, and the following day three others were disabled. However, the bank of clay at the castle at last offered a practicable slope, and during the night, Captain Patton of the engineers examined it closely; he was mortally wounded in returning, yet lived to make his report that it was practicable. Nevertheless the garrison continued, as they had done every night at both breaches, to clear away the ruins, and with bales of wool and other materials to form defences behind the opening. They ranged also a number of huge shells and barrels of powder, with matches fastened to them, along the ramparts, and placed chosen men to defend the breach, each man being supplied with four muskets. In this order they fearlessly awaited another attack, which was soon made. For intelligence now arrived that Drouet's corps was close to Llerena, and that Marmont was on the move from Salamanca; and hence Lord Wellington, seeing that his prey was likely to escape, as a last effort resolved to assault Christoval again. But this time 400 men carrying sixteen long ladders were destined for the attack; the supports were better closed up; the appointed hour was nine instead of twelve, and a greater number of detachments than before were distributed to the right and left to distract the enemy's attention, to cut off his communication with the town, and to be ready to improve any success which might be obtained. On the other side, Phillipon increased the garrison of the fort to 200 men.

The storming party was commanded by Major M'Geechy, the

forlorn hope, again led by the gallant Dyas, was accompanied by Mr. Hunt, an engineer officer, and a little after nine o'clock the leading troops bounding forward, were immediately followed by the support, amidst a shattering fire of musketry which killed Major M'Geechy, Mr. Hunt, and many men upon the glacis. The troops with loud shouts jumped into the ditch, but the French scoffingly called to them to come on, and at the same time rolled the barrels of powder and shells down, while the musketry made fearful and rapid havoc. In a little time the two leading columns united at the main breach, the supports also came up, confusion arose about the ladders, of which only a few could be reared, and the enemy standing on the ramparts, bayoneted the foremost of the assailants, overturned the ladders, and again poured their destructive fire upon the crowd below. When 140 men had fallen the order to retire was given.

An assault on the castle breach might still have been tried, but the troops could not have formed between the top and the retrenchments behind the breach until Christoval was taken, and the guns from thence used to clear the interior of the castle; hence the siege was of necessity raised, because to take Christoval required several days more, and Soult was now ready to advance. The stores were removed on the 10th, and the attack was turned into a blockade.

CHAPTER VIII.

ELBODON—ALDEA DE PONTE—CAPTURE OF CIUDAD RODRIGO.

N intercepted dispatch of Marmont's, revealing the great reinforcements he was about to receive, and that Soult was about to join him with his army, determined Wellington to retire from his position at Albuera, where he had purposed to wait for Soult, should he advance to the relief of Badajos. Lord Wellington knew it would be impossible that the enemy could long subsist their forces when both armies were concentrated, and he patiently waited till they should find it necessary to break up, and this took place in July, when Soult returned to Seville and Marmont to Salamanca. From Albuera the British retired to Fuentes Guinaldo, where an extensive line was taken up, and here they remained about a month without disturbance from the enemy. In the beginning of August Wellington proceeded to the Coa, intending first a blockade and then a siege of Ciudad Rodrigo; but learning that the French had but a day or two before provisioned the place for two months, the first part of the design was abandoned. Preparations for a siege went on till Wellington was informed that Marmont was on his way to relieve the fortress, when he once more formed a blockade, and put his divisions into such a defensive position upon the heights of Guinaldo, as would enable him to concentrate upon Ciudad Rodrigo whenever such a measure was necessary by attempts of the enemy to relieve the fortress. Towards the end of September 1811, the French made their appearance in the plains before Rodrigo, their army at this

time amounting to 60,000 men, of whom 6000 were cavalry, while that of the allies did not exceed 40,000, including 4000 cavalry.

Wellington's position before Rodrigo was very extensive, and therefore very weak. The Agueda, although fordable in many places during fine weather, was liable to sudden freshets, and was on both sides lined with high ridges. The heights occupied by the troops on the left bank were about three miles wide, ending rather abruptly above Pastores and Elbodon, and they were flanked by the great plains and woods which extend from Ciudad to the bed of the Coa. The position of Elbodon itself, which was held by the centre of the army, was, therefore, not tenable against an enemy commanding these plains; and as the wings were distant, their lines of retreat were liable to be cut, if the centre should be briskly pushed back beyond Guinaldo. But at the latter place three field-redoubts had been constructed on the high land, with a view to impose upon the enemy, and so gain time to assemble and feel Marmont's disposition for a battle, because a retreat behind the Coa was to be avoided if possible.

On the 23rd September the French encamped behind the hills to the north-east of Ciudad Rodrigo. Then a strong detachment entered the plain, and having communicated with the garrison and examined the position of the light division on the Vadillo, returned. On the 24th, 6000 cavalry, with four divisions of infantry, crossed the hills in two columns, and placing some troops in observation on the Vadillo, introduced the convoy. On this day the fourth division of the allies was brought up to the position of Guinaldo, and the redoubts were completed, yet no other change was made, for it was thought the French would not advance farther. But on the 25th, soon after daybreak, fourteen squadrons of the imperial guards drove the outposts of the left wing from Caprio across the Azava, and the lancers of Berg crossed that river in pursuit; they were, however, flanked by some infantry in a wood, and then charged and beaten by two squadrons of the 14th and 16th dragoons, who re-occupied the post at Carpio.

During this skirmish 12 battalions of infantry, 30 squadrons of cavalry, and 12 guns, the whole under Montbrun, passed the Agueda by the bridge of Rodrigo and the fords above it,. and marched towards Guinaldo. The road soon divided, one branch turning the Elbodon heights on the right hand, the other leading nearer to the Agueda, and passing through the villages of Pastores, La Encina, and Elbodon; and as the point of divergence was covered by a gentle ridge, it was for some time doubtful which branch the French would follow. In a short time this doubt was decided. Their cavalry poured along the right-hand road leading directly to Guinaldo, the small advanced posts which the allied squadrons had on the plain were rapidly driven in, and the enemy's horsemen, without waiting for their infantry, commenced the combat of

ELBODON.

The position of the third or centre division was completely turned by this movement, and the action began very disadvantageously; for the 74th and 60th regiments were too distant to be called in, and Picton being with three other regiments at Elbodon, could not take any immediate part in the fight. Hence, as the French force was considerable, Wellington sent to Guinaldo for a brigade of the fourth division, and meanwhile directed General Colville to draw up the 77th and 5th British regiments, the 21st Portuguese, and two brigades of artillery of the same nation on the hill over which the road to Guinaldo passed, supporting their flanks with Alten's squadrons. The height thus occupied by the allies was convex towards the enemy, and covered in front and on both flanks by deep ravines; but it was too extensive for their numbers, and before Picton could bring in the troops from the village of Elbodon, the crisis of the combat passed. The Portuguese guns had sent their shot amongst the thickest of Montbrun's horsemen in the plain, but the latter passed the front ravine in half squadrons, and with amazing vigour riding up the rough height, on three sides fell vehemently upon the allies. Neither the loose fire of the infantry nor of the artillery could stop them, but they were checked by the fine fighting of the cavalry, who charged the heads of the ascending masses, not once but twenty times, and always with a good will, thus maintaining the upper ground for above an hour.

It was astonishing to see so few troopers bearing up against that surging multitude, even favoured as the former were by the

K

steep rocky nature of the ground; but Montbrun, obstinate to win, soon brought up his artillery, and his horsemen gaining ground in the centre, cut down some of the gunners and captured the guns; and one of the British squadrons, by charging too far, got entangled in the intricacy of the ravines. The danger was then imminent, when suddenly the 5th regiment, led by Major Ridge, a daring spirit, darted into the midst of the French cavalry and retook the artillery, which again opened its fire; and nearly at the same time the 77th, supported by the 21st Portuguese, repulsed the enemy on the left. However, this charging of a weak line of infantry against a powerful cavalry could only check the foe at that particular point. Montbrun still pressed onward with fresh masses against the left flank of the allies, while other squadrons penetrated between the right flank and the village of Elbodon. From the enclosures and vineyards of that village Picton was at this time with difficulty and some confusion extricating his regiments; the expected brigade of the fourth division was not yet in sight, and the French infantry was rapidly approaching; the position was no longer tenable, and Lord Wellington directed both Picton and Colville to fall back and unite in the plain behind. Colville, forming his battalions in two squares, immediately descended from the hill, but Picton had a considerable distance to move, and at this moment the allied squadrons, fearing to be surrounded by the French, who had completely turned their right, galloped away and took refuge with the Portuguese regiment which was farthest in retreat. Then the 5th and 77th, two weak battalions formed in one square, were quite exposed, and in an instant the whole of the French cavalry came thundering down upon them. The multitudinous squadrons rending the skies with their shouts, and closing upon the glowing squares like the falling edges of a burning crater, were as instantly rejected, scorched, and scattered abroad; and the rolling peal of musketry had scarcely ceased to echo in the hills, when bayonets glittered at the edge of the smoke, and, with firm and even step, the British regiments came forth like the holy men from the Assyrian's furnace. Picton now effected his junction, and the whole retired over the plain to the position at Guinaldo, which was about six miles distant. The French, although fearing to renew the close attack, followed and plied the troops with shot and shell, until about four o'clock in the evening, when the entrenched camp was gained. Here the fourth division presented a fresh front, Pack's brigade and the heavy cavalry being also brought into line, and the action ceased. By this retrograde movement of the left and centre of the third division, the 74th and the 60th regiments, posted at Pastores, were cut off; they, however, crossed the Agueda by a ford, and moving up the right bank, happily reached Guinaldo in the night, after a march of fifteen hours, in the course of which they captured a French cavalry patrol.

During the retreat from Elbodon, the left wing of the army was ordered to fall back on the first division at Nava d'Aver. The seventh division was withdrawn to Albergaria; the light division should have marched to Guinaldo. General Crawfurd received the order at two o'clock; he plainly heard the cannonade, and might easily have reached Guinaldo before midnight, but he only marched to Cespedosa, one league from the Vadillo, which river was immediately passed by 1500 French. The position at Guinaldo was therefore occupied by only 14,000 men, of which about 2600 were cavalry. The left of the army at Nava d'Aver, under Graham, was ten miles distant; the light division was sixteen miles distant, and the fifth division, posted at Payo in the mountains, was twelve miles distant. Meanwhile, Marmont brought up a second division of infantry, and in the course of the night and in the following day united 60,000 men in front of Guinaldo. The situation of the English general was become most critical, yet he would not abandon the light division, which did not arrive until after three o'clock in the evening. Marmont's fortune was fixed in that hour! He knew nothing of the allies' true situation, and having detached a strong column by the valley of the Azava to menace their left, contented himself with making an ostentatious display of the imperial guards in the plain, instead of attacking an adversary who was too weak to fight, and, laughing to see him so employed, soon changed the state of affairs.

In the night, Wellington, by a skilful movement, concentrated the whole army on new ground between the Coa and the sources of the Agueda, twelve miles behind Guinaldo; and it is a curious fact that Marmont had so little knowledge of his own advantages, that instead of harassing the allies in this difficult movement, he also retired during the night, and was actually in march to the rear, when the scouts of the column which had marched by the valley of Azava brought word that the allies were in retreat, and their divisions still widely separated. Dorsenne then insisted that Marmont should wheel round and pursue, but Lord Wellington was already in a strong position behind the stream of the Villa Mayor. The fifth division coming up from Payo, was now on the right at Aldea Velha; the fourth and light divisions, with Victor Alten's cavalry and the heavy dragoons, under Sir Stapleton Cotton, were in the centre, and the line was prolonged by Pack's and M'Mahon's Portuguese brigades; the sixth division, with Anson's cavalry, closed the line. The cavalry piquets were pushed beyond the Villa Mayor in front of Aldea Ponte, in the centre, and towards Furcalhos on the right; and the third and seventh divisions were in reserve behind Alfayates. The position was extensive, but the days were short, serious dispositions were required for a general attack, and the allies could not be turned, because they covered all the practicable roads leading to the bridges and fords of the Coa.

Aldea de Ponte.

The French, moving by the roads of Furcalhos and of Aldea de Ponte, were checked by the piquets of the light division on the former; but on the latter their horsemen drove the cavalry posts from the hills, and across the stream of the Villa Mayor, and about ten o'clock on the 27th September took possession of Aldea de Ponte. At twelve o'clock the head of the infantry came up and immediately attacked General Pakenham, then commanding a brigade of the fourth division, which was posted on the opposite heights. Lord Wellington arrived at the same moment, and directed the 7th fusiliers to charge in line, and he supported them on each flank with a Portuguese regiment in column. The French, who had advanced well up the hill, were driven back, and though they afterwards attempted to turn the brigade by a wood, which was distant about musket-shot from the right, while their cavalry advanced to the foot of the hills, the artillery sufficed to baffle the effort. Then the English general, taking the offensive, directed the 23rd fusiliers and Portuguese caçadores to turn the French left, and seize the opposite hills, which finished the action, and Aldea de Ponte was again occupied by the allies. Wellington, who had been much exposed to the fire, rode to another part of the position, but scarcely had he departed when the French from the Forcalhos road joined those near Aldea de Ponte, and at five o'clock renewing the attack, retook the village. Pakenham, with his fusiliers, immediately recovered it, but the French were very numerous, the country rugged, and so wooded that he could not tell what was passing on the flanks; wherefore, knowing that the chosen ground of battle was behind the Coa, he abandoned Aldea de Ponte and regained his original post.

In the night the allies retreated, and on the morning of the 28th occupied a new and very strong position in front of the Coa. The whole army was enclosed, as it were, in a deep loop of the Coa river, and could only be attacked on a narrow front, and Marmont, who had brought up but a few days' provisions, and could gather none in that country, retired the same day. This terminated the operations. The French placed a fresh garrison in Ciudad Rodrigo; Dorsenne marched to Salamanca; a strong division was posted at Alba de Tormes to communicate with Marmont, and the latter resumed his old position in the valley of the Tagus. At the same time Wellington sent the light division, reinforced by some cavalry, to resume the nominal blockade of Ciudad Rodrigo. Nearly a month had been employed by the French in the preparation and execution of this great operation, which terminated so feebly and so abruptly, because the generals were, as usual, at variance. They had victualled Ciudad Rodrigo, but nothing had been gained in the field, time was lost, and the English general's plans were forwarded.

The numerical inferiority of the British at this time was very great, and Wellington having retired into cantonments on both sides of the Coa, fixed his head-quarters at Frenada. The masterly retreat of Wellington after Elbodon greatly excited the admiration of the French as well as disappointed them, for their plans had been so laid that they fully expected to have secured a thorough and decisive victory. While the allies were in cantonments during the dreary winter months, the active mind of Wellington was ever busy in devising measures whereby the supply of his troops could be improved, and at the same time Marmont, satisfied from the facility with which he had accomplished the relief of Ciudad Rodrigo, rested also tranquilly within his lines. Believing himself in no immediate danger of attack from the British, Marmont afterwards detached several bodies of troops from his main body and sent them in various directions to assist in operations which were being carried on in other parts. The French armies were thus spread over an immense tract of country, and Marmont, deceived by the seemingly careless winter attitude of the allies, left Ciudad Rodrigo without a strong covering force. This was Wellington's opportunity, and over plains covered with snow and under inclement weather, the British army moved towards that place early in January 1812.

SIEGE OF CIUDAD RODRIGO.

The troops disposable for the attack of Ciudad Rodrigo were about 35,000, including cavalry, and seventy pieces of ordnance had been collected at Villa de Ponte. But from the scarcity of transports only thirty-eight guns could be brought to the trenches, and these would have wanted their due supply of ammunition if 8000 shot had not been found amidst the ruins of Almeida. On the 1st of January 1812 a bridge was commenced near the confluence of the Azava with the Agueda, about six miles below Ciudad, and piles driven into the bed of the river above and below, to which trestles were tied to render the whole firm. The fortress was to have been invested on the 6th, but the native carters engaged to bring stores and ammunition from Almeida were two days moving over ten miles of flat and excellent road with empty carts; the operation was thus delayed, and it was dangerous to find fault with these people, because they deserted on the slightest offence. Meanwhile the place being closely examined, it was found that the French, in addition to the old works, had fortified two convents which flanked and strengthened the entrenchments round the suburbs. They had also constructed an enclosed and palisadoed redoubt upon the greater Teson ; and this redoubt, called Francisco, was supported by two guns and a howitzer placed on the flat roof of the convent of that name.

The soil around was exceedingly rocky, except on the Teson itself, and though the body of the place was there better covered by the outworks, and could bring most fire to bear on the trenches, it was more assailable, according to the English general's views, because elsewhere the slope of the ground was such that batteries must have been erected on the very edge of the counterscarp before they could see low enough to breach. This would have been a tedious process, whereas the smaller Teson furnished the means of striking over the crest of the glacis at once, and a deep gully near the latter offered cover for the miners. It was therefore resolved to storm Fort Francisco, form a lodgment there, and opening the first parallel along the greater Teson, to place thirty-three pieces in counter-batteries with which to ruin the defences, and drive the besieged from the convent of Francisco; then working forward by the sap, to construct breaching-batteries on the lesser Teson, and blow in the counterscarp, while seven guns, by battering a weak turret on the left, opened a second breach, with a view to turn any retrenchment behind the principal breach.

The first, third, fourth, and light divisions, and Pack's Portuguese, were destined for the siege; but as the country on the right bank of the Agueda was destitute of fuel and cover, these troops were still to keep their quarters on the left bank; and although there was a very severe frost and fall of snow, yet one division, carrying a day's provisions ready cooked, was to ford the river every twenty-four hours, either above or below the town, and thus alternately carry on the works. Meanwhile, to cover the siege, the Spanish corps of Sanchez and Carlos d'España were posted on the Tormes in observation of the enemy. To obviate the difficulty of obtaining country transport, the English general had previously constructed 800 carts drawn by horses, and these were now his surest dependence for bringing up ammunition; yet so many delays were anticipated from the irregularity of the native carters and muleteers, and the chances of the weather, that he calculated upon an operation of twenty-four days, and yet hoped to steal it from his adversaries, sure, even if he failed, that the clash of his arms would again draw their scattered troops to that quarter, as tinkling bells draw swarming bees to an empty hive.

The 8th of January, the light division and Pack's Portuguese forded the Agueda three miles above the fortress, and making a circuit, took post beyond the great Teson, where they remained quiet during the day; and as there was no regular investment, the enemy believed that the siege was not commenced. But in the evening the troops stood to their arms, and Colonel Colborne, commanding the 52nd, having assembled two companies from each of the British regiments of the light division, stormed the redoubt of Francisco. This he did with so much fury that the assailants appeared to be at one and the same time in the ditch, mounting the parapets, fighting on the top of the rampart, and forcing the gorge of the redoubt, where the explosion of one of the French shells had burst the gate open. Of the defenders a few were killed, not many, and the remainder, about forty in number, were made prisoners. The post being thus taken with the loss of only twenty-four men and officers, working parties were set to labour on the right of it, because the fort itself was instantly covered with shot and shells from the town. This tempest continued through the night, but at daybreak the parallel, 600 yards in length, was sunk three feet deep and four wide, the communication over the Teson to the rear was completed, and the progress of the siege was thus hastened several days by this well-managed assault.

On the 9th, the first division took the trenches in hand. The place was encircled by posts to prevent any external communication, and at night 1200 workmen commenced three counter-batteries, for eleven guns each, under a heavy fire of shells and grape. Before daylight the labourers were under cover, and a ditch was also sunk in the front to provide earth; for the batteries were made eighteen feet thick at top to resist the very powerful artillery of the place.

On the 10th, the fourth division relieved the trenches, and 1000 men laboured, but in great peril, for the besieged had a superabundance of ammunition, and did not spare it. In the night the communication from the parallel to the batteries was opened, and on the 11th the third division undertook the siege. This day the magazines in the batteries were excavated and the approaches widened, but the enemy's fire was destructive, and the shells came so fast into the ditch in front of the batteries that the troops were withdrawn, and the earth was raised from the inside. Great damage was also sustained from salvos of shells with long fuzes, whose simultaneous explosion cut away the parapets in a strange manner, and in the night the French brought a howitzer to the garden of the convent of Francisco, with which they killed many men and wounded others.

On the 12th, the light division resumed the work, and the riflemen, taking advantage of a thick fog, covered themselves in pits, which they dug in front of the trenches, and from thence picked off the enemy's gunners; but in the night the weather was so cold, and the besieged shot so briskly, that little progress was made. The 13th, the first division being on duty, the same causes impeded the labourers, and now also the scarcity of transport baulked the general's operations. One-third only of the native carts expected had arrived, and the drivers of those present were very indolent; much of the twenty-four-pound ammunition was still at Villa de Ponte, and intelligence arrived that Marmont was collecting his forces to succour the place. Wellington, therefore, changing his first plan, resolved to open a breach with his counter-batteries, which were not quite 600 yards from the curtain, and then to storm the place without blowing in the counterscarp; in other words, to overstep the rules of science, and sacrifice life rather than time; for such was the capricious nature of the Agueda that in one night a flood might enable a small French force to relieve the place.

The whole army was immediately brought up from the distant quarters, and posted in the villages on the Coa, ready to cross the Agueda and give battle; and it was at this time that Hill sent a division across the Tagus, lest Marmont, in despair of uniting his force in the north in time to save Ciudad, should act against the line of communication. In the night of the 13th, the batteries were armed with twenty-eight guns, the second parallel and the approaches were continued by the flying sap, and the Santa Cruz convent was surprised by the Germans of the first division, which secured the right flank of the trenches.

On the 14th, the enemy, who had observed that the men in the trenches always went off in a disorderly manner on the approach of the relief, made a sally and overturned the gabions of the sap; they even penetrated to the parallel, and were upon the point of entering the batteries, when a few of the workmen getting together, checked them until a support arrived, and thus the guns were saved. This affair, together with the death of the engineer on duty and the heavy fire from the town, delayed the opening of the breaching-batteries, but at half-past four in the evening, twenty-five heavy guns battered the *fausse braye* and rampart, and two pieces were directed against the convent of Francisco. Then was beheld a spectacle at once fearful and sublime. The enemy replied to the assailants' fire with more than fifty pieces, the bellowing of eighty large guns shook the ground far and wide, the smoke rested in heavy volumes upon the battlements of the place, or curled in light wreaths about the numerous spires, the shells, hissing through the air, seemed fiery serpents leaping from the darkness, the walls crashed to the stroke of the bullet, and the distant mountains, faintly returning the sound, appeared to moan over the falling city. When night put an end to this turmoil, the quick clatter of musketry was heard like the pattering of hail after a peal of thunder, for the 40th regiment assaulted and carried the convent of Francisco, and established itself in the suburb on the left of the attack.

The next day the ramparts were again battered, and fell so fast that it was judged expedient to commence the small breach at the turret, and in the night of the 15th five more guns were mounted. The 16th, at daylight, the besiegers' batteries recommenced, but at eight o'clock a thick fog obliged them to desist; nevertheless the small breach had been opened, and the place was now summoned, but without effect. At night the parallel on the lower Teson was extended, and a sharp musketry was directed from thence against the great breach. The breaching-battery as originally projected was also commenced, and the riflemen of the light division, hidden in the pits, continued to pick off the enemy's gunners.

On the 17th, the fire on both sides was very heavy, and the wall of the place was beaten down in large cantles; but several of the besiegers' guns were dismounted, their batteries injured, and many of their men killed; General Borthwick, the commandant of artillery, was wounded, and the sap was entirely ruined. Even the riflemen in the pits were at first overpowered with grape, yet towards evening they recovered the upper hand, and the French could only fire from the more distant embrasures. In the night the battery intended for the lesser breach was armed, and that on the lower Teson raised so as to afford cover in the daytime. On the 18th, the besiegers' fire was resumed

SIEGE OF CIUDAD RODRIGO.

with great violence. The turret was shaken at the small breach, the large breach became practicable in the middle, and the enemy commenced retrenching it. The sap, however, could make no progress, the superintending engineer was badly wounded, and a twenty-four-pounder having burst in the batteries, killed several men. In the night the battery on the lower Teson was improved, and a field-piece and howitzer being placed there, kept up a constant fire on the great breach to destroy the French retrenchments. On the 19th, both breaches became practicable; Major Sturgeon closely examined the place, and a plan of attack was formed on his report; the assault was then ordered, and the battering-guns were turned against the artillery of the ramparts.

The assault, which was confided to the third and light divisions and Pack's Portuguese, was organised in four parts—the right attack, the centre, the left, and the false attacks.

The right attack was commanded by Colonel O'Toole, of the caçadores. Five hundred volunteers, commanded by Major Manners of the 74th, with a forlorn hope under Mr. Mackie of the 88th, composed the storming party of the third division. Three hundred volunteers led by Major Napier of the 52nd, with a forlorn hope of twenty-five men under Mr. Gurwood of the same regiment, composed the storming party of the light division.

All the troops reached their different posts without seeming to attract the attention of the enemy, but before the signal was given, and while Lord Wellington, who in person had been pointing out the lesser breach to Major Napier, was still at the convent of Francisco, the attack on the right commenced, and was instantly taken up along the whole line. Then the space between the army and the ditch was covered with soldiers and ravaged by a tempest of grape from the ramparts. The storming parties of the third division jumped out of the parallel when the first shout arose, but so rapid had been the movements on their right, that before they could reach the ditch, Ridge, Dunkin, and Campbell, with the 5th, 77th, and 94th regiments, had already scoured the *fausse braye*, and were pushing up the great breach, amidst the bursting of shells, the whistling of grape and muskets, and the shrill cries of the French, who were driven fighting behind the retrenchments. There, however, they rallied, and, aided by the musketry from the houses, made hard battle for their post; none would go back on either side, and yet the British could not get forward, and men and officers falling in heaps choked up the passage, which from minute to minute was raked with grape from two guns flanking the top of the breach at the distance of a few yards. Thus striving and trampling alike upon the dead and the wounded, these brave men maintained the combat.

Meanwhile, the stormers of the light division, who had 300 yards of ground to clear, would not wait for the hay-bags which were prepared for filling up the ditch, but with extraordinary swiftness running to the crest of the glacis, jumped down the scarp, a depth of eleven feet, and rushed up the *fausse braye* under a smashing discharge of grape and musketry. The bottom of the ditch was dark and intricate, and the forlorn hope took too much to their left; but the storming party went straight to the breach, which was so contracted that a gun placed lengthwise across the top nearly blocked up the opening. Here the forlorn hope rejoined the stormers, but when two-thirds of the ascent were gained, the leading men, crushed together by the narrowness of the place, staggered under the weight of the enemy's fire; and such is the instinct or self-defence, that although no man had been allowed to load, every musket in the crowd was snapped. The commander, Major Napier, was at this moment stricken to the earth by a grape-shot which shattered his arm, but he called on his men to trust to their bayonets, and all the officers simultaneously sprang to the front, when the charge was renewed with a furious shout and the entrance was gained. The supporting regiments coming up in sections abreast, then reached the rampart, the 52nd wheeled to the left, the 43rd to the right, and the place was won. During this contest, which lasted only a few minutes after the *fausse braye* was passed, the fighting had continued at the great breach with unabated violence, but when the 43rd and the stormers of the light division came pouring down upon the right flank of the French, the latter bent before the storm. At the same moment the explosion of three wall magazines destroyed many persons, and the third division with a mighty effort broke through the retrenchments. The garrison, indeed, still fought in the streets, but finally fled to the castle, where Mr. Gurwood, who, though wounded, had been amongst the foremost at the lesser breach, received the governor's sword.

SIEGE OF CIUDAD RODRIGO.

The allies now plunged into the streets from all quarters, for O'Toole's attack was also successful, and at the other side of the town Pack's Portuguese, meeting no resistance, had entered the place, and the reserves also came in. Then throwing off the restraints of discipline, the troops committed frightful excesses. The town was fired in three or four places; the soldiers menaced their officers, and shot each other; many were killed in the market-place, intoxication soon increased the tumult, disorder everywhere prevailed, and at last, the fury rising to an absolute madnesss, a fire was wilfully lighted in the middle of the great magazine, when the town and all in it would have been blown to atoms, but for the energetic courage of some officers and a few soldiers who still preserved their senses.

Three hundred French had fallen, 1500 were made prisoners, and besides the immense stores of ammunition, above 150 pieces of artillery, including the battering train of Marmont's army, were captured in the place. The whole loss of the allies was about 1200 soldiers and 90 officers, and of these above 650 men and 60 officers had been slain or hurt at the breaches. General Crawfurd and General Mackinnon, the former a man of great ability, were killed, and with them died many gallant men, amongst others, a captain of the 45th, of whom it has been felicitously said, that "Three generals and seventy other officers had fallen, but the soldiers fresh from the strife only talked of Hardyman." General Vandaleur, Colonel Colborne, and a crowd of inferior rank were wounded, and unhappily the slaughter did not end with the battle, for the next day as the prisoners and their escort were marching out by the breach, an accidental explosion took place and numbers of both were blown into the air. The audacious manner in which Wellington stormed the redoubt of Francisco on the first night of the investment, and the more audacious manner in which he assaulted the place before the fire of the defence had been in any degree lessened, were the true causes of its sudden and rapid capture.

While Rodrigo was being invested, General Hill surprised a French corps at Arroyo de Molinos, taking 1300 prisoners, with a loss of only about forty of his own men.

CHAPTER IX.

SIEGE OF BADAJOS—CAPTAIN GRANT.

HE fall of Ciudad Rodrigo was a cause of profound astonishment to Marmont. That a fortress which had occupied Massena nearly ten months to reduce should have been taken within ten days from its investment, and three from the opening of the besieging batteries, exceeded his powers of expression, and the fine army of 6000 veterans which he had assembled for the relief of the place was broken up and retired to winter quarters. The effect at home and throughout Spain was also great, and further honours were bestowed upon Lord Wellington—England made him an Earl, and Spain created him Duke of Ciudad Rodrigo. Immediately after its surrender, measures were taken to repair the works and put them in a defensible condition. Having accomplished this, and supplied also a good store of provisions, Wellington next determined upon the bold project of transferring his army secretly and suddenly across the Tagus, and reducing Badajos before Marmont and Soult could take effective steps to co-operate for its relief. In all the details of preparation great and prudent caution was observed, as the success of the enterprise depended very much on secrecy and rapidity of movement, and every method was adopted to conceal Wellington's intentions from the enemy till the last moment. On the 16th March the British crossed the Guadiana river, and Badajos was immediately invested by the advance corps of Beresford and Picton, other divisions being posted in positions to repel any relieving force of the enemy.

Siege of Badajos.

The garrison of Badajos, composed of French, Hessian, and Spanish troops, was near 5000 strong, including sick. Phillipon had since the last siege made himself felt in all directions, having continually scoured the vicinity of the place, destroyed many small bands, carried off cattle, almost from under the guns of Elvas and Campo Mayor, and his spies extended their researches from Ciudad Rodrigo to Lisbon, and from Lisbon to Ayamonte. He had also greatly improved the defences of the place. An interior retrenchment was made in the castle, and many more guns were there mounted; the rear of Fort Christoval was also better secured, and a covered communication from the fort itself to the work at the bridge-head was nearly completed. Two ravelins had been constructed on the south side of the town, and a third was commenced, together with counterguards for the bastions; but the eastern front next the castle, which was in other respects the weakest point, was without any outward protection, save the stream of the Rivillas. A second ditch had been dug at the bottom of the great ditch, which was also in some parts filled with water; the gorge of the Pardaleras was enclosed, and that outwork was connected with the body of the place, from whence powerful batteries looked into it. The three western fronts were mined, and on the east, the arch of the bridge behind the San Roque was built up to form an inundation 200 yards wide, which greatly contracted the space by which the place could be approached with troops. All the inhabitants had been obliged, on pain of being expelled, to lay up food for three months, and two convoys with provisions and ammunition had entered the place on the 10th and 16th of February, but Phillipon's stores of powder were still inadequate to his wants, and he was very scantily supplied with shells.

As the former system of attack against Christoval and the castle was now impracticable, Lord Wellington designed to assail one of the western fronts, which would have been a scientific operation; but the engineer represented that he had neither mortars nor miners, nor enough of guns, nor the means of bringing up sufficient stores for such an attack. Indeed, the want of transport had again obliged the allies to draw the stores from Elvas, to the manifest hazard of that fortress, and hence here, as at Ciudad Rodrigo, time was necessarily paid for by the loss of life. The plan finally fixed upon was to attack the bastion of Trinidad, because the counterguard there being unfinished, that bastion could be battered from the hill on which the Picurina stood. The first parallel was therefore to embrace the Picurina, the San Roque, and the eastern front, in such a manner that the counter-batteries there erected might rake and destroy all the defences of the southern fronts which bore against the Picurina hill. The Picurina itself was to be battered and stormed, and from thence the Trinidad and Santa Maria bastions were to be breached; after this all the guns were to be turned against the connecting curtain, which was known to be of weak masonry, that a third breach might be made, and a storming party employed to turn any retrenchments behind the breaches in the bastions. In this way the inundation could be avoided, and although a French deserter declared, and truly, that the ditch was there eighteen feet deep, such was the general's confidence in his troops, and in his own resources for aiding their efforts, that he resolved to storm the place without blowing in the counterscarp.

The battering train, directed by Major Dickson, consisted of fifty-two pieces. This included sixteen 24-pound howitzers for throwing Shrapnel shells, but this species of missile, much talked of in the army at the time, was little prized by Lord Wellington, who had early detected its insufficiency, save as a common shell; and partly to avoid expense, partly from a dislike to injure the inhabitants, neither in this nor in any former siege did he use mortars. Of 900 gunners present, 300 were British, the rest Portuguese, and there were 150 sappers volunteers from the third division, who were indeed rather unskilful, but of signal bravery. The engineer's parc was established behind the heights of St. Michael, and the direction of the siege was given to General Picton. General Kempt, General Colville, and General Bowes alternately commanded in the trenches.

Lord Wellington commenced on the 17th March to break ground before Picurina, within about 160 yards from the fort. The stormy weather favoured the operations of the workmen, who were not discovered by the enemy, and by break of day the approaches were three feet deep. The work continued on the

18th, the relief improving the parallel, while the strongly reinforced garrison kept up a heavy musketry-fire on the labourers, assisted by discharges from field-pieces and a howitzer. In spite of this continuous fire, which fortunately caused but few casualties, the parallels were prolonged during the night and two batteries traced out. While the working parties were busily engaged on the 19th, 1500 French infantry and forty horsemen, commanded by General Vielland, issued unobserved by the Talavera gate from the town, and, with the aid of others from Picurina, fell suddenly on the working parties of the besieging force. Taken by surprise, and being generally unarmed, the men were driven in great confusion from the trench; but being almost immediately rallied by their officers, they in turn vigorously charged and repulsed the French. This sally caused much alarm, but it was too quickly repelled to occasion any more serious loss than the overturning of some of the gabions and a partial filling in of several of the approaches.

Brief as the fight was, it was severe, the French losing above 300 officers and men, and the besiegers about half that number. Some English officers were taken prisoners by the French cavalry, who secured them to their saddles, and attempted to carry them into the fort; but the pursuit became so hot, that they were obliged to free themselves from such encumbrances, and the captives got away. Colonel Fletcher, the chief engineer, was unfortunately wounded. Although thus prevented from continuing a personal superintendence, he possessed Lord Wellington's confidence so highly, that the attack was still forwarded under his direction; and the commander-in-chief came every morning to his tent, accompanied by the staff-officers of the day, with plans of the work executed and in progress, and consulted Colonel Fletcher on the operations as they proceeded.

From this time of the siege the weather became most severe, the rain coming down in torrents, and the labour in the trenches was in consequence both slowly and painfully done; and nothing but the spirit of the troops, united to an earnest zeal in the officers, enabled them to overcome difficulties from which besiegers less determined would have recoiled. The task of excavation was less difficult and toilsome than the other duties laid upon the working parties. Half the day was spent in clearing the trenches of rain-water, and the bottom became so muddy that it became necessary to have it renewed by layers of sand-bags and fascines. Throughout the 22nd the rain continued heavy, and in the afternoon a torrent came down which overflowed the trenches. The floods rose high, the pontoon bridge across the Guadiana was carried away, eleven pontoons sank at their anchors, and the current was so rapid that the flying bridges were worked with difficulty. It thus soon became a question if it would be possible to supply the army with provisions and bring over the guns and ammunition for the attack, and serious apprehensions were entertained that it might become necessary to withdraw from the siege.

These difficulties, however, appeared only to rouse the determination and show the resources of Lord Wellington. By great exertions the bridge was restored, and on the night of the 24th the fifth division invested the place on the right bank of the Guadiana; the weather was fine, and the batteries were armed with ten twenty-fours, eleven eighteens, and seven five-and-a-half-inch howitzers. The next day these pieces opened, but they were so vigorously answered, that one howitzer was dismounted and several artillery and engineer officers were killed. Nevertheless the San Roque was silenced, and the garrison of the Picurina was so galled by the marksmen in the trenches, that no man dared look over the parapet; hence, as the external appearance of that fort did not indicate much strength, General Kempt was charged to assault it in the night.

The outward seeming of the Picurina, however, was fallacious; the fort was very strong; the fronts were well covered by the glacis, the flanks were deep, and the rampart, fourteen feet perpendicular from the bottom of the ditch, was guarded with thick slanting pales above, and from thence to the top there were sixteen feet of an earthen slope. A few palings had, indeed, been knocked off at the covered way, and the parapet was slightly damaged on that side, but this injury was repaired with sand-bags, and the ditch was profound, narrow at the bottom, and flanked by four splinter-proof casemates. Seven guns were mounted on the works, the entrance to which by the rear was protected with three rows of thick paling; the garrison was above 200 strong, and every man had two muskets. The top of the rampart was garnished with loaded shells to push over; a retrenched guard-house formed a second internal defence. Five hundred men of the third division being assembled for the attack, General Kempt ordered 200 under Major Rudd of the 77th to turn the fort on the left; an equal force under Major Shaw of the 74th to turn the fort by the right, and 100 from each of these bodies were directed to enter the communication with San Roque and intercept any succours coming from the town. The flanking columns were to make a joint attack on the fort, and the 100 men remaining were placed under Captain Powis of the 83rd, to form a reserve. The engineers, Holloway, Stanway, and Gips, with twenty-four sappers bearing hatchets and ladders, guided these columns, and fifty men of the light division, likewise provided with axes, were to move out of the trenches at the moment of attack.

The night of the 25th March was fine, the arrangements clearly and skilfully made, and about nine o'clock the two flanking bodies moved forward. The distance was short, and the troops quickly closed on the fort, which, black and silent before, now seemed one mass of fire; then the assailants running up to the palisades in the rear, with undaunted courage endeavoured to break through, and when the destructive musketry of the French and the thickness of the pales rendered their efforts nugatory, they turned against the faces of the work and strove to break in there; but the depth of the ditch and the slanting stakes at the top of the brickwork again baffled them. At this time, the enemy shooting fast and dangerously, the crisis appeared imminent, and Kempt sent the reserve headlong against the front; thus the fight was continued strongly, the carnage became terrible, and a battalion coming from the town to the succour of the fort, was encountered and beaten by the party on the communication. The guns of Badajos and of the castle now opened, the guard of the trenches replied with musketry, rockets were thrown up by the besieged, and the shrill sound of alarm-bells, mixing with the shouts of the combatants, increased the tumult. Still the Picurina sent out streams of fire, by the light of which dark figures were seen furiously struggling on the ramparts, for Powis first escaladed the place in front, where the artillery had beaten down the pales, and the other assailants had thrown their ladders on the flanks in the manner of bridges, from the brink of the ditch to the slanting stakes, and all were fighting hand to hand with the enemy. Meanwhile the axe-men of the light division, compassing the fort like prowling wolves, discovered the gate, and hewing it down, broke in by the rear. Nevertheless the struggle continued. Powis, Holloway, Gips, and Oates of the 88th fell wounded on or beyond the rampart; Nixon of the 52nd was shot two yards within the gate; Shaw, Rudd, and nearly all the other officers had fallen outside; and it was not until half the garrison were killed that Gaspar Thiery, the commandant, and eighty-six men surrendered, while some, not many, rushing out of the gate, endeavoured to cross the inundation and were drowned.

The French governor hoped to have delayed the siege five or six days by the resistance of Picurina, and had the assault been a day later, this would have happened; for a loopholed gallery in the counterscarp and several mines would then have been completed, and the body of the work was too well covered by the glacis to be quickly ruined by fire. His calculations were baffled by this heroic assault, which lasted an hour, and cost four officers and 50 men killed, 15 officers and 250 men wounded; and so vehement was the fight throughout, that the garrison either forgot or had not time to roll over the shells and combustibles arranged on the ramparts. Phillipon did not conceal the danger accruing to Badajos from the loss of the Picurina, but he stimulated his soldiers' courage by calling to their recollection how infinitely worse than death it was to be the inmate of an English hulk!

When the Picurina was taken, three battalions of reserve advanced to secure it, and though a great turmoil and firing from the town continued until midnight, a lodgment in the works and a communication with the first parallel were established, and the second parallel was commenced. However, at daylight, the redoubt was so overwhelmed with fire from the town, that no troops could remain in it, and the lodgment was entirely destroyed. In the evening the sappers effected another lodgment on the flanks, the second parallel was then opened in its whole length, and the next day the counter-batteries on the right of Picurina exchanged a vigorous fire with the town; but one of the besiegers' guns was dismounted, and the Portuguese gunners, from inexperience, produced less effect on the defences than was expected.

In the night of the 27th, a new communication from the first parallel to the Picurina was made, and three breaching-batteries were traced out; but Phillipon had now discovered the true line of attack, and had set strong parties in the night to raise the counter-guard of the Trinidad and the imperfect ravelin covering the menaced front. At daybreak these works, being well furnished with gabions and sand-bags, were lined with musketeers, who severely galled the workmen employed on the breaching-batteries, and the artillery practice also was brisk on both sides. Two of the besiegers guns were dismounted; the gabions placed in front of the batteries to protect the workmen were knocked over, and the musketry then became so destructive that the men were withdrawn and threw up earth from the inside.

In the night of the 27th, the second parallel was extended to the right, with the view of raising batteries to ruin the San Roque, to destroy the dam which held up the inundation, and to breach the curtain behind; but the Talavera road proved so hard, and the moon shone so brightly, that the labourers were quite exposed, and the work was relinquished. On the 28th, the screen of gabions before the batteries was restored, and the workmen resumed their labours outside; the parallel was then improved, and the besieged withdrew their guns from San Roque; but their marksmen still shot from thence with great exactness, and the plunging fire from the castle dismounted two howitzers in one of the counter-batteries, which was therefore dismantled. The enemy had also during the night observed the tracing string which marked the direction of the sap in front of San Roque, and a daring fellow creeping out just before the workmen arrived, brought it in the line of the castle fire, whereby some loss was sustained ere the false direction was discovered. On the 29th, a slight sally made on the right bank of the river was repulsed by the Portuguese, but the sap at the San Roque was ruined by the enemy's fire, and the besieged continued to raise the counter-guard and ravelin of the Trinidad and to strengthen the front attacked. On the other hand, the besiegers during the night carried the sap over the Talavera road, and armed two breaching-batteries with 18 pounders, which the next day opened against the flank of Santa Maria; but they made little impression, and the explosion of an expense magazine killed many men and hurt others.

By the 1st of April the sap was pushed close to the San Roque, the Trinidad bastion crumbled under the stroke of the bullet, and the flank of the Santa Maria, which was casemated and had hitherto resisted the batteries, also began to yield. On the 2nd, the face of the Trinidad was very much broken, but at the Santa Maria, the casemates being laid open, the bullets were lost in their cavities, and the garrison commenced a retrenchment to cut off the whole of the attacked front from the town. In the night a new battery against the San Roque was armed, and two officers with some sappers, gliding behind that outwork, gagged the sentinel, placed powder barrels and a match against the dam of the inundation, and retired undiscovered; but the explosion did not destroy the dam, and the inundation remained. Nor did the sap make progress because of the French musketeers; for though the marksmen set against them slew many, they were reinforced by means of a raft with parapets, which crossed the inundation, and men also passed by a covered communication from the Trinidad gate. On the 3rd, some guns were turned against the curtain behind the San Roque; but the masonry proved hard, ammunition was scarce, and as a breach there would have been useless while the inundation remained, the fire was soon discontinued. The two breaches in the bastion were now greatly enlarged, and the besieged assiduously laboured at the retrenchments behind them, and converted the nearest houses and garden walls into a third line of defence.

The crisis of the siege was now approaching rapidly. The breaches were nearly practicable; Soult, having effected a junction with Drouet and Daricau, was advancing; and as the allies were not in sufficient force to assault the place and give battle at the same time, it was resolved to leave two divisions in the trenches, and to fight at Albuera with the remainder. Graham, therefore, fell back towards that place, and Hill, having destroyed the bridge at Merida, marched from the Upper Guadiana to Talavera Real. Time being now, as in war it always is, a great object, the anxiety on both sides redoubled; but Soult was still at Llerena, when, on the morning of the 5th, the breaches were declared practicable, and the assault ordered for that evening. Leith's division was even recalled to the camp to assist, when a careful personal examination of the enemy's retrenchments caused some doubt in Lord Wellington's mind, and he delayed the storm until a third breach, as originally projected, should be formed in the curtain between the bastions of Trinidad and Maria. This could not, however, be commenced before morning, and during the night the enemy's workmen laboured assiduously at their retrenchments, regardless of the showers of grape with which the besiegers' batteries scoured the ditch and the breach. But on the 6th, the besiegers' guns being all turned against the curtain, the bad masonry crumbled rapidly away; in two hours a yawning breach appeared, and Wellington having again examined the points of attack in person, renewed the order for the assault. Then the soldiers eagerly made themselves ready for a combat, so fiercely fought, so terribly won, so dreadful in all its circumstances, that posterity can scarcely be expected to credit the tale.

The British general was so sensible of Phillipon's firmness and of the courage of his garrison, that he spared them the affront of a summons; yet, seeing the breach strongly entrenched and the enemy's flank fire still powerful, he would not in this dread crisis trust his fortune to a single effort. Eighteen thousand daring soldiers burned for the signal of attack, and as he was unwilling to lose the service of any, to each division he gave a task such as few generals would have the hardihood even to contemplate.

On the right, Picton's division was to file out of the trenches, to cross the Rivillas river, and to scale the castle walls, which were from 18 to 24 feet in height, furnished with all means of destruction, and so narrow at the top that the defenders could easily reach and as easily overturn the ladders.

On the left, Leith's division was to make a false attack on the Pardaleras, and a real assault on the distant bastion of San Vincente, where the glacis was mined, the ditch deep, the scarp 30 feet high, and the parapet garnished with bold troops well provided; for Phillipon, following his old plan, had three loaded muskets placed beside each man, that the first fire might be quick and deadly.

In the centre, the fourth and light divisions, under General Colville and Colonel Andrew Barnard, were to march against the breaches. They were furnished, like the third and fifth divisions, with ladders and axes, and were preceded by storming parties of 500 men each, with their respective forlorn hopes. The light division was to assault the bastion of Santa Maria; the fourth division was to assault the Trinidad and the curtain; and the columns were divided into storming and firing parties, the former to enter the ditch, the latter to keep the crest of the glacis.

Besides these attacks, Major Wilson of the 48th was to storm the San Roque with the guards of the trenches, and on the other side of the Guadiana, General Power was to make a feint on the bridge-head.

At first only one brigade of the third division was to have attacked the castle, but just before the hour fixed upon, a sergeant of sappers having deserted from the enemy, informed Wellington that there was but one communication from the castle to the town, whereupon he ordered the whole division to advance together.

The plan of the assault was well defined, but many nice arrangements filled it up, and some were followed, some disregarded; for it is seldom that all things are strictly attended to in a desperate fight. Nor were the enemy idle, for while it was yet twilight some French cavalry issued from the Pardaleras, escorting an officer who endeavoured to look into the trenches, with a view to ascertain if an assault was intended; but the piquet on that side jumped up, and firing as it ran, drove him and his escort back into the works. Then the darkness fell, and the troops only awaited the signal.

The night was dry but clouded, the air thick with watery exhalations from the river, the ramparts and the trenches unusually still; yet a low murmur pervaded the latter, and in the former lights were seen to flit here and there, while the deep voices of the sentinels at times proclaimed that all was well in Badajos. The French, confiding in Phillipon's direful skill, watched from their lofty station the approach of enemies whom they had twice before baffled, and now hoped to drive a third time blasted and ruined from the walls; the British, standing in deep columns, were as eager to meet that fiery destruction as the others were to pour it down; and both were alike terrible for their strength, their discipline, and the passions awakened in their resolute hearts. Former failures there were to avenge, and on either side

SIEGE OF BADAJOS.

such leaders as left no excuse for weakness in the hour of trial; and the possession of Badajos was become a point of honour, personal with the soldiers of each nation. But the strong desire for glory was in the British dashed with a hatred of the citizens on an old grudge, and recent toil and hardship, with much spilling of blood, had made many incredibly savage. Numbers also were heated with the recollection of Ciudad Rodrigo, and thirsted for spoil. Thus every spirit found a cause of excitement, the wondrous power of discipline bound the whole together as with a band of iron, and, in the pride of arms, none doubted their might to bear down every obstacle that man could oppose to their fury.

At ten o'clock the castle, the San Roque, the breaches, the Pardaleras, the distant bastion of San Vincente, and the bridgehead on the other side of the Guadiana, were to have been simultaneously assailed, and it was hoped that the strength of the enemy would shrivel within that fiery girdle. But many are the disappointments of war. An unforeseen accident delayed the attack of the fifth division; and a lighted carcass, thrown from the castle, falling close to where the men of the third division were drawn up, discovered their array, and obliged them to anticipate the signal by half an hour. Then, everything being suddenly disturbed, the double columns of the fourth and light divisions also moved silently and swiftly against the breaches, and the guard of the trenches rushing forward with a shout, encompassed the San Roque with fire, and broke in so violently that scarcely any resistance was made.

But a sudden blaze of light and the rattling of musketry indicated the commencement of a most vehement combat at the castle. There General Kempt—for Picton, hurt by a fall in the camp and expecting no change in the hour, was not present—there General Kempt led the third division; he had passed the Rivillas in single files by a narrow bridge under a terrible musketry, and then re-forming and running up the rugged hill, had reached the foot of the castle, when he fell severely wounded, and being carried back to the trenches, met Picton, who hastened forward to take the command. Meanwhile, his troops, spreading along the front, reared their heavy ladders, some against the lofty castle, some against the adjoining front on the left, and with incredible courage ascended amidst showers of heavy stones, logs of wood, and bursting shells rolled off the parapet, while from the flanks the enemy plied his musketry with a fearful rapidity, and in front with pikes and bayonets stabbed the leading assailants or pushed the ladders from the walls; and all this attended with deafening shouts, and the crash of breaking ladders, and the shrieks of crushed soldiers answering to the sullen stroke of the falling weights. Still, swarming round the remaining ladders, these undaunted veterans strove who should first climb, until all being overturned, the French shouted victory, and the British, baffled but untamed, fell back a few paces, and took shelter under the rugged edge of the hill. Here when the broken ranks were somewhat re-formed, the heroic Colonel Ridge springing forward, called with a stentorian voice on his men to follow, and seizing a ladder, once more raised it against the castle, to the right of the former attack, where the wall was lower, and an embrasure offered some facility. A second ladder was soon placed alongside of the first by the grenadier officer Canch, and the next instant he and Ridge were on the rampart; the shouting troops pressed after them, the garrison, amazed and in a manner surprised, were driven fighting through the double gate into the town, and the castle was won. A reinforcement sent from the French reserve then came up; a sharp action followed, both sides fired through the gate, and the enemy retired; but Ridge fell, and no man died that night with more glory—yet many died, and there was much glory.

During these events, the tumult at the breaches was such as if the very earth had been rent asunder, and its central fires were bursting upwards uncontrolled. The two divisions had reached the glacis just as the firing at the castle had commenced, and the flash of a single musket discharged from the covered way as a signal showed them that the French were ready; yet no stir was heard, and darkness covered the breaches. Some hay-packs were then thrown, some ladders were placed, and the forlorn hopes and storming parties of the light division, about 500 in all, had descended into the ditch without opposition, when a bright flame shooting upwards displayed all the terrors of the scene. The ramparts, crowded with dark figures and glittering arms, were seen on the one side, and on the other the red columns of the British, deep and broad, were coming on like streams of burning lava; it was the touch of the magician's wand, for a crash of thunder followed, and with incredible violence the storming parties were dashed to pieces by the explosion of hundreds of shells and powder-barrels.

For an instant the light division stood on the brink of the ditch, amazed at the terrific sight, then, with a shout that matched even the sound of the explosion, flew down the ladders, or disdaining their aid, leaped, reckless of the depth, into the gulf below; and nearly at the same moment, amidst a blaze of musketry that dazzled the eyes, the fourth division came running in, and descended with a like fury. There were, however, only five ladders for both columns, which were close together, and a deep cut made in the bottom of the ditch, as far as the counter-guard of the Trinidad, was filled with water from the inundation; into this watery snare the head of the fourth division fell, and it is said that above 100 of the fusiliers, the men of Albuera, were there smothered. Those who followed checked not, but, as if such a disaster had been expected, turned to the left, and thus came upon the face of an unfinished ravelin, which, being rough and broken, was mistaken for the breach, and instantly covered with men; yet a wide and deep chasm was still between them and the ramparts, from whence came a deadly fire wasting their ranks. Thus baffled, they also commenced a rapid discharge of musketry, and disorder ensued; for the men of the light division, whose conducting engineer had been disabled early, and whose flank was confined by an unfinished ditch intended to cut off the bastion of Santa Maria, rushed towards the breaches of the curtain and the Trinidad, which were indeed before them, but which the fourth division were destined to storm.

Great was the confusion, for now the ravelin was quite crowded with men of both divisions, and while some continued to fire, others jumped down and ran towards the breach, many also passed between the ravelin and the counter-guard of the Trinidad; the two divisions got mixed, and the reserves also came pouring in, until the ditch was quite filled, the rear still crowding forward, and all cheering vehemently. The enemy's shouts also were loud and terrible, and the bursting of shells and of grenades, the roaring of the guns from the flanks, answered by the iron howitzers from the battery of the parallel, the heavy roll and horrid explosion of the powder-barrels, the whizzing flight of the blazing splinters, the loud exhortations of the officers, and the continual clatter of the muskets, made a maddening din.

Now a multitude bounded up the great breach as if driven by a whirlwind, but across the top glittered a range of sword-blades, sharp-pointed, keen-edged on both sides, and firmly fixed in ponderous beams, which were chained together and set deep in the ruins; and for ten feet in front the ascent was covered with loose planks, studded with sharp iron points, on which the feet of the foremost being set, the planks moved, and the unhappy soldiers, falling forward on the spikes, rolled down upon the ranks behind. Then the Frenchmen, shouting at the success of their stratagem, and leaping forward, plied their shot with terrible rapidity, for every man had several muskets, and each musket, in addition to its ordinary charge, contained a small cylinder of wood stuck full of leaden slugs, which scattered like hail when they were discharged.

Again the assailants rushed up the breaches, and again the sword-blades, immovable and impassable, stopped their charge, and the hissing shells and thundering powder-barrels exploded unceasingly. Hundreds of men had fallen, and hundreds more were dropping, but still the heroic officers called aloud for new trials, and sometimes followed by many, sometimes by a few, ascended the ruins; and so furious were the men themselves, that in one of these charges the rear strove to push the foremost on to the sword-blades, willing even to make a bridge of their writhing bodies, but the others frustrated the attempt by dropping down; and men fell so fast from the shot that it was hard to know who went down voluntarily, who were stricken, and many stooped unhurt that never rose again. Vain, also, would it have been to break through the sword-blades, for the trench and parapet behind the breach were finished, and the assailants, crowded into even a narrower space than the ditch was, would still have been separated from their enemies, and the slaughter would have continued.

At the beginning of this dreadful conflict, Colonel Andrew Barnard had with prodigious efforts separated his division from the other, and preserved some degree of military array; but now the tumult was such that no command could be heard distinctly, except by those close at hand, and the mutilated carcasses heaped on each other, and the wounded, struggling to avoid being trampled upon, broke the formations; order was impossible. Yet officers of all stations, followed more or less numerously by the men, were seen to start out, as if struck by a sudden madness, and rush into the breach, which yawning and glittering with steel, seemed like the mouth of some huge dragon belching forth smoke and flame. In one of these attempts, Colonel Macleod, of the 43rd, a young man, whose feeble body would have been quite unfit for war if it had not been sustained by an unconquerable spirit, was killed. Wherever his voice was heard there his soldiers gathered, and with such a strong resolution did he lead them up the fatal ruins, that when one behind him, in falling, plunged a bayonet into his back, he complained not, and continuing his course, was shot dead within a yard of the sword-blades. But there was no want of gallant leaders or desperate followers.

Two hours spent in these vain efforts convinced the soldiers that the breach of the Trinidad was impregnable; and as the opening in the curtain, although less strong, was retired, and the approach to it impeded by deep holes and cuts made in the ditch the troops did not much notice it after the partial failure of one attack which had been made early. Gathering in dark groups and leaning on their muskets, they looked up with sullen desperation at the Trinidad, while the enemy, stepping out on the ramparts, and aiming their shots by the light of the fire-balls which they threw over, asked, as their victims fell, "Why they did not come into Badajos?" In this dreadful situation, while the dead were lying in heaps and others continually falling, the wounded crawling about to get some shelter from the merciless fire above, and withal a sickening stench from the burnt flesh of the slain, Captain Nicholas, of the engineers, was observed by Mr. Shaw of the 43rd making incredible efforts to force his way with a few men into the Santa Maria bastion. Shaw, having collected about fifty soldiers of all regiments, joined him, and although there was a deep cut along the foot of this breach also, it was instantly passed, and these two young officers, at the head of their gallant band, rushed up the slope of the ruins; but when they had gained two-thirds of the ascent, a concentrated fire of musketry and grape dashed nearly the whole dead to the earth. Nicholas was mortally wounded, and the intrepid Shaw stood alone! After this no further effort was made at any point, and the troops remained passive, but unflinching, beneath the enemy's shot, which streamed without intermission; for, of the riflemen on the glacis, many leaping early into the ditch had joined in the assault, and the rest, raked by a cross-fire of grape from the distant bastions, baffled in their aim by the smoke and flames from the explosions, and too few in number, had entirely failed to quell the French musketry.

About midnight, when 2000 brave men had fallen, Wellington, who was on a height close to the quarries, sent orders for the remainder to retire and re-form for a second assault; for he had just then heard that the castle was taken, and thinking the enemy would still hold out in the town, was resolved to assail the breaches again. This retreat from the ditch was, however, not effected without further carnage and confusion, for the French fire never slackened, and a cry arose that the enemy were making a sally from the distant flanks, which caused a rush towards the ladders; then the groans and lamentations of the wounded, who could not move, and expected to be slain, increased, many officers, who had not heard of the order, endeavoured to stop the soldiers from going back, and some would even have removed the ladders, but were unable to break the crowd. All this time the third division was lying close in the castle, and either from a fear of risking the loss of a point which ensured the capture of the place, or that the egress was too difficult, made no attempt to drive away the enemy from the breaches. On the other side, however, the fifth division had commenced the false attack on the Pardaleras, and on the right of the Guadiana the Portuguese were sharply engaged at the bridge; thus the town was girdled with fire, for General Walker's brigade having passed on during the feint on the Pardaleras, was escalading the distant bastion of San Vincente. His troops had advanced along the banks of the river, and reached the French guard-house at the barrier-gate undiscovered, for the ripple of the waters smothered the sound of their footsteps; but just then the explosion of the breaches took place, the moon shone out, and the French sentinels, discovering the columns, fired. The British troops immediately springing forward under a sharp musketry, began to hew down the wooden barrier at the covered way, while the Portuguese, being panic-stricken, threw down the scaling-ladders. Nevertheless, the others snatched them up again, and forcing the barrier, jumped into the ditch; but the guiding engineer officer was killed, and when the foremost men succeeded in rearing the ladders, the latter were found too short, for the walls were generally above thirty feet high. Meanwhile the fire of the French was deadly, a small mine was sprung beneath the soldiers' feet, beams of wood and live shells were rolled over on their heads, showers of grape from the flank swept the ditch, and man after man dropped dead from the ladders. Fortunately some of the defenders having been called away to aid in recovering the castle, the ramparts were not entirely manned, and the assailants, having discovered a corner of the bastion where the scarp was only twenty feet high, placed three ladders there under an embrasure which had no gun and was only stopped with a gabion. Some men got up, but with difficulty, for the ladders were still too short, and the first man who gained the top was pushed up by his comrades and then drew others after him, until many had gained the summit; and though the French shot heavily against them from both flanks and from a house in front, they thickened and could not be driven back; half the 4th regiment entered the town itself to dislodge the enemy from the houses, while the others pushed along the rampart towards the breach, and by dint of hard fighting successively won three bastions.

In the last of these combats, General Walker, leaping forward, sword in hand, at the moment when one of the enemy's cannoneers was discharging a gun, fell covered with so many wounds that it was wonderful how he could survive; and some of the soldiers immediately after, perceiving a lighted match on the ground, cried out "A mine!" At that word, such is the power of imagination, those troops whom neither the strong barrier, nor the deep ditch, nor the high walls, nor the deadly fire of the enemy could stop, staggered back appalled by a chimera of their own raising, and in this disorder a French reserve under General Viellande drove on them with a firm and rapid charge, and pitching some men over the walls, and killing others outright, again cleansed the ramparts even to the San Vincente. There, however, Leith had placed Colonel Nugent with a battalion of the 38th as a reserve, and when the French came up, shouting and slaying all before them, this battalion, about 200 strong, arose, and with one close volley destroyed them. Then the panic ceased, the soldiers rallied, and in compact order once more charged along the walls towards the breaches, but the French, although turned on both flanks and abandoned by fortune, did not yet yield; and meanwhile the detachment of the 4th regiment which had entered the town when the San Vincente was first carried, was strangely situated, for the streets were empty and brilliantly illuminated, and no person was seen; yet a low buzz and whisper were heard around, lattices were now and then gently opened, and from time to time shots were fired from underneath the doors of the houses by the Spaniards. However, the troops with bugles sounding, advanced towards the great square of the town, and in their progress captured several mules going with ammunition to the breaches; but the square itself was as empty and silent as the streets, and the houses as bright with lamps—a terrible enchantment seemed to be in operation, for they saw nothing but light, and heard only the low whispers close around them, while the tumult at the breaches was like the crashing thunder.

There, indeed, the fight was still plainly raging, and hence, quitting the square, they attempted to take the garrison in reverse by attacking the ramparts from the town-side; but they were received with a rolling musketry, driven back with loss, and resumed their movement through the streets. At last the breaches were abandoned by the French, other parties entered the place, desultory combats took place in various parts, and finally General Viellande and Phillipon, who was wounded, seeing all ruined, passed the bridge with a few hundred soldiers, and entered San Christoval, where they all surrendered early the next morning upon summons to Lord Fitzroy Somerset, who had with great readiness pushed through the town to the drawbridge ere they had time to organise further resistance. But even in the moment of ruin the night before, the noble governor had sent some horsemen out from the fort to carry the news to Soult's army.

Now commenced that wild and desperate wickedness which tarnished the lustre of the soldiers' heroism. All indeed were not alike, for hundreds risked and many lost their lives in striving to stop the violence, but the madness generally prevailed, and as the worst men were leaders here, all the dreadful passions of human nature were displayed. Shameless rapacity, brutal intemperance, savage lust, cruelty and murder, shrieks and piteous lamentations, groans, shouts, imprecations, the hissing of fires bursting from the houses, the crashing of doors and windows, and the reports of muskets used in violence, resounded for two days and nights in the streets of Badajos! On the third, when the city was sacked, when the soldiers were exhausted by their own excesses, the tumult rather subsided than was quelled. The wounded men were then looked to, the dead disposed of.

Five thousand men and officers fell during this siege, and of these, including 700 Portuguese, 3500 had been stricken in the assault, 60 officers and more than 700 men being slain on the spot. The five generals, Kempt, Harvey, Bowes, Colville, and Picton, were wounded, the first three severely; about 600 men and officers fell in the escalade of San Vincente, as many at the castle, and more than 2000 at the breaches, each division there losing 1200. And how deadly the strife was at that point may be gathered from this—the 43rd and 52nd regiments of the light division alone lost more men than the seven regiments of the third division engaged at the castle.

Let any man picture to himself this frightful carnage taking place in a space of less than 100 square yards. Let him consider that the slain died not all suddenly, nor by one manner of death; that some perished by steel, some by shot, some by water; that some were crushed and mangled by heavy weights, some trampled upon, some dashed to atoms by the fiery explosions; that for hours this destruction was endured without shrinking, and that the town was won at last;—let any man consider this, and he must admit that a British army bears with it an awful power. And false would it be to say that the French were feeble men, for the garrison stood and fought manfully and with good discipline, behaving worthily. Shame there was none on any side. Yet who shall do justice to the bravery of the soldiers? the noble emulation of the officers? Who shall measure out the glory of Ridge, of Macleod, of Nicholas, or of O'Hare of the 95th, who perished on the breach at the head of the stormers, and with him nearly all the volunteers for that desperate service? Who shall describe the springing valour of that Portuguese grenadier who was killed the foremost man at the Santa Maria? or the martial fury of that desperate soldier of the 95th, who, in his resolution to win, thrust himself beneath the chained sword-blades, and there suffered the enemy to dash his head to pieces with the ends of their muskets? Who can sufficiently honour the intrepidity of Walker, of Shaw, of Canch, or the resolution of Ferguson of the 43rd, who having in former assaults received two deep wounds, was here, with his hurts still open, leading the stormers of his regiment, the third time a volunteer, and the third time wounded? Many and signal were the other examples of unbounded devotion, some known, some that will never be known; for in such a tumult much passed unobserved, and often the observers fell themselves ere they could bear testimony to what they saw; but no age, no nation, ever sent forth braver troops to battle than those who stormed Badajos.

When the extent of the night's havoc was made known to Lord Wellington, the firmness of his nature gave way for a moment, and the pride of conquest yielded to a passionate burst of grief for the loss of his gallant soldiers.

Captain Grant.

When the first intelligence that the army of Portugal was concentrating on the Tormes reached Wellington, he sent Captain Colquhoun Grant, a celebrated scouting officer, to watch Marmont's proceedings. That gentleman, in whom the utmost daring was so mixed with subtlety of genius, and both so tempered by discretion, that it is hard to say which quality predominated, very rapidly executed his mission; and the interesting nature of his adventures on this occasion will perhaps excuse a digression concerning them at this point.

Attended by Leon, a Spanish peasant of great fidelity and quickness of apprehension, who had been his companion on many former occasions of the same nature, Grant arrived in the Salamancan district, and passing the Tormes in the night, remained in uniform—for he never assumed any disguise—three days in the midst of the French camp. He thus obtained exact information of Marmont's object, and more especially of his preparations of provisions and scaling ladders, notes of which he sent to Lord Wellington from day to day by Spanish agents. However, on the third night, some peasants brought him a general order, addressed to the French regiments, and saying that the notorious Grant being within the circle of their cantonments, the soldiers were to use their utmost exertions to secure him, for which purpose also guards were placed as it were in a circle round the army. Nothing daunted by this news, Grant consulted with the peasants, and the next morning before daylight entered the village of Huerta, which is close to a ford on the Tormes, and about six miles from Salamanca. Here there was a French battalion, and on the opposite side of the river cavalry videttes were posted, two of which constantly patrolled back and forward for the space of 300 yards, meeting always at the ford. When day broke, the French battalion assembled on its alarm-post, and at that moment Grant was secretly brought with his horse behind the gable of a house, which hid him from the infantry, and was opposite to the ford. The peasants, standing on some loose stones and spreading their large cloaks, covered him from the cavalry videttes, and thus he calmly waited until the latter were separated to the full extent of their beat; then putting spurs to his horse, he dashed through the ford between them, and receiving their fire without damage, reached a wood not very distant, where the pursuit was baffled, and where he was soon rejoined by Leon, who in his native dress met with no interruption.

Grant had already ascertained that the means of storming Ciudad Rodrigo were prepared, and that the French officers openly talked of doing so, but he desired still further to test this project, and to discover if the march of the enemy might not finally be directed by the pass of Perales towards the Tagus; he wished also to ascertain more correctly their real numbers, and therefore placed himself on a wooded hill near Tamames, where the road branches off to the passes and to Ciudad Rodrigo. Here lying perdue until the whole French army had passed by in march, he noted every battalion and gun, and finding that all were directed towards Ciudad, entered Tamames after they had passed, and discovered that they had left the greatest part of their scaling-ladders behind, which clearly proved that the intention of storming Ciudad Rodrigo was not real. This it was which allayed Wellington's fears for that fortress.

When Marmont afterwards passed the Coa in this expedition, Grant preceded him with intent to discover if his farther march would be by Guarda upon Coimbra, or by Sabugal upon Castello Branco; for to reach the latter it was necessary to descend from a very high ridge, or rather succession of ridges, by a pass at the lower mouth of which stands Penamacor. Upon one of the inferior ridges in the pass this persevering officer placed himself, thinking that the dwarf oaks with which the hills were covered would effectually secure him from discovery; but from the higher ridge above the French detected all his movements with their glasses. In a few moments Leon, whose lynx-eyes were always on the watch, called out "The French! the French!" and pointed to the rear, whence some dragoons came galloping up. Grant and his follower instantly darted into the wood for a little space, and then suddenly wheeling, rode off in a different direction; yet at every turn new enemies appeared, and at last the hunted men dismounted and fled on foot through the thickest of the low oaks; but again they were met by infantry, who had been detached in small parties down the sides of the pass, and were directed in their chase by the waving of the French officers' hats on the ridge above. At last Leon fell exhausted, and the barbarians who first came up killed him in despite of his companion's entreaties.

Grant himself they carried, without injury, to Marmont, who, receiving him with apparent kindness, invited him to dinner. The conversation turned upon the prisoner's exploits, and the French marshal affirmed that he had been for a long time on the watch; that he knew all his haunts and his disguises, and had discovered that, only the night before, he had slept in the French head-quarters, with other adventures which had not happened, for this Grant never used any disguise; but there was another Grant, a man also very remarkable in his way, who used to remain for months in the French quarters, using all manner of disguises; hence the similarity of names caused the actions of both to be attributed to one, which is the only palliative for Marmont's subsequent conduct.

Treating his prisoner with great apparent kindness, the French general exacted from him an especial parole, that he would not consent to be released by the guerillas while on his journey through Spain to France, which secured his captive, although

Lord Wellington offered 2000 dollars to any guerilla chief who should rescue him. The exaction of such a parole, however harsh, was in itself a tacit compliment to the man; but Marmont also sent a letter with the escort to the governor of Bayonne, in which, still labouring under the error that there was only one Grant, he designated his captive as a dangerous spy, who had done infinite mischief to the French army, and whom he had only not executed on the spot out of respect to something resembling a uniform which he wore at the time of his capture. He therefore desired that at Bayonne he should be placed in irons and sent up to Paris. This proceeding was too little in accord with the honour of the French army to be supported, and before the Spanish frontier was passed, Grant—it matters not how—was made acquainted with the contents of the letter. Now the custom at Bayonne, in ordinary cases, was for the prisoner to wait on the authorities, and receive a passport to travel to Verdun; and all this was duly accomplished. Meanwhile the delivering of the fatal letter being by certain means delayed, Grant, with a wonderful readiness and boldness, resolved not to escape towards the Pyrenees, thinking that he would naturally be pursued in that direction. He judged that if the governor of Bayonne could not recapture him at once, he would for his own security suppress the letter, in hopes the matter would be no further thought of;—judging in this acute manner, he on the instant inquired at the hotels if any French officer was going to Paris, and finding that General Souham, then on his return from Spain, was so bent, he boldly introduced himself, and asked permission to join his party. The other readily assented; and while thus travelling, the general, unacquainted with Marmont's intentions, often rallied his companion about his adventures, little thinking that he was then himself an instrument in forwarding the most dangerous and skilful of them all.

In passing through Orleans, Grant, by a species of intuition, discovered an English agent, and from him received a recommendation to another secret agent in Paris, whose assistance would be necessary to his final escape; for he looked upon Marmont's double dealing, and the expressed design to take away his life, as equivalent to a discharge of his parole, which was, moreover, only given with respect to Spain. When he arrived at Paris he took leave of Souham, opened an intercourse with the

Parisian agent, from whom he obtained money, and by his advice avoided appearing before the police to have his passport examined. He took a lodging in a very public street, frequented the coffee-houses, and even visited the theatres without fear, because the secret agent, who had been long established and was intimately connected with the police, had ascertained that no inquiry about his escape had been set on foot. In this manner he passed several weeks, at the end of which the agent informed him that a passport was ready for one Jonathan Buck, an American, who had died suddenly on the very day it was to have been claimed. Seizing this occasion, Grant boldly demanded the passport, with which he instantly departed for the mouth of the Loire, because certain reasons, not necessary to mention, led him to expect more assistance there than at any other port. However, new difficulties awaited him, and were overcome by fresh exertions of his surprising talents, which fortune seemed to delight in aiding.

He first took a passage for America in a ship of that nation, but its departure being unexpectedly delayed, he frankly explained his true situation to the captain, who desired him to assume the character of a discontented seaman, and giving him a sailor's dress and forty dollars, sent him to lodge the money in the American consul's hands as a pledge that he would prosecute the captain for ill-usage when he reached the United States; this being the custom on such occasions, the consul gave him a certificate which enabled him to pass from port to port as a discharged sailor seeking a ship.

Thus provided, after waiting some days, Grant prevailed upon a boatman, by a promise of ten napoleons, to row him in the night towards a small island, where, by usage, the English vessels watered unmolested, and in return permitted the few inhabitants to fish and traffic without interruption. In the night the boat sailed, the masts of the British ships were dimly seen on the other side of the island, and the termination of his toils appeared at hand, when the boatman, either from fear or malice, suddenly put about and returned to port. In such a situation, some men would have striven in desperation to force fortune, and so have perished; the spirits of others would have sunk in despair, for the money which he had promised was all that remained of his stock, and the boatman, notwithstanding his breach of contract, demanded the whole; but, with inexpressible coolness and resolution, Grant gave him one napoleon instead of ten, and a rebuke for his misconduct. The other having threatened a reference to the police, soon found that he was no match in subtlety for his opponent, who told him plainly that he would then denounce him as aiding the escape of a prisoner of war, and would adduce the great price of his boat as a proof of his guilt.

This menace was too formidable to be resisted, and Grant in a few days engaged an old fisherman, who faithfully performed his bargain; but now there were no English vessels near the island; however the fisherman cast his nets and caught some fish, with which he sailed towards the southward, where he had heard there was an English ship of war. In a few hours they obtained a glimpse of her, and were steering that way, when a shot from a coast-battery brought them to, and a boat with soldiers put off to board them; the fisherman was steadfast and true; he called Grant his son, and the soldiers, by whom they expected to be arrested, were only sent to warn them not to pass the battery, because the English vessel they were in search of was on the coast. The old man, who had expected this, bribed the soldiers with his fish, assuring them he must go with his son or they would starve, and that he was so well acquainted with the coast he could always escape the enemy. His prayers and presents prevailed; he was desired to wait under the battery till night, and then depart; but under pretence of arranging his escape from the English vessel, he made the soldiers point out her bearings so exactly, that when the darkness came, he ran her straight on board, and the intrepid officer stood in safety on the quarter-deck.

After this Grant reached England and obtained permission to choose a French officer of equal rank with himself, to send to France, that no doubt might remain about the propriety of his escape; and great was his astonishment to find, in the first prison he visited, the old fisherman and his real son, who had meanwhile been captured notwithstanding a protection given to them for their services. Grant, whose generosity and benevolence were as remarkable as the qualities of his understanding, soon obtained their release, and having sent them with a sum of money to France, returned himself to the Peninsula, and within four months from the date of his first capture was again on the Tormes watching Marmont's army! Other strange incidents could be mentioned in the life of this generous and spirited, yet gentle-minded man, who, having served his country nobly and ably in every climate, died, not long after, exhausted by the continual hardships he had endured.

CHAPTER X.

ALMARAZ—THE FORTS OF SALAMANCA.

F the fall of Ciudad Rodrigo was a surprise to the French, the taking of Badajos still further confounded their calculations, as they had not reckoned upon the British army proceeding so actively. Both Soult and Marmont knew that Wellington was on the move, but neither of these marshals brought their armies to the relief of the fortresses, and both now had to retreat —Soult being driven back by the British cavalry, and Marmont being pressed by Wellington, compelling him to retire upon Salamanca. The British, being exhausted by the arduous campaign, went into cantonments for a time, but the energies of its great leader were still actively engaged in the planning of further movements, and he next determined to carry the war beyond the borders of Portugal and enter Spain, and, if possible, isolate Marmont by coming between him and Soult. In furtherance of this, he deemed it necessary to obtain possession of Almaraz, where the enemy had a bridge of boats across the Tagus, protected by the forts of Ragusa and Napoleon, and for this purpose detached General Hill. Owing to difficulties arising through bad roads, Hill found it impossible to take the enemy by surprise, and his movements were discovered before he reached within five miles of Almaraz on the 16th May 1812. General Hill formed his troops in three columns, and made a night march, intending to attack at the same moment the tower of Mirabete, the fortified house in the pass, and the forts at the bridge of Almaraz. The left column, directed against the tower, was commanded by General Chowne. The centre column, with

the dragoons and the artillery, moved by the royal road under the command of General Long. The right column, composed of the 50th, 71st, and 92nd regiments, under the direction of Hill in person, was intended to penetrate by the narrow and difficult way of La Cueva and Roman Gordo against the forts at the bridge. But the day broke before any of the columns reached their destination, and all hopes of a surprise were extinguished. The bad roads had made this untoward beginning unavoidable on the part of the right and centre column; but it would appear that some negligence had retarded General Chowne's column, and that the castle of Mirabete might have been carried by assault before daylight.

The difficulty, great before, was now much increased. An attentive examination of the French defences convinced Hill that to reduce the works in the pass, he must incur more loss than was justifiable, and finish in such plight that he could not afterwards carry the forts at the bridge, which were the chief objects of his expedition. Yet it was only through the pass of Mirabete that the artillery could move against the bridge. In this dilemma, after fruitless attempts to discover some opening through which to reach the valley of Almaraz with his guns, he resolved to leave them on the Sierra with the centre column, and to make a false attack upon the tower with General Chowne's troops, while he himself, with the right column, secretly penetrated by the scarcely practicable line of La Cueva and Roman Gordo to the bridge, intent, with infantry alone, to storm works which were defended by eighteen pieces of artillery and powerful garrisons.

This resolution was even more hardy and bold than it appears without a reference to the general state of affairs. Hill's march had been one of secrecy, amidst various divisions of the enemy; he was four days' journey distant from Merida, which was his first point of retreat; he expected that Drouet would be reinforced and advance towards Medellin, and hence, whether defeated or victorious at Almaraz, that his own retreat would be very dangerous; exceedingly so if defeated, because his fine British troops could not be repulsed with a small loss, and he should have to fall back through a difficult country, with his best soldiers dispirited by failure and burthened with numbers of wounded men. But General Hill was unshaken by such fears.

The troops remained concealed in their position until the evening of the 18th May, and then the general, reinforcing his own column with the 6th Portuguese regiment, a company of the 60th rifles, and the artillerymen of the centre column, commenced the descent of the valley. His design was to storm Fort Napoleon before daylight, and the march was less than six miles, but his utmost efforts could only bring the head of the troops to the fort a little before daylight; the rear was still distant, and it was doubtful if the scaling-ladders, which had been cut in halves to thread the short narrow turns in the precipitous descent, would serve for an assault. Fortunately some small hills concealed the head of the column from the enemy, and at that moment General Chowne commenced the false attack on the castle of Mirabete. Pillows of white smoke rose on the lofty brow of the Sierra, the heavy sound of artillery came rolling over the valley, and the garrison of Fort Napoleon, crowding on the ramparts, were anxiously gazing at these portentous signs of war, when, quick and loud, a British shout broke on their ears, and the gallant 50th regiment, aided by a wing of the 71st, came bounding over the nearest hills.

The French were surprised to see an enemy so close while the Mirabete was still defended; yet they were not unprepared, for a patrol of English cavalry had been seen from the fort on the 17th in the pass of Roman Gordo; and in the evening of the 18th a woman of that village had brought very exact information of Hill's numbers and intentions. This intelligence had caused the commandant, Aubert, to march in the night with reinforcements to Fort Napoleon, which was therefore defended by six companies, including the 39th French and the voltigeurs of a foreign regiment. These troops were ready to fight, and when the first shout was heard, turning their heads, they, with a heavy fire of musketry and artillery, smote the assailants in front, while the guns of Fort Ragusa took them in flank from the opposite side of the river; in a few moments, however, a rise of ground at the distance of only twenty yards from the ramparts, covered the British from the front fire, and General Howard in person leading the foremost troops into the ditch, commenced the escalade. The great breadth of the berm (or space between the foot of the ramparts and the side of the moat) kept off the ends of the shortened ladders from the parapet, but the soldiers who first ascended jumped on to the berm itself, and drawing up the ladders, planted them there, and thus, with a second escalade, forced their way over the rampart; then, closely fighting, friends and enemies went together into the retrenchment round the stone tower. Colonel Aubert was wounded and taken; the tower was not defended, and the garrison fled towards the bridge-head; but the victorious troops would not be shaken off, and entered that work also in one confused mass with the fugitives, who continued their flight over the bridge itself. Still the British soldiers pushed their headlong charge, slaying the hindmost, and they would have passed the river if some of the boats had not been destroyed by stray shots from the forts, which were now sharply cannonading each other; for the artillerymen had turned the guns of Fort Napoleon on Fort Ragusa.

Many of the French leaped into the water and were drowned, but the greatest part were made prisoners, and, to the amazement of the conquerors, the panic spread to the other side of the river; the garrison of Fort Ragusa, although perfectly safe, abandoned that fort also and fled with the others. Some grenadiers of the 92nd immediately swam over and brought back several boats, with which the bridge was restored and Fort Ragusa was gained. The towers and other works were then destroyed, the stores, ammunition, provisions, and boats were burned in the course of the day, and in the night the troops returned to the Sierra above, carrying with them the colours of the foreign regiment and more than 250 prisoners, including a commandant and sixteen other officers. The whole loss on the part of the British was about 180 men, and one officer of artillery was killed by his own mine, placed for the destruction of the tower; but the only officer slain in the actual assault was Captain Candler, a brave man, who fell while leading the grenadiers of the 50th on to the rampart of Fort Napoleon.

This daring attack was executed with a decision similar to that with which it had been planned. The first intention of General Hill was to have directed a part of his column against the bridgehead, and so to have assailed both works together, but when the difficulties of the road marred this project, he attacked the nearest work with the leading troops, leaving the rear to follow as it could.

The works at Mirabete being now cut off from the right bank of the Tagus, General Hill was preparing to reduce them with his heavy artillery, when a report from Sir William Erskine caused him, in conformity with his instructions, to commence a retreat on Merida, leaving Mirabete blockaded by the guerillas of the neighbourhood. It appeared that Soult heard of the allies' march on the 19th, and then desired Drouet to make a diversion in Estremadura without losing his communication with Andalusia; for he did not perceive the true object of the enterprise, and thinking he had to check a movement made for the purpose of reinforcing Wellington in the north, resolved to enforce Hill's stay in Estremadura. In this view he purposed to strengthen Drouet and enable him to fight a battle. But that general, anticipating his orders, had pushed an advanced guard of 4000 men to Dom Benito, and his cavalry patrols, passing the Guadiana, had scoured the roads to Miajadas and Merida, while Lallemand's dragoons drove back the British outposts from Ribera.

Confused by these demonstrations, Sir William Erskine immediately reported to Graham and to Hill that Soult himself was in Estremadura with his whole army, whereupon Graham came up to Badajos, and Hill, fearful of being cut off, retired from Mirabete and reached Merida unmolested. Drouet then withdrew his advanced guards, and Graham returned to Castello de Vide. Notwithstanding this error, Wellington's precautions succeeded, for if Drouet had been aware of Hill's real object, instead of making demonstrations with a part of his force, he would with the whole of his troops, more than 10,000, have marched rapidly to fall on the allies as they issued out of the passes of Truxillo, and before Erskine or Graham could come to their aid; whereas, acting on the supposition that the intention was to cross the Tagus, his demonstrations merely hastened the retreat and saved Mirabete. To meet Hill in the right place would, however, have required very nice arrangements and great activity. Lord Wellington was greatly displeased that this false alarm, given by Erskine, should have rendered the success incomplete; yet he avoided any public expression of discontent, lest the enemy, who had no apparent interest in preserving the post of Mirabete, should be led to keep it, and so embarrass the

THE PENINSULAR CAMPAIGN.

allies when their operations required a restoration of the bridge of Almaraz.

General Hill's success at Almaraz enabled Wellington to establish communications between all the allied forces, and as he had received considerable reinforcements since the beginning of the year, the force that could now be mustered for offensive operations north of the Tagus amounted to about 40,000 infantry and 4000 cavalry. With this force, though fully equal perhaps to cope singly with either of the French armies, Wellington could effect nothing should Marmont and Soult form a junction. Hill held Soult at check, however, and Wellington having formed magazines at Almeida and elsewhere, at length put his forces in motion and advanced towards Salamanca, the periodic rains having ceased, Marmont falling back as the British approached. The French evacuated Salamanca town, and the British entered it amid a great scene of rejoicing; the houses were illuminated, the people singing, shouting, and weeping for joy, giving Lord Wellington a hearty welcome, whilst the army took up a position on the mountain of San Christoval and prepared for the

SIEGE OF THE FORTS AT SALAMANCA.

Four 18-pounders had followed the army from Almeida, three 24-pound howitzers were furnished by the field-artillery, and the battering train used by Hill at Almaraz had passed the bridge of Alcantara on the 11th June. These were the means of offence, but the strength of the forts had been underrated; they contained 800 men, and it was said that thirteen convents and twenty-two colleges had been destroyed in their construction. San Vincente, so called from the large convent it enclosed, was the key-fort. Situated on a perpendicular cliff overhanging the Tormes, and irregular in form but well flanked, it was separated by a deep ravine from the other forts, which were called St. Cajetano and La Merced. These were also on high ground, smaller than San Vincente and of a square form, but with bomb-proofs and deep ditches, having perpendicular scarps and counterscarps.

In the night of the 17th, Colonel Burgoyne, the engineer directing the siege, commenced a battery for eight guns at the distance of 250 yards from the main wall of Vincente, and as the ruins of the destroyed convents rendered it impossible to excavate, earth was brought from a distance; but the moon was up, the night short, the enemy's fire of musketry heavy, the workmen were inexperienced, and at daybreak the battery was still imperfect. Meanwhile an attempt had been made to attach the miner secretly to the counterscarp, and when the vigilance of a trained dog baffled this design, the enemy's piquet was driven in and the attempt openly made; yet it was rendered vain by a plunging fire from the top of the convent.

On the 18th, 800 Germans placed in the ruins mastered all the enemy's fire save that from loopholes, and Colonel May, who directed the artillery service, then placed two field-pieces on a neighbouring convent called San Bernardo, overlooking the fort; these guns could not, however, silence the French artillery. In the night the first battery was armed; covering for two field-pieces as a counter-battery was raised a little to its right, and a second breaching battery for two howitzers was constructed on the Cajetano side of the ravine.

At daybreak on the 19th, seven guns opened, and at nine o'clock the wall of the convent was cut away to the level of the counterscarp. The second breaching-battery, which was lower down the scarp, then commenced its fire; but the iron howitzers proved unmeet battering ordnance, and the enemy's musketry being entirely directed on this point, because the first battery, to save ammunition, had ceased firing, brought down a captain and more than twenty gunners. The howitzers did not injure the wall, ammunition was scarce, and as the enemy could easily cut off the breach in the night, the fire ceased. The 20th at midday, Colonel Dickson arrived with the iron howitzers from Elvas, and the second battery being then reinforced with additional pieces, revived its fire against a re-entering angle of the convent a little beyond the former breach. The wall here was soon broken through, and in an instant a huge cantle of the convent, with its roof, went to the ground, crushing many of the garrison and laying bare the inside of the building. Carcasses were immediately thrown into the opening to burn the convent, but the enemy undauntedly maintained their ground and extinguished the flames. A lieutenant and fifteen gunners were lost this day on the side of the besiegers, and the ammunition being nearly gone, the attack was suspended until fresh stores could come up from Almeida.

During the progress of this siege, the general aspect of affairs had materially changed on both sides. Lord Wellington had been deceived as to the strength of the forts, and intercepted returns of the armies of the south and of Portugal now showed to him that they also were far stronger than he had expected. He had calculated that General Bonet would not quit the Asturias, and that general was in full march for Leon; Caffarelli also was preparing to reinforce Marmont, and thus the brilliant prospect of the campaign was suddenly clouded.

Neither was King Joseph's situation agreeable. The Partidas intercepted his dispatches so surely, that it was the 19th ere Marmont's letter announcing Wellington's advance, and saying that Hill also was in march for the north, reached Madrid. Something was, however, gained in vigour, for the King, no longer depending upon the assistance of the distant armies, gave orders to blow up Mirabete and abandon La Mancha on one side, and the forts of Somosierra and Buitrago on the other, with a view to unite the army of the centre. A detachment of 800 men under Colonel Noizet, employed to destroy Buitrago, was attacked by the Empecinado with 3000, but Noizet, an able officer, defeated him and reached Madrid with little loss. The garrison of Segovia was reinforced to preserve one of the communications with Marmont; that marshal was informed of Hill's true position, and the King advised him to give battle to Wellington, for he supposed the latter to have only 18,000 English troops; but he had 24,000, and had yet left Hill so strong that he desired him to fight Drouet if occasion required.

Meanwhile Marmont united four divisions of infantry and a brigade of cavalry, furnishing about 25,000 men of all arms, with which he marched to the succour of Salamanca. His approach over an open country was descried at a considerable distance, and a brigade of the fifth division was immediately called off from the siege, the battering train was sent across the Tormes, and the army, which was in bivouac on the Salamanca side of San Christoval, formed in order of battle on the top. This position of Christoval was about four miles long, and rather concave, the

THE FORTS AT SALAMANCA.

ascent in front steep and tangled with hollow roads and stone enclosures belonging to the villages, but the summit was broad, even, and covered with ripe corn; the right was flanked by the Upper Tormes, and the left dipped into the country bordering the Lower Tormes; for in passing Salamanca that river makes a sweep round the back of the position. The infantry, the heavy cavalry, and the guns crowned the summit of the mountain, but the light cavalry fell back from the front to the low country on the left, where there was a small stream and a marshy flat. Nothing could be stronger than the position, which completely commanded all the country for many miles; but the heat was excessive, and there was neither shade, nor fuel to cook with, nor water nearer than the Tormes.

About five o'clock in the evening the enemy's horsemen approached, pointing towards the left of the position, as if to turn it by the Lower Tormes; whereupon the British light cavalry made a short forward movement and a partial charge took place; but the French opened six guns, and the British retired to their own ground near Monte Rubio and Villares. The light division, which was held in reserve, immediately closed towards the left of the position until the French cavalry halted, and then returned to the centre. Meanwhile, the main body of the enemy bore in one dark volume against the right, and halting at the very foot of the position, sent a flight of shells on to the lofty summit; nor did this fire cease until after dark, when the French general, after driving back all the outposts, obtained possession of Moresco, and established himself behind that village within gunshot of the allies.

The English general slept that night on the ground amongst the troops, and at the first streak of light the armies were again under arms. Nevertheless, though some signals were interchanged between Marmont and the forts, both sides were quiet until towards evening, when Wellington detached the 68th regiment from the line to drive the French from Moresco. This attack, made with vigour, succeeded; but the troops being recalled just as daylight failed, a body of French coming unperceived through the standing corn, broke into the village as the British were collecting their posts from the different avenues, and did considerable execution. In the skirmish an officer of the 68th named Mackay, being suddenly surrounded, refused to surrender, and singly fighting against a multitude, received more wounds than the human frame was thought capable of sustaining, yet lived to show his honourable scars.

Three divisions and a brigade of cavalry joined Marmont on the 22nd, who having now nearly 40,000 men in hand, extended his left and seized a part of the height in advance of the allies' right wing, from whence he could discern the whole of their order of battle, and attack their right on even terms. However, General Graham, advancing with the seventh division, dislodged this French detachment after a sharp skirmish before it could be formidably reinforced, and that night Marmont withdrew from his dangerous position to some heights about six miles in his rear. It was thought that the French general's tempestuous advance to Moresco with such an inferior force should have been his ruin. Lord Wellington saw clearly enough the false position of his enemy, but he argued that if Marmont came up to fight, it was better to defend a very strong position than to descend and combat in the plain, seeing that the inferiority of force was not such as to ensure the result of the battle being decisive of the campaign; and in case of failure, a retreat across the Tormes would have been very difficult. To this may be added, that during the first evening there was some confusion amongst the allies before the troops of the different nations could form their order of battle. Moreover, as the descent of the mountain towards the enemy was by no means easy, because of the walls and avenues and the two villages which covered the French front, it is probable that Marmont, who had plenty of guns, and whose troops were in perfect order and extremely ready of movement, could have evaded the action until night.

Marmont's new position was skilfully chosen. One flank rested on Cabeza Vellosa, the other at Huerta, the centre was at Aldea Rubia; and Wellington made corresponding dispositions, closing up his left towards Moresco, and pushing the light division along the salient part of his position to Aldea Lengua, where it overhung a ford, which was, however, scarcely practicable at this period. General Graham with two divisions was placed at the fords of Santa Marta, and the heavy German cavalry under General Bock crossed the Tormes to watch the ford of Huerta. By this disposition the allies covered Salamanca and could operate on either side of the Tormes on a shorter line than the French could operate.

The two armies again remained tranquil on the 23rd, but at break of day on the 24th some dropping pistol-shots, and now and then a shout, came faintly from the mist which covered the lower ground beyond the river; the heavy sound of artillery succeeded, and the hissing of the bullets as they cut through the thickened atmosphere plainly told that the French were over the Tormes. After a time the fog cleared up, and the German horsemen were seen in close and beautiful order, retiring before 12,000 French infantry, who in battle-array were marching steadily onwards. At intervals, twenty guns ranged in front would start forwards and send their bullets whistling and tearing up the ground beneath the Germans, while scattered parties of light cavalry, scouting out, capped all the hills in succession, and peering abroad, gave signals to the main body. Wellington immediately sent Graham across the river by the fords of Santa Marta with the first and seventh divisions and Le Marchant's brigade of English cavalry; then concentrating the rest of the army between Cabrerizos and Moresco, he awaited the progress of Marmont's operation. Bock continued his retreat in the same fine and equable order, regardless alike of the cannonade and of the light horsemen on his flanks, until the enemy's scouts had gained a height from whence, at the distance of three miles, they for the first time perceived Graham's 12,000 men and eighteen guns, ranged on an order of battle perpendicular to the Tormes. From the same point also Wellington's heavy columns were to be seen, clustering on the height above the fords of Santa Marta, and the light division was descried at Aldea Lengua, ready either to advance against the French troops left on the position of Aldea Rubia or to pass the river to the aid of Graham. This apparition made the French general aware of his error, whereupon hastily facing about and repassing the Tormes, he resumed his former ground. Wellington's defensive dispositions on this occasion were very skilful, but it would appear that, unwilling to stir before the forts fell, he had again refused the advantage of the moment; for it is not to be supposed that he misjudged the occasion, since the whole theatre of operation was distinctly seen from

San Christoval, and he had passed many hours in earnest observation; his faculties were indeed so fresh and vigorous, that after the day's work he wrote a detailed memoir upon the proposal for establishing a bank in Portugal, treating that and other financial schemes in all their bearings with a master-hand.

When the French retired on the night of the 23rd, the heavy guns had been already brought to the right of the Tormes, and a third battery, to breach San Cajetano, was armed with four pieces; but the line of fire being oblique, the practice, at 450 yards, only beat down the parapet and knocked away the palisades. Time was, however, of vital importance, the escalade of that fort and La Merced was ordered, and the attack commenced at ten o'clock, but in half an hour failed with a loss of 120 men and officers. The wounded were brought off the next day under truce, and the enemy had all the credit of the fight, yet the death of General Bowes must ever be admired. That gallant man, whose rank might have excused his leading so small a force, being wounded early, was having his hurt dressed when he heard that the troops were yielding, and returning to the combat, fell. The siege was now perforce suspended for want of ammunition, and the guns were sent across the river, but were immediately brought back in consequence of Marmont having crossed to the left bank. Certain works were meanwhile pushed forward to cut off the communication between the forts and otherwise to straiten them, and the miner was attached to the cliff on which La Merced stood.

On the 26th, ammunition arrived from Almeida, the second and third batteries were re-armed, the field-pieces were again placed in the convent of San Bernardo, and the iron howitzers, throwing hot shot, set the convent of San Vincente on fire in several places. The garrison again extinguished the flames, and this balanced combat continued during the night; but on the morning of the 27th, the fire of both parties being redoubled, the convent of San Vincente was in a blaze, the breach of San Cajetano was improved, a fresh storming party assembled, and the white flag waved from Cajetano. A negotiation ensued, but Lord Wellington, judging it an artifice to gain time, gave orders for the assault; then the forts fell, for San Cajetano scarcely fired a shot, and the flames raged so violently at San Vincente that no opposition could be made.

THE FORTS AT SALAMANCA.

Seven hundred prisoners, thirty pieces of artillery, provisions, arms, and clothing, and a secure passage over the Tormes were the immediate fruits of this capture, which was not the less prized that the breaches were found to be more formidable than those at Ciudad Rodrigo. The success of a storm would have been very doubtful if the garrison could have gained time to extinguish the flames in the convent of San Vincente, and as it was, the allies had ninety killed; their whole loss since the passage of the Tormes was nearly 500 men and officers, of which 160 men, with fifty horses, fell outside Salamanca, the rest in the siege.

The forts having fallen, and their destruction ordered by Wellington, the opposing forces manœuvred in various directions for a time, till at length Marmont began to concentrate his forces near the Duero, and in these operations he was closely watched and followed up by the British cavalry under Sir Stapleton Cotton, who engaged with the French rear-guard as it was occupied in crossing the river Trabancos, near Castrejon. At daybreak, Cotton's outposts were driven in by the enemy, and the bulk of his cavalry with a troop of horse-artillery immediately formed in front of two infantry divisions, which were drawn up at a considerable distance from each other and separated by a wide ravine. The country was open and hilly, like the downs of England, with here and there water-gulleys, dry hollows, and bold naked heads of land, and behind one of these last, on the other side of the Trabancos, lay the whole French army. Cotton, however, seeing only horsemen, pushed his cavalry towards the river, advancing cautiously by his right along some high table-land, and his troops were soon lost to the view of the infantry, for the morning fog was thick on the stream, and at first nothing could be descried beyond. But very soon the deep tones of artillery shook the ground, the sharp ring of musketry was heard in the mist, and the 43rd regiment was hastily brought through Castrejon to support the advancing cavalry; for besides the ravine which separated the two divisions, there was another ravine with a marshy bottom between the cavalry and infantry, and the village of Castrejon was the only good point of passage.

The cannonade now became heavy and the spectacle surprisingly beautiful, for the lighter smoke and mist, curling up in fantastic pillars, formed a huge and glittering dome tinged of many colours by the rising sun; and through the grosser vapour below, the restless horsemen were seen or lost as the fume thickened from the rapid play of the artillery, while the bluff head of land beyond the Trabancos, covered with French troops, appeared, by an optical deception, close at hand, dilated to the size of a mountain, and crowned with gigantic soldiers, who were continually breaking off and sliding down into the fight. Suddenly a dismounted cavalry officer stalked from the midst of the smoke towards the line of infantry; his gait was peculiarly rigid, and he appeared to hold a bloody handkerchief to his heart, but that which seemed a cloth, was a broad and dreadful wound; a bullet had entirely effaced the flesh from his left shoulder and from his breast, and had carried away part of his ribs; his heart was bared, and its movement plainly discerned. It was a piteous and yet a noble sight, for his countenance, though ghastly, was firm, his step scarcely indicated weakness, and his voice never faltered. This unyielding man's name was Williams; he died a short distance from the field of battle, and, it was said, in the arms of his son, a youth of fourteen, who had followed his father to the Peninsula in hopes of obtaining a commission.

General Cotton maintained this exposed position with skill and resolution from daylight until seven o'clock, at which time Wellington arrived, in company with Beresford, and proceeded to examine the enemy's movements. The time was critical, and the two English generals were like to have been slain together by a body of French cavalry, not very numerous, which came galloping at full speed across the valley. It was for a moment thought they were deserting, but with headlong course they mounted the table-land on which Cotton's left wing was posted, and drove a whole line of British cavalry skirmishers back in confusion. The reserves indeed soon came up, and these furious swordsmen being scattered in all directions, were in turn driven away or cut down; but meanwhile thirty or forty, led by a noble officer, had brought up their right shoulders, and came over the edge of the table-land above the hollow which separated the British wings at the instant when Wellington and Beresford arrived on the same slope. There were some infantry piquets in the bottom, and higher up, near the French, were two guns covered by a squadron of light cavalry, which was disposed in perfect

THE FORTS AT SALAMANCA.   199

order. When the French officer saw this squadron, he reined in his horse with difficulty, and his troopers gathered in a confused body round him as if to retreat. They seemed lost men, for the British instantly charged, but with a shout the gallant fellows soused down upon the squadron, and the latter turning, galloped through the guns; then the whole mass, friends and enemies, went like a whirlwind to the bottom, carrying away Lord Wellington and the other generals, who with drawn swords and some difficulty got clear of the tumult. The French horsemen were now quite exhausted, and a reserve squadron of heavy dragoons coming in, cut most of them to pieces; yet their invincible leader, assaulted by three enemies at once, struck one dead from his horse, and with surprising exertions saved himself from the others, though they rode hewing at him on each side for a quarter of a mile.

While this last charge was being executed, Marmont, having ascertained that only a part of the British army was before him, crossed the Trabancos and marched towards the river Guarena, which, flowing from four branches, unites below Castrillo. The British moved also in the same direction, and for about ten miles the opposing forces marched in sight of each other toward a common goal, the officers on each side pointing forwards with their swords, or touching their caps and waving their hands in courtesy. The Guarena offered a very strong line of defence, and Marmont, hoping to gain it in the first confusion, brought up all his artillery to the front; but Wellington, anticipating this, had ordered other divisions of his army to cross at an upper branch of the river, and these divisions were in line before the French infantry, oppressed by the extreme heat and rapidity of the march, could muster in sufficient strength to attempt the passage of the branch at Vallesa. The sedgy banks of the river would have been difficult to force in face of an enemy, but the British general, Victor Alten, though a very bold man in action, was slow to seize an advantage, and suffered the French cavalry to cross and form in considerable numbers without opposition; he assailed them too late and by successive squadrons instead of by regiments, and the result was unfavourable at first. The 14th and the German hussars were hard pressed, the 3rd dragoons came up in support, but they were immediately driven back again by the fire of some

French infantry; the fight waxed hot with the others, and many fell, but finally General Carier was wounded and taken, and the French retired. During this cavalry action the 27th and 40th regiments coming down the hill, broke the enemy's infantry with an impetuous bayonet charge, and Alten's horsemen being thus disengaged, sabred some of the fugitives.

This combat cost the French, who had advanced too far without support, a general and 500 soldiers; but Marmont concentrated his army at Castrillo in such a manner as to hold both banks of the Guarena. Whereupon Wellington recalled his troops from Vallesa; and as the whole loss of the allies during the previous operations was not more than 600, nor that of the French more than 800, and that both sides were highly excited, the day still young, and the positions, although strong, open and within cannon-shot, a battle was expected. Marmont's troops had, however, been marching for two days and nights incessantly, and Wellington's plan did not admit of fighting unless forced to it in defence, or under such circumstances as would enable him to crush his opponent, and yet keep the field afterwards.

CHAPTER XI.

BATTLE OF SALAMANCA—SIEGE OF BURGOS.

OTH armies now remained quiet for two days, and then commenced a series of marchings and countermarchings, the contending forces manœuvring in almost parallel lines to each other, each occasionally opening fire on the other, and both prepared at any moment to form line of battle. It was not till the morning of the 21st July that the imposing spectacle was presented of the two lines confronting one another in positions facing an oval basin formed by the heights of the Arapiles, and near the Bridge of Salamanca, prepared to fight whenever a false movement or favourable opening gave either side the chance of striking the first blow.

BATTLE OF SALAMANCA.

Marmont's first arrangements had occupied several hours, yet as they gave no positive indication of his designs, Wellington, ceasing to watch him, had retired from the Arapiles. But at three o'clock a report reached him that the French left was in motion and pointing towards the Ciudad Rodrigo road; then starting up, he repaired to the high ground, and observed their movements for some time with a stern contentment, for their left wing was entirely separated from the centre. The fault was flagrant, and he fixed it with the stroke of a thunderbolt. A few orders issued from his lips like the incantations of a wizard, and suddenly the dark mass of troops which covered the English Arapiles was seemingly possessed by some mighty spirit, and rushing violently down the interior slope of the mountain, entered the great basin amidst a storm of bullets which seemed to shear away the whole surface of the earth over which the soldiers moved.

Marmont, from the top of the French Arapiles, saw the country beneath him suddenly covered with enemies at a moment when he was in the act of making a complicated evolution, and when, by the rash advance of his left, his troops were separated into three parts, each at too great a distance to assist the other, and those nearest the enemy neither strong enough to hold their ground, nor aware of what they had to encounter. The third division was, however, still hidden from him by the western heights, and he hoped that the tempest of bullets under which the British line was moving in the basin beneath would check it until he could bring up his reserve divisions, and by the village of Arapiles fall on what was now the left of the allies' position. But even this, his only resource for saving the battle, was weak, for on that point there were still the first and light divisions and Pack's brigade, forming a mass of 12,000 troops with thirty pieces of artillery; the village itself was well disputed, and the English Arapiles rock stood out as a strong bastion of defence. However, the French general, nothing daunted, dispatched officer after officer, some to hasten up the troops from the forest, others to stop the progress of his left wing, and with a sanguine expectation still looked for the victory until he saw Pakenham with the third division shoot like a meteor across the path of Thomieres' corps; then pride and hope alike died within him, and desperately he was hurrying in person to that fatal point, when an exploding shell stretched him on the earth with a broken arm and two deep wounds in his side. Confusion ensued, and the troops, distracted by ill-judged orders and counter-orders, knew not where to move, who to fight, or who to avoid.

It was about five o'clock when Pakenham fell upon Thomieres, and it was at the instant when that general, the head of whose column had gained an open isolated hill at the extremity of the southern range of heights, expected to see the allies in full retreat towards the Ciudad Rodrigo road, closely followed by Marmont from the Arapiles. The counter-stroke was terrible! Two batteries of artillery placed on the summit of the western heights

suddenly took his troops in flank, and Pakenham's massive columns, supported by cavalry, were coming on full in his front, while two-thirds of his own division, lengthened out and unconnected, were still behind in a wood where they could hear, but could not see the storm which was now bursting. From the chief to the lowest soldier all felt that they were lost, and in an instant Pakenham, the most frank and gallant of men, commenced the battle.

The British columns formed lines as they marched, and the French gunners standing up manfully for the honour of their country, sent showers of grape into the advancing masses, while a crowd of light troops poured in a fire of musketry, under cover of which the main body endeavoured to display a front. But bearing onwards through the skirmishers with the might of a giant, Pakenham broke the half-formed lines into fragments, and sent the whole in confusion upon the advancing supports; one only officer, with unyielding spirit, remained by the artillery; standing alone, he fired the last gun at the distance of a few yards, but whether he lived or there died could not be seen for the smoke. Some squadrons of light cavalry fell on the right of the third division, but the 5th regiment repulsed them, and then D'Urban's Portuguese horsemen, reinforced by two squadrons of the 14th dragoons under Felton Harvey, gained the enemy's flank. The Oporto regiment, led by the English major, Watson, instantly charged the French infantry, yet vainly; Watson fell deeply wounded, and his men retired.

Pakenham continued his tempestuous course against the remainder of Thomieres' troops, which were now arrayed on the wooded heights behind the first hill, yet imperfectly, and offering two fronts, the one opposed to the third division and its attendant horsemen, the other to the fifth division, to Bradford's brigade, and the main body of cavalry and artillery, all of which were now moving in one great line across the basin. Meanwhile Bonet's troops, having failed at the village of Arapiles, were sharply engaged with the fourth division, Maucune kept his menacing position behind the French Arapiles, and as Clausel's division had come up from the forest, the connection of the centre and left was in some measure restored; two divisions were however still in the rear, and Boyer's dragoons were in march from Calvariza Ariba.

Thomieres had been killed, and Bonet, who succeeded Marmont, had been disabled, hence more confusion; but the command of the army devolved on Clausel, and he was of a capacity to sustain this terrible crisis.

The fourth and fifth divisions and Bradford's brigade were now hotly engaged and steadily gaining ground; the heavy cavalry, Anson's light dragoons, and Bull's troop of artillery were advancing at a trot on Pakenham's left, and on that general's right D'Urban's horsemen overlapped the enemy. Thus in less than half an hour, and before an order of battle had even been formed by the French, their commander-in-chief and two other generals had fallen, and the left of their army was turned, thrown into confusion and enveloped. Clausel's division had indeed joined Thomieres', and a front had been spread on the southern heights, but it was loose and unfit to resist; for the troops were some in double lines, some in columns, some in squares; a powerful sun shone full in their eyes; the light soil, stirred up by the trampling of men and horses, and driven forward by a breeze which arose in the west at the moment of attack, came full upon them mingled with smoke in such stifling clouds, that, scarcely able to breathe and quite unable to see, their fire was given at random.

In this situation, while Pakenham, bearing onward with a conquering violence, was closing on their flank, and the fifth division advancing with a storm of fire on their front, the interval between the two attacks was suddenly filled with a whirling cloud of dust, which, moving swiftly forward, carried within its womb the trampling sound of a charging multitude. As it passed the left of the third division, Le Marchant's heavy horsemen, flanked by Anson's light cavalry, broke forth from it at full speed, and the next instant 1200 French infantry, though formed in several lines, were trampled down with a terrible clamour and disturbance. Bewildered and blinded, they cast away their arms and ran through the openings of the British squadrons stooping and demanding quarter, while the dragoons, big men and on big horses, rode onwards smiting with their long glittering swords in uncontrollable power, and the third division followed at speed, shouting as the French masses fell in succession before this dreadful charge.

Nor were these valiant swordsmen yet exhausted. Their own general, Le Marchant, and many officers had fallen, but Cotton and all his staff was at their head, and with ranks confused and blended together in one mass, still galloping forward, they sustained from a fresh column an irregular stream of fire which emptied a hundred saddles; yet with fine courage and downright force, the survivors broke through this the third and strongest body of men that had encountered them, and Lord Edward Somerset, continuing his course at the head of one squadron, with a happy perseverance, captured five guns. The French left was entirely broken, more than 2000 prisoners were taken, the French light horsemen abandoned that part of the field, and Thomieres' division no longer existed as a military body. Anson's cavalry, which had passed quite over the hill and had suffered little in the charge, was now joined by D'Urban's troopers, and took the place of Le Marchant's exhausted men; the heavy German dragoons followed in reserve, and, with the third and fifth divisions and the guns, formed one formidable line, two miles in advance of where Pakenham had first attacked; and that impetuous officer with unmitigated strength still pressed forward, spreading terror and disorder on the enemy's left.

While these signal events, which occupied about forty minutes, were passing on the allies' right, a terrible battle raged in the centre. For when the first shock of the third division had been observed from the Arapiles, the fourth division, moving in a line with the fifth, had passed the village of that name under a prodigious cannonade, and vigorously driving Bonet's troops backwards, step by step, to the southern and eastern height, obliged them to mingle with Clausel's and with Thomieres' broken remains. When the combatants had passed the French Arapiles, which was about the time of Le Marchant's charge, Pack's Portuguese assailed that rock, and the front of battle was thus completely defined, because Foy's division was now exchanging a distant cannonade with the first and light divisions. However, Bonet's troops, notwithstanding Marmont's fall and the loss of their own general, fought strongly, and Clausel made a surprising effort, beyond all men's expectations, to restore the battle. Already a great change was visible. Ferey's division arrived in the centre behind Bonet's men; the light cavalry, Boyer's dragoons, and two divisions of infantry from the forest, were also united there, and on this mass of fresh men Clausel rallied the remnants of his own and Thomieres' division. But Clausel, not content with having brought the separated part of his army together and in a condition to effect a retreat, attempted to stem the tide of victory in the very fulness of its strength and roughness. His hopes were founded on a misfortune which had befallen General Pack; for that officer, ascending the French Arapiles in one heavy column, had driven back the enemy's skirmishers and was within thirty yards of the summit, believing himself victorious, when suddenly the French reserves leaped forward from the rocks upon his front and upon his left flank. The hostile masses closed, there was a thick cloud of smoke, a shout, a stream of fire, and the side of the hill was covered to the very bottom with the dead, the wounded, and the flying Portuguese. The result went nigh to shake the whole battle. For the fourth division had just then reached the southern ridge of the basin, and one of the best regiments in the service was actually on the summit when 1200 fresh adversaries arrayed on the reverse slope charged uphill; and as the British fire was straggling and ineffectual, because the soldiers were breathless and disordered by the previous fighting, the French, who came up resolutely and without firing, won the crest. They were even pursuing down the other side when two regiments placed in line below checked them with a destructive volley.

This vigorous counter-blow took place at the moment when Pack's defeat permitted Maucune, who was no longer in pain for the Arapiles hill, to menace the left flank and rear of the fourth division, but the left wing of the 40th regiment immediately wheeled about and with a rough charge cleared the rear. Maucune would not engage himself more deeply at that time, but General Ferey's troops pressed vigorously against the front of the fourth division, and Brennier did the same by the first line of the fifth division. Boyer's dragoons also came on rapidly, and the allies being outflanked and over-matched, lost ground. Fiercely and fast the French followed, and the fight once more raged in the basin below. General Cole had before this fallen deeply wounded, and Leith had the same fortune, but Beresford promptly drew Spry's Portuguese brigade from the second line of the fifth division and thus flanked the advancing columns of the enemy; yet he also fell desperately wounded, and Boyer's dragoons then came freely into action, because Anson's cavalry had been checked after La Marchant's charge by a heavy fire of artillery.

The crisis of the battle had now arrived, and the victory was for the general who had the strongest reserves in hand. Wellington, who was seen that day at every point of the field exactly when his presence was most required, immediately brought up from the second line the sixth division, and its charge was rough, strong, and successful. Nevertheless the struggle was no slight one. The men of General Hulse's brigade, which was on the left, went down by hundreds, and the 61st and 11th regiments won their way desperately and through such a fire as British soldiers only can sustain. Some of Boyer's dragoons also, breaking in between the fifth and sixth divisions, slew many men and caused some disorder in the 53rd; but that brave regiment lost no ground, nor did Clausel's impetuous counter-attack avail at any point, after the first burst, against the steady courage of the allies. The southern ridge was regained, the French general Menne was severely, and General Ferey mortally wounded; Clausel himself was hurt; and the reserve of Boyer's dragoons coming on at a canter, were met and broken by the fire of Hulse's noble brigade. Then the changing current of the fight once more set for the British. The third division continued to outflank the enemy's left, Maucune abandoned the French Arapiles, Foy retired from the ridge of Calvariza, and the allied host righting itself as a gallant ship after a sudden gust, again bore onwards in blood and gloom; for though the air, purified by the storm of the night before, was peculiarly clear, one vast cloud of smoke and dust rolled along the basin, and within it was the battle with all its sights and sounds of terror.

When the English general had thus restored the fight in the centre, he directed the commander of the first division to push between Foy and the rest of the French army, which would have rendered it impossible for the latter to rally or escape; but this order was not executed, and Foy's and Maucune's divisions were skilfully used by Clausel to protect the retreat. The first, posted on undulating ground and flanked by some squadron of dragoons, covered the roads to the fords of Huerta and Encina; the second, reinforced with fifteen guns, was placed on a steep ridge in front of the forest, covering the road to Alba de Tornes; and behind this ridge the rest of the army, then falling back in disorder before the third, fifth, and sixth divisions, took refuge. Wellington immediately sent the light division, formed in two lines and flanked by some squadrons of dragoons, against Foy; and he supported them by the first division in columns, flanked on the right by two brigades of the fourth division, which he had drawn off from the centre when the sixth division restored the fight. The seventh division and the Spaniards followed in reserve; the country was covered with troops, and a new army seemed to have risen out of the earth.

Foy, throwing out a cloud of skirmishers, retired slowly by wings, turning and firing heavily from every rise of ground upon the light division, which marched steadily forward without returning a shot save by its skirmishers; for three miles the march was under this musketry, which was occasionally thickened by a cannonade, and yet very few men were lost, because the French aim was baffled, partly by the twilight, partly by the even order and rapid gliding of the lines. But the French general Desgraviers was killed, and the flanking brigades from the fourth division having now penetrated between Maucune and Foy, it seemed difficult for the latter to extricate his troops from the action; nevertheless he did it and with great dexterity. For having increased his skirmishers on the last defensible ridge, along the foot of which ran a marshy stream, he redoubled his fire of musketry, and made a menacing demonstration with his horsemen just as the darkness fell; the British guns immediately opened their fire, a squadron of dragoons galloped forwards from the left, the infantry crossing the marshy stream, with an impetuous pace hastened to the summit of the hill, and a rough shock seemed at hand, but there was no longer an enemy; the main body of the French had gone into the thick forest on their own left during the firing, and the skirmishers fled swiftly after, covered by the smoke and by the darkness.

Meanwhile Maucune maintained a noble battle. He was outflanked and outnumbered, but the safety of the French army depended on his courage; he knew it, and Pakenham, marking his bold demeanour, advised Clinton, who was immediately in his front, not to assail him until the third division should have turned his left. Nevertheless the sixth division was soon plunged afresh into action under great disadvantage, for after being kept by its commander a long time without reason close under Maucune's batteries, which ploughed heavily through the ranks, it was suddenly directed by a staff officer to attack the hill. Assisted by a brigade of the fourth division, the troops then rushed up, and in the darkness of the night the fire showed from afar how the battle went. On the side of the British a sheet of flame was seen, sometimes advancing with an even front, sometimes pricking forth in spear-heads, now falling back in waving lines, and anon darting upwards in one vast pyramid, the apex of which often approached, yet never gained, the actual summit of the mountain; but the French musketry, rapid as lightning, sparkled along the brow of the height with unvarying fulness, and with what destructive effects the dark gaps and changing shapes of the adverse fire showed too plainly. Yet when Pakenham had again turned the enemy's left and Foy's division had glided into the forest, Maucune's task was completed, the effulgent crest of the ridge became black and silent, and the whole French army vanished as it were in the darkness.

Meanwhile Wellington, who was with the leading regiment of the light division, continued to advance towards the ford of Huerta, leaving the forest to his right, for he thought the Spanish garrison was still in the castle of Alba de Tormes, and that the enemy must of necessity be found in a confused mass at the fords. It was for this final stroke that he had so skilfully strengthened his left wing; nor was he diverted from his aim by marching through standing corn where no enemy could have preceded him; nor by Foy's retreat into the forest, because it pointed towards the fords of Encina and Gonzalo, which that general might be endeavouring to gain, and the right wing of the allies would find him there. A squadron of French dragoons also burst hastily from the forest in front of the advancing troops soon after dark, and firing their pistols, passed at full gallop towards the ford of Huerta, thus indicating great confusion in the defeated army, and confirming the notion that its retreat was in that direction. Had the castle of Alba been held, the French could not have carried off a third of their army, nor would they have been in much better plight if Carlos D'España, who soon discovered his error in withdrawing the garrison, had informed Wellington of the fact. The left wing continued their march to the ford without meeting any enemy, and the night being far spent, were there halted; the right wing, exhausted by long fighting, had ceased to pursue after the action with Maucune, and thus the French gained Alba unmolested; but the action did not terminate without two remarkable accidents. While riding close behind the 43rd regiment, Wellington was struck in the thigh by a spent musket-ball, which passed through his holster; and the night piquets had just been set at Huerta, when Sir Stapleton Cotton, who had gone to the ford and returned a different road, was shot through the arm by a Portuguese sentinel whose challenge he had disregarded. These were the last events of this famous battle, in which the skill of the general was worthily seconded by troops whose ardour may be appreciated by the following anecdotes.

Captain Brotherton of the 14th dragoons, fighting at the Guarena amongst the foremost, as he was always wont to do, had a sword-thrust quite through his side, yet a few days after was again on horseback, and being denied leave to remain in that condition with his own regiment, secretly joined Pack's Portuguese in an undress, and was again hurt in the unfortunate charge at the Arapiles. Such were the officers. A man of the 43rd, one by no means distinguished above his comrades, was shot through the middle of the thigh, and lost his shoes in passing the marshy stream; but refusing to quit the fight, he limped under fire in rear of his regiment, and with naked feet and streaming of blood from his wound, marched for several miles over a country covered with sharp stones. Such were the soldiers; and the devotion of a woman was not wanting to the illustration of this great day.

The wife of Colonel Dalbiac, an English lady of a gentle disposition and possessing a very delicate frame, had braved the dangers and endured the privations of two campaigns with the patient fortitude which belongs only to her sex; and in this battle, forgetful of everything but that strong affection which had so long supported her, she rode deep amidst the enemy's fire, trembling yet irresistibly impelled forwards by feelings more imperious than horror, more piercing than the fear of death.

During the few hours of darkness which succeeded the cessation of the battle, Clausel had with a wonderful diligence passed the Tormes by the narrow bridge of Alba and the fords below it, and at daylight was in full retreat upon Peneranda, covered by an organised rear-guard. Wellington also, having brought up the German dragoons and Anson's cavalry to the front, crossed the river with his left wing at daylight, and moving up the stream, came about ten o'clock upon the French rear, which was winding without much order along the Almar, a small stream at the foot of a height near the village of La Serna. He launched his cavalry against them, and the French squadrons, flying from Anson's troopers towards their own left, abandoned three battalions of infantry, who in separate columns were making up a hollow slope on their right, hoping to gain the crest of the heights before the cavalry could fall on. The two foremost did reach the higher ground and there formed squares, General Foy being in the one, and General Chemineau in the other; but the last regiment, when half-way up, seeing Bock's dragoons galloping hard on, faced about, and being still in column, commenced a disorderly fire. The two squares already formed above also plied their muskets with far greater effect; and as the Germans, after crossing the Almar stream, had to pass a turn of narrow road, and then to clear some rough ground before they could range their squadrons on a charging front, the troopers dropped fast under the fire. By twos, by threes, by tens, by twenties they fell, but the rest keeping together, surmounted the difficulties of the ground, and hurtling on the column, went clean through it; then the squares above retreated, and several hundred prisoners were made by these able and daring horsemen.

This charge had been successful even to wonder, the joyous victors, standing in the midst of their captives and of thousands of admiring friends, seemed invincible; yet those who witnessed the scene, nay, the actors themselves, remained with the conviction of this military truth, that cavalry are not able to cope with veteran infantry save by surprise. The hill of La Serna offered a frightful spectacle of the power of the musket, that queen of weapons, and the track of the Germans was marked by their huge bodies. A few minutes only had the combat lasted, and above 100 had fallen, 51 were killed outright; and in several places man and horse had died simultaneously, and so suddenly, that falling together on their sides, they appeared still alive, the horse's legs stretched out as in movement, the rider's feet in the stirrup, his bridle in his hand, the sword raised to strike, and the large hat fastened under the chin, giving to the grim but undistorted countenance, a supernatural and terrible expression.

Seven thousand prisoners, two eagles, with a number of cannon and other trophies, remained in the hands of the British.

The leader of the allies having accomplished one part of the plan he had projected and entirely cleared the northern frontier of Portugal, now turned to another part by striking at the army of the centre. Leaving a force under General Paget at the Duero to watch the motions of the enemy, Lord Wellington marched against the army of the centre under King Joseph, and on the 7th of August moved towards Madrid, a decisive movement on the part of the British general which had been altogether unforeseen, and for which no preparation had been made to resist. King Joseph had left the capital on the 21st July to the help of Marmont, but on learning the defeat of the French at Salamanca and of the advance of the British towards Madrid, he at once fell back rapidly on the capital. Wellington's march was conducted with all the celerity and good order which at this time distinguished every movement of his magnificent army, and despite various skirmishes by the way, he took possession of Valladolid, capturing there seventeen pieces of artillery, as well as considerable stores, and entered Madrid in triumph on the 12th August—a very memorable event, were it only from the affecting circumstances attending it. He, a foreigner and marching at the head of a foreign army, was met and welcomed to the capital of Spain by the whole remaining population. The multitude, who before that hour had never seen him, came forth to hail his approach, not with feigned enthusiasm, not with acclamations extorted by the fear of a conqueror's power, nor yet excited by the natural proneness of human nature to laud the successful, for there was no tumultuous exultation; famine was amongst them, and long-endured misery had subdued their spirits, but with tears, and every other sign of deep emotion, they crowded around his horse, hung upon his stirrups, touched his clothes, or throwing themselves upon the earth, blessed him aloud as the friend of Spain. His triumph was as pure and glorious as it was uncommon, and he felt it to be so.

Madrid was, however, still disturbed by the presence of the

enemy. The Retiro contained enormous stores, 20,000 stand of arms, more than 180 pieces of artillery, and the eagles of two French regiments, and it had a garrison of 2000 fighting men, besides invalids and followers; but its inherent weakness was soon made manifest. The works consisted of an interior fort called La China, with an exterior entrenchment; but the fort was too small, the entrenchment too large, and the latter could be easily deprived of water. In the lodgings of a French officer also was found an order directing the commandant to confine his real defence to the fort; and accordingly, on the night of the 13th, being menaced, he abandoned the entrenchment, and the next day accepted honourable terms, because La China was so contracted and filled with combustible buildings, that his fine troops would with only a little firing have been smothered in the ruins; yet they were so dissatisfied that many broke their arms, and their commander was like to have fallen a victim to their wrath. They were immediately sent to Portugal, and French writers assert that the escort basely robbed and murdered many of the prisoners. This disgraceful action was perpetrated either at Avila or on the frontier of Portugal, wherefore the British troops, who furnished no escorts after the first day's march from Madrid, are guiltless.

Siege of Burgos.

The situation of Wellington at this time in Madrid was full of peril, as the defeated army of Marmont was still numerous and had been largely reinforced, and General Clausel had also retaken Valladolid. Leaving two divisions to occupy the capital, Wellington, to consolidate his successes in the north, preparatory to the execution of his designs elsewhere, determined to march northwards and attack General Clausel before the other French armies could advance to his support, Early in September the allies again possessed themselves of Valladolid, from which Clausel retired as they approached. There was little fighting in the progress of the march, and on the 19th Wellington reached Burgos and took possession of the town, but the castle was at this time under the command of General Dubreton, an officer of proved skill and undoubted courage. The reduction of the castle Wellington considered to be essential to the success of his further operations, as the French had here collected large stores of ammunition, and the place was required as a point of support in the position he intended to assume. There were 1800 infantry besides artillerymen in the place. Burgos castle and its works enclosed a rugged hill, between which and the river the city of Burgos was situated. An old wall, with a new parapet and flanks constructed by the French, offered the first line of defence; the second line, which was within the other, was earthen, of the nature of a field retrenchment, and well palisaded; the third line was similarly constructed, and contained the two most elevated points of the hill, on one of which was an entrenched building called the White Church, and on the other the ancient keep of the castle; this last was the highest point, and was not only entrenched, but surmounted with a heavy casemated work called the Napoleon battery. Thus there were five separate enclosures.

The Napoleon battery commanded everything around it, save to the north, where at the distance of 300 yards there was a second height, scarcely less elevated than that of the fortress. It was called the hill of San Michael, and was defended by a large hornwork with a hard sloping scarp and a counterscarp. This outwork was unfinished, and only closed by strong palisades, but it was under the fire of the Napoleon battery, was well flanked by the castle defences, and covered in front by slight entrenchments for the out-piquets. The French had already mounted nine heavy guns, eleven field-pieces, and six mortars or howitzers in the fortress, and as the reserve artillery and stores of the army of Portugal were also deposited there, they could increase their armament.

The batteries so completely commanded all the bridges and fords over the Arlanzan, that two days elapsed ere the allies could cross; but on the 19th September 1812, the passage of the river being effected above the town by the first division, Major Somers Cocks, supported by Pack's Portuguese, drove in the French outposts on the hill of San Michael. In the night the same troops, reinforced with the 42nd regiment, stormed the hornwork. The conflict was murderous. For though the ladders were fairly placed by the bearers of them, the storming column, which, covered by a firing party, marched against the front, was beaten with great loss, and the attack would have failed if the gallant leader of the 79th had not meanwhile forced an entrance by the gorge. The garrison was thus actually cut off, but Cocks, though followed by the second battalion of the 42nd regiment, was not closely supported, and the French being still 500 strong, broke through his men and escaped. This assault gave room for censure. The troops complained of each other, and the loss was above 400, while that of the enemy was less than 150.

Wellington was now enabled to examine the defences of the castle. He found them feeble and incomplete, and yet his means were so scant that he had slender hopes of success, and relied more upon the enemy's weakness than upon his own power. It was, however, said that water was scarce with the garrison, and that their provision magazines could be burned.

Colonel Burgoyne conducted the operations of the engineers, Colonel Robe and Colonel Dickson those of the artillery, which consisted of three 18-pounders and the five iron 24-pound howitzers used at the siege of the Salamanca forts; and it was with regard to these slender means, rather than the defects of the fortress, that the line of attack was chosen. When the hornwork fell, a lodgment had been immediately commenced in the interior, and it was continued vigorously, although under a destructive fire from the Napoleon battery, because the besiegers feared the enemy would at daylight endeavour to retake the work by the gorge; good cover was, however, obtained in the night, and the first battery was begun. On the 21st the garrison mounted several fresh field-guns, and at night kept up a heavy fire of grape and shells on the workmen, who were digging a musketry trench in front of the first battery. The fire of the besieged was redoubled on the 22nd, but the besiegers worked with little loss, and their musketeers galled the enemy. In the night the first battery was armed with two 18-pounders and three howitzers, and a secret battery within the hornwork was commenced, and Lord Wellington now resolved to try an escalade against the first line of defence. He selected a point half-way between the suburb of San Pedro and the hornwork, and at midnight 400 men provided with ladders were secretly posted in a hollow road, fifty yards from the wall, which was from 23 to 25 feet high, but had no flanks; this was the main column, and a Portuguese battalion was also assembled in the town of Burgos to make a combined flank attack on that side.

The storm was commenced by the Portuguese, but they were repelled by the fire of the common guard alone, and the principal escalading party, which was composed of detachments from different regiments under Major Lawrie, 79th regiment, though acting with more courage, had as little success. The ladders were indeed placed, and the troops entered the ditch, yet all together and confusedly. Lawrie was killed, and the bravest soldiers who first mounted the ladders were bayoneted; combustible missiles were then thrown down in great abundance, and after a quarter of an hour's resistance the men gave way, leaving half their number behind. The wounded were brought off the next day under a truce. It is said that on the body of one of the officers killed the French found a complete plan of the siege, and it is certain that this disastrous attempt, which delayed the regular progress of the siege for two days, increased the enemy's courage, and produced a bad effect upon the allied troops, some of whom were already dispirited by the attack on the hornwork.

The hollow way from whence the escaladers had advanced, and which at only fifty yards' distance ran along the front of defence, was now converted into a parallel, and connected with the suburb of San Pedro. The trenches were made deep and narrow to secure them from the plunging shot of the castle, and musketeers were also planted to keep down the enemy's fire; but heavy rains incommoded the troops, and though the allied marksmen got the mastery over those of the French immediately in their front, the latter, having a raised and palisaded work on their own right, which in some measure flanked the approaches, killed so many of the besiegers that the latter were finally withdrawn.

In the night a flying sap was commenced from the right of the parallel, and was pushed within twenty yards of the enemy's first line of defence; but the directing engineer was killed, and with him many men; for the French plied their musketry sharply, and rolled large shells down the steep side of the hill. The head of the sap was indeed so commanded as it approached the wall, that a six-feet trench, added to the height of the gabion above, scarcely protected the workmen, wherefore the gallery of a mine was opened, and worked as rapidly as the inexperience of the miners, who were merely volunteers from the line, would permit.

The concealed battery within the hornwork of San Michael being completed, two 18-pounders were removed from the first battery to arm it, and they were replaced by two iron howitzers, which opened upon the advanced palisade below, to drive the French marksmen from that point; but after firing 140 rounds without success, this project was relinquished, and ammunition was so scarce that the soldiers were paid to collect the enemy's bullets. A zigzag was also commenced in front of the first battery and down the face of San Michael, to obtain footing for a musketry-trench to overlook the enemy's defences below; and on the 26th the gallery of the mine was advanced eighteen feet, and the soil was found favourable, but the men in passing the sap were hit fast by the French marksmen, and an assistant-engineer was killed. In the night the parallel was prolonged on the right within twenty yards of the enemy's ramparts, with a view to a second gallery and mine, and musketeers were planted there to oppose the enemy's marksmen and to protect the sap; at the same time the zigzag on the hill of San Michael was continued, and the musket-trench there was completed under cover of gabions, and with little loss, although the whole fire of the castle was concentrated on the spot.

The French were seen strengthening their second line on the 27th, and they had already cut a step along the edge of the counterpart for a covered way, and had palisaded the communication. Meanwhile the besiegers finished the musketry-trench on the right of their parallel, and opened the gallery for the second mine; but the first mine went on slowly; the men in the sap were galled and disturbed by stones, grenades, and small shells, which the French threw into the trenches by hand; and the artillery fire also knocked over the gabions of the musketry-trench on San Michael so fast, that the troops were withdrawn during the day.

In the night a trench of communication forming a second parallel behind the first was begun and nearly completed from the hill of San Michael towards the suburb of San Pedro, and the musketry-trench on the hill was deepened, and next day an attempt was made to perfect this new parallel of communication; but the French fire was heavy, and the shells which passed over came rolling down the hill again into the trench; so the work was deferred until night and was then perfected. The back-roll of the shells continued indeed to gall the troops, but the whole of this trench, that in front of the hornwork above, and that on the right of the parallel below, were filled with men whose fire was incessant. Moreover, the first mine was now completed and loaded with more than a thousand weight of powder, the gallery was strongly tamped for fifteen feet with bags of clay, and all being ready for the explosion, Wellington ordered the third assault.

At midnight the hollow road, fifty yards from the mine, was lined with troops to fire on the defences, and 300 men, composing the storming party, were assembled there, attended by others who carried tools and materials to secure the lodgment when the breach should be carried. The mine was then exploded, the wall fell, and an officer with twenty men rushed forward to the assault. The effect of the explosion was not so great as it ought to have been, yet it brought the wall down, the enemy was stupefied, and the forlorn hope, consisting of a sergeant and four daring soldiers, gained the summit of the breach, and there stood until the French, recovering, drove them down pierced with bayonet wounds. Meanwhile the officer and the twenty men, who were to have been followed by a party of fifty, and these by the remainder of the stormers, missed the breach in the dark, and finding the wall unbroken, returned, and reported that there was no breach. The main body immediately regained the trenches, and before the sergeant and his men returned with streaming wounds to tell their tale, the enemy was reinforced; and such was the scarcity of ammunition, that no artillery practice could be directed against the breach during the night; hence the French were enabled to raise a parapet behind it and to place obstacles on the ascent which deterred the besiegers from renewing the assault at daylight.

This failure arose from the darkness of the night and the want of a conducting engineer; for out of four regular officers of that branch engaged in the siege, one had been killed, one badly wounded, and one was sick, wherefore the remaining one was necessarily reserved for the conducting of the works. The aspect of affairs was gloomy. Twelve days had elapsed since the siege commenced, one assault had succeeded, two had failed, 1200 men had been killed or wounded, little progress had been made, and the troops generally showed symptoms of despondency, especially the Portuguese, who seemed to be losing their ancient spirit. In this state it was essential to make some change in the operations, and as the French marksmen in the advanced palisadoed work below were now become so expert that everything which could be seen from thence was hit, the howitzer battery on San Michael was reinforced with a French 8-pounder, by the aid of which this mischievous post was at last demolished. At the same time the gallery of a second mine was pushed forward, and a new breaching-battery for three guns was constructed behind it, so close to the enemy's defences that the latter screened the work from the artillery fire of their upper fortress; but the parapet of the battery was only made musket-proof, because the besieged had no guns on the lower line of this front.

In the night the three 18-pounders were brought from the hill of San Michael without being discovered, and at daylight, though a very galling fire of muskets thinned the workmen, they persevered until nine o'clock, when the battery was finished and armed. But at that moment the watchful Dubreton brought a howitzer down from the upper works, and with a low charge threw shells into the battery; then making a hole through a flank wall, he thrust out a light gun, which sent its bullets whizzing through the thin parapet at every round, and at the same time his marksmen plied their shot so sharply that the allies were driven from their pieces without firing a shot. More French cannon were now brought from the upper works, the defences of the battery were quite demolished, two of the gun-carriages were disabled, a trunnion was knocked off one of the 18-pounders, and the muzzle of another was split. And it was in vain that the besiegers' marksmen, aided by some officers who considered themselves good shots, endeavoured to quell the enemy's fire, the French being on a height were too well covered, and remained masters of the fight.

In the night a second and more solid battery was formed at a point a little to the left of the ruined one, but at daylight the French observed it; and their fire plunging from above, made the parapet fly off so rapidly, that the English general relinquished his intention and returned to his galleries and mines, and to his breaching-battery on the hill of San Michael. The two guns still serviceable were therefore removed towards the upper battery to beat down a retrenchment formed by the French behind the old breach. It was intended to have placed them in this new position on the night of the 3rd October, but the weather was very wet and stormy, and the workmen, those of the guards only excepted, abandoned the trenches; hence at daylight the guns were still short of their destination, and nothing more could be done until the following night.

On the 4th, at nine o'clock in the morning, the two 18-pounders and three iron howitzers, again opened from San Michael's, and at four o'clock in the evening, the old breach being cleared of all incumbrances, and the second mine being strongly tamped for explosion, a double assault was ordered. The second battalion of the 24th British regiment, commanded by Captain Hedderwick, was selected for this operation, and was formed in the hollow way, having one advanced party under Mr. Holmes pushed forward as close to the new mine as it was safe to be, and a second party under Mr. Fraser in like manner pushed towards the old breach.

At five o'clock the mine was exploded with a terrific effect, sending many of the French up into the air and breaking down 100 feet of the wall; the next instant Holmes and his brave men went rushing through the smoke and crumbling ruins, and Fraser, as quick and brave as his brother officer, was already fighting with the defenders on the summit of the old breach. The supports followed closely, and in a few minutes both points were carried, with a loss to the assailants of 37 killed and 200 wounded, seven of the latter being officers, and amongst them the conducting engineer. During the night lodgments were formed in advance of the old and on the ruins of the new breach, yet very imperfectly, and under a heavy destructive fire from the upper defences. But this happy attack revived the spirits of the army; vessels with powder were coming coastwise from Coruña, a convoy was expected by land from Ciudad Rodrigo, and as a supply of ammunition sent by Sir Home Popham had already reached the camp from Santander, the howitzers continued to knock away the palisades in the ditch, and the battery on San Michael's was directed to open a third breach at a point where the first French line of defence was joined to the second line.

This promising state of affairs was of short duration. On the 5th, at five o'clock in the evening, while the working parties were extending the lodgments, 300 French came swiftly down the hill, and sweeping away the labourers and guards from the trenches, killed or wounded 150 men, got possession of the old breach, destroyed the works, and carried off all the tools. However, in the night the allies repaired the damage and pushed saps from each flank to meet in the centre near the second French line, and to serve as a parallel to check future sallies. Meanwhile the howitzers on the San Michael continued their fire, yet ineffectually, against the palisades; the breaching-battery in the hornwork also opened, but it was badly constructed, and the guns being unable to see the wall sufficiently low, soon ceased to speak, the embrasures were therefore masked. On the other hand, the besieged were unable, from the steepness of the castle-hill, to depress their guns sufficiently to bear on the lodgment at the breaches in the first line, but their musketry was destructive, and they rolled down large shells to retard the approaches towards the second line.

On the 7th the besiegers had got so close to the wall below, that the howitzers above could no longer play without danger to the workmen, wherefore two French field-pieces, taken in the hornwork, were substituted, and did good service. The breaching-battery on San Michael's being altered, also renewed its fire, and at five o'clock had beaten down fifty feet from the parapet of the second line; but the enemy's return was heavy, and another 18-pounder lost a trunnion. However, in the night block-carriages with supports for the broken trunnions were provided, and the disabled guns were enabled to recommence their fire, yet with low charges. But a constant rain had now filled the trenches, the communications were injured, the workmen were negligent, the approaches to the second line went on slowly, and again Dubreton came thundering down from the upper ground, driving the guards and workmen from the new parallel at the lodgments, levelling all the works, carrying off all the tools, and killing or wounding 200 men. Colonel Cocks, promoted for his gallant conduct at the storming of San Michael, restored the fight and repulsed the French, but he fell dead on the ground he had recovered. He was a young man of a modest demeanour, brave, thoughtful, and enterprising, and he lived and died a good soldier.

After this severe check the approaches to the second line were abandoned, and the trenches were extended so as to embrace the whole of the fronts attacked; the battery on San Michael had meantime formed a practicable breach twenty-five feet wide, and the parallel at the old breach of the first line was prolonged by zigzags on the left towards this new breach, while a trench was opened to enable marksmen to fire upon the latter at thirty yards' distance. Nevertheless, another assault could not be risked because the great expenditure of powder had again exhausted the magazines, and without a new supply, the troops might have found themselves without ammunition in front of the French army, which was now gathering head near Briviesca. Heated shot were, however, thrown at the White Church with a view to burn the magazines; and the miners were directed to drive a gallery on the other side of the castle against the church of San Roman, a building pushed out a little beyond the French external line of defence on the side of the city.

The besiegers' ammunition was nearly all gone on the 10th, when a fresh supply arrived from Santander; but no effect had been produced upon the White Church, and Dubreton had strengthened his works to meet the assault; he had also isolated the new breach on one flank by a strong stockade extending at right angles from the second to the third line of defence. The fire from the Napoleon battery had obliged the besiegers again to withdraw their battering guns within the hornwork, and the attempt to burn the White Church was relinquished, but the gallery against San Roman was continued. In this state things remained for several days with little change, save that the French, despite the musketry from the nearest zigzag trench, had scarped eight feet at the top of the new breach and formed a small trench at the back.

The battery in the hornwork was again armed, and the guns pointed to breach the wall of the Napoleon battery; they were, however, overmatched and silenced in three-quarters of an hour, and the embrasures were once more altered, that the guns might bear on the breach in the second line. Some slight works and counter-works were also made on different points, but the besiegers were principally occupied repairing the mischief done by the rain, and in pushing the gallery under San Roman, where the French were now distinctly heard talking in the church; wherefore the mine there was formed and loaded with 900 pounds of powder. On the 17th October, the battery of the hornwork being renewed, the fire of the 18-pounders cleared away the enemy's temporary defences at the breach, the howitzers damaged the rampart on each side, and a small mine was sprung on the extreme right of the lower parallel, with a view to take possession of a cavalier or mound which the French had raised there, and from which they had killed many men in the trenches; it was successful, and a lodgment was effected; but the enemy soon returned in force and obliged the besiegers to abandon it again. However, on the 18th the new breach was rendered practicable, and Wellington ordered it to be stormed. The explosion of the mine under San Roman was to be the signal; that church was also to be assaulted, and at the same time a third detachment was to escalade the works in front of the ancient breach and thus connect the attacks.

At half-past four o'clock the springing of the mine at San Roman broke down a terrace in front of that building, yet with little injury to the church itself; the latter was, however, resolutely attacked by Colonel Browne at the head of some Spanish and Portuguese troops, and though the enemy sprung a counter-mine which brought the building down, the assailants lodged themselves in the ruins. Meanwhile 200 of the foot-guards, with strong supports, poured through the old breach in the first line and escaladed the second line, beyond which, in the open ground between the second and third lines, they were encountered by the French, and a sharp musketry fight commenced. At the same time a like number of the German legion, under Major Wurmb, similarly supported, stormed the new breach on the left of the guards so vigorously, that it was carried in a moment, and some men mounting the hill above, actually gained the third line. Unhappily, at neither of these assaults did the supports follow closely, and the Germans being cramped on their left by the enemy's stockade, extended by their right towards the guards, and at that critical moment Dubreton, who held his reserves well in hand, came dashing like a torrent from the upper ground, and in an instant cleared the breaches. Wurmb and many other brave men fell, and then the French, gathering round the guards, who were still unsupported, forced them beyond the outer line. More than 200 men and officers were killed or wounded in this combat, and the next night the enemy recovered San Roman by a sally. The siege was thus virtually terminated, for though the French were beaten out of San Roman again, and a gallery was opened from that church against the second line, and though two 24-pounders, sent from Santander by Sir Home Popham, had passed Reynosa on their way to Burgos, these were mere demonstrations.

The siege of Burgos was raised on the 21st October, the failure being more attributable to deficiency of means than to want of ardour or devotion in the besiegers, and the army retreated along miserable roads and in bad weather till it once more crossed the Duero, when the British again took nearly the same ground which they had occupied in July before the battle of Salamanca. The French forces now amounting to about 75,000 infantry and 12,000 cavalry, while the allies numbered only 48,000 infantry and 5000 cavalry, Wellington thought the disparity too great to risk a general action, though several minor engagements took place at various points, and continued to retreat farther till he reached the Agueda, and eventually went into cantonments at Ciudad Rodrigo, where dry bivouacs and fuel and the distribution of good rations soon restored the strength and spirits of the men, exhausted by their long marches over the marshy plains in severe weather. Thus ended the campaign of 1812, in all respects one of the most masterly, if not the most brilliant, which Lord Wellington had yet undertaken.

In one of the many minor engagements which took place between the retiring and pursuing forces, Sir Edward Paget was taken prisoner almost in the centre of the allied army. "A detachment of French light troops were concealed in a wood on the road to Ciudad Rodrigo, and Sir Edward Paget observing an interval between the fifth and seventh divisions of infantry, rode alone to the rear to inquire into the cause by which the progress of the latter had been delayed. On his return he missed his way, and fell into the hands of the enemy. By this unlucky accident his country, at a moment of peculiar need, was deprived of the services of one of the bravest and most distinguished of her leaders."

CHAPTER XII.

BATTLE OF VITTORIA—FIRST SIEGE OF SAN SEBASTIAN.

N the early months of 1813 the allied forces were distributed in a very extensive line, and preparations for a general advance were made in the beginning of May, these preparations being of such a character as that, if rightly carried out, they would fully sweep the invaders over their own frontier. The British moved in three bodies—one under Sir Thomas Graham, to pass over the Duero; the right under Sir Rowland Hill, proceeding by Salamanca, and both to concentrate with the centre under Wellington at Valladolid. The enemy were utterly unprepared for these movements, which were carried through with the most perfect success, and the officer commanding at Salamanca had barely time to abandon the town when it was entered by the British cavalry, as the possibility of the allies crossing the Duero within the Portuguese frontier had never been contemplated. The rapid advance of the allies placed Madrid again in peril, and King Joseph abandoned the capital and sought to effect a junction with the army of the north and make a stand at Burgos, a battle for the preservation of which was confidently anticipated, but did not take place. Being vigorously pressed here by General Hill, the French retired from the town, after destroying as far as possible the defences of the castle, and, whether from hurry or negligence or want of skill, the mines exploded outwards at the very moment when a column of infantry was defiling under the castle. Several streets were laid

P

in ruins, thousands of shells and other combustibles which had been left in the place were ignited and driven upwards with a horrible crash, the hills rocked above the devoted column, and a shower of iron, timber, and stony fragments falling on it, in an instant destroyed more than three hundred men.

The French still pursued their way till they reached the Ebro, the passage of which every preparation was made to defend. Resorting to similar tactics here as he pursued at the Duero, Wellington crossed the Ebro at a farther point, and the allied army pushed its way through a difficult country to Vittoria, not without much obstruction from the enemy, who here was compelled to make a decisive stand or be driven ingloriously headlong on the Pyrenees. Wellington halted on the 20th June to rally his columns, as the rear of the British had been much scattered in the previous marches, and taking this opportunity to examine the position of the French armies, observed that they seemed steadfast to fight, whereupon he made his own arrangements and formed his forces for three distinct battles. At Vittoria King Joseph concentrated the various French corps under Generals Drouet, Leval, Gazan, Reille, and Villatte, these having been driven onwards across the country by the different columns of the allies under Hill, Graham, and Lord Wellington, who also had concentrated at this point.

The long-expected conflict was now at hand, and on neither side were the numbers and courage of the troops of mean account. The allies had lost about 200 killed and wounded in the previous operations, and the sixth division, 6500 strong, was left at Medina de Pomar; hence only 60,000 Anglo-Portuguese sabres and bayonets, with 90 pieces of cannon, were actually in the field, but the Spanish auxiliaries were above 20,000, and the whole army, including sergeants and artillerymen, exceeded 80,000 combatants. For the French side, as the regular muster-roll of their troops was lost with the battle, an approximation to their strength must suffice. The number killed and taken in different recent combats was about 2000 men, and some 5000 had marched to France with two convoys. On the other hand, Sarrut's division, the garrison of Vittoria, and the many smaller posts relinquished by the army of the north, had increased the King's forces, and hence, by a comparison with former returns, it would appear that, in the gross, about 70,000 men were present. But in the number and size of their guns the French had the advantage.

The defects of King Joseph's position were apparent both in the general arrangements and in the details. His best line of retreat was on the prolongation of his right flank, which being at Gamara Mayor, close to Vittoria, was too distant to be supported by the main body of the army. Instead of having the rear clear and the field of battle free, many thousand carriages and impediments of all kinds were heaped about Vittoria, blocking all the roads, and creating confusion amongst the artillery parks. Maransin's brigade, placed on the heights above Puebla, was isolated, and too weak to hold that ground. The centre indeed occupied an easy range of hills, its front was open, with a slope to the river, and powerful batteries seemed to bar all access by the bridges; nevertheless many of the guns being pushed with an advanced post into a deep loop of the Zadora, were within musket-shot of a wood on the right bank, which was steep and rugged, so that the allies found good cover close to the river.

There were seven bridges within the scheme of the operations, namely, the bridge of La Puebla, on the French left beyond the defile; the bridge of Nanclares, facing Subijana de Alava and the French end of the defile of Puebla; then three bridges which, placed around the deep loop of the river before mentioned, opened altogether upon the right of the French centre, that of Mendoza being highest up the stream, that of Vellodas lowest down the stream, and that of Tres Puentes in the centre; lastly, the bridges of Gamara Mayor and Ariaga on the Upper Zadora, opposite Vittoria, which were guarded by General Reille, completed the number, and none of the seven were either broken or entrenched.

Wellington formed his plans accordingly. Sir Thomas Graham, moving from Murguia by the Bilbao road, was to fall on Reille, and if possible to force the passage of the river at Gamara Mayor and Ariaga; by this movement the French would be completely turned, and the greatest part of their forces shut up between the Puebla mountains on one side and the Zadora on the other. Sir Rowland Hill was to attack the enemy's left, and his corps, also about 20,000 strong, was composed of Morillo's Spaniards, Sylveira's Portuguese, and the second British division, together with some cavalry and guns. It was destined to force the passage of the Zadora, to assail the French troops on the heights beyond, to thread the defile of La Puebla and to enter the basin of Vittoria, thus turning and menacing all the French left and securing the passage of the Zadora at the bridge of Nanclares.

The centre attack, directed by Wellington in person, consisted of the third, fourth, seventh, and light divisions of infantry, the great mass of the artillery, the heavy cavalry, and D'Urban's Portuguese horsemen, in all nearly 30,000 combatants. They were encamped along the Bayas, from Subijana Morillas to Ulivallo, and had only to march across the ridges which formed the basin of Vittoria on that side to come down to their different points of attack on the Zadora, that is to say, the bridges of Mendoza, Tres Puentes, Villodas, and Nanclares. But so rugged was the country and the communications between the different columns so difficult, that no exact concert could be expected, and each general of division was in some degree master of his movements.

Battle of Vittoria.

At daybreak on the 21st June 1813, the weather being rainy with a thick vapour, the troops moved from their camps on the Bayas, and the centre of the army advancing by columns from the right and left of the line, passed the ridges in front, and entering the basin of Vittoria, slowly approached the Zadora. The left-hand column pointed to Mendoza, the right-hand column skirted the ridge of Morillas, on the other side of which Hill was marching, and that general, having seized the village of Puebla about ten o'clock, commenced passing the river there. Morillo's Spaniards led, and their first brigade, moving on a by-way, assailed the mountain to the right of the great road; the ascent was so steep that the soldiers appeared to climb rather than to walk up; and the second Spanish brigade, being to connect the first with the British troops below, ascended only half way. Little or no opposition was made until the first brigade was near the summit, when a sharp skirmishing commenced, and Morillo was wounded but would not quit the field. His second brigade joined him, and the French, feeling the importance of the height, reinforced Maransin with a fresh regiment. Then Hill succoured Morillo with the 71st regiment and a battalion of light infantry, both

under Colonel Cadogan; yet the fight was doubtful, for though the British secured the summit and gained ground along the side of the mountain, Cadogan, a brave officer and of high promise, fell, and Gazan calling Villatte's division from behind Ariñez, sent it to the succour of his side; and so strongly did these troops fight that the battle remained stationary, the allies being scarcely able to hold their ground. Hill, however, again sent fresh troops to their assistance, and with the remainder of his corps passing the Zadora, threaded the long defile of Puebla, and fiercely issuing forth on the other side, won the village of Subijana de Alava in front of Gazan's line; he thus connected his own right with the troops on the mountain, and maintained this forward position in despite of the enemy's vigorous efforts to dislodge him.

Meanwhile Wellington had brought the fourth and light divisions, the heavy cavalry, the hussars, and D'Urban's Portuguese horsemen down to the Zadora. The fourth division was placed opposite the bridge of Nanclares, the light division opposite the bridge of Villodas; both well covered by rugged ground and woods, and the light division was so close to the water, that their skirmishers could with ease have killed the French gunners of the advanced post in the loop of the river at Villodas. The weather had cleared up, and when Hill's battle began, the riflemen of the light division, spreading along the bank, exchanged a biting fire with the enemy's skirmishers, but no serious effort was made, because the third and seventh divisions, meeting with rough ground, had not reached their point of attack; and it would have been imprudent to push the fourth division and the cavalry over the bridge of Nanclares, and thus crowd a great body of troops in front of the Puebla defile before the other divisions were ready to attack the right and centre of the enemy.

While thus waiting, a Spanish peasant told Wellington that the bridge of Tres Puentes, on the left of the light division, was unguarded, and offered to guide the troops over it. Kempt's brigade of the light division was instantly directed towards this point, and being concealed by some rocks from the French, and well led by the brave peasant, they passed the narrow bridge at a running pace, mounted a steep curving rise of ground, and halted close under the crest on the enemy's side of the river, being then actually behind the King's advanced post, and within a few hundred yards of his line of battle. Some French cavalry immediately approached, and two round shots were fired by the enemy, one of which killed the poor peasant to whose courage and intelligence the allies were so much indebted; but as no movement of attack was made, Kempt called the 15th hussars over the river, and they came at a gallop, crossing the narrow bridge one by one, horseman after horseman, and still the French remained torpid, showing that there was an army there, but no general.

It was now one o'clock; Hill's assault on the village of Subijana de Alava was developed, and a curling smoke, faintly seen far up the Zadora on the enemy's extreme right, being followed by the dull sound of distant guns, showed that Graham's attack had also commenced. Then the King, finding both his flanks in danger, caused his reserve about Gomecha to file off towards Vittoria, and gave Gazan orders to retire by successive masses with the army of the south. But at that moment the third and seventh divisions having reached their ground, were seen moving rapidly down to the bridge of Mendoza; the enemy's artillery opened upon them, a body of cavalry drew near the bridge, and the French light troops, which were very strong there, commenced a vigorous musketry. Some British guns replied to the French cannon from the opposite bank, and the value of Kempt's forward position was instantly made manifest; for Colonel Andrew Barnard, springing forward, led the riflemen of the light division, in the most daring manner, between the French cavalry and the river, taking their light troops and gunners in flank, and engaging them so closely that the English artillerymen, thinking his darkly clothed troops were enemies, played upon both alike. This singular attack enabled a brigade of the third division to pass the bridge of Mendoza without opposition; the other brigade forded the river higher up, and the seventh division and Vandeleur's brigade of the light division followed. The French advanced post immediately abandoned the ground in front of Villodas, and the battle, which had before somewhat slackened, revived with extreme violence. Hill pressed the enemy harder, the fourth division passed the bridge of Nanclares, the smoke and sound of Graham's attack became more distinct, and the banks of the Zadora presented a continuous line of fire. However, the French, weakened in the centre by the draft made of Villatte's division, and having their confidence shaken by the King's order to retreat, were in evident perplexity, and no regular retrograde movement could be made, the allies were too close.

The seventh division and Colville's brigade of the third division, which had forded the river, formed the left of the British, and they were immediately engaged with the French right. Almost at the same time Lord Wellington, seeing the hill in front of Arinez nearly denuded of troops by the withdrawal of Villatte's corps, carried Picton and the rest of the third division in close columns of regiments at a running pace diagonally across the front of both armies towards that central point; this attack was headed by Barnard's riflemen, and followed by the remainder of Kempt's brigade and the hussars, but the other brigade of the light division acted in support of the seventh division. At the same time General Cole advanced with the fourth division from the bridge of Nanclares, and the heavy cavalry, a splendid body, also passing the river, galloped up, squadron after squadron, into the plain ground between Cole's right and Hill's left. The French, thus caught in the midst of their dispositions for retreat, threw out a prodigious number of skirmishers, and fifty pieces of artillery played with astonishing activity. To answer this fire Wellington brought over several brigades of British guns, and both sides were shrouded by a dense cloud of smoke and dust, under cover of which the French retired by degrees to the second range of heights in front of Gomecha, on which their reserve had been posted, but they still held the village of Arinez on the main road. Picton's troops, headed by the riflemen, plunged into that village amidst a heavy fire of musketry and artillery, and in an instant three guns were captured; but the post was important; fresh French troops came down, and for some time the smoke and dust and clamour, the flashing of the fire-arms, and the shouts and cries of the combatants, mixed with the thundering of the guns, were terrible, yet finally the British troops issued forth victorious on the other side. During this conflict the seventh division, reinforced by Vandeleur's brigade of the light division, was heavily raked by a battery at the village of Margarita, until the 52nd regiment, led by Colonel Gibbs, with an impetuous charge drove the French guns away and carried the village, and at the same time the 87th under Colonel Gough won the village of Hermandad. Then the whole advanced fighting on the left of Picton's attack, and on the right hand of that general the fourth division also made way, though more slowly because of the rugged ground.

When Picton and Kempt's brigades had carried the village of Arinez and gained the main road, the French troops near Subijana de Alava were turned, and being hard pressed on their front and on their left flank by the troops on the summit of the mountain, fell back for two miles in a disordered mass, striving to regain the great line of retreat to Vittoria. It was thought that some cavalry launched against them at the moment would have totally disorganised the whole French battle and secured several thousand prisoners, but this was not done; the confused multitude, shooting ahead of the advancing British lines, recovered order, and as the ground was exceedingly diversified, being in some places wooded, in others open, here covered with high corn, there broken by ditches, vineyards, and hamlets, the action for six miles resolved itself into a running fight and cannonade, the dust and smoke and tumult of which filled all the basin, passing onwards towards Vittoria.

Many guns were taken as the army advanced, and at six o'clock the French reached the last defensible height, one mile in front of Vittoria. Behind them was the plain in which the city stood, and beyond the city thousands of carriages and animals and non-combatants, men, women, and children, were crowding together, in all the madness of terror, and as the English shot went booming overhead, the vast crowd started and swerved with a convulsive movement, while a dull and horrid sound of distress arose; but there was no hope, no stay for army or multitude. It was the wreck of a nation. However, the courage of the French soldier was not yet quelled. Reille, on whom everything now depended, maintained his post on the Upper Zadora, and the armies of the south and centre drawing up on their last heights, made their muskets flash like lightning, while more than eighty pieces of artillery massed together pealed with such a horrid uproar that the hills laboured and shook, and streamed with fire and smoke, amidst which the dark figures of the French gunners were seen bounding with a frantic energy.

This terrible cannonade and musketry kept the allies in check,

BATTLE OF VITTORIA.

and scarcely could the third division, which was still the foremost and bore the brunt of this storm, maintain its advanced position. Again the battle became stationary, and the French generals had commenced drawing off their infantry in succession from the right wing, when suddenly the fourth division rushing forward, carried the hill on the French left, and the heights were at once abandoned. It was at this very moment that Joseph, finding the royal road so completely blocked by carriages that the artillery could not pass, indicated the road of Salvatierra as the line of retreat, and the army went off in a confused yet compact body on that side, leaving Vittoria on its left. The British infantry followed hard, and the light cavalry galloped through the town to intercept the new line of retreat, which was through a marsh; but this road also was choked with carriages and fugitive people, while on each side there were deep drains. Thus all became disorder and mischief, the guns were left on the edge of the marsh, the artillerymen and drivers fled with the horses, and, breaking through the miserable multitude, the vanquished troops went off by Metauco towards Salvatierra. However, their cavalry still covered the retreat with some vigour, and many of those generous horsemen were seen taking up children and women to carry off from the dreadful scene.

The result of the last attack had placed Reille, of whose battle it is now time to treat, in great danger. His advanced troops under Sarrut had been placed at the village of Aranguis, and they also occupied some heights on their right, which covered both the bridges of Ariaga and Gamara Mayor, but they had been driven from both the village and the height a little after twelve o'clock by General Oswald, who commanded the head of Graham's column, consisting of the fifth division, Longa's Spaniards, and Pack's Portuguese. Longa then seized Gamara Menor, on the Durango road, while another detachment gained the royal road still farther on the left, and forced the Franco-Spaniards to retire from Durana. Thus the first blow on this side had deprived the King of his best line of retreat, and confined him to the road of Pampeluna. However, Sarrut re-crossed the river in good order, and a new disposition was made by Reille. One of Sarrut's brigades defended the bridge of Ariaga, and the village of Abechuco beyond it; the other was in reserve, equally supporting

Sarrut and La Martiniere, who defended the bridge of Gamara
Mayor and the village of that name beyond the river.

Oswald commenced the attack at Gamara with some guns and
Robinson's brigade of the fifth division. Longa's Spaniards were
to have led, and at an early hour, when Gamara was feebly
occupied, but they did not stir, and the village was meanwhile
reinforced. However, Robinson's brigade being formed in three
columns, made the assault at the running pace. At first the fire
of the artillery and musketry was so heavy that the British troops
stopped and commenced firing also, and the three columns got
intermixed; yet, encouraged by their officers, and especially by
the example of General Robinson, an inexperienced man, but of
high and daring spirit, they renewed the charge, broke through
the village, and even crossed the bridge. One gun was captured,
and the passage seemed to be won, when Reille suddenly turned
twelve pieces upon the village, and La Martiniere, rallying his
division under cover of this cannonade, retook the bridge. It
was with difficulty the allied troops could even hold the village
until they were reinforced. Then a second British brigade came
down, and, the royals leading, the bridge was again carried, but
again these new troops were driven back in the same manner as
the others had been. Thus the bridge remained forbidden ground.

Reille, though considerably inferior in numbers, continued to
interdict the passage of the river until the tumult of Wellington's
battle, coming up the Zadora, reached Vittoria itself, and a part
of the British horsemen rode out of that city upon Sarrut's rear.
Digeon's dragoons kept this cavalry in check for the moment, and
some time before Reille, seeing the retrograde movement of the
King, had formed a reserve of infantry under General Fririon at
Betonia, which now proved his safety. For Sarrut was killed at
the bridge of Ariaga, and General Menne, the next in command,
could scarcely draw off his troops while Digeon's dragoons held
the British cavalry at point; but with the aid of Fririon's reserve,
Reille covered the movement, and rallied all his troops at Betonia.
He had now to make head on several sides, because the allies
were coming down from Ariaga, from Durana, and from Vittoria,
yet he fought his way to Metauco on the Salvatierra road, covering
the general retreat with some degree of order. Vehemently and
closely did the British pursue, and neither the resolute demeanour

BATTLE OF VITTORIA.   235

of the French cavalry, which was covered on the flanks by some light troops, and made several vigorous charges, nor the night, which now fell, could stop their victorious career until the flying masses of the enemy had cleared all obstacles, and passing Metauco, got beyond the reach of further injury. Thus ended the battle of Vittoria; the French escaped, indeed, with comparatively little loss of men, but "they lost all their equipages, all their guns, all their treasure, all their stores, all their papers, so that no man could prove how much pay was due to him; generals and subordinate officers alike were reduced to the clothes on their backs, and most of them were barefooted."

Never was an army more hardly used by its commander, for the soldiers were not half beaten, and never was a victory more complete. The trophies were innumerable. The French carried off but two pieces of artillery from the battle. Jourdan's baton of command, a stand of colours, 143 brass pieces, 100 of which had been used in the fight, all the parks and depôts from Madrid, Valladolid, and Burgos, carriages, ammunition, treasure, everything fell into the hands of the victors. The loss in men did not however exceed 6000, exclusive of some hundreds of prisoners; the loss of the allies was nearly as great, the gross numbers being 5176 killed, wounded, and missing. Of these, 1049 were Portuguese and 553 were Spanish; hence the loss of the English was more than double that of the Portuguese and Spaniards together; and yet both fought well, and especially the Portuguese, but British troops are the soldiers of battle. Marshal Jourdan's baton was taken by the 87th regiment, and the spoil was immense; but to such extent was plunder carried, principally by the followers and non-combatants, for with some exceptions the fighting troops may be said to have marched upon gold and silver without stooping to pick it up, that of five millions and a half of dollars indicated by the French accounts to be in the money-chests, not one dollar came to the public, and Wellington sent fifteen officers with power to stop and examine all loaded animals passing the Ebro and the Duero in hopes to recover the sums so shamefully carried off. Neither was this disgraceful conduct confined to ignorant and vulgar people. Some officers were seen mixed up with the mob and contending for the disgraceful gain.

No victory than that of Vittoria was more decisive and complete

—darkness and the nature of the ground alone favouring the escape of the routed and disorganised French battalions. Of the two guns carried off from the field by the French, one only reached Pampeluna, the other being taken next day; while he who passed over the Pyrenees as a monarch, now re-crossed them a fugitive, and the whole plunder of Spain was disgorged in a moment.

When Lord Wellington first commenced his onward march to Vittoria, he had also put in motion every other armed body of the allies against the French throughout the Peninsula, and in this way Sir John Murray proceeded against General Suchet at Tarragona on the Mediterranean coast; but the English general's operations here were altogether fruitless of good to the general cause. On the 12th April Murray fought the battle of Castalla, in which neither side could claim a victory, but one incident of this engagement may here be given. The ground on which Castalla was fought having an abrupt declination near the top, enabled the French to form a line under cover close to the British, who were lying down waiting for orders to charge; and while the former were unfolding their masses, a grenadier officer, advancing alone, challenged the captain of the 27th grenadiers to single combat. Waldron, an agile vigorous Irishman, and of boiling courage, instantly sprung forward, the hostile lines looked on without firing a shot, the swords of the champions glittered in the sun, the Frenchman's head was cleft in twain, and the next instant the 27th jumping up with a deafening shout, fired a deadly volley at half pistol-shot distance, and then charged with such a shock, that, despite their bravery and numbers, the enemy's soldiers were overthrown, and the side of the sierra was covered with the killed and wounded. Murray also laid siege to Tarragona, but failed completely in all his efforts, and even lost the battering train which had already shook the bloody ramparts of Badajos.

After the battle of Vittoria Sir Thomas Graham was directed to advance on the 22nd June towards Bilboa to intercept General Foy, but the latter, collecting all his detachments, retreated before Graham to Bayonne; whilst Wellington by a series of brilliant attacks drove the French army under King Joseph from post to post till forced to seek safety in a rapid retreat across the Pyrenees. The French garrisons of Pampeluna and San Sebastian now alone remained, and preparations were at once made for the reduction of both these fortresses—the first was blockaded by a force of Spaniards under O'Donnell, and encircled with entrenchments to prevent the escape of the garrison, while Sir Thomas Graham with two divisions invested Sebastian, which place was built on a low sandy isthmus formed by the harbour on one side and the river Urumea on the other. Behind it rose the Monte Orgullo, a rugged cone nearly 400 feet high, washed by the ocean and crowned with the small castle of La Mota. Its southern face, overlooking the town, was cut off from it by a line of defensive works and covered with batteries; but La Mota itself was commanded, at a distance of 1300 yards, by the Monte Olia on the other side of the Urumea.

SAN SEBASTIAN.

When the battle of Vittoria happened, San Sebastian was nearly dismantled; many of the guns had been removed to form battering trains or to arm smaller ports on the coast; there were no bomb-proofs nor palisades nor outworks, the wells were foul and the place was supplied with water by a single aqueduct. Joseph's defeat restored its importance as a fortress. General Emanuel Rey entered it the 22nd of June, bringing with him the escort of a convoy which had quitted Vittoria the day before the battle. The town was thus filled with emigrant Spanish families, with the ministers and other persons attached to the court; the population, ordinarily 8000, was increased to 16,000, and disorder and confusion were predominant. Rey, pushed by necessity, immediately forced all persons not residents to march at once to France, granting them only a guard of 100 men; the people of quality went by sea, the others by land, and fortunately all arrived safely, for the guerillas would have given them no quarter. Before General Graham arrived the French had constructed a redoubt on the heights of San Bartolomeo, and connected it with the convent of that name, which they also fortified. These outworks were supported by posts in the ruined houses of the suburb of San Martin behind, and by a low circular redoubt formed of casks on the main road, half way between the convent and the hornwork. Hence, to reduce the place, working along the isthmus, it was necessary to carry in succession three lines of defence covering the town, and a fourth at the foot of Monte Orgullo, before the castle of La Mota could be assailed. Seventy-six pieces of artillery were mounted upon these works, and others were afterwards obtained from France by sea.

The besieging army consisted of the fifth division under General Oswald, and the independent Portuguese brigades of J. Wilson and Bradford, reinforced by detachments from the first division. Thus, including the artillerymen, some seamen commanded by Lieutenant O'Reilly of the *Surveillante*, and 100 regular sappers and miners, now for the first time used in the sieges of the Peninsula, nearly 10,000 men were employed. The guns available for the attack, in the first instance, were a new battering train, originally prepared for the siege of Burgos, to which were added six 24-pounders lent by the ships of war, and six 18-pounders which had moved with the army from Portugal, making altogether forty pieces, commanded by Colonel Dickson. The distance from the depôt of siege at Passages to the Chofre sandhills was one mile and a half of good road, and a pontoon bridge was laid over the Urumea river above the Chofres, but from thence to the height of Bartolomeo were more than five miles of very bad road.

Early in July the fortress had been twice closely examined by Major Smith, who proposed a plan of siege founded upon the facility furnished by the Chofre hills to destroy the flanks, rake the principal front, and form a breach with the same batteries, the works being at the same time secured, except at low water, by the Urumea. Counter-batteries, to be constructed on the left of that river, were to rake the line of defence in which the breach was to be formed; and against the castle and its outworks he relied principally upon vertical fire, instancing the reduction of Fort Bourbon in the West Indies in proof of its efficacy. This plan would probably have reduced San Sebastian in a reasonable time without any remarkable loss of men, and Lord Wellington approving of it, though he doubted the efficacy of the vertical fire, ordered the siege to be commenced. He renewed his approval afterwards when he had examined the works in person, and all his orders were in the same spirit; but neither the plan nor his orders being followed, the siege, which should have been an ordinary event of war, has obtained a mournful celebrity. Active operations were commenced on the night of the 10th by the construction of two batteries against the convent and redoubt of San Bartolomeo; and on the night of the 13th four batteries to contain twenty of the heaviest guns and four 8-inch howitzers were marked out on the Chofre sandhills, at distances varying from 600 to 1300 yards from the eastern rampart of the town. The river was supposed to be unfordable, wherefore no parallel of support was made, yet good trenches of communications, and subsequently regular approaches, were formed. Two attacks were thus established, and most of the troops were encamped on the right bank to facilitate a junction with the covering army in the event of a general battle.

On the 14th a French sloop entered the harbour with supplies, and the batteries of the left attack, under the direction of the German major, Hartman, opened against San Bartolomeo, throwing hot shot into that building. The besieged responded with musketry from the redoubt, with heavy guns from the town, and with a field-piece which they had mounted on the belfry of the convent itself. On the 15th of July Sir Richard Fletcher took the chief command of the engineers, but Major Smith retained the direction of the attack from the Chofre hills, and Lord Wellington's orders continued to pass through his hands. This day the batteries of the left attack, aided by some howitzers from the right of the Urumea, set the convent on fire, silenced the musketry of the besieged, and so damaged the defences that the Portuguese troops attached to the fifth division were ordered to feel the enemy's post. They were, however, repulsed with great loss, the French sallied, and the firing did not cease until nightfall. A battery for seven additional guns to play against Bartolomeo was commenced on the right of the Urumea, and the original batteries set fire to the convent several times, but the flames were extinguished by the garrison. On the 17th, the convent being nearly in ruins, the assault was ordered without waiting for the effect of the new battery raised on the other side of the Urumea. The storming party was formed in two columns. Detachments from Wilson's Portuguese, supported by the light company of the 9th British regiment and three companies of the royals, composed the right, which, under the direction of General Hay, was destined to assail the redoubt. General Bradford directed the left, which, being composed of Portuguese, supported by three companies of the 9th British regiment under Colonel Cameron, was ordered to assail the convent.

At ten o'clock in the morning two heavy 6-pounders opened against the redoubt; and a sharp fire of musketry in return from the French, who had been reinforced and occupied the suburb of San Martin, announced their resolution to fight. The allied troops were assembled behind the crest of the hill overlooking the convent, and the first signal was given; but the Portuguese advanced slowly at both attacks, and the supporting companies of the 9th regiment on each side passing through them, fell upon the enemy with the usual impetuosity of British soldiers. Colonel Cameron, while leading his grenadiers down the face of the hill, was exposed to a heavy cannonade from the hornwork, but he soon gained the cover of a wall fifty yards from the convent, and there awaited the second signal. However, his rapid advance, which threatened to cut off the garrison from the suburb, joined to the fire of the two 6-pounders and that of some other field-pieces on the farther side of the Urumea, caused the French to abandon the redoubt. Seeing this, Cameron jumped over the wall and assaulted both the convent and the houses of the suburb. At the latter a fierce struggle ensued, and Captain Woodman of the 9th was killed in the upper room of a house after fighting his way up from below; but the grenadiers carried the convent with such rapidity that the French, unable to explode some small mines they had prepared, hastily joined the troops in the suburb. There, however, the fighting continued, and Colonel Cameron's force being very much reduced, the affair was becoming doubtful, when the remaining companies of his regiment, which he had sent for after the attack commenced, arrived, and the suburb was with much fighting entirely won. At the right attack the company of the 9th, although retarded by a ravine, by a thick hedge, by the slowness of the Portuguese, and by a heavy fire, entered the abandoned redoubt with little loss, but the troops were then rashly led against the cask redoubt, contrary to General Oswald's orders, and were beaten back by the enemy.

The loss of the French was 240 men, that of the allies considerable; the companies of the 9th, under Colonel Cameron, alone had seven officers and sixty men killed or wounded. When the action ceased, the engineers made a lodgment in the redoubt, and commenced two batteries for eight pieces to rake the hornwork and the eastern rampart of the place.

The result of the attack on the 20th was not satisfactory, the weather proved bad, the guns mounted on ship-carriages failed, one 24-pounder was rendered unserviceable by the enemy, another became useless from an accident, a captain of engineers was killed, and the besiegers' shot had little effect upon the solid wall. In the night, however, the ship-guns were mounted on better carriages, and a parallel across the isthmus was projected; but the greatest part of the workmen, to avoid a tempest, sought shelter in the suburb of San Martin, and when day broke only one-third of the work was performed.

The besiegers' batteries ceased firing on the 21st, to allow of a summons, but the governor refused to receive the letter and the firing was resumed. The main wall still resisted, yet the parapets and embrasures crumbled away fast, and the batteries on Monte Olia plunged into the hornwork, although at 1600 yards distance, with such effect that the besieged having no bomb-proofs were forced to dig trenches to protect themselves. The counter-fire directed solely against the breaching batteries was feeble, but at midnight a shell thrown from the castle into the bay gave the signal for a sally, and during the firing which ensued several French vessels with supplies entered the harbour. This night also the besieged isolated the breach by cuts in the rampart and other defences. On the other hand, the besiegers' parallel across the isthmus was completed, and in its progress laid bare the mouth of a drain, four feet high and three feet wide, containing the pipe of the aqueduct cut off by the Spaniards. Through this dangerous opening Lieutenant Reid of the engineers, a young and zealous officer, crept even to the counterscarp of the hornwork, and finding the passage there closed by a door returned without an accident. Thirty barrels of powder were placed in this drain, and eight feet was stopped with sandbags, thus forming a globe of compression designed to blow, as through a tube, so much rubbish over the counterscarp as might fill the narrow ditch of the hornwork.

On the 22nd the fire from the batteries, unexampled from its rapidity and accuracy, opened what appeared a practicable breach in the eastern flank wall between two towers. The counter-fire

Q

of the besieged now slackened, but the descent into the town behind the breach was more than twelve feet perpendicular, and the garrison were seen from Monte Olia diligently working at the interior defences to receive the assault : they added also another gun to the battery of St. Elmo to flank the front attack. On the other hand, the besiegers had placed four 68-pound carronades in battery to play on the defences of the breach, but the fire on both sides slackened because the guns were greatly enlarged at the vents with constant practice. On the 23rd, the besiegers judging the breach between the towers quite practicable, turned the guns to break the wall on the right of the main breach, and in the course of the day, the wall being thin, the stroke heavy and quick, a second breach, thirty feet wide, was rendered practicable.

The defensive fire of the besieged being now much diminished, the 10-inch mortars and 68-pound carronades were turned upon the defences of the great breach, and upon a stockade which separated the high curtain, on the land front, from the lower works of the flank against which the attack was conducted. The houses near the breach were soon in flames, which spread rapidly, destroying some of the defences of the besieged and menacing the whole town with destruction. The assault was ordered for the next morning. But when the troops assembled in the trenches the burning houses appeared so formidable that the attack was deferred and the batteries again opened, partly against the second breach, partly against the defences, partly to break the wall in a third place between the half bastion of St. John on the land front and the main breach.

On the night of the 24th, Sir Thomas Graham renewed the order for the assault, when 2000 men of the fifth division filed into the trenches on the isthmus. This force was composed of the third battalion of the royals under Major Frazer, destined to storm the great breach ; the 38th regiment under Colonel Greville, designed to assail the lesser and most distant breach ; the 9th regiment under Colonel Cameron, appointed to support the royals ; finally a detachment, selected from the light companies of all those battalions, was placed in the centre of the royals under the command of Lieutenant Campbell of the 9th regiment. This chosen detachment, accompanied by the engineer Machel with a ladder-party, was intended to sweep the high curtain after the breach should be won.

The distance from the trenches to the points of attack was more than 3000 yards along the contracted space lying between the retaining wall of the hornwork and the river; the ground was strewed with rocks covered by slippery sea-weeds; the tide had left large and deep pools of water; the parapet of the hornwork was entire as well as the retaining wall; the parapets of the other works and the two towers, which closely flanked the breach, although injured, were far from being ruined, and every place was thickly garnished with musketeers. The difficulties of the attack were obvious, and a detachment of Portuguese placed in a trench opened beyond the parallel on the isthmus, within sixty yards of the ramparts, was ordered to quell if possible the fire of the hornwork.

While it was still dark the storming columns moved out of the trenches, and the globe of compression in the drain was exploded with great effect against the counterscarp and glacis of the hornwork. The garrison, astonished by the unlooked-for event, abandoned the flanking parapet, and the troops rushed onwards, the stormers for the main breach leading and suffering more from the fire of their own batteries on the right of the Urumea than from the enemy. Major Frazer and the engineer Harry Jones first reached the breach. The enemy had fallen back in confusion behind the ruins of the still burning houses, and those brave officers rushed up expecting that their troops would follow, but not many followed, for it was extremely dark, the natural difficulties of the way had contracted the front and disordered the column in its whole length, and the soldiers, straggling and out of wind, arrived in small disconnected parties at the foot of the breach. The foremost gathered near their gallant leaders, but the depth of the descent into the town, and the volumes of flames and smoke which still issued from the burning houses behind, awed the stoutest; and more than two-thirds of the storming column, irritated by the destructive flank fire, had broken off to commence a musketry battle with the enemy on the rampart. Meanwhile the shells from the Monte Orgullo fell rapidly, the defenders of the breach rallied, and with a smashing musketry from the ruins and loopholed houses smote the head of the column, while the men in the towers smote them on the flanks; and from every quarter came showers of grape and hand-grenades, tearing the ranks in a dreadful manner.

Major Frazer was killed on the flaming ruins, the intrepid Jones stood there awhile longer amidst a few heroic soldiers, hoping for aid, but none came, and he and those with him were struck down. The engineer Machel had been killed early, and the men bearing ladders fell or were dispersed. Thus the rear of the column was in absolute confusion before the head was beaten. It was in vain that Colonel Greville of the 38th, Colonel Cameron of the 9th, Captain Archimboau of the royals, and many other regimental officers exerted themselves to rally their discomfited troops and refill the breach; it was in vain that Lieutenant Campbell, breaking through the tumultuous crowd with the survivors of his chosen detachment, mounted the ruins; twice he ascended, twice he was wounded, and all around him died. The royals, endeavouring to retire, got intermixed with the 38th, and with some companies of the 9th, which had unsuccessfully endeavoured to pass them and get to the lesser breach. Then, swayed by different impulses and pent up in the narrow way between the hornwork and the river, the mass, reeling to and fro, could neither advance nor go back until the shells and musketry, constantly plied both in front and flank, had thinned the concourse, and the trenches were regained in confusion. At daylight a truce was agreed to for an hour, during which the French, who had already humanely removed the gallant Jones and the other wounded men from the breach, now carried off the more distant sufferers lest they should be drowned by the rising of the tide.

The troops filed out of the long narrow trenches in the night, a tedious operation, and were immediately exposed to a fire of grape from their own batteries on the Chofres. This fire, intended to keep down that of the enemy, should have ceased when the globe of compression was sprung in the drain, but owing to the darkness and the noise the explosion could neither be seen nor heard. The effect of it, however, drove the enemy from the hornwork, the Portuguese on that side advanced to the ditch, and a vigorous escalade would probably have succeeded, but they had no ladders. Again, the stormers of the great breach marched first, filling up the way and rendering the second breach useless, and the ladder-bearers never got to their destination. The attack was certainly ill-digested, and there was a neglect of moral influence followed by its natural consequence, want of vigour in execution.

Lord Wellington repaired immediately to St. Sebastian. The causes of the failure were apparent, and he would have renewed the attack, but wanting ammunition, deferred it until the powder and additional ordnance, which he had written for to England as early as the 26th of June, should arrive. The next day other events caused him to resort to a blockade, and the battering train was transported to Passages, two guns and two howziters only being retained on the Chofres and the Monte Olia. This operation was completed in the night of the 26th, but at daybreak the garrison made a sally from the hornwork, surprised the trenches, and swept off 200 Portuguese and 30 British soldiers. To avoid a repetition of this disaster the guards of the trenches were concentrated in the left parallel, and patrols only were sent out, yet one of those also was cut off on the 1st of August. Thus terminated the first part of the siege of San Sebastian, in which the allies lost 1300 soldiers and seamen.

CHAPTER XIII.

BATTLES OF THE PYRENEES.

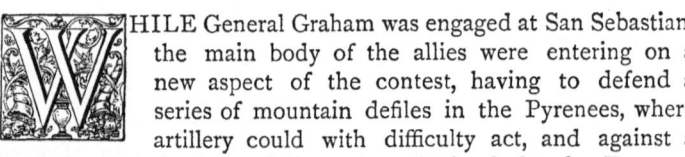HILE General Graham was engaged at San Sebastian, the main body of the allies were entering on a new aspect of the contest, having to defend a series of mountain defiles in the Pyrenees, where artillery could with difficulty act, and against a French marshal whose ability was undoubted, for the Emperor Napoleon had again sent Soult with unlimited authority to recruit and lead the French forces, now organised into one body as the Army of Spain. Soult divided his army into two powerful columns, and prepared to force the passes of Maya and Roncesvalles and relieve the blockade of Pampeluna. The opponents came into contact on the 25th July, commencing the arduous and protracted series of combats known as the Battles of the Pyrenees, the first collision being at Roncesvalles, where the divisions of the allies were under the command of Generals Byng and Morillo.

RONCESVALLES.

On the 23rd July, Marshal Soult issued an order of the day remarkable for its force and frankness. Tracing with a rapid pen the leading events of the past campaign, he showed that the disasters sprang from the incapacity of the king, not from the weakness of the soldiers, whose military virtue he justly extolled, and whose haughty courage he inflamed by allusions to former glories. It is true that, conscious of superior abilities, he did not suppress the sentiment of his own worth as a commander, but he was too proud to depreciate brave adversaries on the eve of battle. "Let us not," he said, "defraud the enemy of the praise which is due to him. The dispositions of the general have been prompt, skilful, and consecutive, the valour and steadiness of his troops have been praiseworthy."

Having thus stimulated the ardour of his troops, he put himself at the head of Clausel's divisions, and on the 25th at daylight led them up against the rocks of Altobiscar. General Byng, warned the evening before that danger was near, and jealous of some hostile indications towards the village of Val Carlos, had sent the 57th regiment down there, but kept the rest of his men well in hand and gave notice to General Cole. Ross's brigade was at Espinal, Anson's brigade was close behind Ross, Stubbs' Portuguese behind Anson, and the artillery was at Linzoain.

Such was the state of affairs when Soult, throwing out a multitude of skirmishers and pushing forward his supporting columns and guns as fast as the steepness of the road and difficult nature of the ground would permit, endeavoured to force Byng's position; but the British general, undismayed at the multitude of assailants, fought strongly; the French fell fast among the rocks, and their rolling musketry pealed in vain for hours along that cloudy field of battle, elevated 5000 feet above the level of the plains. Their numbers, however, continually increased in front, and the national guards, reinforced by Clausel's detachments, skirmished with the Spanish battalions at the foundry of Orbaiceta and threatened to turn the right. About mid-day General Cole arrived at Altobiscar, but his brigades were still distant, and the French, renewing their attack, neglected the Val Carlos to gather more thickly on the front of Byng. He resisted all their efforts, but Reille made progress along the summit of the Airola ridge. Morillo then fell back towards Ibañeta, and the French were already nearer to that pass than the troops at Altobiscar were, when Ross's brigade, coming up the pass of Mendichuri, suddenly appeared on the Lindouz, at the instant when the head of Reille's column was upon the point of cutting the communication with Campbell.

When the head of Ross's column, composed of a wing of the 20th regiment and a company of Brunswickers, reached the summit of the Lindouz, most unexpectedly it encountered Reille's advanced guard. The moment was critical, but Ross, an eager hardy soldier, called aloud to charge, and Captain Tovey of the

20th running forward with his company, crossed a slight wooded hollow, and full against the front of the 6th French light infantry dashed with the bayonet. Brave men fell by that weapon on both sides, but numbers prevailing, these daring soldiers were pushed back again by the French; Ross, however, gained his object, the remainder of his brigade had come up and the pass of Atalosti was secured, yet with a loss of 140 men of the 20th regiment and 41 of the Brunswickers.

During these movements the skirmishing of the light troops continued, but a thick fog coming up the valley prevented Soult from making dispositions for a general attack with his six divisions, and when night fell General Cole still held the great chain of the mountains with a loss of only 380 men killed and wounded. His right was, however, turned by Orbaiceta, he had but 10,000 or 11,000 bayonets to oppose to 30,000, and his line of retreat, being for four or five miles down hill and flanked all the way by the Lindouz, was uneasy and unfavourable. Wherefore putting the troops silently in march after dark, he threaded the passes and gained the valley of Urroz. The great chain was thus abandoned, but the result of the day's operation was unsatisfactory to the French general; he acknowledged a loss of 400 men, he had not gained ten miles, and from the passes now abandoned to Pampeluna the distance was not less than twenty-two miles, with strong defensive positions in the way, where increasing numbers of intrepid enemies were to be expected.

Soult's combinations, contrived for greater success, had been thwarted, partly by fortune, partly by errors of execution the like of which all generals must expect, and the most experienced are the most resigned as knowing them to be inevitable. The interference of fortune was felt in the fog, which rose at the moment when he was ready to thrust forward his heavy masses of troops entire. Soult, however, overrated the force opposed to him, supposing it to consist of two British divisions, besides Byng's brigade and Morillo's Spaniards. He was probably deceived by the wounded men, who, hastily questioned on the field, would declare they belonged to the second and fourth divisions, because Byng's brigade was part of the former; but that general and the Spaniards had without aid sustained Soult's first efforts, and even when the fourth division came up, less than 11,000 men, exclusive of sergeants and officers, were present in the fight. On the 26th the French general put Clausel's wing on the track of Cole, and ordered Reille to follow the crest of the mountains and seize the passes leading from the Bastan in Hill's rear while D'Erlon pressed him in front.

LINZOAIN.

All the columns were in movement at day-break, but every hour brought its obstacle. The fog still hung heavy on the mountain-tops, Reille's guides, bewildered, refused to lead the troops along the crests, and at ten o'clock, having no other resource, he marched down the pass of Mendichuri upon Espinal, and fell into the rear of the cavalry and artillery following Clausel's divisions. Meanwhile Soult, although retarded also by the fog and the difficulties of the ground, overtook Cole's rear-guard in front of Viscayret. The leading troops struck hotly upon some British light companies incorporated under the command of Colonel Wilson of the 48th, and a French squadron passing round their flank fell on the rear; but Wilson facing about, drove off these horsemen, and thus fighting, Cole, about two o'clock, reached the heights of Linzoain, a mile beyond Viscayret, where General Picton met him with intelligence that Campbell had reached Eugui and that the third division was at Zubiri. The junction of all these troops was thus secured, the loss of the day was less than 200, and neither wounded men nor baggage had been left behind. However, the French gathered in front, and at four o'clock seized some heights on the allies' left, which endangered their position, wherefore again falling back a mile, Cole offered battle on the ridge separating the valley of Urroz from that of Zubiri. During this skirmish Campbell, coming from Eugui, showed his Portuguese on the ridges above the right flank of the French, but they were distant, Picton's troops were still at Zubiri, and there was light for an action. Soult, however, disturbed with intelligence received from D'Erlon, and perhaps doubtful what Campbell's troops might be, put off the attack until next morning, and after dark the junction of all the allies was effected. While the combat of Linzoain was in progress, General D'Erlon with three divisions of infantry, numbering about 21,000 men, was operating against the British forces under Generals Pringle and Stewart at the passes of Maya, Aretesque, and Lessessa.

MAYA.

Captain Moyle Sherer, the officer commanding the picquet at the Aretesque pass, was told that at dawn a glimpse had been obtained of cavalry and infantry in movement along the hills in front, some peasants also announced the approach of the French, and at nine o'clock Major Thorne, a staff-officer, having patroled round the great hill in front of the pass, discovered sufficient to make him order up the light companies to support the picquet. These companies had just formed on the ridge with their left at the rock of Aretesque, when D'Armagnac's division mounted the great hill in front, Abbé followed, and General Maransin, with a third division, advanced from Ainhoa and Urdax against the Maya pass, meaning also to turn it by a narrow way leading up the Atchiola mountain.

D'Armagnac's men pushed forwards at once in several columns, and forced the picquet back with great loss upon the light companies, who sustained his vehement assault with infinite difficulty. The alarm guns were now heard from the Maya pass, and General Pringle hastened to the front, but his regiments, moving hurriedly from different camps, were necessarily brought into action one after the other. The 34th came up first at a running pace, yet by companies, not in mass, and breathless from the length and ruggedness of the ascent; the 39th and 28th followed, but not immediately nor together; and meanwhile D'Armagnac, closely supported by Abbé, with domineering numbers and valour combined, despite the desperate fighting of the picquet of the light companies, and of the 34th, had established his columns on the broad ridge of the position.

Colonel Cameron then sent the 50th from the left to the assistance of the overmatched troops, and that fierce and formidable old regiment, charging the head of an advancing column, drove it clear out of the pass of Lessessa in the centre. Yet the French were so many that, checked at one point, they assembled with increased force at another; nor could General Pringle restore the battle with the 39th and 28th regiments, which, cut off from the others, were, though fighting desperately, forced back to a second and lower ridge. They were followed by D'Armagnac, but Abbé continued to press the 50th and 34th, whose natural line of retreat was towards the Atchiola road on the left, because the position trended backward from Aretesque towards that point, and because Cameron's brigade was there. And that officer, still holding the pass of Maya with the left wings of the 71st and 92nd regiments, brought their right wings and the Portuguese guns into action, and thus maintained the fight; but so dreadful was the slaughter, especially of the 92nd, that it is said the advancing enemy was actually stopped by the heaped mass of dead and dying; and then the left wing of that noble regiment, coming down from the higher ground, smote wounded friends and exulting foes alike, as mingled together they stood or crawled before its fire.

It was in this state of affairs that General Stewart reached the field of battle. The passes of Lessessa and Aretesque were lost, that of Maya was still held by the left wing of the 71st, but Stewart, seeing Maransin's men gathered thickly on one side and Abbé's men on the other, abandoned it to take a new position on the first rocky ridge covering the road over the Atchiola; and he called down the 82nd regiment from the highest part of that mountain, and sent messengers to demand further aid from the seventh division. Meanwhile, although wounded himself, he made a strenuous resistance, for he was a very gallant man; but during the retrograde movement, Maransin, no longer seeking to turn the position, suddenly thrust the head of his division across the front of the British line and connected his left with Abbé, throwing as he passed a destructive fire into the wasted remnant of the 92nd, which even then sullenly gave way, for the men fought until two-thirds of the whole had gone to the ground. Still the survivors fought, and the left wing of the 71st came into action, but one after the other all the regiments were forced back, and the first position was lost, together with the Portuguese guns.

Abbé's division now followed D'Armagnac on the road to the town of Maya, leaving Maransin to deal with Stewart's new position, and notwithstanding its extreme strength the French gained ground until six o'clock, for the British, shrunk in numbers, also wanted ammunition, and a part of the 82nd, under Major Fitzgerald, were forced to roll down stones to defend the rocks on which they were posted. In this desperate condition Stewart was upon the point of abandoning the mountain entirely, when a brigade of the seventh division, commanded by General Barnes, arrived from Echallar, and that officer charging at the head of the 6th regiment, drove the French back to the Maya ridge. Stewart thus remained master of the Atchiola, and the Count D'Erlon, who probably thought greater reinforcements had come up, recalled his other divisions from the Maya road and reunited his whole corps on the *Col.* He had lost 1500 men and a general; but he took four guns, and 1400 British soldiers were killed or wounded.

Such was the fight of Maya, a disaster, yet one much exaggerated by French writers, and by an English author misrepresented as a surprise caused by the negligence of the cavalry. General Stewart was surprised, his troops were not, and never did soldiers fight better, seldom so well. The stern valour of the 92nd, principally composed of Irishmen, would have graced Thermopylæ. The Portuguese cavalry patrols, if any went out, which is uncertain, might have neglected their duty; but the infantry picquets, and the light companies so happily ordered up by Major Thorne, were ready, and no man wondered to see the French columns crown the great hill in front of the pass. Stewart deceived himself as to the true point of attack, and did not take proper military precautions on his own front; his position was only half occupied, his troops brought into action wildly, and finally he caused the loss of his guns by a misdirection as to the road. General Stewart was a brave, energetic, zealous, indefatigable man, and of a magnanimous spirit, but he possessed neither the calm reflective judgment nor the intuitive genius which belongs to nature's generals.

Lord Wellington heard of the fight at Maya on his way back from St. Sebastian, but with the false addition that D'Erlon was beaten. As early as the 22nd he had known that Soult was preparing a great offensive movement, but the immovable attitude of the French centre, the skilful disposition of their reserve, which was twice as strong as he at first supposed, together with the preparations made to throw bridges over the Bidassoa at Biriatou, were all calculated to mislead and did mislead him. Soult's complicated combinations to bring D'Erlon's divisions finally into line on the crest of the great chain were impenetrable, and the English general could not believe his adversary would throw himself with only 30,000 men into the valley of the Ebro unless sure of aid from Suchet, and that general's movements indicated a determination to remain in Catalonia; moreover Wellington, in contrast to Soult, knew that Pampeluna was not in extremity, and before the failure of the assault that San Sebastian was. Hence, the operations against his right, their full extent not known, appeared a feint, and he judged the real effort would be to throw bridges over the Bidassoa and raise the siege of San Sebastian. But in the night correct intelligence of the Maya and Roncesvalles affairs arrived, Soult's object was then scarcely doubtful, and Sir T. Graham was ordered to turn the siege into a blockade, to embark his guns and stores, and hold all his spare troops in hand to join Giron, on a position of battle marked out near the Bidassoa. General Cotton was ordered to move the cavalry up to Pampeluna, and O'Donnel was instructed to hold some of his Spanish troops ready to act in advance. This done, Wellington proceeded to San Estevan, which he reached early in the morning; and General Picton, having assumed the command of all the troops in the valley of Zubiri on the evening of the 26th July, recommenced the retreat before dawn on the 27th. Soult followed in the morning, having first sent scouts towards the ridges where Campbell's troops had appeared the evening before. Reille marched by the left bank of the Guy river, Clausel by the right bank, the cavalry and artillery closed the rear, and as the whole moved in compact order the narrow valley was overgorged with troops, a hasty bicker of musketry alone marking the separation of the hostile forces. Meanwhile, the garrison of Pampeluna made a sally, and O'Donnel in great alarm spiked some of his guns, destroyed his magazines, and would have suffered a disaster, if Carlos D'España had not fortunately arrived with his division and checked the garrison. Nevertheless, the danger was imminent, for General Cole, first emerging from the valley of Zubiri, had passed Villalba, only three miles from Pampeluna, in retreat; Picton, following close, was at Huarte, and O'Donnel's Spaniards were in confusion—in fine, Soult was all but successful when Picton, feeling the importance of the crisis, suddenly turned on some steep ridges which, stretching quite across the mouths of the Zubiri and Lanz valleys, screen Pampeluna.

Posting the third division on the right of Huarte he prolonged his line to the left with Morillo's Spaniards, called upon O'Donnel to support him, and directed Cole to occupy some heights between Oricain and Arletta. But that general, having with a surer eye observed a salient hill near Zabaldica, one mile in advance and commanding the road to Huarte, demanded and obtained permission to occupy it instead of the heights first appointed. Two Spanish regiments belonging to the blockading troops were still posted there, and towards them Cole directed his course. Soult had also marked this hill, a French detachment issuing from the mouth of the Val de Zubiri was in full career to seize it, and the hostile masses were rapidly approaching the summit on either side, when the Spaniards, seeing the British so close, vindicated their own post by a sudden charge. This was for Soult the stroke of fate. His double columns just then emerging, exultant, from the narrow valley, were arrested at the sight of 10,000 men which under Cole crowned the summit of the mountain in opposition; and two miles further back stood Picton with a greater number, for O'Donnel had now taken post on Morillo's left. To advance by the Huarte road was impossible, and to stand still was dangerous, because the French army, contracted to a span in front, was cleft in its whole length by the river Guy, and compressed on each side by the mountains, which in that part narrowed the valley to a quarter of a mile. Soult, however, like a great and ready commander, at once shot the head of Clausel's columns to his right across the mountain which separated the Val de Zubiri from the Val de Lanz, and at the same time threw one of Reille's divisions of infantry and a body of cavalry across the mountains on his left, beyond the Guy river, as far as the village of Elcano, to menace the front and right flank of Picton's position at Huarte. The other two divisions of infantry he established at the village of Zabaldica in the Val de Zubiri, close under Cole's right, and meanwhile Clausel seized the village of Sauroren close under that general's left.

While the French general thus formed his line of battle, Lord Wellington, who had quitted Sir Rowland Hill's quarters in the Bastan very early on the 27th, crossed the main ridge and descended the valley of the Lanz without having been able to learn anything of Picton's movements or position, and in this state of uncertainty reached Ostiz, a few miles from Sauroren, where he found General Long with the brigade of light cavalry which had furnished the posts of correspondence in the mountains. Here learning that Picton, having abandoned the heights of Linzoain, was moving on Huarte, he left instructions to stop all the troops coming down the valley of Lanz until the state of affairs at Huarte should be ascertained. Then at racing speed he made for Sauroren. As he entered that village he saw Clausel's divisions moving along the crest of the mountain, and it was clear that the allied troops in the valley of Lanz were intercepted, wherefore, pulling up his horse, he wrote on the parapet of the bridge of Sauroren fresh instructions to turn everything from that valley to the right by a road which led behind the hills to the rear of the position now occupied by Cole. Lord Fitzroy Somerset, the only staff officer who had kept up with him, galloped with these orders out of Sauroren by one road, the French light cavalry dashed in by another, and the English general rode alone up the mountain to reach his troops. One of Campbell's Portuguese battalions first descried him and raised a cry of joy, and the shrill clamour, caught up by the next regiments, swelled as it ran along the line into that stern and appalling shout which the British soldier is wont to give upon the edge of battle, and which no enemy ever heard unmoved. Lord Wellington suddenly stopped in a conspicuous place, he desired that both armies should know he was there, and a spy who was present pointed out Soult, then so near that his features could be plainly distinguished. The English general, it is said, fixed his eyes attentively upon this formidable man, and speaking as if to himself, said, "Yonder is a great commander, but he is a cautious one, and will delay his attack to ascertain the cause of these cheers; that will give time for the sixth division to arrive and I shall beat him." Certain it is that the French general made no serious attack that day.

The position adopted by Cole was the summit of a mountain mass which filled all the space between the Guy and the Lanz rivers as far back as Huarte and Villalba. The front of battle, being less than two miles, was well filled, and the Lanz and Guy river washed the flanks. On the ridges cleft by the waters the second line was posted, at the distance of two miles from, and nearly parallel to, the first position, but on a more extended front. Picton's left was at Huarte, Morillo prolonged Picton's left, and O'Donnel continued the line; Carlos d'España's division maintained the blockade behind the ridges, and the British cavalry under General Cotton took post, the heavy brigades on some open ground behind Picton, the hussar brigade on his right. This second line being on a wider trace than the first, and equally well filled with troops, entirely barred the openings of the two valleys leading down to Pampeluna.

Soult's position was also a mountain filling the space between the two rivers. It was even more rugged than the allies' mountain, and they were only separated by a deep narrow valley. Clausel's three divisions leaned to the right on the village of Sauroren, in the valley of Lanz, and his left was prolonged by two of Reille's divisions, which also occupied the village of Zabaldica in the valley of Zubiri under the right of the allies. The remaining division of this wing and a division of cavalry were thrown forward on the mountains at the other side of the Guy river, menacing Picton and seeking for an opportunity to communicate with the garrison of Pampeluna. Soult's first effort was to gain the Spaniards' hill, and establish himself near the centre of the allies' line of battle. The attack was vigorous, but the French were valiantly repulsed about the time Lord Wellington arrived, and he immediately reinforced that post with the 40th British regiment. There was then a general skirmish along the front, under cover of which Soult carefully examined the whole position, and the firing continued on the mountain side until evening, when a terrible storm, the usual precursor of English battles in the Peninsula, brought on premature darkness, and terminated the dispute. This was the state of affairs at daybreak on the 28th, but a signal alteration took place before the great battle of that day commenced, the various scattered divisions of the British army having come up with the main body under Wellington.

First Battle of Sauroren.

About mid-day on the 28th July, the French gathered at the foot of the position, and their skirmishers rushing forward spread over the face of the mountain, working upward like a conflagration; but the columns of attack were not all prepared when Clausel's division in the valley of Lanz, too impatient to await the general signal of battle, threw out its flankers on the ridge beyond the river and pushed down the valley in one mass. With a rapid pace it turned Cole's left, and was preparing to wheel up on his rear, when a Portuguese brigade of the sixth division, suddenly appearing on the crest of the ridge beyond the river, drove the French flankers back and instantly descended with a rattling fire upon the right and rear of the column in the valley. And almost at the same instant, the main body of the sixth division emerging from behind the same ridge, formed in order of battle across the front. The French, striving to encompass the left of the allies, were themselves encompassed, for two brigades of the fourth division turned and smote them from the left, the Portuguese smote them from the right; and while thus scathed on both flanks with fire, they were violently shocked and pushed back with a mighty force by the sixth division, yet not in flight, but fighting fiercely and strewing the ground with their enemies' bodies as well as with their own.

Clausel's second division, seeing this dire conflict, with a hurried movement assailed the chapel height to draw off the fire from the troops in the valley, and gallantly did the French soldiers throng up the craggy steep, but the general unity of the attack was ruined; neither their third division nor Reille's brigades had yet received the signal, and their attacks, instead of being simultaneous, were made in succession, running from right to left as the necessity of aiding the others became apparent. It was, however, a terrible battle and well fought. One column, darting out of the village of Sauroren, silently, sternly, without firing a shot, worked up to the chapel under a tempest of bullets which swept away whole ranks without abating the speed and power of the mass. The caçadores shrank abashed, and that part of the position was won. Soon, however, they rallied upon General Ross's British brigade, and the whole running forward charged the French with a loud shout and dashed them down the hill. Heavily stricken they were, yet undismayed, and recovering their ranks again, they ascended in the same manner to be again broken and overturned. But the other columns of attack were now bearing upwards through the smoke and flame with which the skirmishers had covered the face of the mountain, and the 10th Portuguese regiment, fighting on the right of Ross's brigade, yielded to their fury; a heavy body crowned the heights,

R.

and wheeling against the exposed flank of Ross, forced that gallant officer also to go back. His ground was instantly occupied by the enemies with whom he had been engaged in front, and the fight raged close and desperate on the crest of the position; charge succeeded charge, and each side yielded and recovered by turns; yet this astounding effort of French valour was of little avail. Lord Wellington brought Byng's brigade forward at a running pace, and sent the 27th and 48th British regiments down from the higher ground in the centre against the crowded masses, rolling them backward in disorder and throwing them one after the other violently down the mountain-side. The two British regiments fell upon the enemy three separate times with the bayonet, and lost more than half their own numbers.

During this battle on the mountain-top, the British brigades of the sixth division, strengthened by a battery of guns, gained ground in the valley of Lanz and arrived on the same front with the left of the victorious troops about the chapel. Lord Wellington then, seeing the momentary disorder of the enemy, ordered Madden's Portuguese brigade, which had never ceased its fire against the right flank of the French column, to assail the village of Sauroren in the rear, but the state of the action in other parts and the exhaustion of the troops soon induced him to countermand this movement. Meanwhile Reille's brigades, connecting their right with the left of Clausel's third division, had environed the Spanish hill, ascended it unchecked, and at the moment when the fourth division was so hardly pressed made the regiment of El Pravia give way on the left of the 40th. A Portuguese battalion rushing forward covered the flank of that invincible regiment, which waited in stern silence until the French set their feet upon the broad summit; but when their glittering arms appeared over the brow of the mountain the charging cry was heard, the crowded mass was broken to pieces, and a tempest of bullets followed its flight. Four times this assault was renewed, and the French officers were seen to pull up their tired men by the belts, so fierce and resolute were they to win. The vehement shout and shock of the British soldier always prevailed, and at last, with thinned ranks, tired limbs, hearts fainting, and hopeless from repeated failures, they were so abashed that three British companies sufficed to bear down a whole brigade. While the battle was thus being fought on the height, the French cavalry beyond the Guy river passed a rivulet, and with a fire of carbines forced the 10th hussars to yield some rocky ground on Picton's right; but the 18th hussars, having better firearms than the 10th, renewed the combat, killed two officers, and finally drove the French over the rivulet again.

Such were the leading events of this sanguinary struggle, which Lord Wellington, fresh from the fight, with homely emphasis called "*bludgeon-work.*" Two generals and 1800 men had been killed or wounded on the French side, a number far below the estimate made at the time by the allies, whose loss amounted to 2600; but the numbers actually engaged were, of French 25,000, of the allies 12,000, and if the strength of the latter's position did not save them from greater loss, their steadfast courage is to be the more admired. On the 29th the armies rested in position without firing a shot, but the wandering divisions on both sides were now entering the line. On Wellington's side the crisis was over. He had vindicated his position with only 16,000 combatants, and now, including the troops still maintaining the blockade, he had 50,000, 20,000 being British, in close military combination. Thirty thousand flushed with recent success were in hand, and Hill's troops were well placed for retaking the offensive.

Soult's situation was proportionably difficult. Finding that he could not force the allies' position in front, he had sent his artillery, part of his cavalry, and his wounded men back to France immediately after the battle, ordering the two former to join Villatte on the Lower Bidassoa, and there await further instructions. Having shaken off this burden, he awaited D'Erlon's arrival by the valley of Lanz, and that general reached Ostiz, a few miles above Sauroren, at mid-day on the 29th, bringing intelligence, obtained indirectly during his march, that General Graham had retired from the Bidassoa and Villatte had crossed that river. This gave Soult a hope that his first movements had disengaged San Sebastian, and he instantly conceived a new plan of operations, dangerous indeed, yet conformable to the critical state of his affairs.

No success was to be expected from another attack, yet he could not, at the moment of being reinforced with 18,000 men, retire by the road he came without some dishonour; nor could he remain where he was, because his supplies of provisions and ammunition, derived from distant magazines by slow and small convoys, was unequal to the consumption. Two-thirds of the British troops, the greatest part of the Portuguese, and all the Spaniards were, as he supposed, assembled in his front under Wellington, or on his right flank under Hill, and it was probable that other reinforcements were on the march; wherefore he resolved to prolong his right with D'Erlon's corps, and then cautiously drawing off the rest of his army, place himself between the allies and the Bastan, in military connection with his reserve and closer to his frontier magazines. Thus posted and able to combine all his troops in one operation, he expected to relieve San Sebastian entirely and profit from the new state of affairs.

In the night of the 29th Soult heard from the deserters that three divisions were to make an offensive movement towards Lizasso on the 30th, and when daylight came he was convinced the men spoke truly, because from a point beyond Sauroren he discerned certain columns descending the ridge of Christoval and the heights above Oricain, while others were in march on a wide sweep apparently to turn Clausel's right flank. These columns were Morillo's Spaniards, Campbell's Portuguese, and the seventh division, the former rejoining Hill, to whose corps they properly belonged, the others adapting themselves to a new disposition of Wellington's line of battle.

At six o'clock in the morning Foy's division of Reille's wing was in march along the crest of the mountain towards Sauroren, where Maucune's division had already relieved Conroux's; the latter, belonging to Clausel's wing, was moving up the valley of Lanz to rejoin that general, who had, with exception of the two flanking regiments before mentioned, concentrated his remaining divisions between Olabe and Ostiz. In this state of affairs Wellington opened his batteries from the chapel height, sent skirmishers against Sauroren, and the fire spreading to the allies' right, became brisk between Cole and Foy. It subsided, however, at Sauroren, and Soult, relying on the strength of the position, ordered Reille to maintain it until nightfall, unless hardly pressed, and went off himself at a gallop to join D'Erlon, for his design was to fall upon the division attempting to turn his right and crush them with superior numbers: a daring project, well and quickly conceived; but he had to deal with a man whose rapid perception and rough stroke rendered sleight-of-hand dangerous. The marshal overtook D'Erlon at the moment when that general, having entered the valley of Ulzema with three divisions of infantry and two divisions of heavy cavalry, was making dispositions to assail Hill, who was between Buenza and Arestegui.

Buenza.

The allies, under Hill, who were about 10,000 fighting men, including Long's brigade of light cavalry, occupied a very extensive mountain ridge. Their right was strongly posted on rugged ground, but the left, prolonged towards Buenza, was insecure, and D'Erlon, who, including his two divisions of heavy cavalry, had not less than 20,000 sabres and bayonets, was followed by La Martiniere's division of infantry now coming from Lanz. Soult's combination was therefore extremely powerful. The light troops were already engaged when he arrived, and the same soldiers on both sides who had so strenuously combated at Maya on the 25th were again opposed to each other.

D'Armagnac's division was directed to make a false attack upon Hill's right; Abbé's division, emerging by Lizasso, endeavoured to turn the allies' left and gain the summit of the ridge in the direction of Buenza. Maranzin followed Abbé, and the divisions of cavalry entering the line supported and connected the two attacks. The action was brisk at both points, but D'Armagnac pushing his feint too far became seriously engaged, and was beaten by Da Costa and Ashworth's Portuguese, aided by a part of the 28th British regiment. Nor were the French at first more successful on the other flank, being repeatedly repulsed, until Abbé, turning that wing, gained the summit of the mountain and rendered the position untenable. General Hill, who had lost about 400 men, then retired to the heights of Equaros, thus drawing towards Marcalain with his right and throwing back his left. Here being joined by Campbell and Morillo, he again offered battle, but Soult, whose principal loss was in D'Armagnac's division, had now gained his main object; he had turned Hill's left, secured a fresh line of retreat, a shorter communication with Villatte by the pass of Doña Maria, and withal the great Irurzun road to Toloza, distant only one league and a half, was in his power. His first thought was to seize it and march through Lecumberri either upon Toloza or Andoain and Ernani. There was nothing to oppose except the light division, but neither the French marshal nor General Hill knew of its presence, and the former thought himself strong enough to force his way to San Sebastian, and there unite with Villatte and his artillery, which, following his previous orders, was now on the Lower Bidassoa.

This project was feasible. La Martiniere's division of Reille's wing, coming from Lanz, was not far off. Clausel's three divisions were momentarily expected, and Reille's during the night. On the 31st, therefore, Soult, with at least 50,000 men, would have broken into Guipuscoa, thrusting aside the light division in his march, and menacing Sir Thomas Graham's position in reverse while Villatte's reserve attacked it in front. The country about Lecumberri was, however, very strong for defence, and Lord Wellington would have followed, yet scarcely in time, for he did not suspect his views and was ignorant of his strength, thinking D'Erlon's force to be originally two divisions of infantry and now only reinforced with a third division, whereas that general had three divisions originally, and was now reinforced by a fourth division of infantry and two of cavalry. This error, however, did not prevent him from seizing, with the rapidity of a great commander, the decisive point of operation, and giving a counterstroke which Soult, trusting to the strength of Reille's position, little expected.

When Wellington saw that La Martiniere's division and the cavalry had abandoned the mountains, he ordered Picton, reinforced with two squadrons of cavalry and a battery of artillery, to enter the valley of Zubiri and turn the French left; the seventh division was directed to sweep over the hills beyond the Lanz river upon the French right. The fourth division was to assail Foy's position, but, respecting its great strength, the attack was to be measured according to the effect produced on the flanks. Meanwhile Byng's brigade and the sixth division, the latter having a battery of guns and some squadrons of cavalry, were combined to assault Sauroren.

SECOND BATTLE OF SAUROREN.

These movements began at daylight. Picton's advance was rapid. He gained the valley of Zubiri and threw his skirmishers at once on Foy's flank, and about the same time General Inglis, one of those veterans who purchase every step of promotion with their blood, advancing with only 500 men of the seventh division, broke at one shock the two French regiments covering Clausel's right, and drove them down into the valley of Lanz. He lost, indeed, one-third of his own men, but instantly spreading the remainder in skirmishing order along the descent, opened a biting fire upon the flank of Conroux's division, which was then moving up the valley from Sauroren, sorely amazed and disordered by this sudden fall of two regiments from the top of the mountain into the midst of the column.

Foy's division, marching to support Conroux and Maucune, was on the crest of the mountains between Zabaldica and Sauroren at the moment of attack, but too far off to give aid, and his own light troops were engaged with the skirmishers of the fourth division; and Inglis had been so sudden and vigorous, that before the evil could be well perceived it was past remedy. For Wellington instantly pushed the sixth division, now commanded by General Pakenham, Pack having been wounded on the 28th, to the left of Sauroren, and shoved Byng's brigade headlong down from the chapel height against that village, which was defended by Maucune's division. Byng's vigorous assault was simultaneously enforced from the opposite direction by Madden's Portuguese of the sixth division, and at the same time the battery near the chapel sent its bullets crashing through the houses and booming up the valley towards Conroux's column, which Inglis never ceased to vex, and he was closely supported by the remainder of the seventh division.

The village and bridge of Sauroren and the straits beyond were now covered with a pall of smoke, the musketry pealed frequent and loud, and the tumult and affray, echoing from mountain to mountain, filled all the valley. Byng with hard fighting carried the village of Sauroren, and 1400 prisoners were made, for the two French divisions, thus vehemently assailed in the front and flank, were entirely broken. Part retreated along the valley towards Clausel's other divisions, which were now beyond Ostiz, part fled up the mountain-side to seek refuge with Foy, who had remained on the summit a helpless spectator of this rout; but though he rallied the fugitives in great numbers, he had soon to look to himself, for by this time his skirmishers had been driven up the mountain by those of the fourth division, and his left was infested by Picton's detachments. Thus pressed, he abandoned his strong position, and fell back along the summit of the mountain between the valley of Zubiri and valley of Lanz, and the woods enabled him to effect his retreat without much loss; but he dared not descend into either valley, and thinking himself entirely cut off, sent advice of his situation to Soult, and then retired into the Alduides by the pass of Urtiaga. Meanwhile Wellington, pressing up the valley of Lanz, drove Clausel as far as Olague, and the latter, now joined by Martiniere's division, took a position in the evening covering the roads of Lanz and Lizasso. The English general, whose pursuit had been damped by hearing of Hill's action at Buenza, also halted near Ostiz.

The allies lost 1900 men killed and wounded, or taken, in the two battles of this day, and of these nearly 1200 were Portuguese, the soldiers of that nation having borne the brunt of both fights. On the French side the loss was enormous. Conroux's and Maucune's divisions were completely disorganised; Foy, with 8000 men, including the fugitives he had rallied, was entirely separated from the main body; 2000 men, at the lowest computation, had been killed or wounded, many were dispersed in the woods and ravines, and 3000 prisoners were taken. This blow, joined to former losses, reduced Soult's fighting men to 35,000, of which the 15,000 under Clausel and Reille were dispirited by defeat, and the whole were placed in a most critical situation. Hill's force, now increased to 15,000 men by the junction of Morillo and Campbell, was in front, and 30,000 were on the rear in the valley of Lanz, or on the hills at each side; for the third division, finding no more enemies in the valley of Zubiri, had crowned the heights in conjunction with the fourth division.

Wellington, expecting Soult would rejoin Clausel and make for the Bastan by the pass of Vellate, intended to confine and press him closely in that district. But the French marshal was in a worse position than his adversary imagined, being too far advanced

SECOND BATTLE OF SAUROREN.

towards Buenza to return to Lanz; in fine, he was between two fires, and without a retreat save by the pass of Doña Maria upon San Estevan. Wherefore calling in Clausel, and giving D'Erlon, whose divisions, hitherto successful, were in good order and undismayed, the rear-guard, he commenced his march soon after midnight towards the pass. But mischief was thickening around him. Sir Thomas Graham, having only the blockade of San Sebastian to maintain, was at the head of 20,000 men, ready to make a forward movement, and there remained, besides, the light division under Charles Alten. That general took post on the mountain of Santa Cruz on the 27th. From thence on the evening of the 28th he marched to gain Lecumberri, on the great road of Irurzun; but, whether by orders from Sir Thomas Graham or in default of orders, the difficulty of communication being extreme in those wild regions, he commenced his descent into the valley of Lerins very late. His leading brigade, getting down with some difficulty, reached Leyza beyond the great chain by the pass of Goriti or Zubieta; but darkness caught the other brigade, and the troops dispersed in that frightful wilderness of woods and precipices. Many made faggot torches, waving them as signals, and thus moving about, the lights served indeed to assist those who carried them, but misled and bewildered others who saw them at a distance. The heights and the ravines were alike studded with these small fires, and the soldiers calling to each other for directions filled the whole region with their clamour. Thus they continued to rove and shout, until morning showed the face of the mountain covered with tired and scattered men and animals, who had not gained half a league of ground beyond their starting-place, and it was many hours ere they could be collected to join the other brigade at Leyza.

General Alten, who had now been separated for three days from the army, sent mounted officers in various directions to obtain tidings, and at six o'clock in the evening renewed his march. At Areysa he halted for some time, without suffering fires to be lighted, for he knew nothing of the enemy, and was fearful of discovering his situation; but at night he again moved, and finally established his bivouacs near Lecumberri early on the 30th. The noise of Hill's battle at Buenza was clearly heard in the course of the day, and the light division was thus again comprised in the immediate system of operations directed by Wellington in person. Had Soult continued his march upon Guipuscoa, Alten would have been in great danger; but the French general being forced to retreat, the light division was a new power thrown into his opponent's hands.

Soult's object being to get through the pass of Doña Maria, he commenced his retreat in the night of the 30th, and Wellington, deceived as to the real state of affairs, did not take the most fitting measures to stop his march; that is to say, he continued in his first design, halting in the valley of Lanz, while Hill passed his front, to enter the Bastan, into which district he sent Byng's brigade, as belonging to the second division. But early on the 31st, when Soult's real strength became known, he directed the seventh division to aid Hill, followed Byng through the pass of Vellate with the remainder of his forces, and thinking the light division might be at Zubieta, in the valley of Lerins, sent Alten orders to head the French, if possible, at San Estevan or at Sumbilla; in fine, to cut in upon their line of march somewhere. Longa also was ordered to come down to the defiles at Yanzi, thus aiding the light division to block the way on that side, and Sir Thomas Graham was advertised to hold his army in readiness to move in the same view, and the routes of the sixth and third divisions were also changed for a time.

Doña Maria.

At ten o'clock in the morning of the 31st General Hill overtook Soult's rear-guard between Lizasso and the Puerto. The seventh division, coming from the hills above Olague, was already ascending the mountain on his right, and the French only gained a wood on the summit of the pass, under the fire of Hill's guns. There, however, they turned, and throwing out their skirmishers, made strong battle. General Stewart, leading the attack of the second division, now engaged with D'Erlon's troops, was again wounded, and his first brigade was repulsed; but General Pringle, who succeeded to the command, renewed the attack with the second brigade, and the 34th regiment leading, broke the enemy at the moment that the seventh division did the same on the right. Some prisoners were taken, but a thick fog prevented further pursuit, and the loss of the French in the action is unknown, probably less than that of the allies, which was something short of 400 men.

The seventh division remained on the mountain, but Hill fell back to Lizasso, and then, following his orders, moved by a short but rugged way, leading between the passes of Doña Maria and Vellate over the great chain to Almandoz, to join Wellington, who had during the combat descended into the Bastan by the pass of Vellate. Meanwhile Byng reached Elizondo, and captured a large convoy of provisions and ammunition left there under guard of a battalion by D'Erlon on the 29th; he made several hundred prisoners also after a sharp skirmish, and then pushed forward to the pass of Maya. Wellington now occupied the hills through which the road leads from Elizondo to San Estevan, and full of hope to strike a terrible blow; for Soult, not being pursued after passing Doña Maria, had halted in San Estevan, although by his scouts he knew that the convoy had been taken at Elizondo. He was in a deep narrow valley, and three British divisions, with one of Spaniards, were behind the mountains overlooking the town; the seventh division was on the mountain of Doña Maria; the light division and Sir Thomas Graham's Spaniards were marching to block the Vera and Echallar exits from the valley; Byng was already at Maya, and Hill was moving by Almandoz, just behind Wellington's own position. A few hours gained, and the French must surrender or disperse. Wellington gave strict orders to prevent the lighting of fires, the straggling of soldiers, or any other indication of the presence of troops; and he placed himself amongst some rocks at a commanding point from whence he could observe every movement of the enemy. Soult seemed tranquil, and four of his gens-d'armes were seen to ride up the valley in a careless manner. Some of the staff proposed to cut them off; the English general, whose object was to hide his own presence, would not suffer it, but the next moment three marauding English soldiers entered the valley, and were instantly carried off by the horsemen. Half an hour afterwards the French drums beat to arms, and their columns began to move out of San Estevan towards Sumbilla. Thus the disobedience of three plundering knaves, unworthy of the name of soldiers, deprived one commander of the most splendid success, and saved another from the most terrible disaster.

The captives walked from their prison, but their chains hung upon them. The way was narrow, the multitude great, and the baggage, and wounded men borne on their comrades' shoulders, filed with such long procession, that Clausel's divisions forming the rear-guard were still about San Estevan on the morning of the 1st of August, and scarcely had they marched a league of ground, when the skirmishers of the fourth division and the Spaniards thronging along the heights on the right flank opened a fire to which little reply could be made. The troops and baggage then got mixed with an extreme disorder, numbers of the former fled up the hills, and the commanding energy of Soult, whose personal exertions were conspicuous, could scarcely prevent a general dispersion. However, prisoners and baggage fell at every step into the hands of the pursuers, the boldest were dismayed at the peril, and worse would have awaited them in front, if Wellington had been on other points well seconded by his subordinate generals.

The head of the French column, instead of taking the first road leading from Sumbilla to Echallar, had passed onward towards that leading from the bridge near Yanzi; the valley narrowed to a mere cleft in the rocks as they advanced, the Bidassoa was on their left, and there was a tributary torrent to cross, the bridge of which was defended by a battalion of Spanish caçadores detached to that point by General Barceñas. The front was now as much disordered as the rear, and had Longa or Barceñas reinforced the caçadores, those only of the French who, being near Sumbilla, could take the road from that place to Echallar would have escaped; but the Spanish generals kept aloof, and D'Erlon won the defile. However, Reille's divisions were still to pass, and when they came up a new enemy had appeared.

The light division had been directed to head the French army at San Estevan or Sumbilla. This order was received on the evening of the 31st, and the division reached Elgoriaga about mid-day on the 1st of August, having then marched twenty-four miles, and being little more than a league from Estevan and about the same distance from Sumbilla. The movement of the French along the Bidassoa was soon discovered, but the division, instead of moving on Sumbilla, turned to the left, clambered up the great mountain of Santa Cruz, and made for the bridge of Yanzi. The weather was exceedingly sultry, the mountain steep and hard to overcome, many men fell and died convulsed and frothing at the mouth, while others, whose spirit and strength had never before been quelled, leaned on their muskets and muttered in sullen tones that they yielded for the first time. Towards evening, after marching for nineteen consecutive hours over forty miles of mountain roads, the head of the exhausted column reached the edge of a precipice near the bridge of Yanzi. Below, within pistol-shot, Reille's divisions were seen hurrying forward along the horrid defile in which they were pent up, and a fire of musketry commenced, slightly from the British on the high rock, more vigorously from some low ground near the bridge of Yanzi, where the riflemen had ensconced themselves in the brushwood. The scene which followed is thus described by an eye-witness:—

"We overlooked the enemy at stone's-throw, and from the summit of a tremendous precipice. The river separated us, but the French were wedged in a narrow road with inaccessible rocks on one side and the river on the other. Confusion impossible to describe followed; the wounded were thrown down in the rush and trampled upon, the cavalry drew their swords and endeavoured to charge up the pass of Echallar, but the infantry beat them back, and several, horses and all, were precipitated into the river; some fired vertically at us, the wounded called out for quarter, while others pointed to them, supported as they were on branches of trees, on which were suspended great-coats clotted with gore, and blood-stained sheets taken from different habitations to aid the sufferers."

On these miserable supplicants brave men could not fire, and so piteous was the spectacle that it was with averted or doubtful aim they shot at the others, although the latter rapidly plied their muskets in passing, and some, in their veteran hardihood, even dashed across the bridge of Yanzi to make a counter-attack. It was a soldier-like but a vain effort! The night found the British in possession of the bridge, and though the great body of the enemy escaped by the road to Echallar, the baggage was cut off, and fell, together with many prisoners, into the hands of the light troops which were still hanging on the rear in pursuit from San Estevan.

During the night Soult rallied his divisions about Echallar, and on the morning of the 2nd occupied the "*Puerto*" of that name. His left was placed at the rocks of Zagaramurdi; his right at the rock of Ivantelly, communicating with the left of Villatte's reserve, which was in position on the ridges between Soult's right and the head of the great Rhune mountain. Meanwhile Clausel's three divisions, now reduced to 6000 men, took post on a strong hill between the "*Puerto*" and town of Echallar. This position was momentarily adopted by Soult to save time, to examine the country, and to make Wellington discover his final object, but that general would not suffer the affront. He had sent the third and sixth divisions to reoccupy the passes of Roncesvalles and the Alduides; Hill had reached the Col de Maya, and Byng was at Urdax; the fourth, seventh, and light divisions remained in hand, and with these he resolved to fall upon Clausel, whose position was dangerously advanced.

Echallar and Ivantelly.

The light division held the road running from the bridge of Yanzi to Echallar until relieved by the fourth division, and then marched by Lesaca to Santa Barbara, thus turning Clausel's right. The fourth division marched from Yanzi upon Echallar to attack his front, and the seventh moved from Sumbilla against his left; but Barnes's brigade, contrary to Lord Wellington's intention, arrived unsupported before the fourth and light divisions were either seen or felt, and, without awaiting the arrival of more troops, assailed Clausel's strong position. The fire became vehement, but neither the steepness of the mountain nor the overshadowing multitude of the enemy clustering above in support of their skirmishers could arrest the assailants, and then was seen the astonishing spectacle of 1500 men driving, by sheer valour and force of arms, 6000 good troops from a position so rugged that there would have been little to boast of if the numbers had been reversed and the defence made good.

The British soldiers, their natural fierceness stimulated by the remarkable personal daring of their general, Barnes, were excited by the pride of success; and the French divisions were those which had failed in the attack on the 28th, which had been utterly defeated on the 30th, and which had suffered so severely the day before about Sumbilla. Such, then, is the preponderance of moral power. The men who had assailed the terrible rocks above Sauroren, with a force and energy that all the valour of the hardiest British veterans scarcely sufficed to repel, were now, only five days afterwards, although posted so strongly, unable to sustain the shock of one-fourth of their own numbers. And at this very time eighty British soldiers, the comrades and equals of those who achieved this wonderful exploit, having wandered to plunder, surrendered to some French peasants, whom, Lord Wellington truly observed, "*they would under other circumstances have ate up!*"

Clausel, thus dispossessed of the mountain, fell back fighting to a strong ridge beyond the pass of Echallar, having his right covered by the Ivantelly mountain, which was strongly occupied. Meanwhile the light division, emerging by Lesaca from the narrow valley of the Bidassoa, ascended the broad heights of Santa Barbara without opposition, and halted there until the operations of the fourth and seventh divisions were far enough advanced to render it advisable to attack the Ivantelly. This lofty mountain lifted its head on the right, rising as it were out of the Santa Barbara heights, and separating them from the ridges through which the French troops beaten at Echallar were now retiring. Evening was coming on; a thick mist capped the crowning rocks, which contained a strong French regiment; the British soldiers, besides their long and terrible march the previous day, had been for two days without sustenance, and were leaning, weak and fainting, on their arms, when the advancing fire of Barnes's action about Echallar indicated the necessity of dislodging the enemy from Ivantelly. Colonel Andrew Barnard instantly led five companies of his riflemen to the attack, and four companies of the 43rd followed in support. The misty cloud had descended, and the riflemen were soon lost to the view, but the sharp clang of their weapons, heard in distinct reply to the more sonorous rolling musketry of the French, told what work was going on. For some time the echoes rendered it doubtful how the action went, but the following companies of the 43rd could find no trace of an enemy save the killed and wounded. Barnard had fought his way unaided and without a check to the summit, where his dark-clothed swarthy veterans raised their victorious shout from the highest peak, just as the coming night showed the long ridges of the mountains beyond sparkling with the last musket-flashes from Clausel's troops retiring in disorder from Echallar.

This day's fighting cost the British 400 men, and Lord Wellington narrowly escaped the enemy's hands. He had carried with him towards Echallar half a company of the 43rd as an escort, and placed a sergeant named Blood with a party to watch in front while he examined his maps. The French, who were close at hand, sent a detachment to cut the party off; and such was the nature of the ground, that their troops, rushing on at speed, would infallibly have fallen unawares upon Lord Wellington, if Blood, a young intelligent man, seeing the danger, had not with surprising activity, leaping rather than running down the precipitous rocks he was posted on, given the general notice; and as it was, the French arrived in time to send a volley of shot after him as he galloped away.

Soult now caused Count D'Erlon to reoccupy the hills about Ainhoa, Clausel to take post on the heights in advance of Sarre, and Reille to carry his two divisions to St. Jean de Luz in second line behind Villatte's reserve. Foy, who had rashly uncovered St. Jean Pied de Port by descending upon Cambo, was ordered to return and reinforce his troops with all that he could collect of national guards and detachments. Wellington had on the 1st directed General Graham to collect his forces and bring up pontoons for crossing the Bidassoa, but he finally abandoned this design, and the two armies therefore rested quiet in their respective positions, after nine days of continual movement, during which they had fought ten serious actions.

CHAPTER XIV.

SAN SEBASTIAN—SAN MARCIAL—VERA.

N the 31st July the enemy was discovered to be in full retreat, and the allies became again masters of the passes through the mountains, being on the 1st of August established nearly in the same positions they had occupied previous to the beginning of the attacks ten days before, and these positions they now strengthened by redoubts and entrenchments. It was at once decided upon to reopen the siege of San Sebastian by Sir Thomas Graham, a fresh battering train having arrived from England. On the 5th of August the guns were landed and the works against the fortress resumed. On the 8th, a notion having spread that the enemy was mining under the cask redoubt, the engineers seized the occasion to exercise their inexperienced miners by sinking a shaft and driving a gallery. The men soon acquired expertness, and as the water rose in the shaft at twelve feet, the work was discontinued when the gallery had attained eighty feet. Meanwhile the old trenches were repaired, the heights of San Bartolomeo were strengthened, and the convent of Antigua, built on a rock to the left of those heights, was fortified and armed with two guns to scour the open beach and sweep the bay. The siege, however, languished for want of ammunition; and during this forced inactivity the garrison of San Sebastian received supplies and reinforcements by sea, their damaged works were repaired, new defences constructed, the magazines filled, and sixty-seven pieces of artillery put in a condition to play. Eight hundred and fifty men had been killed and wounded since the commencement of the attack

in July, but as fresh men came by sea, more than 2600 good soldiers were still present under arms; and to show that their confidence was unabated, they celebrated the emperor's birthday by crowning the castle with a splendid illumination, encircling it with a fiery legend to his honour in characters so large as to be distinctly read by the besiegers.

On the 19th of August the battering train of fifteen heavy pieces was placed in battery, eight at the right attack, and seven at the left. A second battering train came on the 23rd, augmenting the number of pieces of various kinds to 117, including a large Spanish mortar; but with characteristic negligence this enormous armament had been sent out from England with no more shot and shells than would suffice for one day's consumption! On the 24th the attack was recommenced with activity. The Chofre batteries were enlarged to contain forty-eight pieces, and two batteries for thirteen pieces were begun on the heights of Bartolomeo, designed to breach at 700 yards' distance the faces of the left demi-bastion of the horn-work, that of St. John on the main front, and the end of the high curtain, for these works, rising in gradation one above another, were in the same line of shot. The approaches on the isthmus were now also pushed forward by the sap, but the old trenches were still imperfect, and before daylight next day, the French coming from the horn-work swept the left of the parallel, injured the sap, and made some prisoners before they were repulsed. On the 25th and 26th the batteries were all armed on both sides of the Urumea, and fifty-seven pieces opened with a general salvo, and continued to play with astounding noise and rapidity. The firing from the Chofre hills destroyed the revêtement of the demi-bastion of St. John, and nearly ruined the towers near the old breach, together with the wall connecting them; but at the isthmus the batteries, although they injured the horn-work, made little impression on the main front, from which they were too distant.

Lord Wellington, present at this attack and discontented with the operation, now ordered a battery for six guns to be constructed amongst some ruined houses on the right of the parallel, only 300 yards from the main front, and two shafts were sunk with a view to drive galleries for the protection of this new battery against the enemy's mines, but the work was slow because of the sandy nature of the soil. At three o'clock in the morning of the 27th the boats of the squadron, commanded by Lieutenant Arbuthnot of the *Surveillante*, and carrying 100 soldiers of the 9th regiment under Captain Cameron, pulled to attack the island of Santa Clara. A heavy fire was opened on them, and the troops landed with some difficulty; but the island was then easily taken and a lodgment made with the loss of only twenty-eight men and officers, of which eighteen were seamen.

In the night of the 27th, about three o'clock, the French sallied against the new battery on the isthmus; but as Colonel Cameron of the 9th regiment met them on the very edge of the trenches with the bayonet the attempt failed, yet it delayed the arming of the battery. At daybreak the renewed fire of the besiegers, especially that from the Chofres sand-hills, was extremely heavy, and the shrapnel shells were supposed to be very destructive; nevertheless the practice with that missile was very uncertain; the bullets frequently flew amongst the guards in the parallel, and one struck the field-officer. In the course of the day another sally was commenced, but the enemy, being discovered and fired upon, did not persist. The trenches were now furnished with banquettes and parapets as fast as the quantity of gabions and fascines would permit. Lord Wellington again visited the works this day, and in the night the advanced battery, which, at the desire of Sir Richard Fletcher, had been constructed for only four guns, was armed. It opened on the 29th, but an accident had prevented the arrival of one gun, and the fire of the enemy soon dismounted another, so that only two instead of six guns, as Lord Wellington had designed, smote at short range the face of the demi-bastion of St. John and the end of the high curtain. However, the general firing was severe both upon the castle and the town-works, and great damage was done to the defences. By this time the French guns were nearly silenced, and as additional mortars were mounted on the Chofre batteries, making in all sixty-three pieces, of which twenty-nine threw shells or spherical case-shot, the superiority of the besiegers was established.

The Urumea was now discovered to be fordable. Captain Alexander Macdonald of the artillery, without orders, waded across in the night, passed close under the works to the breach, and returned safely; wherefore, as a few minutes would suffice to bring the enemy into the Chofre batteries, to save the guns from being spiked, their vents were covered with iron plates fastened by chains; and this was also done at the advanced battery on the isthmus. The trenches leading from the parallel on the isthmus were now very wide and good, the sap was pushed on the right close to the demi-bastion of the horn-work, and the sea-wall supporting the high-road into the town, which had increased the march and cramped the formation of the columns in the first assault, was broken through to give access to the strand and shorten the approach to the breaches. The crisis was at hand, and in the night of the 29th a false attack was ordered, to make the enemy spring his mines; a desperate service, and bravely executed by Lieutenant Macadam of the 9th regiment. The order was sudden, no volunteers were demanded, no rewards offered, no means of excitement resorted to; yet such is the inherent bravery of British soldiers, that seventeen men of the royals—the nearest at hand—immediately leaped forth ready and willing to encounter what seemed certain death. With a rapid pace, all the breaching batteries playing hotly at the time, they reached the foot of the breach unperceived, and then mounted in extended order, shouting and firing; but the French were too steady to be imposed upon, and their musketry laid the whole party low, with the exception of their commander, who returned alone to the trenches.

On the 30th the batteries continued their fire, and about three o'clock Lord Wellington, after examining the enemy's defence, resolved to make a lodgment on the breach, and in that view, ordered the assault to be made the next day at eleven o'clock, when the ebb of tide would leave full space between the horn-work and the water. The galleries in front of the advanced battery on the isthmus were now pushed close up to the sea-wall, under which three mines were formed, with the double view of opening a short and easy way for the troops to reach the strand, and rendering useless any subterranean works the enemy might have made in that part. At two o'clock in the morning of the 31st they were sprung, and opened three wide passages, which were immediately connected, and a traverse of gabions six feet high was run across the mouth of the main trench on the left, to screen the opening from the grape-shot of the castle. Everything was now ready for the assault; but before describing that terrible event it will be fitting to show the state of the besieged in defence.

Sir Thomas Graham had been before the place for fifty-two days, during thirty of which the attack was suspended. All this time the garrison had laboured incessantly, and though the heavy fire of the besiegers appeared to have ruined the defences of the enormous breach in the sea-flank, it was not so. A perpendicular fall behind of more than twenty feet barred progress, and beyond that, amongst the ruins of the burned houses, was a strong counter-wall fifteen feet high, loopholed for musketry, and extending in a parallel direction with the breaches, which were also cut off from the sound part of the rampart by traverses at the extremities. The only really practicable road into the town was by the narrow end of the high curtain above the half-bastion of St. John. In front of the counter-wall, about the middle of the great breach, stood the tower of Los Hormos, and beneath it a mine, charged with twelve hundredweight of powder. The streets were all trenched, and furnished with traverses, to dispute the passage and to cover a retreat to the Monte Orgullo; but before the assailants could reach the main breach it was necessary either to form a lodgment in the hornwork, or to pass, as in the former assault, under a flanking fire of musketry for a distance of nearly 200 yards. And the first step was close under the sea-wall, covering the salient angle of the covered way, where two mines, charged with 800 pounds of powder, were prepared to overwhelm the advancing columns. Neither the resolution of the governor nor the courage of the garrison were abated, but the overwhelming fire of the last few days had reduced the number of fighting men; General Rey had only 250 men in reserve, and he demanded of Soult whether his brave garrison should be exposed to another assault. "The army would endeavour to succour him," was the reply, and he abided his fate.

STORMING OF SAN SEBASTIAN.

Lord Wellington thought the fifth division discouraged at the former failure, and demanded fifty volunteers from each of the fifteen regiments composing the first, fourth, and light divisions, "*men who could show other troops how to mount a breach.*" This was the phrase employed, and 750 gallant soldiers instantly marched to San Sebastian in answer to the appeal. Colonel Cooke and Major Robertson led the guards and Germans of the first division, Major Rose commanded the men of the fourth division, and Colonel Hunt, a daring officer who had already won his promotion at former assaults, was at the head of the fierce rugged veterans of the light division. It being at first supposed that Lord Wellington merely designed a simple lodgment on the great breach, the volunteers and one brigade of the fifth division only were ordered to be ready; but in a council held at night Major Smith maintained that the orders were misunderstood, as no lodgment could be formed unless the high curtain was gained. General Oswald, being called to the council, was of the same opinion, whereupon the remainder of the fifth division was brought to the trenches, and General Bradford, having offered the services of his Portuguese brigade, was told he might ford the Urumea and assail the farthest breach if he judged it advisable.

Sir James Leith had resumed the command of the fifth division, and being assisted by General Oswald, directed the attack from the isthmus. He was extremely offended by the arrival of the volunteers, and would not suffer them to lead the assault; some he spread along the trenches to keep down the fire of the horn-work; the remainder were held as a reserve along with the fifth division. To General Robinson's brigade the assault was confided, and Sir Thomas Graham overlooked the whole operations from the right bank of the river.

The morning of the 31st broke heavily; a thick fog hid every object, and the besiegers' batteries could not open until eight o'clock. From that hour a constant shower of heavy missiles was poured upon the besieged until eleven, when Robinson's brigade, getting out of the trenches, passed through the openings in the sea-wall and was launched bodily against the breaches. While the head of the column was still gathering on the strand, about thirty yards from the salient angle of the horn-work, twelve men, commanded by a sergeant whose heroic death has not sufficed to preserve his name, running violently forward, leaped upon the covered way with intent to cut the sausage of the enemy's mines. The French, startled by this sudden assault, fired the train prematurely, and though the sergeant and his brave followers were all destroyed and the high sea-wall thrown with a dreadful crash upon the head of the advancing column, not more than forty men were crushed by the ruins, and the rush of the troops was scarcely checked. The forlorn hope had already passed beyond the play of the mine, and now speeded along the strand amidst a shower of grape and shells; the leader, Lieutenant Macguire of the 4th regiment, conspicuous from his long white plume, his fine figure, and his swiftness, bounded far ahead of his men in all the pride of youthful strength and courage, but at the foot of the great breach he fell dead, and the stormers went sweeping like a dark surge over his body. Many died, however, with him, and the trickling of wounded men to the rear was incessant.

At this time there was a broad strand left by the retreating tide, and the sun had dried the rocks, yet they disturbed the order and closeness of the formation. The distance to the main breach was still nearly 200 yards, and the French, seeing the first mass of assailants pass the horn-work regardless of its broken bastion, immediately abandoned the front, and crowding on the river-face of that work, poured their musketry into the flank of the second column as it rushed along a few yards below them; but the soldiers, still running forward towards the breach, returned this fire without slackening their speed. The batteries of the Monte Orgullo and the St. Elmo now sent their showers of shot and shells, the two pieces on the cavalier swept the face of the breach in the bastion of St. John, and the 4-pounder in the horn-work, being suddenly mounted on the broken bastion, poured grape-shot into their rear. Thus scourged with fire from all sides, the stormers, their array broken alike by the shot, and by the rocks they passed over, reached their destinations, and the head of the first column gained the top of the great breach; but the gulf below could only be passed at a few places where portions of the burned houses were still attached to the rampart, and the deadly clatter of the French muskets from the loopholed wall beyond soon strewed the narrow crest of the ruins with dead. In vain the following multitude covered the ascent, seeking an entrance at every part; to advance was impossible, and the mass of assailants, slowly sinking downwards, remained stubborn and immovable on the lower part of the breach. Here they were covered from the musketry in front, but from several isolated points the French still smote them with small-arms, and the artillery poured shells and grape without intermission.

Such was the state of affairs at the great breach, and at the half-bastion of St. John it was even worse. The access to the top of the high curtain being quite practicable, the efforts to force a way were more persevering and constant, and the slaughter was in proportion; for the traverse on the flank, cutting it off from the cavalier, was defended by French grenadiers, who would not yield; the two pieces on the cavalier itself swept along the front face of the opening, and the 4-pounder and the musketry from the horn-work swept in like manner along the river-face. In the midst of this destruction some sappers and a working party attached to the assaulting columns endeavoured to form a lodgment, but no artificial materials had been provided, and most of the labourers were killed before they could raise the loose rocky fragments into a cover. During this time the besiegers' artillery kept up a constant counter-fire, which killed many of the French, and the reserve brigades of the fifth division were pushed on by degrees to feed the attack, until the left wing of the 9th regiment only remained in the trenches. The volunteers also, who had been with difficulty restrained in the trenches, " calling out to know why they had been brought there if they were not to lead the assault," these men, whose presence had given such offence to General Leith that he would have kept them altogether from the assault, being now let loose, went like a whirlwind to the breaches, and again the crowded masses swarmed up the face of the ruins, but reaching the crest-line, they came down like a fallen wall; crowd after crowd were seen to mount, to totter, and to sink; the deadly French fire was unabated, the smoke floated away, and the crest of the breach bore no living man.

Sir Thomas Graham, standing on the nearest of the Chofre batteries, beheld this frightful destruction with a stern resolution to win at any cost; and he was a man to have put himself at the head of the last company, and died sword in hand upon the breach rather than sustain a second defeat; but neither his confidence nor his resources were yet exhausted. He directed an attempt to be made on the horn-work, and turned all the Chofre batteries and one on the isthmus, that is to say, the concentrated fire of fifty heavy pieces, upon the high curtain. The shot ranged over the heads of the troops who now were gathered at the foot of the breach, and the stream of the missiles thus poured along the upper surface of the high curtain broke down the traverses, and in its fearful course shattering all things, strewed the rampart with the mangled limbs of the defenders. When this flight of bullets first swept over the heads of the soldiers a cry arose "to retire, because the batteries were firing on the stormers;" but the veterans of the light division under Hunt, being at that point, were not to be so disturbed, and in the very heat and fury of the cannonade effected a solid lodgment in some ruins of houses actually within the rampart on the right of the great breach.

For half an hour this horrid tempest smote upon the works and the houses behind, and then suddenly ceasing, the small clatter of the French muskets showed that the assailants were again in activity; and at the same time the 13th Portuguese regiment, led by Major Snodgrass, and followed by a detachment of the 24th under Colonel Macbean, entered the river from the Chofres. The ford was deep, the water rose above the waist, and when the soldiers reached the middle of the stream, which was 200 yards wide, a heavy gun struck on the head of the column with a shower of grape; the havoc was fearful, but the survivors closed and moved on. A second discharge from the same piece tore the ranks from front to rear; still the regiment moved on, and amidst a confused fire of musketry from the ramparts, and of artillery from St. Elmo, from the castle, and from the Mirador, landed on the left bank and rushed against the third breach. Macbean's men, who had followed with equal bravery, then reinforced the great breach, about eighty yards to the left of the other, although the line of ruins seemed to extend the whole way. The fighting now became fierce and obstinate again at all the breaches, but the French musketry still rolled with deadly effect, the heaps of slain increased, and once more the great mass of stormers sank to the foot of the ruins unable to win; the living sheltered themselves as they could, but the dead and wounded lay so thickly that hardly could it be judged whether the hurt or unhurt were most numerous.

It was now evident that the assault must fail unless some accident intervened, for the tide was rising, the reserves all engaged, and no greater effort could be expected from men whose courage had been already pushed to the verge of madness. In this crisis fortune interfered. A number of powder-barrels, live shells, and combustible materials which the French had accumulated behind the traverses for their defence caught fire, a bright consuming flame wrapped the whole of the high curtain, a succession of loud explosions were heard, hundreds of the French grenadiers were destroyed, the rest were thrown into confusion, and while the ramparts were still involved with suffocating eddies of smoke the British soldiers broke in at the first traverse. The defenders, bewildered by this terrible disaster, yielded for a moment, yet soon rallied, and a close desperate struggle took place along the summit of the high curtain; but the fury of the stormers, whose numbers increased every moment, could not be stemmed. The French colours on the cavalier were torn away by Lieutenant Gethin of the 11th regiment. The horn-work and the land front below the curtain and the loopholed wall behind the great breach were all abandoned; the light division soldiers, who had already established themselves in the ruins on the French left, immediately penetrated to the streets, and at the same moment the Portuguese at the small breach, mixed with British who had wandered to that point seeking for an entrance, burst in on their side.

Five hours the dreadful battle had lasted at the walls, and now the stream of war went pouring into the town. The undaunted governor still disputed the victory for a short time with the aid of his barricades, but several hundreds of his men being cut off and taken in the horn-work, his garrison was so reduced that even to effect a retreat behind the line of defences which separated the town from the Monte Orgullo was difficult. Many of his troops flying from the horn-work along the harbour flank of the town broke through a body of the British who had reached the vicinity of the fortified convent of Santa Téresa before them, and this post was the only one retained by the French in the town. It was thought by some that Monte Orgullo might have been carried on this day, if a commander of sufficient rank to direct the troops had been at hand; but whether from wounds or accident, no general entered the place until long after the breach had been won. The commanders of battalions were embarrassed for want of orders, and a thunderstorm, which came down from the mountains with unbounded fury immediately after the place was carried, added to the confusion of the fight. This storm seemed to be the signal of hell for the perpetration of villainy which would have shamed the most ferocious barbarians of antiquity. At Ciudad Rodrigo intoxication and plunder had been the principal object; at Badajos lust and murder were joined to rapine and drunkenness; but at San Sebastian the direst and most revolting cruelty was added to the catalogue of crimes. Some order was at first maintained, but the resolution of the troops to throw off discipline was quickly made manifest. A British staff-officer was pursued with a volley of small-arms, and escaped with difficulty from men who mistook him for the provost-martial of the fifth division; a Portuguese adjutant, who endeavoured to prevent some atrocity, was put to death in the market-place, not with sudden violence from a single ruffian, but deliberately by a number of English soldiers. Many officers exerted themselves to preserve order, many men were well conducted, but the rapine and violence commenced by villains soon spread, the camp-followers crowded into the place, and the disorder continued until the flames, following the steps of the plunderer, put an end to his ferocity by destroying the whole town.

Three generals, Leith, Oswald, and Robinson, had been hurt in the trenches; Sir Richard Fletcher, the chief engineer, a brave man who had served his country honourably, was killed; and Colonel Burgoyne, the next in command of that arm, was wounded. The carnage at the breaches was appalling. The volunteers, although brought late into the action, had nearly half their number struck down, most of the regiments of the fifth division suffered in the same proportion, and the whole loss since the renewal of the siege exceeded 2500 men and officers.

The town being thus taken, the Monte Orgullo was to be attacked, but it was very steep and difficult to assail. The castle served as a citadel, and just below it four batteries connected with masonry stretched across the face of the hill. From the Mirador and Queen's batteries, at the extremities of this line, ramps, protected by redans, led to the convent of Santa Téresa, which was the most salient part of the defence. On the side of Santa Clara and behind the mountain were some sea batteries, and if all these works had been of good construction, the troops fresh and well supplied, the siege would have been long and difficult; but the garrison was shattered by the recent assault, most of the engineers and leaders killed, the governor and many others wounded, 500 men were sick or hurt, the soldiers fit for duty did not exceed 1300, and they had 400 prisoners to guard. The castle was small, the bomb-proofs scarcely sufficed to protect the ammunition and provisions, and only ten guns remained in a condition for service, three of which were on the sea-line. There was very little water, and the troops were forced to lie out on the naked rock, exposed to the fire of the besiegers. General Rey and his brave garrison were, however, still resolute to fight, and they received nightly by sea supplies of ammunition, though in small quantities.

Lord Wellington arrived the day after the assault. Regular approaches could not be carried up the steep naked rock; he doubted the power of vertical fire, and ordered batteries to be formed on the captured works of the town, intending to breach the enemy's remaining lines of defence and then storm the Orgullo. And as the convent of Santa Téresa would enable the French to sally by the rampart on the left of the allies' position in the town, he composed his first line with a few troops strongly barricaded, placing a supporting body in the market-place, and strong reserves on the high curtain and flank ramparts. Meanwhile from the convent, which, being actually in the town, might have been easily taken at first, the enemy killed many of the besiegers, and when after several days it was assaulted, they set the lower part on fire, and retired by a communication made from the roof to a ramp on the hill behind. All this time the flames were destroying the town, and the Orgullo was overwhelmed with shells shot upwards from the besiegers' batteries.

On the 3rd of September, the governor being summoned to surrender, demanded terms inadmissible; his resolution was not to be shaken, and the vertical fire was therefore continued day and night, though the British prisoners suffered as well as the enemy. The new breaching batteries were now commenced, one for three pieces on the isthmus, the other for seventeen pieces on the land front of the horn-work. These guns were brought from the Chofres at low water across the Urumea, at first in the night, but the difficulty of labouring in the water during darkness induced the artillery officers to transport the remainder in daylight, and within reach of the enemy's batteries, which did not fire a shot. In the town the besiegers' labours were impeded by the flaming houses, but near the foot of the hill the ruins furnished shelter for the musketeers employed to gall the garrison, and the guns on the island of Santa Clara being reinforced, were actively worked by the seamen. The besieged replied but little; their ammunition was scarce, and the horrible vertical fire subdued their energy. In this manner the action was prolonged until the 8th of September, when fifty-nine heavy battering-pieces opened at once from the island, the isthmus, the horn-work, and the Chofres. In two hours both the Mirador and the Queen's battery were broken, the fire of the besieged was entirely extinguished, and the summit and face of the hill torn and furrowed in a frightful manner; the bread-ovens were destroyed, a magazine exploded, and the castle, small and crowded with men, was overlaid with the descending shells. Then the governor, proudly bending to his fate, surrendered. On the 9th this brave man and his heroic garrison, reduced to one-third of their original number, and leaving 500 wounded behind them in the hospital, marched out with the honours of war. The Spanish flag was hoisted under a salute of twenty-one guns, and the siege terminated, after sixty-three days' open trenches, precisely when the tempestuous season, beginning to vex the coast, would have rendered a continuance of the sea blockade impossible.

While the siege of San Sebastian was in progress, Soult fought battles at San Marcial and at Vera with the covering force, not willingly nor with much hope of success, but he was averse to let San Sebastian fall without another effort, and thought a bold demeanour would best hide his real weakness. Guided, however, by the progress of the siege, which he knew perfectly through his sea communication, he awaited the last moment of action, striving meanwhile to improve his resources and to revive the confidence of the army and of the people. He was in no manner deceived as to his enemy's superior strength of position, number, and military confidence; but his former efforts on the side of Pampeluna had interrupted the attack of San Sebastian, and another offensive movement would necessarily produce a like effect; wherefore he hoped by repeating the disturbance, as long as a free intercourse by sea enabled him to reinforce and supply the garrison, to render the siege a wasting operation for the allies. To renew the movement against Pampeluna was most advantageous, but it required 50,000 infantry for the attack, and 20,000 as a corps of observation on the Lower Bidassoa, and he had not such numbers to dispose of. The subsistence of his troops also was uncertain, because the loss of all the military carriages at Vittoria was still felt, and the resources of the country were reluctantly yielded by the people. To act on the side of St. Jean Pied de Port was therefore impracticable; and to attack the allies' centre, at Vera, Echallar, and the Bastan, was unpromising, seeing that two mountain-chains were to be forced before the movement could seriously affect Lord Wellington; moreover, the ways being impracticable for artillery, success, if such should befall, would lead to no decisive result. It only remained to attack the left of the allies by the great road of Irun.

Against that quarter Soult could bring more than 40,000 infantry, but the positions were of perilous strength. The Upper Bidassoa was in Wellington's power, because the light division, occupying Vera and the heights of Santa Barbara on the right bank, covered all the bridges; but the Lower Bidassoa, flowing from Vera with a bend to the left, separated the hostile armies, and against this front, about nine miles wide, Soult's operations were directed at daylight of the 31st August, by an attack on the allied troops occupying a detached mountain ridge at

San Marcial.

During the action two bridges were thrown over the river, partly on trestles, partly on boats, below the fords, and the head of Villatte's reserve crossing ascended the ridge and maintained the fight vigorously; one brigade reached the chapel of San Marcial, and the left of the Spanish line was shaken; but the 85th regiment, belonging to Lord Aylmer's brigade, advanced a little way to support it, and at that moment Lord Wellington rode up with his staff from San Sebastian. Then the Spaniards dashed their adversaries down with so much violence that many were driven into the river, and some of the French pontoon boats coming to their succour were overloaded and sunk. It was several hours before the broken and confused masses could be rallied and the bridges, which had been broken up to let the boats save the drowning men, repaired. When this was effected, Soult, who overlooked the action from the summit of the mountain Louis XIV., sent the remainder of Villatte's reserve over the river, and calling up Foy's division, prepared a more formidable and better-arranged attack; and he expected greater success, inasmuch as operations begun on the side of Vera were now making considerable progress up the Peña de Haya on the allies' right.

VERA.

General Clausel had descended the Bayonette and Commissary mountains immediately after daybreak, under cover of a thick fog, but at seven o'clock the weather cleared, and three divisions formed in heavy columns were seen by the troops on Santa Barbara making for the fords below Vera in the direction of two hamlets called the Silinas and the Bario de Lesaca. A fourth French division and the guns remained stationary on the slopes of the mountain, and the artillery opened now and then upon the little town of Vera, from which the picquets of the light division were recalled, with exception of one post in a fortified house commanding the bridge. About eight o'clock the enemy's columns began to pass the fords covered by the fire of their artillery, but the first shells thrown fell into the midst of their own ranks, and the British troops on Santa Barbara cheered the French battery with a derisive shout. Their march, however, was sure, and a battalion of chosen light troops, without knapsacks, quickly commenced the battle on the left bank of the river with the Portuguese brigade, and by their extreme activity and rapid fire forced the latter to retire up the slopes of the mountain. General Inglis then reinforced the line of skirmishers, and the whole of his brigade was soon afterwards engaged; but Clausel menaced his left flank from the lower ford, and the French troops still forced their way upwards in front without a check, until the whole mass disappeared fighting amidst the asperities of the Peña de la Haya. Inglis lost 270 men and 22 officers, but he finally halted on a ridge commanding the intersection of the roads leading from Vera and Lesaca to Irun and Oyarzun, somewhat below where the fourth division, having now recovered its Portuguese brigade, was, in conjunction with Longa's Spaniards, so placed as to support and protect equally the left of Inglis and the right of Freyre on San Marcial.

These operations, from the great height and asperity of the mountain, occupied many hours, and it was past two o'clock before even the head of Clausel's columns reached this point; but thinking the allies at Echallar and Santa Barbara were only awaiting the proper moment to take him in flank and rear, by the bridges of Vera and Lesaca, if he engaged farther up the mountain, Clausel now abated his efforts, and sent word of his views and intentions to Soult. The battle was, however, arrested by a tempest, which, commencing in the mountains about three o'clock, raged for several hours with wonderful violence. Huge branches were torn from the trees and whirled through the air like feathers on the howling winds, while the thinnest streams, swelling into torrents, dashed down the mountains, rolling innumerable stones along with a frightful clatter. Amidst this turmoil and under cover of night the French recrossed the Bidassoa.

Clausel, having received the order to retire early in the evening, when the storm had already put an end to all fighting, repassed the fords in person and before dark at the head of two brigades, ordering General Vandermaesen to follow with the remainder of his divisions. It would appear that he expected no difficulty, since he did not take possession of the bridge of Vera, nor of the fortified house covering it; and, apparently ignorant of the state of his own troops on the other bank of the river, occupied himself with suggesting new projects displeasing to Soult. Meanwhile Vandermaesen's situation became critical. Many of his soldiers attempting to cross were drowned by the rising waters, and finally, unable to effect a passage at the fords, that general marched up the stream to seize the bridge of Vera. His advanced guard surprising a corporal's picquet, rushed over, but was driven back by a rifle company posted in the fortified house. This happened about three o'clock in the morning, and the riflemen defended the passage until daylight, when a second company and some Portuguese caçadores came to their aid. But the French reserve left at Vera, seeing how matters stood, opened a fire of guns against the fortified house from a high rock just above the town, and their skirmishers approached it on the right bank, while Vandermaesen plied his musketry from the left bank. The two rifle captains and many men fell under this cross fire, and the passage was forced, but Vandermaesen, urging the attack in person, was killed, and more than 200 of his soldiers were hurt.

Soult, now learning that all offensive movements on the side of Maya had ceased, contemplated another attack on San Marcial; but in the course of the 31st August General Rey's report of the assault on San Sebastian reached him, and at the same time he heard that General Hill was in movement on the side of St. Jean Pied de Port. This state of affairs brought reflection. San Sebastian was lost; a fresh attempt to carry off the wasted garrison from the castle would cost 5000 or 6000 good soldiers, and the safety of the whole army would be endangered by pushing headlong amongst the terrible asperities of the mountains. For Wellington could throw his right wing and centre, forming a mass of at least 35,000 men, upon the French left during the action, and he would be nearer to Bayonne than the French right when once the battle was engaged beyond the Lower Bidassoa. The army had lost in recent actions 3600 men. General Vandermaesen had been killed, and four other generals wounded. The remaining superior officers agreed that a fresh attempt would be most dangerous, and serious losses might draw on an immediate invasion of France before the necessary defensive measures were completed. Yielding to these reasons, he resolved to recover his former positions, and thenceforward remain entirely on the defensive, for which his vast knowledge of war, his foresight, his talent for methodical arrangement, and his firmness of character peculiarly fitted him. Twelve battles or combats, fought in seven weeks, bore testimony that he had striven hard to regain the offensive for the French army, and willing still to strive, if it might be so, he had called upon Suchet to aid him,, and demanded fresh orders from the Emperor; but Suchet helped him not, and Napoleon's answer indicated at once his own difficulties and his reliance upon the Duke of Dalmatia's capacity and fidelity: " I have given you my confidence, and can add neither to your means nor to your instructions."

CHAPTER XV.

PASSAGE OF THE BIDASSOA—VERA—FALL OF PAMPELUNA.

OULT, now on the defensive, was yet fearful of an attack along the Nive, and his uneasy movements made the allies think he was again preparing for offensive operations. This double misunderstanding did not, however, last long, and each army resumed its former position.

The fall of San Sebastian had given Lord Wellington a new port and point of support, had increased the value of Passages as a depôt, and let loose a considerable body of troops for field operations. Austria, Prussia, and Russia were all in league against the Emperor Napoleon, whose fortunes were evidently now on the wane; and it seemed, therefore, certain that Wellington would immediately invade France. The English cabinet had promised the continental sovereigns that it should be so when the French were expelled from Spain; and newspaper editors were, as usual, actively deceiving the people of all countries by their absurd projects and assumptions. Meanwhile the partisans of the Bourbons were secretly endeavouring to form a conspiracy in the south, and the Duke of Berri desired to join the British army, pretending that 20,000 Frenchmen were already armed and organised, at the head of which he would place himself. In fine, all was exultation and extravagance. But Lord Wellington, well understanding the inflated nature of such hopes and promises, while affecting to rebuke the absurdity of the newspapers, took the opportunity to check similar folly in higher places, by observing, "that if he had done all that was expected, he should have been before that period in the moon."

Having shaken off the weight of the continental policy, Lord Wellington proceeded to consider the question of invading France simply as a military operation, which might conduce to or militate against the security of the Peninsula while Napoleon's power was weakened by the war in Germany; and such was his inflexible probity of character, that no secret ambitious promptings, no desire for personal reputation, diverted him from this object, all the renown of which he already enjoyed—the embarrassments, mortifications, and difficulties, although to the surface-seeing public there appeared none, alone remaining.

The French position at the Bidassoa was the base of a triangle of which Bayonne was the apex, and the great roads leading from thence to Irun and St. Jean Pied de Port were the sides. A rugged mass of mountains intervened between the left and centre, but nearly all the valleys and communications coming from Spain beyond the Nieve centred at St. Jean Pied de Port, and were embraced by an entrenched camp which General Foy occupied in front of that fortress. Finally, the whole system of defence was tied to that of St. Jean Pied de Port by the double bridge-head at Cambo, which secured the junction of Foy with the rest of the army.

The French worked diligently on their entrenchments, yet they were but little advanced when the castle of San Sebastian surrendered, and Wellington had even then matured a plan of attack as daring as any undertaken during the whole war. This was to seize the great Rhune mountain and its dependents, and at the same time to force the passage of the Lower Bidassoa and establish his left wing in the French territory. He would thus bring the Rhune, Commissary, and Bayonette mountains, forming a salient menacing point of great altitude and strength towards the French centre, within his own system, and shorten his communications by gaining the command of the road running along the river from Irun to Vera. Thus also he would obtain the port of Fuenterabia, which, though bad in winter, was some advantage to a general whose supplies came from the ocean, and with scanty means of land-transport. He designed this operation for the middle of September, immediately after the castle of San Sebastian fell, and before the French works acquired strength; but some error retarded the arrival of his pontoons, the weather became bad, and the attack, which depended upon the state of the tides and fords, was of necessity deferred until the 7th of October. Meanwhile, to mislead Soult, to ascertain Foy's true position about St. Jean Pied de Port, and to strengthen his own right, he brought part of Del Parque's force up from Tudela to Pampeluna. The Andalusian division, which had remained at the blockade after the battle of Sauroren, then rejoined Giron at Echallar, and at the same time Mina's troops gathered in the neighbourhood of Roncesvalles. Wellington himself repaired to that quarter on the 1st of October, and in his way he caused General Campbell to surprise some isolated posts on the rock of Airola; a French scouting detachment was also cut off near the foundry of Baygorry, and 2000 sheep were swept from the valley.

These affairs awaked Soult's jealousy. He was in daily expectation of an attack without being able to ascertain on what quarter the blow would fall, and at first, deceived by false information that the fourth division had reinforced Hill, he thought the march of Mina's troops and the Andalusians was intended to mask an offensive movement by the Val de Baygorry. The arrival of light cavalry in the Bastan, Lord Wellington's presence at Roncesvalles, and the loss of the post at Airola seemed to confirm this; but he knew the pontoons were at Oyarzun, and some deserters told him that the real object of the allies was to gain the great Rhune. On the other hand, a French commissary, taken at San Sebastian and exchanged, after remaining twelve days at Lesaca, assured him that nothing at Wellington's headquarters indicated a serious attack, although the officers spoke of one, and there were many movements of troops; and this weighed much with the French general, because the slow march of the pontoons and the wet weather had caused a delay contradictory to the reports of the spies and deserters. It was also beyond calculation that Wellington should, against his military judgment, push his left wing into France merely to meet the wishes of the allied sovereigns in Germany, and as the most obvious line for a permanent invasion was by his right and centre, there was no apparent cause for deferring his operations.

The true reason of the procrastination, namely, the state of the tides and fords on the Lower Bidassoa, was necessarily hidden from Soult, who finally inclined to the notion that Wellington only designed to secure his blockade at Pampeluna from interruption by menacing the French and impeding their labours, the results of which were now becoming visible. However, as all the deserters and spies came with the same story, he recommended increased vigilance along the whole line. And yet so little did he anticipate the nature of his opponent's project, that on the 6th he reviewed D'Erlon's divisions at Ainhoa, and remained that night at Espelette, doubting if any attack was intended, and no way suspecting that it would be against his right. But Wellington could not diminish his troops on the side of Roncesvalles and the Alduides, lest Foy and Paris, and the light cavalry under Pierre Soult, should unite at St. Jean Pied de Port to raise the blockade of Pampeluna; the troops at Maya were already posted offensively, menacing Soult between the Nive and the Nivelle, and it was therefore only with his left wing and left centre, and against the French right, that he could act. Early in October a reinforcement of 1200 British soldiers arrived from England. Mina was then in the Ahescoa, on the right of General Hill, who was thus enabled to relieve Campbell's Portuguese in the Alduides; and the latter, marching to Maya, replaced the third division, which, shifting to its left, occupied the heights above Zagaramurdi, to enable the seventh division to relieve Giron's Andalusians in the Puerto de Echallar.

These dispositions were made with a view to the attack of the great Rhune and its dependents. For the assault on these positions Wellington designed to employ the first and fifth divisions and the unattached brigades of Wilson and Lord Aylmer, in all about 15,000 men. By the help of Spanish fishermen he had secretly discovered three fords, practicable at low water, between the bridge of Behobia and the sea, and his intent was to pass his column at the old fords above, and at the new fords below the bridge, and this though the tides rose sixteen feet, leaving at the ebb open heavy sands not less than half a mile broad. The left bank of the river also was completely exposed to observation from the enemy's hills, which, though low in comparison of the mountains above the bridge, were nevertheless strong ridges of defence; but relying on his previous measures to deceive the enemy, the

English general disdained these dangers, and his anticipations were not belied by the result.

Passage of the Bidassoa.

The night of October 6th set in heavily. A sullen thunderstorm gathering about the craggy summit of the Peña de Haya came slowly down its flanks, and towards morning rolling over the Bidassoa, fell in its greatest violence upon the French positions. During this turmoil Wellington, whose pontoons and artillery were close up to Irun, disposed a number of guns and howitzers along the crest of San Marcial, and the different columns attained their respective stations along the banks of the river. The second brigade of guards and the Germans of the first division were concealed near Irun, close to a ford below the bridge of Behobia called the Great Jonco. The British brigades of the fifth division covered themselves behind a large river embankment opposite Andaya; Sprye's Portuguese and Lord Aylmer's brigade were posted in the ditch of Fuenterabia.

As all the tents were left standing in the camps of the allies, the enemy could perceive no change on the morning of the 7th October, but at seven o'clock the fifth division and Lord Aylmer's brigade, emerging from their concealment, took the sands in two columns, that on the left pointing against the French camp of the Sans Culottes, that on the right against the ridge of Andaya. No shot was fired, but when they had passed the fords of the low-water channel a rocket was sent up from the steeple of Fuenterabia as a signal. Then the guns and howitzers opened from San Marcial, the troops near Irun, covered by the fire of a battery, made for the Jonco ford, and the passage above the bridge also commenced. From the crest of San Marcial seven columns could be seen at once, attacking on a line of five miles; those above the bridge plunging at once into the fiery contest, those below it appearing in the distance like huge sullen snakes winding over the heavy sands. The Germans, missing the Jonco ford, got into deep water, but quickly recovered the true line; and the French, completely surprised, permitted even the brigades of the fifth division to gain the right bank and form their lines before a hostile musket flashed. The cannonade from San Marcial was heard by Soult at Espelette, and at the same time the sixth division made a false attack on D'Erlon's positions; the Portuguese brigade under Colonel Douglas were, however, pushed too far, and repulsed with the loss of 150 men; and the French marshal, instantly detecting the true nature of this attack, hurried to his right, but his camps on the Bidassoa were lost before he arrived.

When the British artillery first opened, Maucune's troops had assembled at their different posts of defence, and the French guns, established principally near the mountain of Louis XIV. and the Caffé Republicain, commenced firing. The alarm spread, and Boyer's corps marched from the second line behind Urogne to support Maucune without waiting for the junction of the working parties; but his brigades moved separately as they could collect, and before the first came into action Sprye's Portuguese, forming the extreme left of the allies, menaced the camp of the Sans Culottes. Thither, therefore, one of Boyer's regiments was ordered, while the others advanced by the royal road towards the Croix des Bouquets. But Andaya, guarded only by a picquet, was abandoned, and Reille, thinking the camp of the Sans Culottes would be lost before Boyer's men reached it, sent a battalion there from the centre, thus weakening his force at the chief point of attack; for the British brigades of the fifth division were now advancing left in front from Andaya, and bearing under a sharp fire of artillery and musketry towards the Croix des Bouquets.

By this time the columns of the first division had passed the river, one above the bridge, one below, who, aided by the fire of the guns on San Marcial, drove back the enemy's advanced posts, won the Caffé Republicain, the mountain of Louis XIV., and drove the French from those heights to the Croix des Bouquets. This was the key of the position, and towards it guns and troops were now hastening from every side. The Germans, who had lost many men in the previous attack, were here brought to a check, for the heights were very strong, and Boyer's leading battalions were now close at hand; but at this critical moment Colonel Cameron arrived with the 9th regiment of the fifth division, and passing through the German skirmishers, rushed with great vehemence to the summit of the first height. The French infantry instantly opened their ranks to let their guns retire, and then retreated themselves at full speed to a second ridge, somewhat lower, but where they could only be approached on a narrow front. Cameron as quickly threw his men into a single column and bore against this new position, which curving inwards enabled the French to pour a concentrated fire upon his regiment; nor did his violent course seem to dismay them until he was within ten yards, when, appalled by the furious shout and charge of the 9th, they gave way, and the ridges of the Croix des Bouquets were won as far as the royal road. The British regiment, however, lost many men and officers, and during the fight the French artillery and scattered troops, coming from different points and rallying on Boyer's battalions, were gathered on the ridges to the French left of the road.

The entrenched camp above Biriatu and the Bildox had been meanwhile defended with success in front, but Freyre turned them with his right wing, which, being opposed only by a single battalion, soon won the Mandale mountain, and the French fell back from that quarter. Reille, thus beaten at the Croix des Bouquets and his flanks turned, retreated in great disorder along the royal causeway and the old road of Bayonne. He passed through the village of Urogne, and the British skirmishers at first entered it in pursuit, but they were beaten out again by the second brigade of Boyer's division; for Soult now arrived with part of Villatte's reserve and many guns, and by his presence and activity restored order and revived the courage of the troops at the moment when the retreat was degenerating into a flight. Reille lost eight pieces of artillery and about 400 men; the allies did not lose more than 600, of which half were Spaniards, so slight and easy had the skill of the general rendered this stupendous operation. But if the French commander, penetrating Wellington's design, and avoiding the surprise, had opposed all his troops, amounting, with what Villatte could spare, to 16,000, instead of the 5000 actually engaged, the passage could scarcely have been forced; and a check would have been tantamount to a terrible defeat, because in two hours the returning tide would have come with a swallowing flood upon the rear.

Equally unprepared and equally unsuccessful were the French on the side of Vera, although the struggle there proved more fierce and constant. At daybreak Giron had descended from the Ivantelly rocks, and General Alten from Santa Barbara. One brigade drew up in column on an open space to the right of Vera. The other brigade, under Colonel Colborne, was disposed on the left of Vera. Half of Longa's division was between these brigades; the other half, after crossing the ford of Salinas, drew up on Colborne's left. The whole of the narrow vale of Vera was thus filled with troops ready to ascend the mountains, and General Cole, displaying his force to advantage on the heights of Santa Barbara, presented a formidable reserve.

Taupin's division guarded the enormous positions in front of the allies. His right was on the Bayonette, from whence a single slope descended to a small plain about two parts down the mountain. From this platform three distinct tongues shot into the valley below; each was defended by an advanced post, and the platform itself secured by a star redoubt, behind which, about half-way up the single slope, there was a second entrenchment with abattis. Another large redoubt and an unfinished breastwork on the superior crest completed the system of defence for the Bayonette. The Commissary, which is a continuation of the Bayonette towards the great Rhune, was covered by a profound gulf thickly wooded and defended with skirmishers, and between this gulf and another of the same nature the main road, leading from Vera over the Puerto, pierced the centre of the French position. Rugged and ascending with short abrupt turns, this road was blocked at every uncovered point with abattis and small retrenchments; each obstacle was commanded, at half-musket shot, by small detachments placed on all the projecting parts overlooking the ascent, and a regiment connected the troops on the crest of the Bayonette and Commissary with those on the saddle-ridge, against which Giron's attack was directed. Between Alten's right and Giron's left was an isolated ridge called by the soldiers the Boar's back, the summit of which, about half a mile long and rounded at each end, was occupied by four French companies. This huge cavalier, thrown as it were into the gulf to cover the Puerto and saddle ridges, although of mean height in comparison of the towering ranges behind, was yet so great that the few warning shots fired from the summit by the enemy reached the allies at its base with that slow singing sound which marks the dying force of a musket-ball. It was essential to take the Boar's back before the general attack commenced, and five companies of British riflemen, supported by the 17th Portuguese regiment, were ordered to assail it at the Vera end, while a battalion of Giron's Spaniards, preceded by a detached company of the 43rd, attacked it on the other.

Second Combat of Vera.

Soon after seven o'clock a few cannon-shot from some mountain-guns, of which each side had a battery, were followed by the Spanish musketry on the right, and the next moment the Boar's back was simultaneously assailed at both ends. The riflemen on the Vera side ascended to a small pine-wood two-thirds of the way up, and there rested; but soon resuming their movement with a scornful gallantry, they swept the French off the top, disdaining to use their rifles beyond a few shots down the reverse side, to show that they were masters of the ridge. This was the signal for the general attack. The 17th Portuguese followed the victorious sharp-shooters; the 43rd, preceded by their own skirmishers and by the remainder of the riflemen of the right wing, plunged into the rugged pass; Longa's troops entered the gloomy wood of the ravine on the left; and beyond them Colborne's brigade, moving by narrow paths and throwing out skirmishers, assailed the Bayonette; the 52nd took the middle tongue, the caçadores and riflemen the two outermost, and all bore with a concentric movement against the star redoubt on the platform above. Longa's second brigade quietly followed the riflemen in reserve.

Soon the open slopes of the mountains were covered with men and with fire, a heavy confused sound of mingled shouts and musketry filled the deep hollows between, and the white smoke came curling up above the dark forest trees which covered their gloomy recesses. The French, compared with their assailants, seemed few and scattered on the mountain-side, and Kempt's brigade soon forced its way without a check through all the retrenchments on the main pass, his skirmishers spreading wider and breaking into small detachments of support as the depth of the ravine lessened and the slopes melted into the higher ridges. When about half-way up an open platform gave a clear view over the Bayonette slopes, and all eyes were turned that way. Longa's

SECOND COMBAT OF VERA.

right brigade, fighting in the gulf between, seemed labouring and overmatched; but beyond, on the broad open space in front of the star fort, the caçadores and riflemen of Colborne's brigade were seen coming out, in small bodies, from a forest which covered the three tongues of land up to the edge of the platform. Their fire was sharp, their pace rapid, and in a few moments they closed upon the redoubt in a mass as if resolved to storm it. The 52nd were not then in sight, and the French, thinking from the dark clothing that all were Portuguese, rushed in close order out of the entrenchment; they were numerous and very sudden, and this rough charge sent the scattered assailants back over the rocky edge of the descent. With shrill cries the French followed, but just then the 52nd appeared, partly in line, partly in column, on the platform, and raising their shout, rushed forward. The red uniform and full career of this regiment startled the hitherto adventurous French; they stopped short, wavered, and then turning, fled to their entrenchment. The 52nd, following hard, entered the works with them; the riflemen and caçadores, who had meanwhile rallied, passed it on both flanks, and for a few moments everything was hidden by a dense volume of smoke. Soon, however, the British shout pealed again, and the whole mass emerged on the other side, the French, now the fewer, flying, the others pursuing, until the second entrenchment, half-way up the parent slope, enabled the retreating troops to make another stand.

The exulting and approving cheers of Kempt's brigade now echoed along the mountain-side, and with renewed vigour the men continued to scale the craggy mountain, fighting their toilsome way to the top of the Puerto. Meanwhile Colborne, after having carried the second entrenchment above the star fort, was brought to a check by the works on the very crest of the mountain, from whence the French not only plied his troops with musketry at a great advantage, but rolled huge stones down the steep. These works were extensive, well lined with men, and strengthened by a large redoubt on the right; but the defenders soon faltered, for their left flank was turned by Kempt, and the effects of Lord Wellington's skilful combinations were now felt in another quarter. Freyre's Spaniards, after carrying the Mandale mountain, had pushed to a road leading to St. Jean de Luz, and this was the line of retreat from the crest of the Bayonette for Taupin's right wing; but Freyre's

Spaniards got there first, and if Longa's brigade, instead of slowly following Colborne, had spread out widely on the left, a military line would have been completed from Giron to Freyre. Still Taupin's right was cut off on that side, and he was forced to file under fire along the crest of the Bayonette to reach the Puerto de Vera road, where he was joined by his centre. He effected this, but lost his mountain battery and 300 men. These last, apparently the garrison of the large fort on the extreme right of the Bayonette crest, were captured by Colborne in a remarkable manner. Accompanied by only one of his staff and half-a-dozen riflemen, he crossed their march unexpectedly, and with great presence of mind and intrepidity ordered them to lay down their arms, an order which they, thinking themselves entirely cut off, obeyed. Meanwhile the French skirmishers in the deep ravine, between the two lines of attack, being feebly pushed by Longa's troops, retreated too slowly, and getting amongst some rocks from whence there was no escape, surrendered to Kempt's brigade. The right and centre of Taupin's division being now completely beaten, fled down the side of the mountain; they were pursued by a part of the allies until they rallied upon Villatte's reserve, which was in order of battle on a ridge extending across the gorge of Olette. The Bayonette and Commissary, with the Puerto de Vera, were thus won after five hours' incessant fighting and toiling up their craggy sides. Nevertheless the battle was still maintained by the French troops on the Rhune.

When Giron's left wing was rendered free to move by the capture of the Boar's back, he fought his way up abreast with the British line until near the saddle-ridge, a little to his own right of the Puerto. There, however, he was arrested by a strong line of abattis, from behind which two French regiments poured a heavy fire. The Spaniards stopped, and though Downie, a Spanish general, encouraged them with his voice and they kept their ranks, they seemed irresolute and did not advance. There happened to be present an officer of the 43rd regiment named Havelock, who, being attached to General Alten's staff, was sent to ascertain Giron's progress. His fiery temper could not brook the check. He took off his hat, he called upon the Spaniards to follow him, and putting spurs to his horse, at one bound cleared the abattis and went headlong amongst the enemy. Then the soldiers, shouting for "*El chico blanco*," "The fair boy," as they called him—for

SECOND COMBAT OF VERA.

he was very young and had light hair—with one shock broke through the French, and this at the very moment when their centre was flying under the fire of Kempt's skirmishers from the Puerto de Vera.

The two regiments thus defeated by the Spaniards retired by their left along the saddle-ridge to the flanks of the Rhune, so that Clausel had now eight regiments concentrated on this great mountain. Two occupied the crest, including the highest rock called the Hermitage; four were on the flanks; the remaining two occupied a lower and parallel crest behind called the Small Rhune. In this situation they were attacked at four o'clock by Giron's right wing. The Spaniards first dislodged a small body from a detached pile of crags about musket-shot below the summit, and then assailed the bald staring rocks of the Hermitage itself, endeavouring at the same time to turn it by their right. In both objects they were defeated with loss. The Hermitage was impregnable; the French rolled down stones large enough to sweep away a whole column at once, and the Spaniards resorted to a distant musketry which lasted until night.

The success was not complete, for while the French kept possession of the summit of the Rhune the allies' new position was insecure. The front and the right flank of the great mountain were impregnable, but Lord Wellington, observing that the left flank descending towards Sarre, was less inaccessible, concentrated the Spaniards on that side on the 8th, designing a combined attack against the mountain itself, and against the camp of Sarre. At three o'clock in the afternoon the rocks which studded the lower parts of the Rhune slope were assailed by the Spaniards, and at the same time detachments of the seventh division descended from the Puerto de Echallar upon the fort of San Barbe, and other outworks covering the advanced French camp of Sarre. The Andalusians soon won the rocks and an entrenched height that commanded the camp; for Clausel, too easily alarmed at some slight demonstrations made by the sixth division in rear of his left, thought he should be cut off from his great camp, and very suddenly abandoned not only the slope of the mountain, but all his advanced works in the basin below, including the fort of San Barbe. His troops were thus concentrated on the height behind Sarre, still holding with their right the smaller Rhune, but the consequences of his error were soon made apparent. Wellington immediately established a strong body of the Spanish troops close up to the rocks of the Hermitage, and the two French regiments there, seeing the lower slopes and the fort of San Barbe given up, imagined they also would be cut off, and without orders abandoned the impregnable rocks of the Hermitage and retired in the night to the smaller Rhune. The next morning some of the seventh division rashly pushed into the village of Sarre, but they were quickly repulsed, and would have lost the camp and works taken the day before if the Spaniards had not succoured them.

The whole loss on the three days of fighting was about 1400 French and 1600 of the allies, one-half being Spaniards; but many of the wounded were not brought in until the third day after the actions, and several perished miserably where they fell, it being impossible to discover them in those vast solitudes. Some men were also lost from want of discipline; having descended into the French villages, they got drunk, and were taken the next day by the enemy. With exception of two slight checks, the course of these operations had been eminently successful, and surely the bravery of troops who assailed and carried such stupendous positions must be admired. To them the unfinished state of the French works was not visible. Day after day, for more than a month, entrenchment had risen over entrenchment, covering the vast slopes of mountains, which were scarcely accessible from their natural steepness and roughness. This they could see, yet cared neither for the growing strength of the works, the height of the mountains, nor the breadth of the river, with its heavy sands and its mighty rushing tide; all were despised; and while they marched with this confident valour, it was observed that the French fought in defence of their dizzy steeps with far less fierceness than when, striving against insurmountable obstacles, they attempted to storm the lofty rocks of Sauroren. Continual defeat had lowered their spirit, but the feebleness of the defence on this occasion may be traced to another cause. It was a general's, not a soldier's, battle. Wellington had with overmastering combinations overwhelmed each point of attack.

The project of the passage of the Bidassoa was one of bold conception, and the success of Lord Wellington in executing this daring and difficult operation in the presence of an opponent like Marshal Soult, whose circumspection was equal to his ability, is a sterling proof of the great military genius of the leader of the allied forces. While the struggle at the Bidassoa was going on, Pampeluna was at last forced to surrender—an event produced by a long blockade, less fertile of incident than the siege of San Sebastian, yet very honourable to the firmness of the governor-general, Cassan.

Fall of Pampeluna.

Pampeluna had been partially blockaded by Mina for eighteen months previous to the battle of Vittoria, and when King Joseph arrived, after the action, the place was badly provisioned. The stragglers of his army increased the garrison to something more than 3500 men of all arms, who were immediately invested by the allies. Many of the inhabitants went off during the short interval between the king's arrival and departure, and General Cassan, finding his troops too few for action, and yet too many for the food, abandoned two outworks on the south, demolished everything which could interfere with his defence outside, and commenced such works as he deemed necessary to improve it inside. Moreover, foreseeing that the French army might possibly make a sudden march, without guns, to succour the garrison, he prepared a field-train of forty pieces to meet the occasion.

Wellington, although at first inclined to besiege Pampeluna, finally established a blockade and ordered works of contravallation to be constructed. Cassan's chief object was then to obtain provisions, and on the 28th and 30th of June he sustained actions outside the place to cover his foragers. On the 1st of July he burned the suburb of Madalina, beyond the river Arga, and forced many inhabitants to quit the place before the blockaders' works were completed. Skirmishes now occurred almost daily, the French always seeking to gather the grain and vegetables which were ripe and abundant beyond the walls, and the allies endeavouring to set fire to the standing corn within range of the guns of the fortress. On the 14th of July, O'Donnel's Andalusians were permanently established as the blockading force, and the next day the garrison made a successful forage on the south side of the town. This operation was repeated towards the east beyond the Arga on the 19th, when a sharp engagement of cavalry took place, during which the remainder of the garrison carried away a great deal of corn.

On the 26th the sound of Soult's artillery reached the place, and Cassan, judging rightly that the marshal was in march to succour Pampeluna, made a sally in the night by the Roncesvalles road. He was driven back, but the next morning he came out again with 1100 men and two guns, overthrew the Spanish outguards, and advanced towards Villalba at the moment when Picton was falling back with the third and fourth divisions. Then O'Donnel evacuated some of the entrenchments, destroyed a great deal of ammunition, spiked a number of guns, and but for the timely arrival of Carlos d'España's division would have abandoned the blockade altogether.

Soon the battle on the mountains of Oricain commenced; the smoke rose over the intervening heights of Escava and San Miguel, the French cavalry appeared on the slopes above El Cano, and the baggage of the allies was seen filing in the opposite direction along the road of Irurzun. The garrison thought deliverance sure, and having reaped a good harvest, withdrew into the place. The bivouac fires of the French army cheered them during the night, and the next morning a fresh sally being made with the greatest confidence, a great deal of corn was gathered with little loss of men. Several deserters from the foreign regiments in the English service also came over with intelligence exaggerated and coloured, after the manner of such men, and the French re-entered the place elated with hope; but in the evening the sound of the conflict ceased, and the silence of the next day showed that the battle was not to the advantage of Soult. However, the governor, losing no time, made another sally, and again obtained provisions from the south side.

The 30th the battle recommenced, but the retreating fire of the French told how the conflict was decided, and the spirit of the soldiers fell. Nevertheless their indefatigable officers led another sally on the south side, whence they carried off grain and some ammunition which had been left in one of the abandoned outworks.

On the 31st Carlos d'España's troops and 2000 of O'Donnel's

FALL OF PAMPELUNA.

Andalusians, in all about 7000 men, resumed the blockade, and maintained it until the middle of September, when a division of Del Parque's army relieved the Andalusians, who rejoined their own corps near Echallar. The allies' works of contravallation were now augmented, and part of Mina's troops occupied the valleys leading to Pampeluna, and made entrenchments to bar the escape of the garrison that way.

In October Cassan put his fighting men upon rations of horse-flesh, four ounces to each, with some rice, and he turned more families out of the town, but this time they were fired upon by their countrymen and forced to re-enter; and Baron Maucune, who conducted most of the sallies during the blockade, attacked and carried some fortified houses on the east side of the place; he was immediately assailed by the Spanish cavalry, but he beat them and pursued the fugitives close to Villalba. Carlos d'España then advanced to their aid in person with a greater body, and the French were driven in with the loss of eighty men; yet the Spaniards lost a far greater number; Carlos d'España himself was wounded, and the garrison obtained some corn, which was their principal object.

The soldiers were now feeding on rats and other disgusting animals; seeking also for roots beyond the walls, many in their hunger poisoned themselves with hemlock, and a number of others, unable to bear their misery, deserted. In this state Cassan made a general sally, on the 10th of October, to ascertain the strength of the lines around him, with a view to breaking through; but after some fighting his troops were driven in with the loss of seventy men, and all hope of escape vanished. Yet he still spoke of attempting it, and the public manner in which he increased the mines under the citadel induced Wellington to reinforce the blockade, and to bring up his cavalry into the vicinity of Pampeluna.

The scurvy now invaded the garrison. One thousand men were sick, 800 had been wounded; the deaths by battle and disease exceeded 400, 120 had deserted, and the governor, moved by the great misery, offered on the 26th to surrender if he was allowed to retire into France with his troops and six pieces of cannon. This being refused, he proposed to yield on condition of not serving for a year and a day, which being also denied, he broke off the negotiation, giving out that he would blow up the works of the fortress and break through the blockade. To deter him a menacing letter was thrown to his outposts, and Lord Wellington, being informed of his design, denounced it as contrary to the laws of war, and directed Carlos d'España to put him, all his officers and non-commissioned officers, and a tenth of the soldiers to death when the place should be taken, if any damage were done to the works.

Cassan's object being merely to obtain better terms, this order remained dormant, and happily so, for the execution would never have borne the test of public opinion. To destroy the works of Pampeluna and break through the blockading force would have been a very noble exploit, and a useful one for the French army if Soult's plan of changing the theatre of war by descending into Aragon had been followed. There could, therefore, be nothing contrary to the laws of war in a resolute action of that nature. On the other hand, if the governor, having no chance whatever of success, made a hopeless attempt the pretence for destroying a great fortress belonging to the Spaniards and depriving the allies of the fruits of their long blockade and glorious battles, the conquerors might have justly exercised that severe but undoubted right of war, refusing quarter to an enemy. A few days longer the governor and garrison endured their distress, and then capitulated, having defended themselves more than four months with great constancy. The officers and soldiers became prisoners of war. The first were allowed to keep their arms and baggage, the second their knapsacks, expressly on the ground that they had treated the inhabitants well during the investment.

There was no stronghold now retained by the French in the north of Spain except Santona, and as the blockade of that place had been exceedingly tedious, Lord Wellington, whose sea-communications were interrupted by the privateers from thence, formed a small British corps under Lord Aylmer with a view to attack Laredo, which, being on the opposite point of the harbour to Santona, commanded the anchorage. Accidental circumstances, however, prevented this body from proceeding to its destination, and Santona remained in the enemy's possession. With this exception the contest in the northern parts of Spain was terminated, and the south of France was now to be invaded.

CHAPTER XVI.

BATTLE OF THE NIVELLE.

FTER crossing the Bidassoa, Lord Wellington fixed his head-quarters at Vera, and now being actually in France, and the war in Germany having taken a favourable turn, he prepared to commence operations in the French territory—the fall of Pampeluna having removed the last hindrance to the carrying out of his designs, and the capture of San Sebastian having set free a large number of troops to join the main body of the allies. The Peninsula had at length been delivered by the genius of Wellington, his army was cantoned within the territory of France, Soult had been repeatedly defeated, the fortresses had fallen, and except a detached and useless force under Suchet at Catalonia, there remained no longer a single French soldier in Spain. Such were the tidings which reached the Emperor Napoleon from his Spanish frontier after his disastrous retreat from Moscow, and at the very moment when it was necessary for him to make head against the Russians, Germans, and Austrians, chiefly armed and supplied at the cost of Britain, and now rapidly concentrating in great masses on different points of the Rhine, with the purpose of forcing their way to Paris and causing the usurper to resign. At this time, too, not a few of Napoleon's own ministers, hopeless of breathing in peace while that insatiable spirit continued at the head of affairs, were well prepared to take a part in his overthrow; nor was it long ere these enemies were content to overlook their own differences and work together for the one issue.

On the failure of his efforts in the Pyrenees, Soult had formed a strong line of defence many miles in extent, stretching from the sea across the Nivelle to the heights of the Rhune mountains behind Ainhoe. This position he strengthened with a series of formidable redoubts—every road was defended by abattis and entrenchments, every eminence crowned by a field-work, and all were so disposed that the fire of each might protect and enfilade the works in its neighbourhood, while at the same time the forces were being added to by large reinforcements. The weather became extremely inclement, the crests of the mountains were covered with snow, and many of the roads being rendered nearly impassable, it was not till the beginning of November that the allied army found it possible to advance against the new position Soult had taken up. This advance was eagerly desired by the allies, as their position among the mountains had been one of extreme discomfort and privation; one portion of the army were for two days without provisions, being blocked up by the snow.

Soult's weakest point of general defence was the opening between the Rhune mountains and the Nivelle. Gradually narrowing as it approached the bridge of Amotz, this space was the most open, the least fortified, and the Nivelle, being fordable above that bridge, could not hamper the allies' movements. Wherefore a powerful force acting in this direction could pass by D'Erlon's first line, and breaking in upon the main position, between the right of that general's second line and Clausel's left, turn both by the same attack.

Before Clausel's right position could be assailed, the smaller Rhune which covered it was to be stormed. This mountain outwork was a hog's-back ridge rising abruptly out of table-land, and parallel with the greater Rhune. It was inaccessible along its front, which was precipitous and from fifty to two hundred feet high; but on the enemy's left these rocks gradually decreased, descending by a long slope to the valley of Sarre, and about two-thirds of the way down the 34th French regiment was placed, with an advanced post on some isolated crags situated in the hollow between the two Rhunes. On the enemy's right the hog's-back sank by degrees into the plain or platform. It was, however, covered at that point by a marsh scarcely passable, and the attacking troops were therefore first to move up against the perpendicular rocks in front, and then to file to their left under fire, between the marsh and the lower crags, until they gained an accessible point from whence they could fight their way along the narrow ridge of the hog's-back. But the bristles of the latter were huge perpendicular crags connected with walls of loose stones so as to form several small forts or castles communicating with each other by narrow footways, and rising one above another until the culminant point was attained. The table-land beyond this ridge was extensive, and terminated in a very deep ravine on every side, save a narrow space on the right of the marsh, where the enemy had drawn a traverse of loose stones, running perpendicularly from behind the hog's-back, and ending in a star fort which overhung the edge of the ravine.

This rampart and fort, and the hog's-back itself, were defended by Barbot's brigade of Maransin's division, and the line of retreat was towards a low narrow neck of land which, bridging the deep ravine, linked the Rhune to Clausel's main position: a reserve was placed here, partly to sustain the 34th French regiment posted on the slope of the mountain towards Sarre, partly to protect the neck of land on the side of that village. As this neck was the only approach to the French position in that part, to storm the smaller Rhune was a necessary preliminary to the general battle, wherefore Alten, filing his troops after dark on the 9th from the Hermitage, the Commissary mountain, and the Puerto de Vera, collected them at midnight on that slope of the greater Rhune which descended towards Ascain. The main body of the light division, turning the marsh by the left, was to assail the stone traverse and lap over the star fort by the ravine beyond; Longa, stretching still farther on the left, was to turn the smaller Rhune altogether; and the 43rd regiment, supported by the 17th Portuguese, was to assail the hog's-back. One battalion of riflemen and the mountain-guns were, however, left on the summit of the greater Rhune, with orders to assail the craggy post between the Rhunes and connect Alten's attack with that of Giron's Spaniards. All these troops gained their respective stations so secretly that the enemy had no suspicion of their presence, although for several hours the columns were lying within half musket-shot of the works. Towards morning, indeed, five or six guns, fired in a hurried manner from the low ground near the sea, broke the stillness; but the French on the Rhune remained quiet, and the British troops awaited the rising of the sun, when three guns fired from the Atchubia mountain were to give the signal of attack.

BATTLE OF THE NIVELLE.

The 10th of November broke with great splendour, and as the first ray of light played on the summit of the lofty Atchubia, the signal-guns were fired in rapid succession from its summit. The soldiers instantly leaped up, and the French beheld with astonishment several columns rushing forward from the flank of the great Rhune. Running to their defences with much tumult, they opened a few pieces, which were answered from the top of the greater Rhune by the mountain-artillery, and at the same moment two companies of the 43rd were detached to cross the marsh if possible, and keep down the enemy's fire from the lower part of the hog's-back. The action being thus commenced, the remainder of the regiment, formed partly in line, partly in a column of reserve, turned the marsh by the right and advanced against the high rocks. From these crags the French shot fast and thickly, but the quick even movement of the British line deceived their aim, and the soldiers, running forward very swiftly, though the ground was rough, turned suddenly between the rocks and the marsh, and were immediately joined by the two companies, which had passed that obstacle notwithstanding its depth. Then all together jumped into the lower works, but the men, exhausted by their exertions—for they had passed over half a mile of very difficult ground with a wonderful speed—remained for a few minutes inactive within half pistol-shot of the first stone castle, from whence came a sharp and biting musketry. When they had recovered breath they arose, and with a stern shout commenced the assault.

The defenders were as numerous as the assailants, and for six weeks they had been labouring on their well-contrived castles; but strong and valiant in arms must the soldiers have been who stood in that hour before the veterans of the 43rd. One French grenadier officer only dared to sustain the rush. Standing alone on the high wall of the first castle, and flinging large stones with both his hands, a noble figure, he fought to the last and fell, while his men, shrinking on each side, sought safety among the rocks on his flanks. Close and confused then was the action, man met man at every turn, but with a rattling fire of musketry, sometimes struggling in the intricate narrow paths, sometimes climbing the loose stone walls, the British soldiers won their desperate way until they had carried the second castle, called by the French the place of arms, and the magpie's nest, because of a lofty pillar of rock which rose above it, and on which a few marksmen were perched. From these points the defenders were driven into their last castle, which being higher and larger than the others, and covered by a natural ditch or cleft in the rocks fifteen feet deep, was called the Donjon. Here they made a stand, and the assailants, having advanced so far as to look into the rear of the rampart and star fort on the table-land below, suspended the vehement throng of their attack for a while, partly to gather a head for storming the Donjon, partly to fire on the enemy beneath them, who were now warmly engaged with the two battalions of riflemen, the Portuguese caçadores, and the 17th Portuguese. This last regiment was to have followed the 43rd, but seeing how rapidly and surely the latter were carrying the rocks, had moved at once against the traverse on the other side of the marsh; and very soon the French defending the rampart, being thus pressed in front, and warned by the direction of the fire that they were turned on the ridge above, seeing also the 52nd, forming the extreme left of the division, now emerging from the deep ravine beyond the star fort on the other flank, abandoned their works. Then the 43rd, gathering a strong head, stormed the Donjon. Some leaped with a shout down the deep cleft in the rock, others turned it by the narrow paths on each flank, and the enemy abandoned the loose walls at the moment they were being scaled. Thus in twenty minutes 600 old soldiers were hustled out of this labyrinth; yet not so easily but that the victors lost eleven officers and sixty-seven men.

The whole mountain was now cleared of the French, for the riflemen, dropping perpendicularly down from the greater Rhune upon the post of crags in the hollow between the Rhunes, seized it with small loss; but they were ill-seconded by Giron's Spaniards, and were severely handled by the 34th French regiment, which, maintaining its post on the slope, covered the flight of the confused crowd which came rushing down the mountain behind them towards the neck of land leading to the main position. At that point they all rallied, and seemed inclined to renew the action, but after some hesitation continued their retreat. This favourable moment for a decisive stroke had been looked for by the commander of the 43rd, but the officer entrusted with the reserve companies of the regiment had thrown them needlessly into the fight, thus rendering it impossible to collect a body strong enough to assail such a heavy mass.

The contest at the stone rampart and star fort, being shortened by the rapid success on the hog's-back, was not very severe, but General Kempt, always conspicuous for his valour, was severely wounded; nevertheless he did not quit the field, and soon re-formed his brigade on the platform he had thus so gallantly won. Meanwhile the 52nd, having turned the position by the ravine, was now approaching the enemy's line of retreat, when General Alten, following his instructions, halted the division partly in the ravine itself to the left of the neck, partly on the table-land, and during this action Longa's Spaniards, having got near Ascain, were in connection with Freyre's Gallicians. In this position, with the enemy now and then cannonading Longa's people and the troops in the ravine, Alten awaited the progress of the army on his right, for the columns there had a long way to march, and it was essential to regulate the movements.

The signal-guns from the Atchubia which sent the light division against the Rhune, had also put the fourth and seventh divisions in movement against the redoubts of San Barbe and Grenada. Eighteen guns were immediately placed in battery against the former, and while they poured their stream of shot the troops advanced with scaling-ladders, and the skirmishers of the fourth division got into the rear of the work, whereupon the French leaped out and fled. Ross's battery of horse artillery, galloping to a rising ground in rear of the Grenada fort, drove the enemy from there also, and then the fourth and seventh divisions carried the village of Sarre and the position beyond it, and advanced to the attack of Clausel's main position.

From the smaller Rhune at eight o'clock a splendid spectacle of war opened upon the view. On one hand, British ships of war, slowly sailing to and fro, were exchanging shots with the fort of Socoa; Sir John Hope, menacing the French lines in the low ground, sent the sound of a hundred pieces of artillery bellowing up the rocks, and they were answered by nearly as many from the

BATTLE OF THE NIVELLE.

tops of the mountains. On the other hand, the summit of the great Atchubia was just lighted by the rising sun, and 50,000 men, rushing down its enormous slopes with ringing shouts, seemed to chase the receding shadows into the deep valley. The plains of France, so long overlooked from the towering crags of the Pyrenees, were to be the prize of battle, and the half-famished soldiers in their fury broke through the iron barrier erected by Soult as if it were but a screen of reeds.

The principal action was on a space of seven or eight miles, but the skirts of battle spread wide, and in no point had Wellington's combinations failed. Far on the right General Hill, after a long and difficult night-march, had got within reach of the enemy a little before seven o'clock. Opposing Morillo's and Mina's Spaniards to Abbé's troops on the Mondarain and Atchuleguy rocks, he directed the second division against D'Armagnac's brigade, and brushed it back from the forge of Urdax and the village of Ainhoa. Meanwhile, the aid of the sixth division and Hamilton's Portuguese being demanded by him, they passed the Nivelle lower down and bent their march along the right bank towards the bridge of Amotz. Thus while Mina's battalion and Morillo's division kept Abbé in check on the mountains, the three Anglo-Portuguese divisions, marching left flank in advance, approached D'Erlon's second position, but the country being very rugged, it was eleven o'clock before they got within cannon-shot of the French redoubts. Each of these contained 500 men, and they were placed along the summit of a high ridge, which, being thickly clothed with bushes and covered by a deep ravine, was very difficult to attack. However, General Clinton, leading the sixth division on the extreme left, turned this ravine and drove the enemy from the works covering the approaches to the bridge, after which, wheeling to his right, he advanced against the nearest redoubt, and the garrison, not daring to await the assault, abandoned it. Then the Portuguese division, passing the ravine and marching on the right of the sixth, menaced the second redoubt, and the second division in like manner approached the third redoubt. D'Armagnac's troops now set fire to their hutted camp and retreated behind San Pé, pursued by the sixth division. Abbé's second brigade, forming the French left, was separated by a ravine from D'Armagnac's ground, but he also, after some hesitation, retreated towards Espelette and Cambo, where his other brigade, which had meanwhile fallen back from the Mondarain before Morillo, rejoined him.

It was the progress of the battle on the left of the Nive that rendered D'Erlon's defence so feeble. After the fall of the St. Barbe and Grenada redoubts Conroux's right and centre endeavoured to defend the village and heights of Sarre; but while the fourth and seventh divisions, aided by the 94th regiment, detached from the third division, attacked and carried those points, the third division, being on their right and less opposed, pushed rapidly towards the bridge of Amotz, forming in conjunction with the sixth division the narrow end of the wedge into which Beresford's and Hill's corps were now thrown. The French were thus driven from all their new unfinished works covering the approaches to that bridge on both sides of the Nivelle, and Conroux's division, spreading from Sarre to Amotz, was broken by superior numbers at every point. That general, indeed, vigorously defended the old works around the bridge itself, but he soon fell mortally wounded, his troops were again broken, and the third division seized the bridge and established itself on the heights between that structure and the redoubt of Louis XIV., which, having been also lately commenced, was unfinished. This happened about eleven o'clock, and D'Erlon, fearing to be cut off from San Pé, yielded at once to the attack of the sixth division, and at the same time the remainder of Conroux's troops fell back in disorder from Sarre, closely pursued by the fourth and seventh divisions, which were immediately established on the left of the third. Thus the communication between Clausel and D'Erlon was cut, the left flank of one and the right flank of the other broken, and a direct communication between Hill and Beresford secured by the same blow.

D'Erlon abandoned his position, but Clausel stood firm with Taupin's and Maransin's divisions. The latter, now completed by the return of Barbot's brigade from the smaller Rhune, occupied the redoubt of Louis XIV., and, supported with eight field-pieces, attempted to cover the flight of Conroux's troops. The guns opened briskly, but they were silenced by Ross's battery of horse artillery, the only one which had surmounted the difficulties of the ground after passing Sarre; the infantry were then assailed,

BATTLE OF THE NIVELLE.

in front by the fourth and seventh divisions, in flank by the third division; the redoubt of Louis XIV. was stormed, the garrison bayoneted; Conroux's men continued to fly; Maransin's, after a stiff combat, were cast headlong into the ravines behind their position, and Maransin himself was taken, but escaped in the confusion. Giron's Spaniards now came up on the left of the fourth division, somewhat late, however, and after having abandoned the riflemen on the lower slopes of the smaller Rhune.

On the French side Taupin's division and a large body of conscripts, forming Clausel's right wing, still remained to fight. The left rested on a large work called the signal redoubt, which had no artillery, but overlooked the whole position; the right was covered by two redoubts overhanging a ravine which separated them from the camp of Serres, and some works in the ravine itself protected the communication by the bridge of Ascain. Behind the signal redoubt, on a ridge crossing the road to San Pé, and along which Maransin's and Conroux's beaten divisions were now flying in disorder, there was another work called the redoubt of Harastaguia, and Clausel, thinking he might still dispute the victory if his reserve division, posted in the camp of Serres, could come to his aid, drew the 31st French regiment from Taupin, and posted it in front of this redoubt of Harastaguia. His object was to rally Maransin's and Conroux's troops there and so form a new line, the left on the Harastaguia, the right on the signal redoubt, into which last he threw 600 of the 88th regiment. In this position, having a retreat by the bridge of Ascain, he resolved to renew the battle; but his plan failed at the moment of conception, because Taupin could not stand before the light division, which was now again in full action.

About half-past nine General Alten, seeing the whole of the columns on his right, as far as the eye could reach, well engaged with the enemy, had crossed the low neck of land in his front. It was first passed by the 52nd regiment with a rapid pace and a very narrow front, under a destructive cannonade and fire of musketry from the entrenchments which covered the side of the opposite mountain; a road coming from Ascain by the ravine led up the position, and as the 52nd pushed their attack along it the enemy abandoned his entrenchments on each side, and forsook even his crowning works above. This formidable regiment was followed by the remainder of Alten's troops, and Taupin, though his division was weak from its losses on the 7th of October, and now still further diminished by the absence of the 31st regiment, awaited the assault above, being supported by the conscripts drawn up in his rear. But at this time Longa, having turned the smaller Rhune, approached Ascain, and being joined by part of Freyre's troops, their skirmishers opened a distant musketry against the works covering that bridge on Taupin's right; a panic immediately seized the French, the 70th regiment abandoned the two redoubts above, and the conscripts were withdrawn. Clausel ordered Taupin to retake the forts, but this only added to the disorder; the 70th regiment, instead of facing about, disbanded entirely, and were not reassembled until next day. There remained only four regiments unbroken; one, the 88th, was in the signal redoubt, two under Taupin in person kept together in rear of the works on the right, and the 31st covered the fort of Harastaguia, now the only line of retreat.

In this emergency Clausel, anxious to bring off the 88th regiment, ordered Taupin to charge on one side of the signal redoubt, intending to do the same himself on the other at the head of the 31st regiment; but the latter was now vigorously attacked by the Portuguese of the seventh division, and the fourth division was rapidly interposing between that regiment and the signal redoubt. Moreover, Alten, previous to this, had directed the 43rd, preceded by Barnard's riflemen, to turn at the distance of musket-shot the right flank of the signal redoubt; wherefore Taupin, instead of charging, was himself charged in front by the riflemen, and being menaced at the same time in flank by the fourth division, retreated, closely pursued by Barnard until that intrepid officer fell dangerously wounded. During this struggle the seventh division broke the 31st; the rout was complete; the French fled to the different bridges over the Nivelle, and the signal redoubt was left to its fate.

This formidable work barred the way of the light division, but it was of no value to the defence when the forts on its flanks were abandoned. Colborne approached it in front with the 52nd regiment, Giron's Spaniards menaced it on Colborne's right, the fourth division was passing to its rear, and Kempt's brigade was turning it on the left. Colborne, whose military judgment was seldom at fault, halted under the brow of the conical hill on which the work was situated, but some of Giron's Spaniards, making a vaunting though feeble demonstration of attacking it on his right, were beaten back, and at that moment a staff-officer, without warrant—for General Alten sent no such order—rode up and directed Colborne to advance. It was not a moment for remonstrance, and his troops, covered by the steepness of the hill, reached the flat top, which was about forty yards across to the redoubt; then they made their rush, but a wide ditch, thirty feet deep, well fraised and palisaded, stopped them short, and the fire of the enemy stretched all the foremost men dead. The intrepid Colborne, escaping miraculously—for he was always at the head and on horseback—immediately led the regiment under cover of the brow to another point, and thinking to take the French unawares, made another rush, yet with the same result. At three different places did he rise to the surface in this manner, and each time the French fire swept away the head of his column. Resorting then to persuasion, he held out a white handkerchief and summoned the commandant, pointing out to him how his work was surrounded and how hopeless his defence; whereupon the garrison yielded, having had only one man killed, whereas on the British side there fell 200 soldiers of a regiment never surpassed in arms since arms were first borne by men.

During this affair Clausel's divisions had crossed the Nivelle in great disorder, Maransin's and Conroux's troops near San Pé, the 31st regiment at Harastaguia, Taupin between that place and the bridge of Serres. They were pursued by the third and seventh divisions, and the skirmishers of the former, crossing by Amotz and a bridge above San Pé, entered that place while the French were in the act of passing the river below. It was now past two o'clock; Cornoux's troops pushed on to a fortified position on the road from San Pé to Bayonne, where they were joined by Taupin and by D'Erlon with D'Armagnac's division; but Clausel rallied Maransin's men and took post on some heights immediately above San Pé. Meanwhile Soult had hurried from St. Jean de Luz to the camp of Serres, with all his reserve artillery and spare troops, to menace the allies' left flank by Ascain, and Wellington thereupon halted the fourth and light divisions, and Giron's Spaniards, on the reverse slopes of Clausel's original position, facing the camp of Serres, waiting until the sixth division, then following D'Armagnac's retreat on the right of the Nivelle, was well advanced. When he was assured of Clinton's progress, he crossed the Nivelle with the third and seventh divisions and drove Maransin from his new position after a hard struggle, in which General Inglis was wounded and the 51st and 68th regiments handled very roughly. This ended the battle in the centre, for darkness was coming on and the troops were exhausted, especially the sixth division, which had been marching or fighting for twenty-four hours. However, three divisions were firmly established in rear of Soult's right wing, under Reille, of whose operations it is now time to treat.

In front of Reille's entrenchments were two advanced positions, the camp of the Sans Culottes on the right, the Bons Secours in the centre covering Urogne. The first had been attacked and carried early in the morning by the fifth division. The second, after a short cannonade, was taken by Halket's Germans and the guards, and immediately afterwards the 85th regiment, of Lord Alymer's brigade, drove a French battalion out of Urogne. The first division, being on the right, then menaced the camp of Belchena, and the German skirmishers passed a small stream covering this part of the line, but they were driven back by the enemy, whose musketry and cannonade were brisk along the whole front. Meanwhile Freyre, advancing in two columns on the right of the first division, placed eight guns in battery against the Nassau redoubt, a large work constructed on the ridge occupied by Villatte to cover the approaches to Ascain. The Spaniards were here opposed by their own countrymen under Casa Palacio, who commanded the remains of King Joseph's Spanish guards, and during the fight General Freyre's skirmishers on the right united with Longa's men. Thus a kind of false battle was maintained along the whole line to the sea until nightfall, with equal loss of men but great advantage to the allies, because it entirely occupied Reille's two divisions and Villatte's reserve, and prevented the troops in the camp of Serres from passing by the bridge of Ascain to aid Clausel, who was thus overpowered. When that event happened and Lord Wellington had passed the Nivelle at San Pé, Daricau and the Italian brigade withdrew from Serres, and Villatte's reserve occupied it, whereupon Freyre and Longa entered the town of Ascain. Villatte, however, held the camp

BATTLE OF THE NIVELLE.

above until Reille had withdrawn into St. Jean de Luz and destroyed all the bridges on the Lower Nivelle; when that was effected the whole retired, and at daybreak reached the heights of Bidart on the road to Bayonne. During the night the allies halted on the position they had gained in the centre, but an accidental conflagration, catching a wood, completely separated the piquets towards Ascain from the main body, and spreading far and wide over the heath, lighted up all the hills—a blazing sign of war to France.

On the 11th the army advanced in order of battle. Sir John Hope, on the left, forded the river above St. Jean de Luz with his infantry, and marched on Bidart. Marshal Beresford, in the centre, moved by the roads leading upon Arbonne. General Hill, communicating by his right with Morillo, brought his left forward into communication with Beresford, and with his centre took possession of Suraide and Espelette, facing towards Cambo. The time required to restore the bridges for the artillery at Ciboure, and the change of front on the right rendered these movements slow, and gave Soult time to rally his army upon a third line of fortified camps which he had previously commenced, the right resting on the coast at Bidart, the centre at Helbacen Borda, the left at Ustaritz on the Nive. This front was about eight miles, but the works were only slightly advanced, and Soult, dreading a second battle on so wide a field, drew back his centre and left, broke down the bridges on the Nive at Ustaritz, and at two o'clock a slight skirmish, commenced by the allies in the centre, closed the day's proceedings. The next morning the French retired to the ridge of Beyris, having their right in advance at Anglet and their left in the entrenched camp of Bayonne. During this movement a dense fog arrested the allies, but when the day cleared Sir John Hope took post at Bidart on the left, and Beresford occupied the hill of San Barbe, in the centre. General Hill endeavoured to pass the fords and restore the broken bridges of Ustaritz, and he also made a demonstration against the works at Cambo, but the rain which fell heavily in the mountains on the 11th rendered the fords impassable, and both points were defended successfully by Foy, whose operations had been distinct from the rest. In the night of the 9th D'Erlon, mistrusting the strength of his own position, had sent that general orders to march to Espelette, but the messenger did not arrive in time, and on the morning of the 10th, about eleven o'clock, Foy, following Soult's previous instructions, drove Mina's battalions from the Gorospil mountain; then pressing against the flank of Morillo, he forced him also back fighting to the Puerto de Maya. However, D'Erlon's battle was at this period receding fast, and Foy, fearing to be cut off, retired with the loss of a colonel and 150 men, having, however, taken a quantity of baggage and 100 prisoners. Continuing his retreat all night, he reached Cambo and Ustaritz on the 11th, just in time to relieve Abbé's division at those posts, and on the 12th defended them against General Hill. Such were the principal circumstances of the battle of the Nivelle, whereby Soult was driven from a mountain position which he had been fortifying for three months. He lost 4265 men and officers, including 1200 or 1400 prisoners, and one general was killed. His field-magazines at St. Jean de Luz and Espelette fell into the hands of the victors, and 51 pieces of artillery were taken, the greater part having been abandoned in the redoubts of the low country to Sir John Hope. The allies had two generals, Kempt and Byng, wounded, and they lost 2694 men and officers.

In the report of the battle Lord Wellington, from some oversight, did but scant and tardy justice to the light division. Acting alone—for Longa's Spaniards went off towards Ascain and scarcely fired a shot—this division, furnishing only 4700 men and officers, first carried the smaller Rhune defended by Barbot's brigade, and then beat Taupin's division from the main position, thus driving superior numbers from the strongest works. In fine, being less than one-sixth of the whole force employed against Clausel, they defeated one-third of that general's corps. Many brave men they lost, and two who fell in this battle may be mentioned.

The first, low in rank, for he was but a lieutenant, rich in honour, for he bore many scars, was young of days. He was only nineteen. But he had seen more combats and sieges than he could count years. So slight in person and of such surpassing and delicate beauty that the Spaniards often thought him a girl disguised in man's clothing, he was yet so vigorous, so active, so brave, that the most daring and experienced veterans watched his looks on the field of battle, and, implicitly following where he led, would like children obey his slightest sign in the most difficult situations.

His education was incomplete, yet were his natural powers so happy, the keenest and best-furnished intellects shrank from an encounter of wit, and every thought and aspiration was proud and noble, indicating future greatness if destiny had so willed it. Such was Edward Freer of the 43rd, one of three brothers who, covered with wounds, all died in the service. Assailed the night before the battle with that strange anticipation of coming death so often felt by military men, he was pierced with three balls at the first storming of the Rhune rocks, and the sternest soldiers in the regiment wept even in the middle of the fight when they heard of his fate.

On the same day and at the same hour was killed Colonel Thomas Lloyd. He likewise had been a long time in the 43rd. Under him Freer had learned the rudiments of his profession, but in the course of the war promotion placed Lloyd at the head of the 94th, and it was leading that regiment he fell. In him also were combined mental and bodily powers of no ordinary kind. A graceful symmetry combined with Herculean strength, and a countenance at once frank and majestic, gave the true index of his nature, for his capacity was great and commanding, and his military knowledge extensive both from experience and study. His mirth and wit, so well known in the army, he used without offence, yet so as to increase his ascendency over those with whom he held intercourse; for, though gentle, he was valiant, ambitious, and conscious of his fitness for great exploits. He, like Freer, was prescient of and predicted his own fall, yet with no abatement of courage. When he received the mortal wound, a most painful one, he would not suffer himself to be moved, but remained watching the battle, and making observations upon the changes in it, until death came. It was thus, at the age of thirty, that the good, the brave, the generous Lloyd died. Tributes to his merit have been published by Lord Wellington and by one of his own poor soldiers—by the highest and by the lowest!

CHAPTER XVII.

BATTLES IN FRONT OF BAYONNE.

DEFEATED and disheartened, the French retreated towards the Nive and the Adour, while for the allies Nivelle was followed by a short period of quiet. The hardships and privations endured on the mountains by the allied troops were beneficial to them as an army. The fine air and the impossibility of the soldiers committing their usual excesses in drink had rendered them unusually healthy, while the facility of enforcing a strict discipline, and their natural impatience to win the fair plains spread out before them, had raised their moral and physical qualities in a wonderful degree. Danger was their sport, and their experienced general, in the prime and vigour of life, was as impatient for action as his soldiers. Neither the works of the Bayonne camp nor the barrier of the Nive, suddenly manned by a beaten and dispirited army, could have long withstood the progress of such a fiery host, and if Wellington could have let their strength and fury loose in the first days succeeding the battle of the Nivelle, France would have felt his conquering footsteps to her centre. But the country at the foot of the Pyrenees is a deep clay, quite impassable after rain, except by the royal road near the coast, and that of St. Jean Pied de Port, both of which were in the power of the French. On the by-roads the infantry sank to the mid-leg, the cavalry above the horses' knees, and even to the saddle-girth in some places. The artillery could not move at all. The rain commenced on the 11th November; the mist in the early part of the 12th had given Soult time to regain his camp and secure the high-road to St. Jean Pied

de Port, by which his troops easily gained their proper posts on the Nive, while his adversary, fixed in the swamps, could only make some ineffectual demonstrations.

The bad weather, however, was not the only obstacle to the English general's operations. On the very day of the battle of Nivelle Freyre's and Longa's soldiers, entering Ascain, pillaged it and murdered several persons; the next day the whole of the Spanish troops continued these excesses in various places, and on the right Mina's battalions, some of whom were also in a state of mutiny, made a plundering and murdering incursion from the mountains towards Hellette. The Portuguese and British soldiers of the left wing had commenced the like outrages, and two French persons were killed in one town; however, the adjutant-general, Pakenham, arriving at the moment, saw and instantly put the perpetrators to death, thus nipping this wickedness in the bud, but at his own risk, for legally he had not that power. This general, whose generosity, humanity, and chivalric spirit excited the admiration of every honourable person who approached him, afterwards fell at New Orleans. Terrified by these excesses, the French people fled even from the larger towns, but Wellington quickly relieved their terror. Although looking forward to a battle, he put to death all the Spanish marauders he could take in the act, and then, with many reproaches, and despite of the discontent of their generals, forced the whole to withdraw into their own country. He disarmed the insubordinate battalions under Mina, quartered Giron's Andalusians in the Bastan, where O'Donnel resumed the command, sent Freyre's Gallicians to the district between Irun and Ernani, and Longa over the Ebro. Morillo's division alone remained with the army. These decisive proceedings, marking the lofty character of the man, proved not less politic than resolute. The French people immediately returned, and finding the strictest discipline preserved, and all things paid for, adopted an amicable intercourse with the invaders. However, the loss of such a mass of troops, and the effects of weather on the roads, reduced the army for the moment to a state of inactivity; the head-quarters were fixed at St. Jean de Luz, and the troops were established in permanent cantonments. These occupying, however, only a confined space between the sea and the river Nive, while the enemy occupied the whole ground beyond that river, and had thus unlimited supplies, Lord Wellington determined to cross the Nive and drive the French from the strong position they occupied between the Nive and the Adour, and then advance towards Bayonne. These new operations for forcing the passage of the Nive began on the 9th December 1813.

The Nive, the Adour, and the Gave de Pau, which falls into the Adour many miles above Bayonne, were all navigable, the first as far as Ustaritz, the second to Dax, the third to Peyrehorade, and the great French magazines were collected at the two latter places. But the army was fed with difficulty, and hence to restrain Soult to the country beyond the Nive, to intercept his communications with St. Jean Pied de Port, to bring a powerful cavalry into activity, and to obtain secret intelligence from the interior of Spain were Wellington's inducements to force a passage over the Nive. Yet to place the troops on both sides of a navigable river, with communications bad at all times, and subject to entire interruptions from rain—to do this in face of an army possessing short communications, good roads, and entrenched camps for retreat, was a delicate and dangerous operation.

On the 9th Sir John Hope and Charles Alten, with the first, fifth, and light divisions, the unattached brigades of infantry, Vandeleur's cavalry, and twelve guns, in all about 24,000 combatants, were to drive back the French advanced posts along the whole front of the entrenched camp between the Nive and the sea. This movement was partly to examine the course of the Lower Adour with a view to subsequent operations, but principally to make Soult discover his dispositions of defence on that side, and to keep his troops in check while Beresford and Hill crossed the Nive. To support this double operation the fourth and seventh divisions were secretly brought up from Ascain and Espelette, the latter to the hill of San Barbe, from whence it detached one brigade to relieve the posts of the third division. There remained the second, the third, and the sixth divisions, Hamilton's Portuguese, and Morillo's Spaniards for the passage. Beresford, leading the third and sixth, reinforced with six guns and a squadron of cavalry, was to cross at Ustaritz with pontoons; Hill, having the second division, Hamilton's Portuguese, Vivian's and Victor Alten's cavalry, and fourteen guns, was to ford the river at Cambo and Larressore. Both generals were then to repair the bridges at these respective points with materials prepared beforehand; and to cover Hill's movement on the right and protect the valley of the Nive from General Paris, who, being at Lahoussoa, might have penetrated to the rear of the army during the operations, Morillo's Spaniards were to cross at Itzassu. At this time Foy's division was extended from Halzou, in front of Larressore, to the fords above Cambo. The rest of D'Erlon's troops remained on the heights of Moguerre in front of Mousserolles.

Passage of the Nive.

At Ustaritz the French had broken both bridges, but the island connecting them was in possession of the British. Beresford laid his pontoons down on the hither side in the night of the 8th December, and next morning a beacon lighted on the heights above Cambo gave the signal of attack. The passage was immediately forced under the fire of the artillery, the second bridge was laid, and D'Armagnac's brigade was driven back by the sixth division; but the swampy nature of the country between the river and the high-road retarded the allies' march and gave the French time to retreat with little loss. At the same time Hill's troops, also covered by the fire of artillery, forced the passage in three columns above and below Cambo with slight resistance, though the fords were so deep that several horsemen were drowned, and the French strongly posted, especially at Halzou, where there was a deep and strong mill-race to cross as well as the river.

Foy seeing, by the direction of Beresford's fire, that his retreat was endangered, retired hastily with his left, leaving his right wing under General Berlier at Halzou without orders. Hence, when General Pringle attacked the latter from Larressore, the sixth division was already on the high-road between Foy and Berlier, who escaped by cross-roads towards Hasparen, but did not rejoin his division until two o'clock in the afternoon. Meanwhile Morillo crossed at Itzassu, and Paris retired to Hellette, where he was joined by a regiment of light cavalry belonging to Pierre Soult, who was then on the Bidouse river. Morillo followed, and in one village near Hellette his troops killed fifteen peasants, amongst them several women and children.

General Hill, having won the passage, placed a brigade of infantry at Urcurray to cover the bridge of Cambo, and to support the cavalry which he despatched to scour the roads towards Lahoussoa, St. Jean Pied de Port, and Hasparen, and to observe Paris and Pierre Soult. With the rest of his troops he marched to the heights of Lormenthoa in front of the hills of Moguerre and Villefranque, and was there joined by the sixth division, the third remaining to cover the bridge of Ustaritz. It was now about one o'clock, and Soult, coming hastily from Bayonne, approved of the disposition made by D'Erlon, and offered battle, his line being extended so as to bar the high-road. D'Armagnac's brigade, which had retired from Ustaritz, was now in advance at Villefranque, and a heavy cannonade and skirmish ensued along the front, but no general attack was made, because the deep roads had retarded the rear of Hill's columns. However, the Portuguese of the sixth division, descending from Lormenthoa about three o'clock, drove D'Armagnac's brigade, with sharp fighting and after one repulse, out of Villefranque. A brigade of the second division was then established in advance, connecting Hill's corps with the troops in Villefranque. Thus three divisions of infantry, wanting the brigade left at Urcurray, hemmed up four French divisions; and as the latter, notwithstanding their superiority of numbers, made no advantage of the broken movements of the allies caused by the deep roads, the passage of the Nive may be judged a surprise. Wellington thus far overreached his able adversary, yet he had not trusted to this uncertain chance alone. The French masses falling upon the heads of his columns at Lormenthoa, while the rear was still labouring in the deep roads, might have caused some disorder, but could not have driven either Hill or Beresford over the river again, because the third division was close at hand to reinforce the sixth, and the brigade of the seventh, left at San Barbe, could have followed by the bridge of Ustaritz, thus giving the allies the superiority of numbers. The greatest danger was that Paris, reinforced by Pierre Soult's cavalry, should have returned and fallen either upon Morillo or the brigade left at Urcurray in the rear, while Soult, reinforcing D'Erlon with fresh divisions brought from the other side of the Nive, attacked Hill and Beresford in front. It was to prevent this that Hope and Alten, whose operations are now to be related, pressed the enemy on the left bank.

The first-named general, having twelve miles to march from St. Jean de Luz before he could reach the French works, put his troops in motion during the night, and about eight o'clock passed between the tanks in front of Barrouilhet with his right, while his left descended from the platform of Bidart and crossed the valley towards Biaritz. The French outposts retired fighting, and Hope sweeping with a half-circle to his right, and being preceded by the fire of his guns and many skirmishers, arrived in front of the entrenched camp about one o'clock. His left then rested on the Lower Adour, his centre menaced a very strong advanced work on the ridge of Beyris beyond Anglet, and his right was in communication with Alten. That general, having a shorter distance to move, halted about Bussussary and Arcangues until Hope's fiery crescent was closing on the French camp, and then he also advanced; but with the exception of a slight skirmish at the fortified house, there was no resistance. Three divisions, some cavalry, and the unattached brigades, equal to a fourth division, sufficed, therefore, to keep six French divisions in check on this side. When evening closed the allies fell back towards their original positions, but under heavy rain, and with great fatigue to Hope's wing, for even the royal road was knee-deep of mud, and his troops were twenty-four hours under arms. The whole day's fighting cost about 800 men for each side, the loss of the allies being rather greater on the left bank of the Nive than on the right.

Wellington's wings being now divided by the Nive, the French general resolved to fall upon one of them with the whole of his forces united; and misled by the prisoners, who assured him that the third and fourth divisions were both on the heights of Lormenthoa, he resolved, being able to assemble his troops with greater facility on the left of the Nive, where also the allies' front was most extended, to choose that side for his counter-stroke. The garrison of Bayonne was 8000 strong, partly troops of the line, partly national guards, with which he ordered the governor to occupy the entrenched camp of Mousserolles; then stationing ten gunboats on the Upper Adour to watch that river as high as the confluence of the Gave de Pau, he made D'Erlon file his four divisions over the bridge of boats between the fortress and Mousserolles, directing him to take post behind Clausel's corps on the other side of the river. He thus concentrated nine divisions of infantry and Villatte's reserve, a brigade of cavalry, and forty guns, furnishing in all about 60,000 combatants, including conscripts, to assail a quarter where the allies, although stronger by one division than the French general imagined, had yet only 30,000 infantry, with twenty-four pieces of cannon.

The French marshal's first design was to burst with his whole army on the table-land of Bussussary and Arcangues, and then to act as circumstances should dictate; and he judged so well of his position that he desired the minister of war to expect good news for the next day. Indeed, the situation of the allies, although better than he knew of, gave him some right to anticipate success. On no point was there any expectation of this formidable counter-attack. Lord Wellington was on the left of the Nive preparing to assault the heights where he had last seen the French the evening before. Hope's troops, with the exception of Wilson's Portuguese, now commanded by General Campbell and posted at Barrouilhet, had retired to their cantonments; the first division was at St. Jean de Luz and Ciboure, more than six miles distant from the outposts; the fifth division was between those places and Bidart, and all exceedingly fatigued. The light division had orders to retire from Bussussary to Arbonne, a distance of four miles, and part of the second brigade had already marched, when fortunately General Kempt, somewhat suspicious of the enemy's movements, delayed obedience until he could see what was going on in his front. He thus, as the event proved, saved the position.

The extraordinary difficulty of moving through the country even for single horsemen, the numerous enclosures and copses which denied any distinct view, the easy success of the operation to cross the Nive, and a certain haughty confidence, the sure attendant of a long course of victory, seem to have rendered the English general at this time somewhat negligent of his own security. Undoubtedly the troops were not disposed as if a battle was expected. The general position, composed of two distinct parts, was indeed very strong; the ridge of Barrouilhet could only be attacked along the royal road on a narrow front between the tanks, and he had directed entrenchments to be made; but there was

BATTLES IN FRONT OF BAYONNE. 329

only one brigade there, and a road made with difficulty by the engineers supplied a bad flank communication with the light division. This Barrouilhet ridge was prolonged to the platform of Bussussary, but in its winding bulged out too near the enemy's works in the centre to be safely occupied in force, and behind it there was a deep valley or basin extending to Arbonne.

The ridge of Arcangues, on the other side of this basin, was the position of battle for the centre. Three tongues of land shot out from this part to the front, and the valleys between them as well as their slopes were covered with copse-woods, almost impenetrable. The church of Arcangues, a senator's house, and parts of the village furnished rallying points of defence for the piquets, which were necessarily numerous because of the extent of front. At this time the left-hand ridge or tongue of land was occupied by the 52nd regiment, which had also posts in the great basin separating the Arcangues position from that of Barrouilhet; the central tongue was held by the piquets of the 43rd with supporting companies placed in succession towards Bussussary, where was an open common, across which troops in retreat would have to pass to the church of Arcangues. The third tongue was guarded partly by the 43rd, partly by the riflemen, but the valley between was not occupied, and the piquets on the extreme right extended to an inundation, across a narrow part of which there was a bridge: the facility for attack there, however, was small. One brigade of the seventh division continued this line of posts to the Nive, holding the bridge of Urdains; the rest of the division was behind San Barbe, and belonged rather to Ustaritz than to this front. The fourth division was several miles behind the right of the light division.

In this state of affairs, if Soult had, as he first designed, burst with his whole army upon Bussussary and Arcangues, it would have been impossible for the light division, scattered as it was over such an extent of difficult ground, to have stopped him for half-an-hour; and there was no support within several miles, no superior officer to direct the concentration of the different divisions. Lord Wellington had, indeed, ordered all the line to be entrenched, but the works were commenced on a great scale, and, as is common when danger does not spur, the soldiers had laboured so carelessly that, beyond a few abattis, the tracing of some lines and redoubts, and the opening of a road of communication, the ground remained in its natural state. The French general would therefore quickly have gained the broad open hills beyond Arcangues, separated the fourth and seventh divisions from the light division, and cut them off from Hope. Soult, however, in the course of the night, changed his project, and at daybreak Reille marched with Boyer's and Maucune's divisions, Sparre's cavalry, and from twenty to thirty guns against Hope by the main road. He was followed by Foy and Villatte, but Clausel assembled his troops under cover of the ridges near the fortified house in front of Bussussary, and one of D'Erlon's divisions approached the bridge of Urdains.

A heavy rain fell in the night, yet the morning of the 10th broke fair, and soon after dawn the French infantry were observed by the piquets of the 43rd pushing each other about as if at gambols, yet lining by degrees the nearest ditches; a general officer was also seen behind a farmhouse close to the sentinels, and at the same time the heads of columns could be perceived in the rear. Thus warned, some companies of the 43rd were thrown on the right into the basin to prevent the enemy from penetrating that way to the small plain between Bussussary and Arcangues. General Kempt was with the piquets, and his foresight in delaying his march to Arbonne now saved the position, for he immediately placed the reserves of his brigade in the church and mansion-house of Arcangues. Meanwhile the French, breaking forth with loud cries and a rattling musketry, fell at a running pace upon the piquets of the 43rd both on the tongue and in the basin, and a cloud of skirmishers descending on their left, penetrating between them and the 52nd regiment, sought to turn both. The right tongue was in like manner assailed, and at the same time the piquets at the bridge near the senator's house were driven back.

The assault was so strong and rapid, the enemy so numerous, and the ground so extensive that it would have been impossible to have reached the small plain beyond Bussussary in time to regain the church of Arcangues if any serious resistance had been attempted; wherefore, delivering their fire at pistol-shot distance, the piquets fell back in succession, and never were the steadiness and intelligence of veteran soldiers more eminently displayed; for though it was necessary to run at full speed to gain the small plain before the enemy, who was constantly outflanking the line of posts by the basin, though the ways were so deep and narrow that no formation could be preserved, though the fire of the French was thick and close, and their cries vehement as they rushed on in pursuit, the instant the open ground at Bussussary was attained, the apparently disordered crowd of fugitives became a compact and well-formed body, defying and deriding the fruitless efforts of their adversaries. The 52nd being about half-a-mile to the left, though only slightly assailed, fell back also to the main ridge; for though the closeness of the country did not permit Colonel Colborne to observe the strength of the enemy, he could see the rapid retreat of the 43rd, and thence judging how serious the affair was, so well did the regiments of the light division understand each other's qualities, withdrew his outposts to secure the main position. And in good time he did so.

On the right-hand tongue the troops were not so fortunate, for whether they delayed their retreat too long, or that the country was more intricate, the enemy, moving by the basin, reached Bussussary before the rear arrived, and about one hundred of the 43rd and riflemen were thus intercepted. The French were in a hollow road and careless, never doubting that the officer of the 43rd, Ensign Campbell, a youth scarcely eighteen years of age, would surrender; but he, with a shout, broke into their column sword in hand, and though the struggle was severe and twenty of the 43rd and thirty of the riflemen, with their officer, remained prisoners, reached the church with the rest. D'Armagnac's division of D'Erlon's corps now pushed close up to the bridge of Urdains, and Clausel assembled his three divisions by degrees at Bussussary, opening meanwhile a sharp fire of musketry. The position was, however, safe. The mansion-house on the right, covered by abattis and not easily accessible, was defended by a rifle battalion and the Portuguese. The church and churchyard were occupied by the 43rd, who were supported with two mountain-guns, their front being covered by a declivity of thick copse-wood filled with riflemen, and only to be turned by narrow hollow roads leading on each side to the church. On the left the 52nd, now supported by the remainder of the division, spread as far as the great basin which separated the right wing from the ridge of Barrouilhet, towards which some small posts were pushed, but there was still a great interval between Alten's and Hope's positions.

The skirmishing fire grew hot; Clausel brought up twelve guns to the ridge of Bussussary, with which he threw shot and shells into the churchyard of Arcangues, and 400 or 500 infantry then made a rush forwards, but a heavy fire from the 43rd sent them back over the ridge where their guns were posted. Yet the practice of the latter, well directed at first, would have been murderous if this musketry from the churchyard had not made the French gunners withdraw their pieces a little behind the ridge, which caused their shot to fly wild and high. General Kempt, thinking the distance too great, was at first inclined to stop this fire, but the moment it lulled the French gunners pushed their pieces forwards again, and their shells knocked down eight men in an instant. The small-arms then recommenced, and the shells again flew high. The French were in like manner kept at bay by the riflemen in the village and mansion-house, and the action, hottest where the 52nd fought, continued all day. It was not very severe, but the real battle was at Barrouilhet.

On that side Reille, advancing with two divisions about nine o'clock, drove Campbell's Portuguese from Anglet, and the French cavalry, charging during the fight, cut down a great many men. The French infantry then assailed the ridge at Barrouilhet, but moving along a narrow ridge and confined on each flank by the tanks, only two brigades could get into action by the main road, and the rain of the preceding night had rendered all the by-roads so deep that it was mid-day before the French line of battle was filled. This delay saved the allies, for the attack here also was so unexpected, that the first division and Lord Alymer's brigade were at rest in St. Jean de Luz and Bidart when the action commenced. The latter did not reach the position before eleven o'clock; the foot-guards did not march from St. Jean until after twelve, and only arrived at three o'clock in the afternoon, when the fight was done; all the troops were exceedingly fatigued, only ten guns could be brought into play, and part of the infantry were at first without ammunition.

Robinson's brigade of the fifth division first arrived to support Campbell's Portuguese and fight the battle. The French spread their skirmishers along the whole valley in front of Biaritz, but their principal effort was directed by the great road and against the platform of Barrouilhet about the mayor's house, where the ground was so thick of hedges and coppice-wood that a most confused fight took place. The assailants, cutting ways through the hedges, poured on in smaller or larger bodies as the openings allowed, and were immediately engaged with the defenders; at some points they were successful, at others beaten back, and few knew what was going on to the right or left of where they stood. By degrees Reille engaged both his divisions, and some of Villatte's reserve also entered the fight, and then Bradford's Portuguese and Lord Aylmer's brigade arrived on the allies' side, which enabled Colonel Greville's brigade of the fifth division, hitherto kept in reserve, to relieve Robinson's; that general was, however, dangerously wounded and his troops suffered severely.

A very notable action was now performed by the 9th regiment under Colonel Cameron. This officer was on the extreme left of Greville's brigade, Robinson's being then shifted in second line and towards the right; Bradford's brigade was at the mayor's house, some distance to the left of the 9th regiment, and the space between was occupied by a Portuguese battalion. There was in front of Greville's brigade a thick hedge, but immediately opposite the 9th was a coppice-wood possessed by the enemy, whose skirmishers were continually gathering in masses and rushing out as if to assail the line; they were as often driven back, yet the ground was so broken that nothing could be seen beyond the flanks; and when some time had passed in this manner, Cameron, who had received no orders, heard a sudden firing along the main road close to his left. His adjutant was sent to look out, and returned immediately with intelligence that there was little fighting on the road, but a French regiment, which must have passed unseen in small bodies through the Portuguese between the 9th and the mayor's house, was rapidly filing into line on the rear. The 4th British regiment was then in close column at a short distance, and its commander, Colonel Piper, was directed by Cameron to face about, march to the rear, and then bring up his left shoulder, when he would infallibly fall in with the French regiment. Piper marched, but whether he misunderstood the order, took a wrong direction, or mistook the enemy for Portuguese, he passed them. No firing was heard; the adjutant again hurried to the rear, and returned with intelligence that the 4th regiment was not to be seen, but the enemy's line was nearly formed. Cameron, leaving fifty men to answer the skirmishing fire which now increased from the copse, immediately faced about and marched in line against the new enemy, who was about his own strength, as fast as the rough nature of the ground would permit. The French fire, slow at first, increased vehemently as the distance lessened; but when the 9th, coming close up, sprang forwards to the charge, the adverse line broke and fled to the flanks in the utmost disorder. Those who made for their own right brushed the left of Greville's brigade, and even carried off an officer of the royals in their rush; yet the greatest number were made prisoners, and the 9th, having lost about eighty men and officers, resumed their old ground.

The final result of the battle at Barrouilhet was the repulse of Reille's divisions; but Villatte still menaced the right flank, and Foy, taking possession of the narrow ridge connecting Bussussary with the platform of Barrouilhet, threw his skirmishers into the great basin leading to Arbonne, and connecting his right with Reille's left, menaced Hope's flank at Barrouilhet. This was about two o'clock. Soult, whose columns were now all in hand, gave orders to renew the battle, and his masses were beginning to move, when Clausel reported that a large body of fresh troops, apparently coming from the other side of the Nive, was menacing D'Armagnac's division from the heights above Urdains. Unable to account for this, Soult, who saw the guards and Germans moving up fast from St. Jean de Luz and all the unattached brigades already in line, hesitated, suspended his own attack, and ordered D'Erlon, who had two divisions in reserve, to detach one to the support of D'Armagnac. Before this disposition could be completed the night fell.

The fresh troops seen by Clausel were the third, fourth, sixth, and seventh divisions, whose movements during the battle it is time to notice. When Lord Wellington, who remained on the right of the Nive during the night of the 9th, discovered at daybreak that the French had abandoned the heights in Hill's front, he directed that officer to occupy them, and push parties close up to the entrenched camp of Mousseroles, while his cavalry spread beyond Hasparen and up the Adour. Meanwhile, the cannonade on the left bank of the Nive being heard, he repaired in person to that side, first making the third and sixth divisions repass the river, and directing Beresford to lay another bridge of communication lower down the Nive, to shorten the line of movement. When he reached the left of the Nive and saw how the battle stood, he made the seventh division close to the left from the hill of San Barbe, placed the third division at Urdains, and brought up the fourth division to an open heathy ridge on a hill about a mile behind the church of Arcangues. From this point General Cole sent Ross's brigade down into the basin on the left of Colborne, to cover Arbonne, being prepared himself to march with his whole division if the enemy attempted to penetrate in force between Hope and Alten. These dispositions were for the most part completed about two o'clock, and thus Clausel was held in check at Bussussary, and the renewed attack by Foy, Villatte, and Reille's divisions on Barrouilhet prevented.

This day's battle cost the Anglo-Portuguese more than 1200 men killed and wounded; two generals were amongst the latter, and about 300 men were made prisoners. The French had one general, Villatte, wounded, and lost about 2000 men; but when the action terminated two regiments of Nassau and one of Frankfort, the whole under the command of a Colonel Kruse, came over to the allies. These men were not deserters. Their prince, having abandoned Napoleon in Germany, sent secret instructions to his troops to do so likewise, and in good time, for orders to disarm them reached Soult the next morning. The generals on each side, the one hoping to profit, the other to prevent mischief, immediately transmitted notice of this event to Catalonia, where several regiments of the same nations were serving under Suchet, whose corps was here held in check by a force of allies under Sir William Clinton. Lord Wellington's message failed, but Suchet disarmed his Germans with reluctance, thinking they could be trusted; and the Nassau troops at Bayonne were perhaps less influenced by patriotism than by an old quarrel, for when belonging to the army of the centre they had forcibly foraged Soult's district early in the year, and carried off the spoil in defiance of his authority, which gave rise to bitter disputes at the time, and was probably not forgotten by him.

Combat of the 11th December.

In the night of the 10th Reille withdrew behind the tanks as far as Pucho; Foy and Villatte likewise drew back along the connecting ridge towards Bussussary, thus uniting with Clausel's left and D'Erlon's reserve, so that on the morning of the 11th the French army, with the exception of D'Armagnac's division, which remained in front of Urdains, was concentrated, for Soult feared a counter-attack. The French deserters, indeed, declared that Clausel had formed a body of 2000 choice grenadiers to assault the village and church of Arcangues, but the day passed without any event in that quarter save a slight skirmish, in which a few men were wounded. Not so on the side of Barrouilhet. There was a thick fog, and Lord Wellington, desirous to ascertain what the French were about, directed the 9th regiment about ten o'clock to open a skirmish beyond the tanks towards Pucho, and to push the action if the French augmented their force. Cameron did so, and the fight was becoming warm, when Colonel Delancy, a staff-officer, rashly directed the 9th to enter the village. The error was soon and sharply corrected, for the fog cleared up, and Soult, who had 24,000 men at that point, observing the 9th unsupported, ordered a counter-attack, which was so strong and sudden that Cameron only saved his regiment with the aid of some Portuguese troops hastily brought up by Sir John Hope. The fighting then ceased, and Lord Wellington went to the right, leaving Hope with orders to push back the French picquets, and re-establish his former outposts on the connecting ridge towards Bussussary.

Soult had hitherto appeared undecided, but roused by this second insult, he ordered Darricau's division to attack Barrouilhet along the connecting ridge, while Boyer's division fell on by the main road between the tanks. This was about two o'clock, and the allies, expecting no battle, had dispersed to gather fuel, for the time was wet and cold. In an instant the French penetrated in all directions; they outflanked the right, they passed the tanks, seized the out-buildings of the mayor's house, and occupied the coppice in front of it; they were, indeed, quickly driven from the out-buildings by the royals, but the tumult was great, and the coppice was filled with men of all nations intermixed and fighting in a perilous manner. Robinson's brigade was very hardly handled, the officer commanding it was wounded, a squadron of French cavalry suddenly cut down some of the Portuguese near the wood, and on the right the colonel of the 84th, having unwisely engaged his regiment in a hollow road where the French possessed the high bank, was killed, with a great number of men. However, the 9th regiment, posted on the main road, plied Boyer's flank with fire, the 85th regiment of Lord Aylmer's brigade came into action, and Sir John Hope, conspicuous from his gigantic stature and heroic courage, was seen wherever danger pressed, rallying and encouraging the troops; at one time he was in the midst of the enemy, his clothes were pierced with bullets, and he received a severe wound in the ankle, yet he would not quit the field, and by his great presence of mind and calm intrepidity restored the battle. The French were finally beaten back from the position of Barrouilhet, yet they had recovered their original posts, and continued to gall the allies with a fire of shot and shells until the fall of night. The total loss in this fight was about 600 men of a side, and as the fifth division was now considerably reduced in numbers, the first division took its place on the front line. Meanwhile Soult sent his cavalry over the Nive to Mousseroles to check the incursions of Hill's horsemen.

Combat of the 12th December.

The rain fell heavily in the night, and though the morning broke fair, neither side seemed inclined to commence hostilities. The advanced posts were, however, very close to each other, and about ten o'clock a misunderstanding arose. The French general, observing the fresh regiments of the first division close to his posts, imagined the allies were going to attack him, and immediately reinforced his front; this movement causing an English battery to fall into a like error, it opened upon the advancing French troops, and in an instant the whole line of posts was engaged. Soult then brought up a number of guns, the firing continued without an object for many hours, and 300 or 400 men of a side were killed and wounded; but the great body of the

French army remained concentrated and quiet on the ridge between Barrouilhet and Bussussary.

Lord Wellington as early as the 10th had expected Soult would abandon this attack to fall upon Hill, and therefore had given Beresford orders to carry the sixth division to that general's assistance by the new bridge, and the seventh division by Ustaritz, without waiting for further instructions, if Hill was assailed; now observing Soult's tenacity at Barrouilhet, he drew the seventh division towards Arbonne. Beresford had, however, made a movement towards the Nive, and this, with the march of the seventh division and some changes in the position of the fourth division, caused Soult to believe the allies were gathering with a view to attack his centre on the morning of the 13th; and it is remarkable that the deserters at this early period told him the Spaniards had re-entered France, although orders to that effect were not given until the next day. Convinced then that his bolt was shot on the left of the Nive, he left two divisions and Villatte's reserve in the entrenched camp, and marched with the other seven to Mousseroles, intending to fall upon Hill.

That general had pushed his scouting parties to the Gambouri, and when General Sparre's horsemen arrived at Mousseroles on the 12th, Pierre Soult advanced from the Bidouze with all the light cavalry. He was supported by the infantry of General Paris, and drove the allies' posts from Hasparen. Colonel Vivian, who commanded there, immediately ordered Major Brotherton to charge with the 14th dragoons across the bridge, but it was an ill-judged order, and the impossibility of succeeding so manifest, that when Brotherton, noted throughout the army for his daring, galloped forward, only two men and one subaltern, Lieutenant Southwell, passed the narrow bridge with him, and they were all taken. Vivian then, seeing his error, charged with his whole brigade to rescue them, yet in vain; he was forced to fall back upon Urcuray, where Morillo's Spaniards had relieved the British infantry brigade on the 11th. This threatening movement induced General Hill to put the British brigade in march again for Urcuray on the 12th, but he recalled it at sunset, having then discovered Soult's columns passing the Nive by the boat-bridge above Bayonne.

Lord Wellington, now feeling the want of numbers, brought

forward a division of Gallicians and one of Andalusians, and, to prevent their plundering, fed them from the British magazines. The Gallicians were to support Hope, the Andalusians to watch the upper valley of the Nive and protect the rear of the army from Paris and Pierre Soult, who could easily be reinforced by a strong body of national guards. Meanwhile Hill had taken a position of battle on a front of two miles. His left, under General Pringle, occupied a wooded and broken range crowned by the château of Villefranque; it covered the new pontoon bridge of communication, which was a mile and a half higher up the river, but it was separated from the centre by a small stream forming a chain of ponds in a very deep and marshy valley. The centre, placed on both sides of the high-road, near the hamlet of St. Pierre, occupied a crescent-shaped height, broken with rocks and close brushwood on the left hand, and on the right hand enclosed with high and thick hedges, one of which, covering at the distance of a hundred yards part of the line, was nearly impassable. Here Ashworth's Portuguese and Barnes's brigade of the second division were posted. Ashworth's Portuguese were posted in advance immediately in front of St. Pierre, and their skirmishers occupied a small wood covering their right. Twelve guns, under Colonels Ross and Tullock, were concentrated in front of the centre, looking down the great road, and half-a-mile in rear of this point Lecor's Portuguese division was stationed with two guns as a reserve.

The right, under Byng, was composed of the 3rd, 57th, 31st, and 66th. One of these regiments—the 3rd—was posted on a height running nearly parallel with the Adour, called the ridge of Partouhiria, or Old Moguerre, because a village of that name was situated upon the summit. This regiment was pushed in advance to a point where it could only be approached by crossing the lower part of a narrow swampy valley which separated Moguerre from the heights of St. Pierre. The upper part of this valley was held by Byng with the remainder of his brigade, and his post was well covered by a mill-pond leading towards the enemy and nearly filling all the valley.

One mile in front of St. Pierre was a range of counter-heights belonging to the French, but the basin between was broad, open, and commanded in every part by the fire of the allies, and in all parts the country was too heavy and too much enclosed for the action of cavalry. Nor could the enemy approach in force, except on a narrow front of battle and by the high-road, until within cannon-shot, when two narrow difficult lanes branched off to the right and left, and crossing the swampy valleys on each side, led, the one to the height where the 3rd regiment was posted on the extreme right of the allies, the other to General Pringle's position on the left. In the night of the 12th the rain swelled the Nive and carried away the allies' bridge of communication. It was soon restored, but on the morning of the 13th General Hill was completely cut off from the rest of the army; and while seven French divisions of infantry, furnishing at least 35,000 combatants, approached him in front, an eighth, under General Paris, and the cavalry division of Pierre Soult menaced him in rear. To meet the French in his front he had less than 14,000 men and officers, with fourteen guns in position; and there were only 4000 Spaniards, with Vivian's cavalry, at Urcuray.

Battle of St. Pierre.

The morning broke with a heavy mist, under cover of which Soult formed his order of battle. D'Erlon, having D'Armagnac's, Abbé's, and Daricau's divisions of infantry, Sparre's cavalry, and twenty-two guns, marched in front; he was followed by Foy and Maransin, but the remainder of the French army was in reserve, for the roads would not allow of any other order. The mist hung heavily, and the French masses, at one moment quite shrouded in vapour, at another dimly seen, or looming sudden and large and dark at different points, appeared like thunder-clouds gathering before the storm. At half-past eight Soult pushed back the British picquets in the centre; the sun burst out at that moment, the sparkling fire of the light troops spread wide in the valley and crept up the hills on either flank, while the bellowing of forty pieces of artillery shook the banks of the Nive and the Adour. Daricau, marching on the French right, was directed against General Pringle. D'Armagnac, moving on their left, and taking Old Moguerre as the point of direction, was ordered to force Byng's right. Abbé assailed the centre at St. Pierre, where

General Stewart commanded; for Sir Rowland Hill had taken his station on a commanding mount in the rear, from whence he could see the whole battle and direct the movements.

Abbé, a man noted for vigour, pushed his attack with great violence, and gained ground so rapidly with his light troops, on the left of Ashworth's Portuguese, that Stewart sent the 71st regiment and two guns from St. Pierre to the latter's aid; the French skirmishers likewise won the small wood on Ashworth's right, and half of the 50th regiment was also detached from St. Pierre to that quarter. The wood was thus retaken, and the flanks of Stewart's position secured; but his centre was very much weakened, and the fire of the French artillery was concentrated against it. Abbé then pushed on a column of attack there with such a power that, in despite of the play of musketry on his flanks and a crashing cannonade in his front, he gained the top of the position, and drove back the remainder of Ashworth's Portuguese and the other half of the 50th regiment which had remained in reserve.

General Barnes, who had still the 92nd regiment in hand behind St. Pierre, immediately brought it on with a strong counter-attack. The French skirmishers fell back on each side, leaving two regiments composing the column to meet the charge of the 92nd. It was rough, and pushed home; the French mass wavered and gave way. Abbé immediately replaced it; and Soult, redoubling the heavy play of his guns from the height he occupied, sent forward a battery of horse artillery, which, galloping down the valley, opened its fire close to the allies with most destructive activity. The cannonade and musketry rolled like a prolonged peal of thunder, and the second French column, regardless of Ross's guns, though they tore the ranks in a horrible manner, advanced so steadily up the high-road that the 92nd, yielding to the tempest, slowly regained its old position behind St. Pierre. The Portuguese guns, their British commanding officer having fallen wounded, then limbered up to retire, and the French skirmishers reached the impenetrable hedge in front of Ashworth's right. General Barnes, now seeing that hard fighting only could save the position, made the Portuguese guns resume their fire, and the wing of the 50th and the caçadores gallantly held the small wood on the right; but Barnes was soon wounded, the greatest part of his and General Stewart's staff were hurt, and the matter seemed desperate; for the light troops, overpowered by numbers, were all driven in except those in the wood, the artillerymen were falling at the guns, Ashworth's line of Portuguese crumbled away rapidly before the musketry and cannonade, the ground was strewed with the dead in front, and the wounded crawling to the rear were many.

If the French light troops could then have penetrated through the thick hedge in front of the Portuguese, defeat would have been inevitable on this point, for the main column of attack still steadily advanced up the main road, and a second column launched on its right was already victorious, because the colonel of the 71st had shamefully withdrawn that gallant regiment out of action and abandoned the Portuguese. Pringle was, indeed, fighting strongly against Daricau's superior numbers on the hill of Villefranque, but on the extreme right the colonel of the 3rd regiment had also abandoned his strong post to D'Armagnac, whose leading brigade was thus rapidly turning Byng's other regiments on that side. And now Foy's and Maransin's divisions, hitherto retarded by the deep roads, were coming into line ready to support Abbé, and this at the moment when the troops opposed to him were deprived of their reserve; for when General Hill beheld the retreat of the 3rd and 71st regiments he descended in haste from his mount, met and turned the latter back to renew the fight, and then in person leading one brigade of Le Cor's reserve division to the same quarter, sent the other against D'Armagnac on the hill of Old Moguerre. Thus at the decisive moment of the battle the French reserve was augmented, and that of the allies thrown as a last resource into action. However, the right wing of the 50th and Ashworth's caçadores, both spread as skirmishers, never lost the small wood in front, upholding the fight there and towards the high-road with such unflinching courage that the 92nd regiment had time to re-form behind the hamlet of St. Pierre. Then its gallant colonel, Cameron, once more led it down the road with colours flying and music playing, resolved to give the shock to whatever stood in the way. At this sight the British skirmishers on the flanks, suddenly changing from retreat to attack, rushed forward and drove those of the enemy back on each side; yet the battle seemed hopeless, for

Ashworth was badly wounded, his line was shattered to atoms, and Barnes, who had not quitted the field for his former hurt, was now shot through the body.

The 92nd was but a small body compared with the heavy mass in its front, and the French soldiers seemed willing enough to close with the bayonet; but an officer riding at their head suddenly turned his horse, waved his sword, and appeared to order a retreat; then they faced about and immediately retired across the valley to their original position, in good order, however, and scarcely pursued by the allies, so exhausted were the victors. This retrograde movement—for there was no panic or disorder—was produced partly by the gallant advance of the 92nd and the returning rush of the skirmishers, partly by the state of affairs immediately on the right of the French column; for the 71st, indignant at their colonel's conduct, had returned to the fight with such alacrity, and were so well aided by Le Cor's Portuguese, Generals Hill and Stewart each in person leading an attack, that the hitherto victorious French were overthrown there also, in the very moment when the 92nd came with such a brave show down the main road. Le Cor was, however, wounded.

This double action in the centre being seen from the hill of Villefranque, Daricau's division, already roughly handled by Pringle, fell back in confusion; and meantime, on the right, Buchan's Portuguese, detached by Hill to recover the Moguerre or Partouhiria ridge, crossed the valley, and ascending under a heavy flank fire from Soult's guns, rallied the 3rd regiment; in happy time, for D'Armagnac's first brigade, having already passed the flank of Byng's regiments at the mill-pond, was actually in rear of the allies' lines. It was now twelve o'clock, and while the fire of the light troops in the front and the cannonade in the centre continued, the contending generals restored their respective orders of battle. Soult's right wing had been quite repulsed by Pringle, his left was giving way before Buchan, and the difficult ground forbade his sending immediate succour to either; moreover, in the exigency of the moment, he had called D'Armagnac's reserve brigade to sustain Abbé's retiring columns. However, that brigade and Foy's and Maransin's divisions were in hand to renew the fight in the centre, and the allies could not, unsuccoured, have sustained a fresh assault; for their ranks were wasted with fire, nearly all the staff had been killed or wounded, and three generals had quitted the field badly hurt.

In this crisis General Hill, seeing that Buchan was now well and successfully engaged on the Partouhiria ridge, and that Byng's regiments were quite masters of their ground in the valley of the mill-pond, drew the 57th regiment from the latter place to reinforce his centre. At the same time, the bridge above Villefranque having been restored, the sixth division, which had been marching since daybreak, appeared in order of battle on the mount from whence Hill had descended to rally the 71st. It was soon followed by the fourth division, and that again by the brigades of the third division; two other brigades of the seventh division were likewise in march. With the first of these troops came Lord Wellington, who had hurried from Barrouilhet when the first sound of the cannon reached him; yet he arrived only to witness the close of the battle; the crisis was past; Hill's day of glory was complete. Soult had, according to the French method, made indeed another attack, or rather demonstration, against the centre, to cover his new dispositions, an effort easily repulsed; but at the same moment Buchan drove D'Armagnac headlong off the Partouhiria ridge. The sixth division then appeared on the commanding mount in the rear of St. Pierre, and though the French masses still maintained a menacing position on the high-road and on a hillock rising between the road and the mill-pond, they were quickly dispossessed; for the English general, being now supported by the sixth division, sent Byng with two battalions against the hillock, and some troops from the centre against those on the high-road. At this last point the generals and staff had been so cut down that Colonel Currie, the aide-de-camp who brought the order, could find no superior officer to deliver it to, and led the troops himself to the attack, but both charges were successful; and two guns of the light battery sent down in the early part of the fight by Soult, and which had played without ceasing up to this moment, were taken.

The battle now abated to a skirmish of light troops, under cover of which the French endeavoured to carry off their wounded and rally their stragglers, but at two o'clock Lord Wellington commanded a general advance of the whole line. Then the French retreated fighting, and the allies, following close on the side of the Nive, plied them with musketry until dark. Yet they maintained their line towards the Adour, for Sparre's cavalry, passing out that way, rejoined Pierre Soult on the side of Hasparen. This last-named general and Paris had during the day menaced Morillo and Vivian's cavalry at Urcuray; however, not more than thirty men of a side were hurt, and when Soult's ill-success became known the French retired to Bonloc.

In this bloody action Soult had designed to employ seven divisions of infantry with one brigade of cavalry on the front, and one brigade of infantry with a division of cavalry on the rear; but the state of the roads and the narrow front he was forced to move upon did not permit more than five divisions to act at St. Pierre, and only half of those were seriously engaged. His loss was certainly 3000, making a total of the five days' fighting of 6000 men, with two generals, Villatte and Maucomble, wounded. The estimate made by the British at the time far exceeded this number, and one French writer makes their loss 10,000, including probably the Nassau and Frankfort regiments. The same writer, however, estimates the loss of the allies at 16,000! Whereas Hill had only three generals and about 1500 men killed and wounded on the 13th, and Morillo lost but twenty-six men at Urcuray. The real loss of the allies in the whole five days' fighting was only 5019, including, however, five generals, Hope, Robinson, Barnes, Le Cor, and Ashworth. Of this number 500 were prisoners.

An unusual incident, illustrative of both courage and cowardice, took place in one of these later battles of the war. The colonel of an infantry regiment, being hard pressed, showed a disposition not only to run away himself, but to order his regiment to retire. In fact, a retrograde movement had commenced, when Lord Charles Churchill, aide-de-camp to Sir William Stewart, dashed forward, and seizing the colours of the regiment, exclaimed, "If your colonel will not lead you, follow me, my boys!" The gallantry of this youth, then only eighteen years of age, so animated the regiment and restored their confidence, that they rallied and shared in the glories of the day.—*Gronow's Recollections.*

CHAPTER XVIII.

PASSAGE OF THE GAVES—GARRIS—THE ADOUR.

HE fierce and stormy contest which had raged from the 9th to the 13th December was the last military operation of the campaign of 1813, and there followed a calm of some duration, the enemy not venturing to disturb the allies in their winter quarters. In this interval of inaction, during which the weather was very severe, Soult received considerable reinforcements, and the position he now occupied was well chosen either for aggression or defence. His wings were well advanced, the right flank protected by the camp and fortress of Bayonne, the left by St. Jean Pied de Port, while in the centre, having the command of the Adour and the Gave de Pau, he was enabled to concentrate his troops in force should opportunity occur for an offensive movement. How and where to cross the Adour and invest Bayonne in the face of Soult's position was an object of solicitude to Wellington. The Adour was a great river, with a strong current, and well protected by troops and gunboats above Bayonne, and it was still greater below the town, where also were several gunboats and a sloop-of-war to keep the passage; but in spite of all these difficulties he resolved to cross, and the means adopted were proportionate to the design.

To draw the attention of the French army by an attack on their left, near the roots of the Pyrenees, would be sure to keep the Lower Adour free from any formidable defensive force, because the rapidity and breadth of the stream there denied the use of common pontoons, and the mouth, about six miles below Bayonne, was so barred with sand, so beaten by surges, and so difficult of navigation even with the help of the land-marks, some of which had been removed, that the French would never expect small vessels fit for constructing a bridge could enter that way. Yet it was thus Lord Wellington designed to achieve his object. He had collected forty large sailing-boats of from fifteen to thirty tons burden, called *chasse marées*, as if for the commissariat service, but he secretly loaded them with planks and other materials for his bridge. These and some gunboats he designed, with the aid of the navy, to run up the Adour to a certain point, upon which he meant also to direct the troops and artillery, and then with hawsers and pontoons formed into rafts, to throw over a covering body and destroy a small battery near the mouth of the river.

While Wellington was thus preparing for offensive operations the French general was active in defensive measures. He had fortified all the main passes of the rivers by the great roads leading against his left, but the recall of some of his divisions, together with artillery and cavalry, by Napoleon in January, obliged him to withdraw his outposts from Anglet, which enabled Lord Wellington to examine the whole course of the Adour below Bayonne and arrange for the passage with more facility. Soult immediately concentrated his left wing against the allies' right beyond the Nive, endeavouring to throw his adversary entirely upon the defensive. Thus, on the 26th of January 1814, Morillo having taken possession of an advanced post near Mendionde not properly belonging to him, Soult, who desired to ascertain the feelings of the Spaniards about the English alliance, caused Harispe, under pretence of remonstrating, to sound him ; he did not respond, and Harispe then drove him, not without a vigorous resistance, from the post.

The French marshal had, however, no hope of checking the allies long by these means. He judged justly that Wellington was resolved to obtain Bordeaux and the line of the Garonne, and foreseeing that his own line of retreat must ultimately be in a parallel direction with the Pyrenees, he desired to organise in time a strong defensive system in the country behind him, and to cover Bordeaux if possible. In this view he sent General Darricau, a native of the Landes, to prepare an insurgent levy in that wilderness, and directed Maransin to the High Pyrenees to extend the insurrection of the mountaineers already commenced in the Lower Pyrenees by Harispe. The castle of Jaca was held by 800 men, but they were starving, and a convoy collected at Navarrens, being stopped by the snow in the mountain-passes, made a surrender inevitable.

Soult, knowing nothing of the various difficulties, financial and political, which at this time peculiarly harassed Lord Wellington, fully supposed that the allied forces numbered about 120,000 infantry and 12,000 cavalry, while in reality, on the morning of the 13th February, when the new operations began, the whole force did not exceed 70,000 men of all arms, nearly 10,000 being cavalry, but of these about 30,000 were engaged in enterprises in other directions.

Passage of the Gaves.

In the second week of February the weather set in with a strong frost, the roads became practicable, and the English general, eagerly seizing the long-expected opportunity, advanced at the moment when General Paris had again marched with the convoy from Navarrens to make a last effort for the relief of Jaca. But the troops were at this time receiving the clothing which had been so long delayed in England, and the regiments, wanting the means of carriage, marched to the stores; the English general's first design was, therefore, merely to threaten the French left, and turn it by the sources of the rivers with Hill's corps, which was to march by the roots of the Pyrenees, while Beresford kept the centre in check upon the lower parts of the same rivers. Soult's attention would thus, he hoped, be drawn to that side, while the passage of the Adour was being made below Bayonne. And it would seem that, uncertain if he should be able to force the passage of the tributary rivers with his right, he intended, if his bridge was happily thrown, to push his main operations on that side, and thus turn the Gaves by the right bank of the Adour.

On the 12th and 13th Hill's corps, which, including Picton's division and five regiments of cavalry, furnished 20,000 combatants with sixteen guns, being relieved by the sixth and seventh divisions in front of Mousseroles and on the Adour, was concentrated about Urcuray and Hasparen. The 14th it marched in two columns—one by Bonloc to drive the French posts beyond the Joyeuse; another by the great road of St. Jean Pied de Port against Harispe, who was at Hellette. This second column had the Ursouia mountain on the right, and a third, composed of Morillo's Spaniards, having that mountain on its left, marched against the same point. Harispe, who had only three brigades, principally conscripts, retired skirmishing in the direction of St. Palais, and took a position for the night at Meharin. Not more than thirty men on each side were hurt, but the line of the Joyeuse was turned by the allies, the direct communication with St. Jean Pied de Port cut, and that place was immediately invested by Mina's battalions.

On the 15th Hill, leaving the 57th regiment at Hellette to observe the road to St. Jean Pied de Port, marched through Meharin upon Garris, eleven miles distant, but that road being impracticable for artillery, the guns moved by Armendaritz more to the right. Harispe's rear-guard was overtaken and pushed back fighting, and meanwhile Lord Wellington directed Beresford to send a brigade of the seventh division across the Gamboury to the Bastide de Clerence. The front, being thus extended from Urt towards Garris, a distance of more than twenty miles, was too attenuated; wherefore he caused the fourth division to occupy La Costa in support of the troops at the Bastide. At the same time learning that the French had weakened their force at Mousseroles, and thinking that might be to concentrate on the heights of Anglet, which would have frustrated his plan for throwing a bridge over the Adour, he directed Hope secretly to occupy the back of those heights in force, and to prevent any intercourse between Bayonne and the country.

Soult knew of the intended operations against his left on the 12th, but hearing the allies had collected boats and constructed a fresh battery near Urt on the Upper Adour, and that the pontoons had reached Urcuray, he thought Lord Wellington designed to turn his left with Hill's corps, to press him on the Bidouze with Beresford's, and to keep the garrison of Bayonne in check with the Spaniards, while Hope crossed the Adour above that fortress. Wherefore, on the 14th, when Hill's movement commenced, he repaired to the Bastide de Clerence, and made his dispositions to dispute the passage, first of the Bidouze and the Soissons or Gave of Mauleon, and then of the Gave of Oleron. He had four divisions in hand, with which he occupied a position on the 15th along the Bidouze; and he recalled General Paris, pôsting him on the road between St. Palais and St. Jean Pied de Port, with a view to watch Mina's battalions, which he supposed to be more numerous than they really were. Jaca, thus abandoned, capitulated on the 17th, the garrison returning to France on condition of not serving until exchanged. Harispe, having General Paris under his command, and being supported by Pierre Soult with a brigade of light cavalry, now covered the road from St. Jean Pied de Port with his left, and the upper line of the Bidouze with his right. Lower down that river, Villatte occupied Ilharre, Taupin was on the heights of Bergoney below Villatte, and Foy guarded the banks of the river from Came to its confluence with the Adour. The rest of the army remained under D'Erlon on the right of the latter river.

Combat of Garris.

Harispe had just taken a position in advance of the Bidouze, on a height called the Garris mountain, which stretched to St. Palais, when his rear-guard came plunging into a deep ravine in his front, closely followed by the light troops of the second division. Upon the parallel counter-ridge thus gained by the allies General Hill's corps was immediately established, and, though the evening was beginning to close, the skirmishers descended into the ravine, and two guns played over it upon Harispe's troops. These last, to the number of 4000, were drawn up on the opposite mountain, and in this state of affairs Wellington arrived. He was anxious to turn the line of the Bidouze before Soult could strengthen himself there, and seeing that the communication with General Paris by St. Palais was not well maintained, sent Morillo by a flank march along the ridge now occupied by the allies towards that place; then menacing the enemy's centre with Le Cor's Portuguese division, he at the same time directed the 39th and 28th regiments, forming Pringle's brigade, to attack, observing with a concise energy, "*You must take the hill before dark.*"

The expression caught the attention of the troops, and it was repeated by Colonel O'Callaghan as he and General Pringle placed themselves at the head of the 39th, which, followed by the 28th, rushed with loud and prolonged shouts into the ravine. The French fire was violent, Pringle fell wounded, and most of the mounted officers had their horses killed; but the troops, covered by the thick wood, gained with little loss the summit of the Garris mountain, on the right of the enemy, who thought from the shouting that a larger force was coming against them and retreated. The 39th then wheeled to their own right, intending to sweep the summit, but soon the French, discovering their error, came back at a charging pace, and receiving a volley without flinching, tried the bayonet. Colonel O'Callaghan, distinguished by his strength and courage, received two strokes of that weapon, but repaid them with fatal power in each instance, and the French, nearly all conscripts, were beaten off. Twice, however, they came back and fought, until the fire of the 28th was beginning to be felt, when Harispe, seeing the remainder of the second division ready to support the attack, Le Cor's Portuguese advancing against the centre, and the Spaniards in march towards St. Palais, retreated to that town, and calling in Paris from the side of Mauleon, immediately broke down the bridges over the Bidouze. He lost on this day nearly 500 men, of whom 200 were prisoners, and he would hardly have escaped if Morillo had not been slow. The allies lost only 160, of whom not more than fifty fell at Garris, and these chiefly in the bayonet contest, for the trees and the darkness screened them at first.

During these operations at Garris, Picton moved from Bonloc to Oreque, on Hill's left, menacing Villatte; but though Beresford's scouting parties, acting on the left of Picton, approached the Bidouze facing Taupin and Foy, his principal force remained on the Gamboury, the pivot upon which Wellington's line hinged, while the right, sweeping forward, turned the French positions. Foy, however, though in retreat, observed the movement of the fourth and seventh divisions on the heights between the Nive and the Adour, pointing their march, as he thought, towards the French left, and his reports to that effect reached Soult at the moment that General Blondeau gave notice of the investment of St. Jean Pied de Port. The French general, being thus convinced that

Lord Wellington's design was not to pass the Adour above Bayonne, but to gain the line of that river by constantly turning the French left, made new dispositions.

The line of the Bidouze was strong, if he could have supported Harispe at St. Palais, and guarded at the same time the passage of the Soissons at Mauleon; but this would have extended his front, already too wide, wherefore he resolved to abandon both the Bidouze and the Soissons, and take the line of the Gave d'Oleron, placing his right at Peyrehorade and his left at Navarrens. In this view D'Erlon was ordered to pass the Adour by the flying bridge at the Port de Landes, and take post on the left bank of that river; while Harispe, having Paris's infantry still attached to his division, defended the Gave de Mauleon, and pushed parties on his left towards the town of that name. Villatte occupied Suaveterre, where the bridge was fortified with a head on the left bank, and from thence Taupin lined the right bank to Sordes, near the confluence of the Gave de Pau. Foy occupied the works of the bridge-head at Peyrehorade and Hastingues, guarding that river to its confluence with the Adour; this line was prolonged by D'Erlon towards Dax, but Soult still kept advanced parties on the Lower Bidouze, at the different entrenched passages of that river. One brigade of cavalry was in reserve at Suaveterre, another distributed along the line. Head-quarters were transported to Orthes, and the park of artillery to Aire. The principal magazines of ammunition were, however, at Bayonne, Navarrens, and Dax; and the French general, seeing that his communications with all these places were likely to be intercepted before he could remove his stores, anticipated distress, and wrote to the minister of war to form new depôts.

On the 16th Lord Wellington repaired the broken bridges of St. Palais, after a skirmish in which a few men were wounded. Hill then crossed the Bidouze, the cavalry and artillery by the repaired bridge, the infantry by the fords; but the day being spent in the operation, the head of the column only marched beyond St. Palais. Meanwhile the fourth and part of the seventh divisions occupied the Bastide de Clerence, on the right of the Joyeuse, and the light division came up in support to the heights of La Costa on the left bank of that river. On the 17th Hill, marching at eight o'clock, passed towards the Soissons, while the third division on his left passed to the heights of Somberraute, both corps converging upon General Paris, who was in position at Arriveriete to defend the Soissons above its confluence with the Gave d'Oleron. The French outposts were immediately driven across the Gave. General Paris attempted to destroy the bridge of Arriveriete, but Lord Wellington was too quick; the 92nd regiment, covered by the fire of some guns, crossed at a ford above the bridge, and beating two French battalions from the village, secured the passage. The allies then halted for the day near Arriveriete, having marched only five miles and lost one man killed with twenty-three wounded. Paris relinquished the Soissons, but remained between the two rivers during the night, and retired on the morning of the 18th. The allies then seized the great road, which here runs from Sauveterre to Navarrens up the left bank of the Oleron Gave.

Harispe, Villatte, and Paris, supported by a brigade of cavalry, were now at Sauveterre, occupying the bridge-head on the left bank. Taupin's division was opposite the Bastide de Bearn, lower down on the right, Foy on the right of Taupin, and D'Erlon on the left of the Adour, above its confluence with the Gave de Pau. Meanwhile the fourth division advanced to Bidache, on the Bidouze, and the light division followed in support to the Bastide de Clerence, the seventh division remaining as before, partly in that vicinity, partly extended on the left to the Adour. The cavalry of the centre, under Sir Stapleton Cotton, arrived also on the banks of the Bidouze, connecting the fourth with the third division at Somberraute. In this state of affairs Hill sent Morillo up the Soissons to guard the fords, then spreading Fane's cavalry and the British and Portuguese infantry between that river and the Gave d'Oleron, he occupied all the villages along the road to Navarrens, and at the same time cannonaded the bridge-head of Sauveterre.

Soult, thrown from the commencement of the operations entirely upon the defensive, was at a loss to discover his adversary's object. The situation of the seventh division, and the march of the fourth and light divisions, led him to think his works at Hastingues and Peyrehorade would be assailed. The weakness of his line, he having only Taupin's division to guard the river between Sauveterre and Sordes, a distance of ten miles, made him fear the passage of the Gave would be forced near the Bastide de Bearn, to which post there was a good road from Came and Bidache. On the other hand, the prolongation of Hill's line up the Gave towards Navarrens indicated a design to march on Pau, or it might be to keep him in check on the Gaves while the camp at Bayonne was assaulted. In this uncertainty he sent Pierre Soult, with a cavalry brigade and two battalions of infantry, to act between Oleron and Pau. That done, he decided to hold the Gaves as long as he could, and when they were forced, to abandon the defensive, concentrate his whole force at Orthes, and fall suddenly upon the first of the allies' converging columns that approached him.

The French general's various conjectures embraced every project but the true one of the English general. The latter did, indeed, design to keep him in check upon the rivers, not to obtain an opportunity of assaulting the camp of Bayonne, but to throw his stupendous bridge over the Adour; yet his combinations were so made that, failing in that, he could still pursue his operations on the Gaves. When, therefore, he had established his offensive line strongly beyond the Soissons and the Bidouze, and knew that his pontoon train was well advanced towards Garris, he on the 19th returned rapidly to St. Jean de Luz. Everything there depending on man was ready, but the weather was boisterous with snow for two days, and Wellington, fearful of letting Soult strengthen himself on the Gave of Oleron, returned on the 21st to Garris, having decided to press his operations on that side in person, and leave to Sir John Hope and Admiral Penrose the charge of effecting

The Passage of the Adour.

The heights of Anglet had been occupied since the 15th February by the guards and Germans, small parties were cautiously pushed towards the river through the pine-forest, called the Wood of Bayonne, and the fifth division, now commanded by General Colville, occupied Bussussary and the bridge of Urdains. On the 21st Colville relieved the sixth division in the blockade of Mousseroles on the right of the Nive. To replace these troops at Bussussary, Freyre's Spaniards passed the Bidassoa, but the Andalusians and Del Parque's troops and the heavy British and Portuguese cavalry were still retained within the frontiers of Spain. Sir John Hope had therefore only two British and two Spanish divisions, three independent brigades of Anglo-Portuguese infantry, and Vandeleur's brigade of cavalry, furnishing altogether about 28,000 men and officers, with twenty pieces of artillery. There were, however, two regiments which had been sent to the rear sick, and several others expected from England, destined to join him.

In the night of the 22nd the first division, six 18-pounders, and the rocket-battery, were cautiously filed from the causeway near Anglet towards the Adour; but the road was deep and heavy, and one of the guns falling into a ditch delayed the march. Nevertheless at daybreak the whole reached some sand-downs which extended behind the pine-forest to the river. The French picquets were then driven into the entrenched camp at Beyris, the pontoon train and the field-artillery were brought down to the Adour, opposite to the village of Boucaut, and the 18-pounders were placed in battery on the bank. The light troops meanwhile moved to the edge of the marsh which covered the right of the French camp, and Carlos España's division taking post on the heights of Anglet, in concert with the independent brigades, which were at Arcangues and the bridge of Urdains, attracted the enemy's attention by false attacks, which were prolonged beyond the Nive by the fifth division. It was intended that the arrival of the gunboats and chasse-marées at the mouth of the Adour should have been simultaneous with that of the troops; but the wind having continued contrary none were to be seen, and Sir John Hope, whose firmness no untoward event could ever shake, resolved to attempt the passage with the army alone. The French flotilla opened its fire on his columns about nine o'clock; his artillery and rockets retorted upon the French gunboats and the sloop-of-war so fiercely, that three of the former were destroyed and the sloop so hardly handled that about one o'clock the whole took refuge higher up the river. Meanwhile sixty men of the guards were rowed in a pontoon across the mouth of the river in the face of a French picquet, which, seemingly bewildered, retired without firing. A raft was then formed with the remainder of the pontoons, and a hawser being stretched across, 600 of the guards and the 60th regiment, with a part of the rocket-battery, the whole under Colonel Stopford, passed, yet slowly, and at slack water only, for the tide ran strongly and the waters were wide.

During this operation General Thouvenot, commanding at Bayonne, deceived by spies and prisoners, thought that the light division was with Hope as well as the first division, and that 15,000 men were embarked at St. Jean de Luz to land between Cape Breton and the Adour. Wherefore, fearing to endanger his garrison by sending a strong force to any distance down the river, when he heard that Stopford's detachment was on the right bank, he detached two battalions under General Macomble to ascertain the state of affairs, for the pine-forest and a great bending of the river prevented him from obtaining any view from Bayonne. Macomble made a show of attacking Stopford; but the latter, flanked by the field-artillery from the left bank, received him with a discharge of rockets, projectiles which, like the elephants in ancient warfare, often turn upon their own side. This time, however, amenable to their directors, they smote the French column, and it fled amazed, with a loss of thirty wounded. It is, nevertheless, obvious that if Thouvenot had kept strong guards, with a field-battery, on the right bank of the Adour, Sir John Hope could not have passed over the troops in pontoons, nor could any vessels have crossed the bar—no resource save that of disembarking troops between the river and Cape Breton would then have remained. This error was fatal to the French. The British continued to pass all night, and until twelve o'clock on the 24th, when the British flotilla was seen under a press of sail making with a strong breeze for the mouth of the river.

To enter the Adour is, from the flatness of the coast, never an easy task; it was now most difficult, because the high winds of the preceding days had raised a great sea, and the enemy had removed one of the guiding flag-staves by which the navigation was ordinarily directed. In front of the flotilla came the boats of the men-of-war, and ahead of all the naval captain, O'Reilly, ran his craft, a chosen Spanish vessel, into the midst of the breakers, which, rolling in a frightful manner over the bar, dashed her on to the beach. That brave officer, stretched senseless on the shore, would have perished with his crew but for the ready succour of the soldiers; however, a few only were drowned, and the remainder, with an intrepid spirit, launched their boat again to aid the passage of the troops, which was still going on. O'Reilly was followed, and successfully, by Lieutenant Debenham, in a six-

oared cutter; but the tide was falling, wherefore the remainder
of the boats, the impossibility of passing until high water being
evident, drew off, and a pilot was landed to direct the line of
navigation by concerted signals.

When the water rose again the crews were promised rewards
in proportion to their successful daring, and the whole flotilla
approached in close order; but with it came black clouds and a
driving gale, which covered the whole line of coast with a rough
tumbling sea, dashing and foaming without an interval of dark
water to mark the entrance of the river. The men-of-war's boats
first drew near this terrible line of surge, and Mr. Bloye, of the
Lyra, having the chief pilot with him, heroically led into it; but
in an instant his barge was engulfed, and he and all with him
were drowned. The *Lyra's* boat thus swallowed up, the following
vessels swerved in their course, and shooting up to the right and
left, kept hovering, undecided, on the edge of the tormented waters.
Suddenly Lieutenant Cheyne, of the *Woodlark*, pulled ahead, and
striking the right line, with courage and fortune combined, safely
passed the bar. The wind then lulled, the waves, as if conquered,
abated somewhat of their rage, and the chasse-marées, manned
with Spanish seamen, but having an engineer officer with a party
of sappers in each, who compelled them to follow the men-of-war's
boats, came plunging one after another through the huge breakers,
and reached the point designed for the bridge. Thus was achieved
this perilous and glorious exploit; but Captain Elliot, of the
Martial, with his launch and crew and three transports' boats,
perished close to the shore in despite of the most violent efforts
made by the troops to save them; three other vessels, cast on the
beach, lost part of their crews; and one large chasse-marée, full of
men, after passing the line of surf safely, was overtaken by a swift
bellying wave, which, breaking on her deck, dashed her to pieces.

The whole of the first division and Bradford's Portuguese—
in all 8000 men—being now on the right bank, took post on the
sand-hills for the night. The next morning, sweeping in a half-
circle round the citadel and its entrenchments, they placed their
left on the Adour above the fortress, and their right on the same
river below the place; for the water here made such a bend in
their favour that their front was little more than two miles wide,
and for the most part covered by a marshy ravine. This nice

operation was effected without opposition, because the entrenched camps, menaced by the troops on the other side of the Adour, were so enormous that Thouvenot's force was scarcely sufficient to maintain them. Meanwhile the bridge was constructed, about three miles below Bayonne, at a place where the river was contracted to 800 feet by strong retaining walls, built with a view of sweeping away the bar by increasing the force of the current. The plan of the bridge and boom were the conception of Colonel Sturgeon and Major Todd, but the execution was confided entirely to the latter, who, with a mind less brilliant than Sturgeon's, but more indefatigable, very ably and usefully served his country throughout this war.

Twenty-six of the chasse-marées, moored head and stern at distances of forty feet, reckoning from centre to centre, were bound together with ropes; two thick cables were then carried loosely across their decks, and the ends, being cast over the walls on each bank, were strained and fastened in various modes to the sands. They were sufficiently slack to meet the spring-tides, which rose fourteen feet, and planks were laid upon them without any supporting beams. The boom, moored with anchors above and below, was a double line of masts connected with chains and cables, so as to form a succession of squares, in the design that if a vessel broke through the outside it should, by the shock, turn round in the square and become entangled with the floating wrecks of the line through which it had broken. Gunboats, with aiding batteries on the banks, were then stationed to protect the boom and to keep off fire-vessels; many row-boats were furnished with grappling-irons. The whole was, by the united labour of seamen and soldiers, finished on the 26th. Contrary to the general opinion on such matters, Major Todd found the soldiers, with minds quickened by the wider range and variety of knowledge attendant on their service, more ready of resource, and their efforts, combined by a more regular discipline, of more avail, with less loss of time, than the irregular activity of the seamen.

The agitation of the water in the river from the force of the tides was generally so great that to maintain a pontoon bridge on it was impossible. A knowledge of this had rendered the French officers too careless of watch and defence, and this year the shifting sands had given the course of the Adour such a slanting direction towards the west that it ran for some distance almost parallel to the shore; the outer bank, thus acting as a breakwater, lessened the agitation within, and enabled the large two-masted boats employed to ride safely and support the heaviest artillery and carriages. Nevertheless, this fortune, the errors of the enemy, the matchless skill and daring of the British seamen, and the discipline and intrepidity of the British soldiers, all combined by the genius of Wellington, were necessary to the success of this stupendous undertaking, which must always rank amongst the prodigies of war.

When the bridge was finished Sir John Hope resolved to contract his line of investment round the citadel. This was a serious affair. The position of the French outside that fort was exceedingly strong, for the flanks were protected by ravines, the sides of which were covered with fortified villas; and in the centre a ridge, along which the great roads from Bordeaux and Peyrehorade led into Bayonne, was occupied by the village and church of St. Etienne, both situated on rising points of ground strongly entrenched and under the fire of the citadel guns. The allies advanced in three converging columns covered by skirmishers. Their wings easily attained the edges of the ravines at either side, resting their flanks on the Adour above and below the town, at about 900 yards from the enemy's works. But a severe action took place in the centre. The assailing body, composed of Germans and a brigade of guards, was divided into three parts, which should have attacked simultaneously, the guards on the left, the light battalions of Germans on the right, and their heavy infantry in their centre. The flanks were retarded by some accident, and the centre first attacked the heights of St. Etienne. The French guns immediately opened from the citadel, and the skirmishing fire became heavy, but the Germans stormed church and village, forced the entrenched line of houses, and took a gun, which, however, they could not carry off under the close fire from the citadel. The wings then gained their positions, and the action ceased for a time; but the people of Bayonne were in such consternation that Thouvenot, to reassure them, sallied at the head of his troops. He charged the Germans twice and fought well, but was wounded, and finally lost his gun and the position of St. Etienne. There is no return of the allies' loss; it could not have been less than 500 men and officers, of which 400 were Germans. The new position thus gained was defended by ravines on each flank, and the centre, being close to the enemy's works on the ridge of St. Etienne, was entrenched. Preparations for besieging the citadel were then commenced under the direction of the German Colonel Hartmann, a code of signals was established, and infinite pains taken to protect the bridge and to secure a unity of action between the three investing bodies. The communications, however, required complicated arrangements; for the ground on the right bank of the river, being low, was overflowed every tide, and would have occasioned great difficulty but for the retaining wall, which, being four feet thick, was made use of as a carriage-road.

While these events were in progress at Bayonne, Lord Wellington pushed his operations on the Gaves with great vigour. On the 21st he returned to Garris; the pontoons had already reached that place, and on the 23rd they were carried beyond the Gave de Mauleon. During his absence the sixth and light divisions had come up, and thus six divisions of infantry and two brigades of cavalry were concentrated beyond that river on the Gave d'Oleron, between Sauveterre and Navarrens. Beresford meanwhile held the line of the Bidouze down to its confluence with the Adour, and, apparently to distract the enemy, threw a battalion over the latter river near Urt, and collected boats as if to form a bridge there. In the evening he recalled this detachment, yet continued the appearance of preparations for a bridge until late in the 23rd, when he moved forward and drove Foy's posts from the works on the lower parts of the Oleron Gave into the entrenchments of the bridge-head at Peyrehorade. The allies lost fifty men, principally Portuguese, but Soult's right and centre were thus held in check; for Beresford, having the fourth and seventh divisions and Vivian's cavalry, was strong enough for both Foy and Taupin. The rest of the French army was distributed at Orthes and Sauveterre, feeling towards Navarrens, and on the 24th Wellington put his troops in motion to pass the Gave d'Oleron. During the previous days his movements and the arrival of his reinforcements had again deceived the French general, who seems to have known nothing of the presence of the light division, and imagined the first division was at Came, as well as the fourth and seventh divisions. However, his dispositions remained the same; he did not expect to hold the Gave, and looked to a final concentration at Orthes.

On the 24th Morillo, reinforced with a strong detachment of cavalry, moved to the Laussette, a small river running in front of Navarrens, where rough ground concealed his real force, while his scouters beat back the French outposts, and a battalion marching higher up menaced the fords of the Gave at Doguen, with a view to draw the attention of the garrison of Navarrens from the ford of Ville Nave. This ford, about three miles below Doguen, was the point where Lord Wellington designed really to pass, and a great concentric movement was now in progress towards it. Le Cor's Portuguese division marched from Gestas, the light division from Aroue crossing the Soissons at Nabas; the second division, three batteries of artillery, the pontoons, and four regiments of cavalry moved from other points. Favoured by the hilly nature of the country, the columns were well concealed from the enemy, and at the same time the sixth division advanced towards the fords of Montfort, about three miles below that of Ville Nave. A battalion of the second division was sent to menace the ford of Barraute below Montfort, while the third division, reinforced with a brigade of hussars and the batteries of the second division, marched against the bridge-head of Sauveterre, with orders to make a feint of forcing a passage there. The bulk of the light cavalry remained in reserve under Cotton, but Vivian's hussars, coming up from Beresford's right, threatened all the fords between Picton's left and the Bastide of Bearn; and below this Bastide some detachments were directed upon the fords of Sindos Castagnhede and Hauterive. During this movement Beresford, keeping Foy in check at Peyrehorade with the seventh division, sent the fourth above the confluence of the Gaves to seek a fit place to throw a bridge. Thus the whole of the French front was menaced on a line of twenty-five miles, but the great force was above Sauveterre.

The first operations were not happily executed. The columns directed on the side of Sindos missed the fords. Picton opened a cannonade against the bridge-head of Sauveterre, and made four companies of Keane's brigade and some cavalry pass the Gave in the vicinity of the bridge; they were immediately assailed by a

French regiment, and driven across the river again with a loss of ninety men and officers, of whom some were drowned and thirty were made prisoners, whereupon the cavalry returned to the left bank and the cannonade ceased. Nevertheless the diversion was complete, and the general operations were successful. Soult on the first alarm drew Harispe from Sauveterre, and placed him on the road to Orthes, where a range of hills running parallel to the Gave of Oleron separates it from that of Pau; thus only a division of infantry and Berton's cavalry remained under Villatte at Sauveterre; and that general, notwithstanding his success against the four companies, alarmed by the vigour of Picton's demonstrations, abandoned his works on the left bank and destroyed the bridge. Meanwhile the sixth division passed without opposition at Montfort above Sauveterre, and at the same time the great body of the other troops, coming down upon the ford of Ville Nave, met only with a small cavalry piquet, and crossed with no more loss than two men drowned: a happy circumstance, for the waters were deep and rapid, the cold intense, and the ford so narrow that the passage was not completed before dark. To have forced it in face of an enemy would have been exceedingly difficult and dangerous, and it was remarkable that Soult, who was with Harispe, only five miles from Montfort and about seven from Ville Nave, should not have sent that general down to oppose the passage. The heads of the allies' columns immediately pushed forward to the range of hills, the right being established near Loubeing, the left towards Sauveterre, from whence Villatte and Berton had been withdrawn by Clausel, who, commanding at this part, seems to have kept a bad watch.

The French divisions now took a position to give time for Taupin to retire from the lower parts of the Gave of Oleron towards the bridge of Berenx on the Gave of Pau, for both he and Foy had received orders to march upon Orthes and break down all the bridges as they passed. When the night fell Soult sent Harispe's division also over the bridge of Orthes, and D'Erlon was already established in that town, but General Clausel remained until the morning at Orion to cover the movement.

On the 25th, at daylight, Lord Wellington, with some cavalry and guns, pushed Clausel's rear-guard into the suburb of Orthes, which covered the bridge of that place on the left bank. He also cannonaded the French troops beyond the river, and the Portuguese of the light division, skirmishing with the French in the houses to prevent the destruction of the bridge, lost twenty-five men. The second, sixth, and light divisions, Hamilton's Portuguese, five regiments of cavalry, and three batteries were now massed in front of Orthes; the third division and a brigade of cavalry was in front of the broken bridge at Berenx, about five miles lower down the Gave; the fourth and seventh divisions, with Vivian's cavalry, were in front of Peyrehorade, from whence Foy retired by the great Bayonne road to Orthes. Affairs being in this state, Morillo was directed to invest Navarrens; and as Mina's battalions were no sure guarantee against the combined efforts of the garrison of St. Jean Pied de Port and the warlike inhabitants of Baygorry, five British regiments, which had gone to the rear for clothing and were now coming up separately, were ordered to halt at St. Palais in observation, relieving each other in succession as they arrived at that place.

On the morning of the 26th Beresford, finding that Foy had abandoned the French works at Peyrehorade, passed the Gave, partly by a pontoon bridge, partly by a ford, where the current ran so strong that a column of the seventh division was like to have been carried away bodily. He had previously detached the 18th hussars to find another ford higher up, and this being effected under the guidance of a miller, the hussars gained the high-road about half-way between Peyrehorade and Orthes, and drove back the French cavalry. The French, rallying upon their reserves, turned and beat back the foremost of the pursuers, but they would not await the shock of the main body, now reinforced by Vivian's brigade and commanded by Beresford in person. In this affair Major Sewell, an officer of the staff, who had frequently distinguished himself by his personal prowess, happening to be without a sword, pulled a large stake from a hedge, and with that weapon overthrew two French hussars in succession, and only relinquished the combat when a third had cut his club in twain.

Beresford now threw out a detachment to Habas, on his left, to intercept the enemy's communication with Dax, and Lord Wellington immediately ordered Lord Edward Somerset's cavalry and the third division to cross the Gave by fords below the broken bridge of Berenx. Then directing Beresford to take a position for the night on some heights near the village of Baights, he proceeded to throw a pontoon bridge at Berenx, and thus, after a circuitous march of more than fifty miles with his right wing, he again united it with his centre, and secured a direct communication with Hope. During the 25th and 26th he had carefully examined Soult's position. The bridge of Orthes could not be easily forced. That ancient and beautiful structure consisted of several irregular arches, with a high tower in the centre, the gateway of which was built up by the French, the principal arch in front of the tower was mined, and the houses on both sides contributed to the defence. The river above and below was deep and full of tall pointed rocks, but above the town the water spreading wide with flat banks presented the means of crossing. Lord Wellington's first design was to pass there with Hill's troops and the light division, but when he heard that Beresford had crossed the Gave he suddenly changed his design, and passed the third division over and threw his bridge at Berenx. This operation was covered by Beresford, while Soult's attention was diverted by the continual skirmish at the suburbs of Orthes, by the appearance of Hill's columns above, and by Wellington's taking cognisance of the position near the bridge so openly as to draw a cannonade.

The English general did not expect Soult would, when he found Beresford and Picton were over the Gave, await a battle, and his emissaries reported that the French army was already in retreat, a circumstance to be borne in mind because the next day's operation required success to justify it. Hope's happy passage of the Adour being now known, that officer was instructed to establish a line of communication to the port of Landes, where a permanent bridge was to be formed wlth boats brought up from Urt. A direct line of intercourse was thus secured with the army at Bayonne. Lord Wellington felt that he was pushing his operations beyond his strength if Suchet should send reinforcements to Soult; wherefore he called up Freyre's Spaniards, ordering that general to cross the Adour below Bayonne, with two of his divisions and a brigade of Portuguese 9-pounders, and join him by the port of Landes. O'Donnel's Andalusians and the Prince of Anglona's troops were also directed to be in readiness to enter France. These orders were given with the greatest reluctance.

CHAPTER XIX.

ORTHES—AIRE—BORDEAUX.

THE feeble resistance made by the French in the difficult country already passed left Wellington without much uneasiness as to the power of Soult's army in the field, but his disquietude was extreme about the danger of an insurgent warfare. "Maintain the strictest discipline; *without that we are lost*," was his expression to General Freyre, and he issued a proclamation authorising the people of the districts he had overrun to arm themselves for the preservation of order under the direction of their mayors. He invited them to arrest all straggling soldiers and followers of the army, and all plunderers and evil-doers, and convey them to head-quarters with proof of their crimes, promising to punish the culpable and to pay for all damages. At the same time he confirmed all the local authorities who chose to retain their offices, on the sole condition of having no political or military intercourse with the countries still possessed by the French army. Nor was his proclamation a dead letter, for the inhabitants of a village situated near the road leading from Sauveterre to Orthes shot one English soldier dead and wounded a second who had come with others to plunder. Lord Wellington caused the wounded man to be hung as an example, and he also forced an English colonel to quit the army for suffering his soldiers to destroy the municipal archives of a small town.

Soult had no thought of retreating. His previous retrograde movements had been effected with order, his army was concentrated with its front to the Gave, and every bridge, except the noble structure at Orthes, the ancient masonry of which resisted his mines, had been destroyed. One regiment of cavalry was detached on the right to watch the fords as far as Peyrehorade, three others, with two battalions of infantry, under Pierre Soult, watched those between Orthes and Pau, and a body of horsemen and gens-d'armes covered the latter town from Morillo's incursions. Two regiments of cavalry remained with the army, and the French general's intention was to fall upon the head of the first column which should cross the Gave. But the negligence of the officer stationed at Puyoo, who had suffered Vivian's hussars to pass on the 26th February, without opposition and without making any report of the event, enabled Beresford to make his movement in safety when otherwise he would have been assailed by at least two-thirds of the French army. It was not until three o'clock in the evening that Soult received intelligence of his march, and his columns were then close to Baïghts, on the right flank of the French army, his scouters were on the Dax road in its rear, and at the same time the sixth and light divisions were seen descending by different roads from the heights beyond the river pointing towards Berenx.

In this crisis the French marshal hesitated whether to fall upon Beresford and Picton while the latter was still passing the river, or take a defensive position, but finally judging that he had not time to form his columns of attack, he decided upon the latter. Wherefore, under cover of a skirmish, sustained near Baïghts by a battalion of infantry, which, coming from the bridge of Berenx, was joined by the light cavalry from Puyoo, he hastily threw D'Erlon's and Reille's divisions on a new line across the road from Peyrehorade. The right extended to the heights of St. Boës, along which runs the road from Orthes to Dax, and this line was prolonged by Clausel's troops to Caste Tarbe, a village close to the Gave. Having thus opposed a temporary front to Beresford, he made his dispositions to receive battle the next morning, bringing Villatte's infantry and Pierre Soult's cavalry from the other side of Orthes through that town, and it was this movement that led Lord Wellington's emissaries to report that the army was retiring.

Soult's new line was on a ridge of hills partly wooded, partly naked. In the centre was an open rounded hill, from whence long narrow tongues were pushed out; the front was generally covered by a deep and marshy ravine, broken by two short tongues of land which jutted out from the principal hill. Behind the centre a succession of undulating bare heathy hills trended for several miles to the rear, but behind the right the country was low and deep. General Reille, having Taupin's, Roguet's, and Paris's divisions under him, commanded on the right. Count D'Erlon, commanding Foy's and D'Armagnac's divisions, was on the left of Reille. He placed the first along a ridge extending towards the road of Peyrehorade, the second in reserve. In rear of this last Villatte's division and the cavalry were posted above the village of Rontun, on the open hills behind the main position. Harispe, whose troops, as well as Villatte's, were under Clausel, occupied Orthes and the bridge, having a regiment near the ford of Souars above the town. Thus the French army extended from St. Boës to Orthes, but the great mass was disposed towards the centre.

At daybreak on the 27th February the sixth and light divisions, having passed the Gave near Berenx, by the pontoon bridge thrown in the night, wound up a narrow way between high rocks to the great road of Peyrehorade. The third division and Lord Edward Somerset's cavalry were already established there in columns of march, with skirmishers pushed forwards to the edge of the wooded height occupied by D'Erlon's left, and Beresford, with the fourth and seventh divisions and Vivian's cavalry, had meanwhile gained the ridge of St. Boës, and approached the Dax road beyond. Hill remained with the second British and Le Cor's Portuguese divisions, menacing the bridge of Orthes and the ford of Souars. Between Beresford and Picton, a distance of a mile and a half, there were no troops; but about half-way, exactly in front of the French centre, was a Roman camp crowning an isolated hill of singular appearance, and nearly as lofty as the centre of Soult's position.

On this camp, now covered with vineyards, but then open and grassy, with a few trees, Lord Wellington, after viewing the country on Beresford's left, stopped for an hour or more to examine the enemy's disposition for battle. During this time the two divisions were coming up from the river, but so hemmed in by rocks that only a few men could march abreast, and their point of union with the third division was little more than cannon-shot from the enemy's position. The moment was critical. Picton did not conceal his disquietude, but Wellington, undisturbed as the deep sea, continued his observations without seeming to notice the dangerous position of his troops. When they had reached the main road he reinforced Picton with the sixth, and drew the light division by cross-roads behind the Roman camp, thus connecting his wings and forming a central reserve. From this point by-ways led, on the left to the high church of Baïghts and the Dax road, on the right to the Peyrehorade road; and two others led straight across the marsh to the French position.

This marsh, the open hill about which Soult's guns and reserves were principally gathered, the form and nature of the ridges on the flanks, all combined to forbid an attack in front, and the flanks were scarcely more promising. The extremity of the French left sank, indeed, to a gentle undulation in crossing the Peyrehorade road, yet it would have been useless to push troops on that line towards Orthes, for the town was strongly occupied by Harispe, and was there covered by an ancient wall and the bed of a torrent. It was equally difficult to turn the St. Boës flank, because of the low marshy country into which the troops must have descended beyond the Dax road; and the brows of the hills, trending backwards from the centre of the French position, would have enabled Soult to oppose a new and formidable front at right angles to his actual position. The whole of the allied army must, therefore, have made a circuitous flank movement within gun-shot, and through a most difficult country, or Beresford's left must have been dangerously extended and the whole line weakened. Nor could the movement be hidden, because the hills, although only moderately high, were abrupt on that side, affording a full view of the low country, and Soult's cavalry detachments were in observation on every brow.

It only remained to assail the French flanks along the ridges, making the principal efforts on the side of St. Boës, with intent, if successful, to overlap the French right beyond and seize the road of St. Sever, while Hill passed the Gave at Souars and cut off the road to Pau, thus enclosing the beaten army in Orthes. This was, however, no slight affair. On Picton's side it was easy to obtain a footing on the flank ridge near the high-road, but beyond that the ground rose rapidly and the French were gathered thickly, with a narrow front and plenty of guns. On Beresford's side they could only be assailed along the summit of the St. Boës ridge, advancing from the high church of Baïghts and the Dax road. But the village of St. Boës was strongly occupied, the ground immediately behind it was strangled to a narrow pass by the ravine, and the French reserve of sixteen guns, placed on the Dax road, behind the hill in the centre of Soult's line, and well covered from counter-fire, was in readiness to crush the head of any column which should emerge from the gorge of St. Boës.

Battle of Orthes.

During the whole morning of February 27th a slight skirmish, with now and then a cannon-shot, had been going on with the third division on the right, and the French cavalry at times pushed parties forward on each flank, but at nine o'clock Wellington commenced the real attack. The third and sixth divisions won without difficulty the lower part of the ridges opposed to them, and endeavoured to extend their left along the French front with a sharp fire of musketry; but the main battle was on the other flank. There General Cole, keeping Anson's brigade of the fourth division in reserve, assailed St. Boës with Ross's British brigade and Vasconcellos' Portuguese. His object was to get on to the open ground beyond it, but fierce and slaughtering was the struggle. Five times breaking through the scattered houses did Ross carry his battle into the wider space beyond; yet ever as the troops issued forth the French guns from the open hill smote them in front, and the reserved battery on the Dax road swept through them with grape from flank to flank. Then Taupin's supporting masses rushed forwards with a wasting fire, and lapping the flanks with skirmishers, which poured along the ravines on either hand, forced the shattered columns back into the village. It was in vain that, with desperate valour, the allies time after time broke through the narrow way and struggled to spread a front beyond. Ross fell, dangerously wounded, and Taupin, whose troops were clustered thickly and well supported,

2 A

defied their utmost efforts. Nor was Soult less happy on the other side. The nature of the ground would not permit the third and sixth divisions to engage many men at once, so that no progress was made; and one small detachment which Picton extended to his left, having made an attempt to gain the smaller tongue jutting out from the central hill, was suddenly charged as it neared the summit by Foy, and driven down again in confusion, losing several prisoners.

When the combat had thus continued with unabated fury on the side of St. Boës for about three hours, Lord Wellington sent a caçadore regiment of the light division from the Roman camp to protect the right flank of Ross's brigade against the French skirmishers; but this was of no avail, for Vasconcellos' Portuguese, unable to sustain the violence of the enemy any longer, gave way in disorder, and the French pouring on, the British troops retreated through St. Boës with difficulty. As this happened at the moment when the detachment on Picton's left was repulsed, victory seemed to declare for the French; and Soult, conspicuous on his commanding open hill, the knot of all his combinations, seeing his enemies thus broken and thrown backwards on each side, put all his reserves in movement to complete the success. It is said that in the exultation of the moment he smote his thigh, exclaiming, "At last I have him!" Whether this be so or not, it was no vainglorious speech, for the moment was most dangerous. There was, however, a small black cloud rising just beneath him, unheeded at first amidst the thundering din and tumult that now shook the field of battle, but which soon burst with irresistible violence. Wellington, seeing that St. Boës was inexpugnable, had suddenly changed his plan of battle. Supporting Ross with Anson's brigade, which had not hitherto been engaged, he backed both with the seventh division and Vivian's cavalry, now forming one heavy body, towards the Dax road. Then he ordered the third and sixth divisions to be thrown in mass upon Foy's left flank, and at the same time sent the 52nd regiment down from the Roman camp, with instructions to cross the marsh in front, to mount the French ridge beyond, and to assail the flank and rear of the troops engaged with the fourth division at St. Boës.

Colonel Colborne, so often distinguished in this war, immediately led the 52nd down and crossed the marsh under fire, the men sinking at every step above the knees, in some places to the middle, but still pressing forwards with that stern resolution and order to be expected from the veterans of the light division, soldiers who had never yet met their match in the field. They soon obtained footing on firm land, and ascended the heights in line at the moment that Taupin was pushing vigorously through St. Boës; Foy and D'Armagnac, hitherto more than masters of their positions, being at the same time seriously assailed on the other flank by the third and sixth divisions. With a mighty shout and a rolling fire the 52nd soldiers dashed forwards between Foy and Taupin, beating down a French battalion in their course, and throwing everything before them into disorder. General Bechaud was killed in Taupin's division, Foy was dangerously wounded, and his troops, discouraged by his fall and by this sudden burst from a quarter where no enemy was expected—for the march of the 52nd had been hardly perceived save by the skirmishers—got into confusion, and the disorder spreading to Reille's wing, he also was forced to fall back and take a new position to restore his line of battle. The narrow pass behind St. Boës was thus opened, and Wellington, seizing the critical moment, thrust the fourth and seventh divisions, Vivian's cavalry, and two batteries of artillery through, and spread a front beyond.

The victory was thus secured; for the third and sixth divisions had now won D'Armagnac's position and established a battery of guns on a knoll, from whence their shot ploughed through the French masses from one flank to another. Suddenly a squadron of French chasseurs came at a hard gallop down the main road of Orthes to charge these guns, and sweeping to their right, they rode over some of the sixth division which had advanced too far, but pushing this charge too madly, got into a hollow lane, and were nearly all destroyed. The third and seventh divisions then continued to advance, and the wings of the army were united. The French general rallied all his forces on the open hills beyond the Dax road, and with Taupin's, Roguet's, Paris's, and D'Armagnac's divisions made strong battle to cover the reformation of Foy's disordered troops, but his foes were not all in front. This part of the battle was fought with only two-thirds of the allied army. Hill, who had remained with 12,000 combatants, cavalry and infantry, before the bridge of Orthes, received orders, when Wellington changed his plan of attack, to force the passage of the Gave, partly in view of preventing Harispe from falling upon the flank of the sixth division, partly in the hope of a successful issue to the attempt; and so it happened. Hill, though unable to force the bridge, forded the river above at Souars, and driving back the troops posted there, seized the heights above, cut off the French from the road to Pau, and turned the town of Orthes. He thus menaced Soult's only line of retreat by Salespice, on the road to St. Sever, at the very moment when, the 52nd having opened the defile of St. Boës, the junction of the allies' wings was effected on the French position.

Clausel immediately ordered Harispe to abandon Orthes and close towards Villatte on the heights above Rontun, leaving, however, some conscript battalions on a rising point beyond the road of St. Sever, called the Motte de Turenne. Meanwhile in person he endeavoured to keep General Hill in check by the menacing action of two cavalry regiments and a brigade of infantry; but Soult arrived at the moment, and seeing that the loss of Souars had rendered his whole position untenable, gave orders for a general retreat.

This was a perilous matter. The heathy hills upon which he was now fighting, although for a short distance they furnished a succession of parallel positions favourable enough for defence, soon resolved themselves into a low ridge running to the rear on a line parallel with the road to St. Sever; and on the opposite side of that road, about cannon-shot distance, was a corresponding ridge, along which General Hill, judging by the firing how matters went, was now rapidly advancing. Five miles distant was the Luy de Bearn, and four miles beyond that the Luy de France, two rivers, deep and with difficult banks. Behind these the Lutz, the Gabas, and the Adour crossed the line, and though, once beyond the wooden bridge of Sault de Navailles on the Luy de Bearn, these streams would necessarily cover the retreat, to carry off by one road and one bridge a defeated army still closely engaged in front seemed impossible. Nevertheless Soult did so. For Paris sustained the fight on his right until Foy and Taupin's troops rallied; and when the impetuous assault of the 52nd and the rush of the fourth and seventh divisions drove Paris back,

D'Armagnac interposed to cover him until the union of the allies' wings was completed; then both retired, being covered in turn by Villatte. In this manner the French yielded, step by step and without confusion, the allies advancing with an incessant deafening musketry and cannonade, yet losing many men, especially on the right, where the third division were very strongly opposed. However, as the danger of being cut off at Salespice by Hill became more imminent, the retrograde movements were more hurried and confused. Hill, seeing this, quickened his pace, until at last both sides began to run violently, and so many men broke from the French ranks, making across the fields towards the fords, and such a rush was necessarily made by the rest to gain the bridge of Sault de Navailles, that the whole country was covered with scattered bands. Sir Stapleton Cotton, then breaking with Lord Edward Somerset's hussars through a small covering body opposed to him by Harispe, sabred 200 or 300 men, and the 7th Hussars cut off about 2000, who threw down their arms in an enclosed field; yet some confusion or mismanagement occurring, the greatest part, recovering their weapons, escaped, and the pursuit ceased at the Luy de Bearn.

The French army appeared to be entirely dispersed; but it was more disordered in appearance than reality, for Soult passed the Luy de Bearn and destroyed the bridge with the loss of only six guns and less than 4000 men killed, wounded, and prisoners. Many thousands of conscripts, however, threw away their arms, and one month afterwards the stragglers still amounted to 3000. Nor would the passage of the river have been effected so happily if Lord Wellington had not been struck by a musket-ball just above the thigh, which caused him to ride with difficulty, whereby the vigour and unity of the pursuit was necessarily abated. The loss of the allies was 2300, of which fifty, with three officers, were taken; but among the wounded were Lord Wellington, General Walker, General Ross, and the Duke of Richmond, then Lord March. He had served on Lord Wellington's personal staff during the whole war without a hurt; but being made a captain in the 52nd, like a good soldier joined his regiment the night before the battle. He was shot through the chest a few hours afterwards, thus learning by experience the difference between the labours and dangers of staff and regimental officers.

General Berton, stationed between Pau and Orthes during the battle, had been cut off by Hill's movement; yet skirting that general's march, he retreated with his cavalry, picking up two battalions of conscripts on the road. Meanwhile Soult, having no position to rally upon, continued his retreat in the night to St. Sever, breaking down all the bridges behind him. Lord Wellington pursued at daylight in three columns. At St. Sever he hoped to find the enemy still in confusion, but he was too late; the French were across the river, the bridge was broken, and the army halted. The result of the battle was, however, soon made known far and wide; and Darricau, who with a few hundred soldiers was endeavouring to form an insurgent levy at Dax, the works of which were incomplete and still unarmed, immediately destroyed part of the stores, and retreated through the Landes to the Garonne.

From St. Sever, which offered no position, Soult turned short to the right and moved upon Barcelona, higher up the Adour; but he left D'Erlon with two divisions of infantry, some cavalry, and four guns at Caceres on the right bank, and sent Clausel to occupy Aire on the other side of the river. He thus abandoned his magazines at Mont Marsan, and left open the direct road to Bordeaux; but holding Caceres with his right, he commanded another road by Roquefort to that city, while his left, being at Aire, protected the magazines and artillery-park at that place and covered the road to Pau. Meanwhile the main body at Barcelona equally supported Clausel and D'Erlon, and covered the great roads leading to Agen and Toulouse on the Garonne, and to the mountains by Tarbes.

In this situation it was difficult to judge what line of operations he meant to adopt. Wellington, however, passed the Adour about one o'clock, partly by the repaired bridge of St. Sever, partly by a deep ford below, and immediately detached Beresford with the light division and Vivian's cavalry to seize the magazines at Mont Marsan; at the same time he pushed the head of a column towards Caceres, where a cannonade and charge of cavalry had place, and a few men and officers were hurt on both sides. The next day Hill's corps reached the Adour between St. Sever and Aire, and D'Erlon was again assailed on the right bank and driven back skirmishing to Barcelona. This event proved that Soult had abandoned Bordeaux; but the English general could not push the pursuit more vigorously, because every bridge was broken, and a violent storm on the evening of the 1st March had filled the smaller rivers and torrents, carried away the pontoon-bridges, and cut off all communication between the troops and the supplies.

The bulk of the army was now necessarily halted on the right bank of the Adour until the bridges could be repaired; but Hill, who was on the left bank, marched to seize the magazines at Aire. Moving in two columns on the 2nd, he reached his destination about three o'clock, with two divisions of infantry, a brigade of cavalry, and a battery of horse artillery. He expected no serious opposition; but General Clausel had arrived a few hours before, and was in order of battle, covering the town with Villatte's and Harispe's divisions and some guns. The French occupied a steep ridge in front of Aire, high and wooded on the right where it overlooked the river, but merging on the left into a wide table-land, over which the great road led to Pau. The position was strong for battle, yet it could be readily outflanked on the left by the table-land, and was an uneasy one for retreat on the right, where the ridge was narrow, the ravine behind steep and rugged, with a mill-stream at the bottom between it and the town. A branch of the Adour also flowing behind Aire cut it off from Barcelona, while behind the left wing was the greater Lees, a river with steep banks and only one bridge.

AIRE.

General Hill, arriving about two o'clock, attacked without hesitation. General Stewart with two British brigades fell on the French right, a Portuguese brigade assailed their centre, and the other brigades followed in columns of march. The action was, however, very sudden. The Portuguese were pushed forward in a slovenly manner by General Da Costa, a man of no ability, and the French under Harispe met them on the flat summit of the height with so rough a charge that they gave way in flight. The rear of the allies' column being still in march, the battle was like to be lost; but General Stewart, having by this time won the heights on the French right, where Villatte, fearing to be enclosed, made but a feeble resistance, immediately detached General Barnes with the 50th and 92nd regiments to the aid of the Portuguese. The vehement charge of these troops turned the stream of battle, the French were broken in turn and thrown back on their reserves; yet they rallied and renewed the action with great courage, fighting obstinately until General Byng's British brigade came up, when Harispe was driven towards the river Lees, and Villatte quite through the town of Aire into the space between the two branches of the Adour behind.

General Reille, who was at Barcelona when the action began, brought up Roguet's division to support Villatte; the combat was thus continued until night at that point. Meanwhile Harispe crossed the Lees and broke the bridge, but the French lost many men. Two generals were wounded, a colonel of engineers was killed, one hundred prisoners were taken, many of Harispe's conscripts threw away their arms and fled to their homes, and the magazines fell into the conqueror's hands. The loss of the British troops was 150, General Barnes was wounded, and Colonel Hood killed. The loss of the Portuguese was never officially stated, yet it could not have been less than that of the British, and the vigour of the action proved that the French courage was very little abated by the battle of Orthes. Soult immediately retreated up the Adour by both banks, and was not followed, for new combinations were now opened to the generals on both sides.

The victory of Orthes showed the superiority of the allies as conspicuously as any former battle in the Peninsular campaigns, and but for the hurt Lord Wellington had received the result might perhaps have been more decisive. The following up of the enemy was further delayed by a sudden rise of the Adour and its tributaries, the bridges over these having also to be replaced, as the French had destroyed them in their disorderly flight, for it was a retreat no longer. Extremely perilous and disheartening was the situation of the French general. His army was greatly reduced by his losses in battle and by the desertion of the conscripts, and 3000 stragglers (old soldiers who ought to have rejoined their eagles) were collected by different generals, into whose districts they had wandered, and employed to strengthen detached corps instead of being restored to the army. All his magazines were taken, discontent, the natural offspring of misfortune, prevailed amongst his officers, a powerful enemy was in front, no certain resources of men or money behind, and his efforts were ill seconded by the civil authorities.

On the 3d and 4th March he retreated towards Rabastens, where he halted, covering Tarbes, his design being to keep in mass and await the development of the allies' plans. In this view he called in the detachments of cavalry and infantry which had been left on the side of Pau before the battle of Orthes, and hearing that Darricau was at Langon with 1000 men, he ordered him to join the army immediately. He likewise put the national guards and gens-d'armes in activity on the side of the Pyrenees, and directed the commanders of the military districts in his rear to keep their old soldiers, of which there were still many scattered through the country, in readiness to aid the army.

Soult was mistaken as to the real force of the allies in the recent operations. In other respects he displayed clear views and great activity. He reorganised his army in six divisions, called in his detachments, urged the imperial commissioners and local authorities to hasten the levies and restore deserters, and he prepared a plan of action for the partisans which had been organised towards the mountains. Nevertheless his difficulties increased.

Nor was Wellington without embarrassments. The storms prevented him following up his victory while the French army was in confusion. Now it was reorganised on a new line, and could retreat for many days in a direction parallel to the Pyrenees with strong defensive positions. Should he press it closely? His army, weakened at every step, would have to move between the mountains and the Garonne, exposing its flanks and rear to the operations of any force which the French might be able to collect on those boundaries; that is to say, all the power of France beyond the Garonne. It was essential to find some counterpoise and to increase his field army. To establish a Bourbon party at Bordeaux was an obvious mode of attaining the first object. To seize that city by a detachment he must employ 12,000 men, and remain with 26,000 to oppose Soult, who he erroneously believed was being joined by 10,000 men which Suchet had sent. The five regiments detached for their clothing had rejoined the army, and all the reserves of cavalry and artillery were now called up, but the reinforcements from England and Portugal, amounting to 20,000 men, upon which he had calculated, were detained. Wherefore, driven by necessity, he directed Freyre to join him with two divisions of the Gallician army, a measure which was instantly followed by innumerable complaints of outrages and excesses, although the Spaniards were entirely provided from the English military chest. He determined to seize Bordeaux, and meanwhile repaired the destroyed bridges, brought up one of Morillo's brigades to the vicinity of Aire, sent Campbell's Portuguese dragoons to Roquefort, General Fane with two regiments of cavalry and a brigade of infantry to Pau, and pushed posts towards Tarbes and Vic Bigorre.

Soult meantime, fearing the general apathy and ill-will of the people would become fatal to him, endeavoured to arouse the energies of the people and the army by a proclamation, which has been unreasonably railed at by several English writers, for it was a judicious, well-timed, and powerful address.

It was in this state of affairs that the English general detached Beresford with 12,000 men against Bordeaux, giving him instructions to occupy that city and acquire the Garonne as a port for the allies. On the 8th March Beresford marched towards Langon with the fourth and seventh divisions, Vivian's horsemen, and some guns; he was joined on the road by some of Vandeleur's cavalry from Bayonne, and he had orders to observe the enemy's movements towards Agen, for it was still in Soult's power, by a forced march on that side, to cross the Garonne and enter Bordeaux before him. Long before this epoch Soult, foreseeing that the probable course of the war would endanger Bordeaux, had given orders to place the forts in a state of defence.

Entering Bordeaux on the 12th March, Beresford met the municipality and a great body of Bourbonists, at the head of whom was the mayor, Count Lynch, decorated with the scarf of his office and the legion of honour, both conferred upon him by the sovereign he was then going to betray. After some formal discourse, in which Beresford explicitly made known his instructions, Lynch very justly tore the tricolor, the emblem of his country's glory, from his own shoulders; the white flag was then displayed, and the allies took peaceable possession of the city. The Duke of Angoulême arrived on the same day, and Louis the Eighteenth was formally proclaimed. This event, the act of a party, was not generally approved, and the mayor, conscious of weakness, immediately issued, with the connivance of the Duke of Angoulême, a proclamation, in which he asserted that "the British, Portuguese, and Spanish armies were united in the south, as the other nations were united in the north, solely to destroy Napoleon, and replace him by a Bourbon king, who was conducted thither by these generous allies, and only by accepting that king could the French appease the resentment of the Spaniards." At the same time the Duke of Angoulême, as if quite master of the country, appointed prefects and other authorities in districts beyond the limits of Bordeaux.

Both the duke and the mayor soon repented of their precipitancy. The English fleet, which should have acted simultaneously with the troops, had not arrived; the *Regulus*, a French seventy-four, with several inferior vessels of war, were anchored below Blaye, and Beresford was recalled with the fourth division and Vivian's cavalry. Lord Dalhousie remained with only the seventh division and three squadrons to oppose the French corps which were now on the Garonne. He could not guard the river below Bordeaux, and some French troops re-crossing again took possession of the fort of Grave near the mouth; a new army was forming under General Decaen beyond the Garonne, the Napoleonists, recovering from their first stupor, began to stir themselves, and a partisan officer, coming down to St. Macaire, surprised fifty men which Lord Dalhousie had sent across the Garonne from Langon to take possession of a French magazine. In the Landes the peasants burned the houses of the gentlemen who had joined the white standard, and in Bordeaux itself a counter-insurrection was preparing, whenever Decaen should be ready to advance.

The prince, frightened at these symptoms of reaction, desired Lord Dalhousie to bring his troops into Bordeaux to awe the Napoleonists, and meanwhile each party strove to outvie the other in idle rumours and falsehoods relating to the emperor. Victories and defeats were invented or exaggerated, Napoleon was dead from illness, had committed suicide, was poisoned, stabbed; and all these things were related as certain, with most circumstantial details. Meanwhile Wellington, writing to the

Duke of Angoulême, denied the veracity of the mayor's proclamation, and expressed his trust that the prince was not a party to such a mendacious document. The latter, however, with some excuses about hurry and confusion, avowed his participation in its publication, and defended the mayor's conduct. He also forwarded a statement of the danger his party was exposed to, and demanded aid of men and money, supporting his application by a note of council in which, with more ingenuity than justice, it was argued that as civil government could not be conducted without executive power, and as Lord Wellington had suffered the Duke of Angoulême to assume the civil government at Bordeaux without an adequate executive force, he was bound to supply the deficiency from his army, and even to furnish money until taxes could be levied under the protection of the soldiers.

The English general was not a man to bear with such sophistry in excuse for a breach of faith. Sorry he was, he said, to find that the principle by which he regulated his conduct towards the Bourbon party had made so little impression that the duke could not perceive how inconsistent it was with the mayor's proclamation. Most cautious, therefore, must be his future conduct, seeing that, as the chief of an army and the confidential agent of three independent nations, he could not permit his views to be misrepresented upon such an important question. Angoulême had better, he continued, conduct his policy and compose his manifestoes in such a manner as not to force a public contradiction of them. His royal highness was free to act as he pleased for himself, but he was not free to adduce the name and authority of the allied governments in support of his measures when they had not been consulted, nor of their general, when he had been consulted, but had given his opinion against those measures.

When Beresford marched to rejoin the army the line of occupation was too extensive for Lord Dalhousie, and Lord Wellington ordered him to keep clear of the city and hold his troops together, observing that his own projected operations on the Upper Garonne would keep matters quiet on the lower part of that river. Nevertheless, if the war had continued for a month that officer's situation would have been critical; for when Napoleon knew that Bordeaux had fallen, he sent General Decaen to Libourne to form the "*army of the Gironde.*" For this object General Despeaux, acting under Soult's orders, collected a body of gens-d'armes, custom-house officers, and national guards on the Upper Garonne, and it was one of his detachments that surprised Lord Dalhousie's men at St. Macaire on the 18th. A battery of eight guns was sent down from Narbonne, other batteries were despatched from Paris, and 300 or 400 cavalry joined L'Huillier, who, with 1000 infantry, was in position beyond the Dordogne. Behind these troops all the national guards, custom-house officers, and gens-d'armes of five departments were ordered to assemble and march to the Dordogne; but the formidable part of the intended army was a body of Suchet's veterans, 6000 in number, under General Beurman, who had been directed upon Libourne.

Decaen entered Mucidan on the 1st of April, but Beurman's troops had not then reached Perigeaux, and Lord Dalhousie's cavalry were in Libourne, between him and L'Huillier. The power of concentration was thus denied to the French, and meanwhile Admiral Penrose had secured the command of the Garonne. It appears Lord Wellington thought this officer dilatory, but on the 27th March he arrived with a seventy-four and two frigates, whereupon the *Regulus* and other French vessels made sail up the river, and escaped through a narrow channel on the north side and cast anchor under some batteries. Previous to this event Mr. Ogilvy, a commissary, being on the river in a boat manned with Frenchmen, discovered the *Requin* sloop, half French, half American, pierced for twenty-two guns, lying at anchor not far below Bordeaux, and at the same time he saw a sailor leap hastily into a boat above him and row for the vessel. This man, being taken, proved to be the armourer of the *Requin*. He said there were not many men on board; and Mr. Ogilvie, observing his alarm and judging that the crew would also be fearful, with ready resolution bore down upon the *Requin*, boarded and took her without any opposition either from her crew or that of his own boat, although she had fourteen guns mounted and eleven men with two officers on board. The naval co-operation being thus assured, Lord Dalhousie crossed the Garonne above the city, drove the French posts beyond the Dordogne, and sending his cavalry over that river, intercepted Decaen's and L'Huillier's communications; the former was thus forced to remain at

Mucidan with 250 gens-d'armes, awaiting the arrival of Beurman, and he found neither arms nor ammunition nor a willing spirit to enable him to organise the national guards.

The English horsemen repassed the Dordogne on the 2nd of April, but on the 4th Lord Dalhousie crossed it again lower down with about 3000 men, intending to march upon Blaye, but hearing that L'Huillier had halted at Etauliers, he turned suddenly upon him. The French general formed his line on an open common, occupying some woods in front with his detachments. Overmatched in infantry, he had 300 cavalry opposed to one weak squadron, and yet his troops would not stand the shock of the battle. The allied infantry cleared the woods in a moment, the artillery then opened upon the main body, which retired in disorder, horsemen and infantry together, leaving behind several scattered bodies, upon whom the British cavalry galloped and made 200 or 300 men and thirty officers prisoners.

If the 6000 old troops under Beurman had arrived at this time in Lord Dalhousie's rear, his position would have been embarassing, but they were delayed on the road. Meanwhile Admiral Penrose, having observed the French flotilla, consisting of fifteen armed vessels and gunboats, coming down to join the *Regulus*, sent the boats of his fleet to attack them, whereupon the French vessels ran on shore, and the crews, aided by 200 soldiers, lined the beach to protect them. Lieutenant Dunlop, who commanded the English boats, landing all his seamen and marines, beat these troops and carried off or destroyed the whole flotilla with a loss to himself of only six men wounded and missing. This operation completed, the admiral, now reinforced with a second ship of the line, resolved to attack the French squadron and the shore batteries, but in the night the enemy set fire to their vessels. Captain Harris of the *Belle Poule* frigate then landed with 600 seamen and marines, and destroyed the batteries and forts on the right bank. By this time treason had done its work at Paris, and Napoleon was overthrown. The war was virtually over, but on the side of Toulouse and Bayonne the armies, ignorant of this great event, were still battling with unabated fury.

CHAPTER XX.

VIC BIGORRE—TARBES—TOULOUSE—BAYONNE.

HILE Beresford was moving upon Bordeaux, Soult and Wellington remained in observation, each thinking the other stronger than himself, for the English general, having intelligence of Beurman's march, believed that his troops were intended to reinforce and had actually joined Soult. On the other hand, that marshal, who knew not of Beresford's march until the 13th March, concluded Wellington still had the 12,000 men detached to Bordeaux. The numbers on each side were, however, nearly equal. The French army was 31,000, infantry and cavalry; yet 3000 being stragglers, Soult could only put into line, exclusive of conscripts without arms, 28,000 sabres and bayonets, with thirty-eight pieces of artillery. On the allies' side 27,000 sabres and bayonets were under arms, with forty-two guns, but from this number detachments had been sent to Pau and Roquefort, and the cavalry scouts were pushed to the Upper Garonne.

Lord Wellington, expecting Soult would retreat upon Auch, and designing to follow him, had caused Beresford to keep the bulk of his troops towards the Upper Garonne that he might the sooner rejoin the army; but the French general, having early fixed his line of retreat by St. Gaudens, was only prevented from retaking the offensive on the 9th or 10th by the loss of his magazines, which forced him first to organise a system of requisition for the subsistence of his army. Meanwhile his equality of force passed away. On the 13th Freyre came up with 8000 Spanish infantry, and the next day Ponsonby's heavy cavalry arrived. Lord

Wellington was then the strongest, yet he still awaited Beresford's troops, and was uneasy about his own situation, and he dreaded the junction of Suchet's army with Soult. The French general, having obtained exact intelligence of Beresford's march to Bordeaux, now resolved to attack the allies, and the more readily that Napoleon had recently sent him instructions to draw the war to the side of Pau, keeping his left resting on the Pyrenees, which accorded with his own designs. Lord Wellington's main body was now concentrated round Aire and Barcelona, yet divided by the Adour, and the advanced guards were on a semicircle to the front and about half a march in advance. Soult thought to strike a good blow, and purposed to throw himself upon the high tabular land between Pau and Aire, and then act according to circumstances.

The country was suited to the action of all arms, offering a number of long and nearly parallel ridges of moderate height, the sides of which were sometimes covered with vineyards, but the summits commonly so open that troops could move along them without much difficulty, and between these ranges a number of small rivers and muddy fords descended from the Pyrenees to the Adour. This conformation determined the order of the French general's march, which followed the course of these rivers. Leaving one regiment of cavalry to watch the valley of the Adour, he moved with the rest of his army down the smaller Lees. In this position the head of the columns, pointing direct upon Aire, separated Viella from Garlin, which was the right of General Hill's position, and menaced that general's posts on the great Lees. Meanwhile Pierre Soult, marching with three regiments of cavalry along the high land between the two Lees, covered the left flank of the French army, and pushed Fane's cavalry posts back with the loss of two officers taken and a few men wounded. During this movement Berton, advancing with two regiments of cavalry on the right flank of the French army, endeavoured to cross the Saye river at a difficult muddy ford near the broken bridge. Sir John Campbell, leading a squadron of the 4th Portuguese cavalry, overthrew the head of his column; but the Portuguese horsemen were too few to dispute the passage, and Berton, finally getting a regiment over higher up, gained the table-land above, and charging the rear of the retiring troops in a narrow way leading to the Aire road, killed several and took some prisoners.

This terminated the French operations for the day, and Lord Wellington, imagining the arrival of Suchet's troops had made Soult thus bold, resolved to keep on the defensive until his reinforcements and detachments could come up. Hill, however, passed the greater Lees partly to support his posts, partly to make out the force and true direction of the French movement; but he re-crossed that river during the night, and finally occupied the strong platform between Aire and Garlin, which Soult had designed to seize. Lord Wellington immediately brought the third and sixth division and the heavy cavalry over the Adour to his support, leaving the light division with the hussar brigade still on the right bank. The bulk of the army thus occupied a strong position parallel with the Pau road. On the morning of the 14th, Soult, intending to fall on Hill, whose columns he had seen the evening before on the right of the Lees, drove in the advanced posts which had been left to cover the retrograde movement, and then examined the allies' new position; but these operations wasted the day, and towards evening he disposed his army on the heights between the two Lees. Meanwhile Pierre Soult carried three regiments of cavalry to Clarac, on the Pau road, to menace the right flank of the allies, against which the whole French army was now pointing. Fane's outposts, being thus assailed, retired with some loss at first; but they were soon supported, and drove the French horsemen in disorder clear off the Pau road to Carere.

Soult now seeing the strength of the position above Aire, and hearing from the peasants that 40,000 or 50,000 men were concentrated there, feared to attack; but changing his plan, resolved to hover about the right flank of the allies in the hopes of enticing them from their vantage-ground. Lord Wellington, on the other hand, drew his cavalry posts down the valley of the Adour, and keeping close on that side, massed his forces on the right in expectation of an attack. In fine, each general, acting upon false intelligence of the other's strength, was afraid to strike. The English commander's error as to the junction of Suchet's troops was encouraged by Soult, who had formed his battalions upon two ranks instead of three to give himself an appearance of strength, and in the same view had caused his reserve of conscripts to move in rear of his line of battle. And he also judged the allies' strength by what it might have been rather than by what it was; for though Freyre's Spaniards and Ponsonby's dragoons were now up, the whole force did not exceed 36,000 men, including the light division and the hussars, who were on the right bank of the Adour. This number was, however, increasing every hour by the arrival of detachments and reserves; and it behoved Soult, who was entangled in a country extremely difficult if rain should fall, to watch that Wellington, while holding the French in check with his right wing, did not strike with his left, and thus cast them upon the mountains about Lourdes.

This danger, and the intelligence now obtained of the fall of Bordeaux, induced the French general to retire before day on the 16th and occupy both sides of the two branches of the Lees and the heights between them; however, his outposts remained at Conchez, and Pierre Soult, again getting upon the Pau road, detached a hundred chosen troopers against the allies' communication with Orthes. Captain Dania, commanding these men, making a forced march, reached Hagetnau at nightfall, surprised six officers and eight medical men with their baggage, and made a number of other prisoners. This enterprise, extended to such a distance from the army, was supposed to be executed by bands of peasants, and seemed to indicate a disposition for insurrection; wherefore Lord Wellington, to check it, seized the civil authorities at Hagetnau, and declared that he would hang all the peasants caught in arms and burn their villages.

The offensive movement of the French general had now terminated. He sent his conscripts at once to Toulouse, and prepared for a rapid retreat on that place. His recent operations had been commenced too late; he should have been on the Lees when there were not more than 20,000 infantry and 2500 cavalry to oppose him. On the other hand, the passive state of Wellington was now also at an end; all his reinforcements and detachments were either up or close at hand, and he could put in motion six Anglo-Portuguese and three Spanish divisions of infantry, numbering 40,000 bayonets, with five brigades of cavalry, furnishing nearly 6000 sabres, and from fifty to sixty pieces of artillery. On the evening of the 17th March the English general pushed the hussars up the valley of the Adour, supporting them with the light division; and on the 18th, at daylight, the whole army was in movement, the hussars with the light and the fourth division forming the left;

VIC BIGORRE.

Hill's troops forming the right, keeping a detachment on the road to Pau in observation of Pierre Soult's cavalry, and the main body moved in the centre under Wellington in person. The French right was thus turned by the valley of the Adour, while General Hill with a sharp skirmish, in which about eighty British and Germans were killed and wounded, drove back their outposts upon Lembege.

Soult retired during the night to a strong ridge having a small river with rugged banks, called the Laiza, in his front, and his right under D'Erlon was extended towards Vic Bigorre on the great road of Tarbes. Meanwhile Berton's cavalry, one regiment of which, retreating from Viella, disengaged itself with some difficulty and loss, reached Maubourget, and took post in column behind that place, the road being confined on each side by deep and wide ditches. Pressed here by Bock's cavalry, which preceded the centre column of the allies, the French horsemen suddenly charged the Germans, at first with success, taking an officer and some men, but finally they were beaten and retreated through Vic Bigorre. Soult, thinking a flanking column only was on this side in the valley of the Adour, resolved to fall upon it with his whole army; but he recognised the skill of his opponent when he found that the whole of the allies' centre had been thrown on to the Tarbes road while he was retiring from Lembege. This heavy mass was now approaching Vic Bigorre; the light division, coming up the right bank of the Ardour, were already near Rabastens, upon which place the hussars had already driven the French cavalry left in observation when the army first advanced. Vic Bigorre was thus turned, Berton's horsemen had passed it in retreat, and the danger was imminent. The French general immediately ordered Berton to support the cavalry regiment at Rabastens and cover that road to Tarbes. Then, directing D'Erlon to take post at Vic Bigorre and check the allies on the main road, he marched, in person and in all haste, to Tarbes by a circuitous road. D'Erlon, not seeming to comprehend the crisis, moved slowly, with his baggage in front, and having the river Lechez to cross, rode on before his troops, expecting to find Berton at Vic Bigorre, but he met the German cavalry there. Then, indeed, he hurried his march, yet he had only time to place Darricau's division, now under General Paris, amongst some vineyards, two miles in front of Vic Bigorre, when Picton came to the support of the cavalry and fell upon him.

Vic Bigorre.

The French left flank was secured by the Lechez river, but their right, extending towards the Ardour, being loose, was menaced by the German cavalry, while the front was attacked by Picton. The action commenced about two o'clock, and General Paris was soon driven back in disorder; but then D'Armagnac's division entered the line, and extending to the Adour, renewed the fight, which lasted until D'Erlon, after losing many men, saw his right turned beyond the Adour by the light division and by the hussars, who were now close to Rabastens, whereupon he likewise fell back behind Vic Bigorre, and took post for the night. The action was vigorous. About 250 Anglo-Portuguese men and officers fell, and amongst them died Colonel Henry Sturgeon.

Soult's march through the deep sandy plains was harassing, and would have been dangerous if Lord Wellington had sent Hill's cavalry, now reinforced by two regiments of heavy dragoons, in pursuit; but the country was unfavourable for quick observation, and the French covered their movements with rear-guards whose real numbers it was difficult to ascertain. One of these bodies was posted on a hill the end of which abutted on the high-road, the slope being clothed with trees and defended by skirmishers. Lord Wellington was desirous to know whether a small or a large force thus barred his way, but all who endeavoured to ascertain the fact were stopped by the fire of the enemy. At last Captain William Light made the trial. He rode forward as if he would force his way through the French skirmishers, but when in the wood dropped his reins and leaned back as if badly wounded; his horse appeared to canter wildly along the front of the enemy's light troops, and they, thinking him mortally hurt, ceased their fire and took no further notice. He thus passed unobserved through the wood to the other side of the hill, where there were no skirmishers, and ascending to the open summit above, put spurs to horse and galloped along the French main line, counting their regiments as he passed. His sudden appearance, his blue undress, his daring confidence, and his speed, made the French doubt if he was an enemy, and a few shots only were discharged, while he, dashing down the opposite declivity, broke from the rear through the very skirmishers whose fire he had first essayed in front. Reaching the spot where Lord Wellington stood, he told him there were but five battalions on the hill.

Soult now felt that a rapid retreat upon Toulouse was inevitable, yet determined to dispute every position which offered the least advantage. His army was on the morning of the 20th again in line of battle on the heights two or three miles behind Tarbes, and he still held Tarbes with Clausel's corps, which was extended on the right towards Trie, as if to retain a power of retreat by that road to Toulouse. The plain of Tarbes, although apparently open, was full of deep ditches, which forbade the action of horsemen, wherefore he sent his brother with five regiments of cavalry to the Trie road, with orders to cover the right flank and observe the route to Auch, for he feared lest Wellington should intercept his retreat by that line. At daybreak the allies again advanced in two columns. The right, under Hill, moved along the highroad. The left, under Wellington in person, was composed of the light division and hussars, Ponsonby's heavy cavalry, the sixth division, and Freyre's Spaniards.

TARBES.

The Adour separated Wellington's columns, but when the left approached Tarbes, the light division and the hussars, bringing up their right shoulders, attacked the centre of Harispe's division, which occupied the heights and commanded the road with two guns. Under cover of this attack General Clinton made a flank movement to his left, and opening a cannonade against Harispe's right, endeavoured to get between that general and Soult's main position. Meanwhile General Hill, moving by the other bank of the Adour, assailed the town and bridge of Tarbes, which was defended by Villatte's division. These operations were designed to envelop and crush Clausel's two divisions, which seemed the more easy because there appeared to be only a fine plain, fit for the action of all the cavalry, between him and Soult. The latter, however, having sent his baggage and encumbrances off during the night, saw the movement without alarm; he was better acquainted with the nature of the plain behind Harispe, and had made roads to enable him to retreat without passing through Tarbes. Nevertheless Clausel was in some danger, for while Hill menaced his left at Tarbes, the light division, supported with cavalry and guns, fell upon his centre, and General Clinton, opening a brisk cannonade, penetrated between Harispe and Pierre Soult, and cut the latter off from the army.

The action was begun about twelve o'clock. Hill's artillery thundered on the right, Clinton's answered it on the left, and Alten threw the light division in mass upon the centre, where Harispe's left brigade, posted on a strong hill, was suddenly assailed by the three rifle battalions. Here the fight was short, yet wonderfully fierce and violent; for the French, probably thinking their opponents to be Portuguese on account of their green dress, charged with great hardiness, and being encountered by men not accustomed to yield, they fought muzzle to muzzle, and it was difficult to judge at first who would win. At last the French gave way, and Harispe's centre being thus suddenly overthrown, he retired rapidly through the fields before Clinton could get into his rear. Meanwhile Hill forced the passage of the Adour at Tarbes, and Villatte also retreated along the high-road under a continued cannonade. The flat country was now covered with confused masses of pursuers and pursued, all moving precipitately with an eager musketry, the French guns also replying as they could to the allies' artillery. The situation of the retreating troops seemed desperate, but, as Soult had foreseen, the deep ditches and enclosures, and the small copses, villages, and farm-houses, prevented the British cavalry from acting; Clausel, therefore, extricating his troops with great ability from their dangerous situation, finally gained the main position, where four fresh divisions were drawn up in order of battle, and immediately opened all their batteries on the allies. The pursuit was thus checked, and before Lord Wellington could make arrangements for a new attack darkness came on, and the army halted. The loss of the French is unknown; that of the allies did not exceed 120, but of that number twelve officers and eighty men were of the rifle battalions. During the night Soult retreated in two columns, one by the main road, the other on the left of it, guided by fires lighted on different hills as points of direction. A forced march of more than thirty miles was made with a view to gain Toulouse in the most rapid manner; for the French general, having now seen nearly all Wellington's infantry and his 5000 horsemen, feared that the allies would suddenly gain the plains and intercept his retreat upon Toulouse, which was his great depôt, the knot of all his future combinations, and the only position where he could hope to make a successful stand with his small army.

The allies, owing to the heavy roads and the encumbrance of a heavy pontoon train, moved very slowly in pursuit, and did not reach the Garonne till the 27th of March, and here they halted on the left bank of the river, in front of Toulouse. From a strategic point of view the passage of the Garonne should have been made below the town, but observing that the south side of the city was the most open to attack, the English general resolved to cast his bridge at Portet, six miles above Toulouse, designing to throw his right wing suddenly into the open country between the Garonne and the canal of Languedoc, while with his centre and left he assailed the suburb of St. Cyprien. With this object, at eight o'clock in the evening of the 27th, some men of one of Hill's brigades were ferried over and the bridge was commenced, the remainder of that general's troops being to pass at midnight. But when the river was measured the width was found too great for the pontoons, and there were no means of substituting trestles, wherefore this plan was abandoned. Had it been executed some considerable advantage would probably have been gained, since it does not appear that Soult knew of the attempt until two days later.

Wellington, thus baffled, tried another scheme; he drove the enemy from the Touch river on the 28th, and collected the infantry of his left and centre about Portet, masking the movement with his cavalry. In the course of the operation a single squadron of the 18th hussars, under Major Hughes, being inconsiderately pushed by Colonel Vivian across the bridge of Touch, suddenly came upon a whole regiment of French cavalry. The rashness of the act, as often happens in war, proved the safety of the British; for the enemy, thinking that a strong support must be at hand, discharged their carbines and retreated at a canter. Hughes followed, the speed of both sides increased, and as the nature of the road did not admit of any egress to the sides, this great body of French horsemen was pushed headlong by a few men under the batteries of St. Cyprien.

During these movements Hill's troops were withdrawn to St. Roques; but in the night of the 30th, a new bridge being laid two miles above the confluence of the Arriege, that general passed the Garonne with two divisions of infantry, Morillo's Spaniards, Gardiner's and Maxwell's artillery, and Fane's cavalry, in all 13,000 sabres and bayonets, eighteen guns, and a rocket brigade. The advanced guard moved with all expedition by the great road, having orders to seize the stone bridge of Cintegabelle, and on the march to secure a ferry-boat known to be at Vinergue. The remainder of the troops followed, the intent being to pass the Arriege river hastily at Cintegabelle, and so come down the right bank to attack Toulouse on the south, while Lord Wellington assailed St. Cyprien. This march was to have been made privily in the night, but the new bridge, though ordered for the evening of the 30th, was not finished until five o'clock in the morning of the 31st. Soult thus got notice of the enterprise in time to observe, from the heights of Old Toulouse, the strength of the column, and to ascertain that the great body of the army still remained in front of St. Cyprien. The marshy nature of the country on the right of the Arriege was known to him, and the suburbs of St. Michel and St. Etienne being now in a state to resist a partial attack, the matter appeared a feint to draw off a part of his army from Toulouse while St. Cyprien was assaulted or the Garonne passed below the city. In this persuasion he kept his infantry in hand, and sent only his cavalry up the right bank of the Arriege to observe the march of the allies; but he directed General Lafitte, who had collected some regular horsemen and the national guards of the department, to hang upon their skirts and pretend to be the van of Suchet's army. He was, however, somewhat disquieted, because the baggage, which, to avoid encumbering the march, had been sent up the Garonne to cross at Carbonne, being seen by his scouts, was reported to be a second column, increasing Hill's force to 18,000 men.

While in this uncertainty he heard of the measurement of the river made at Portet on the night of the 27th, and that many guns were still collected there; wherefore, being ignorant of the cause why the bridge was not thrown, he concluded there was a design to cross there also when Hill should descend the Arriege. To meet this danger he put four divisions under Clausel, with orders to fall upon the head of the allies if they should attempt the passage before Hill came down, resolving in the contrary case to fight in the suburbs of Toulouse and on the Mont Rave, because the positions on the right of the Arriege were all favourable to the assailants. He was, however, soon relieved from anxiety. General Hill effected, indeed, the passage of the Arriege at Cintegabelle, but his artillery were quite unable to move in the deep country there; and as success and safety alike depended on rapidity, he returned during the night and recrossed the Garonne, taking up his pontoons and leaving only a flying bridge, with a small guard of infantry and cavalry on the right bank. His retreat was followed by Lafitte's horsemen, who picked up a few stragglers and mules; but no other event occurred, and Soult remained well pleased that his adversary had thus lost three or four important days.

The French general was now sure the next attempt would be below Toulouse, but having completed his works of defence for the city and the suburbs, and fortified all the bridges over the canal, he concluded not to abandon Toulouse under any circumstances, and therefore set his whole army and all the working population to entrench the Mont Rave, between the canal and the Ers river, thinking he might thus securely meet the shock of battle, let it come on which side it would. Meanwhile the Garonne continued so full and rapid that Lord Wellington was forced to remain inactive before St. Cyprien until the 3rd April; then the waters falling, the pontoons were carried in the night fifteen miles below Toulouse, where the bridge was at last thrown, and thirty guns placed in battery on the left bank to protect it. The third, fourth, and sixth divisions of infantry and three brigades of cavalry, the whole under Beresford, immediately passed, and the cavalry, being pushed out two leagues on the front and flanks, captured a large herd of bullocks destined for the French army. But now the river again swelled so fast that the light division and the Spaniards were unable to follow, the bridge got damaged, and the pontoons were taken up.

This passage was made known to Soult immediately by his

cavalry scouts, yet he knew not the exact force which had crossed, and he imagined that the greatest part of the allied army was still over the Garonne. Wherefore, merely observing Beresford with his cavalry, he continued to strengthen his field of battle about Toulouse, his resolution to keep that city being confirmed by hearing on the 7th that the allied sovereigns had entered Paris.

On the 8th the waters subsided, the allies' bridge was again laid down, Freye's Spaniards and the Portuguese artillery crossed, and Lord Wellington, taking the command in person, advanced to within five miles of Toulouse. Marching up both banks of the Ers, his columns were separated by that river, which was impassable without pontoons, and it was essential to secure as soon as possible one of the stone bridges. Hence Vivian's horsemen drove Berton's cavalry up the right of the Ers towards the bridge of Bordes, and the 18th hussars descended towards that of Croix d'Orade. The latter was defended by Vial's dragoons, and after some skirmishing the hussars were suddenly menaced by a regiment in front of the bridge, the opposite bank of the river being lined with dismounted carbineers. The two parties stood facing each other, hesitating to begin, until the approach of some British infantry, when both sides sounded a charge at the same moment; but the English horsemen were so quick, the French were in an instant jammed up on the bridge, their front ranks were sabred, and the mass, breaking away to the rear, went off in disorder, leaving many killed and wounded, and above a hundred prisoners in the hands of the victors. They were pursued through the village of Croix d'Orade, but beyond it they rallied on the rest of their brigade and advanced again; the hussars then recrossed the bridge, which was now defended by the British infantry, whose fire stopped the French cavalry. The communication between the allied columns was thus secured.

Lord Wellington now carefully examined the French general's position, and resolved to attack on the 9th. Meanwhile, to shorten his communications with General Hill, he directed the pontoons to be removed and relaid higher up. The light division were to cross at daybreak, but the bridge was not relaid until late in the day; and the English general, extremely incensed at the failure, was forced to defer his battle until the 10th.

Soult's combinations were now crowned with success. He had

by means of his fortresses, his battles, the sudden change of his line of operations after Orthes, his rapid retreat from Tarbes, and his clear judgment in fixing upon Toulouse as his next point of resistance, reduced the strength of his adversary to an equality with his own. He had gained seventeen days for preparation, had brought the allies to deliver battle on ground naturally adapted for defence, and well fortified; where one-third of their force was separated by a great river from the rest, where they could derive no advantage from their numerous cavalry, and were overmatched in artillery, notwithstanding their previous superiority in that arm.

His position covered three sides of Toulouse. Defending St. Cyprien on the west with his left, he guarded the canal on the north with his centre, and with his right held the Mont Rave on the east. His reserve manned the ramparts of Toulouse, and the urban guards, while maintaining tranquillity, aided to transport the artillery and ammunition to different posts. Hill was opposed to his left; but while the latter, well fortified at St. Cyprien, had short and direct communication with the centre by the great bridge of Toulouse, the former could only communicate with the main body under Wellington by the pontoon bridge, this being a circuit of ten or twelve miles.

It was not till the 10th of April that the allied army was in a position to commence offensive operations against the city on the south side, where Toulouse was weakest in defence. Wellington, having well observed the ground on the 8th and 9th April, made the following disposition of attack. General Hill was to menace St. Cyprien, augmenting or abating his efforts to draw the enemy's attention according to the progress of the battle on the right of the Garonne, which he could easily discern. The third and light divisions and Freyre's Spaniards, being already on the banks of the river Ers, were to advance against the northern front of Toulouse. The two first, supported by Bock's German cavalry, were to make demonstrations against a line of canal defended by Darricau. That is to say, Picton was to menace the bridge of Jumeaux and the convent of the Minimes, while Alten maintained the communication between him and Freyre, who, reinforced with the Portuguese artillery, was to carry the hill of Pugade and then halt to cover Beresford's column of march. This last, composed of the fourth and sixth divisions with three batteries, was, after passing the bridge of Croix d'Orade, to move round the left of the Pugade and along the low ground between the French heights and the Ers, until the rear should pass the road of Lavaur, when the two divisions were to wheel into line and attack the platform of St. Sypiere. Freyre was then to assail that of Calvinet, and Ponsonby's dragoons, following close, were to connect that general's left with Beresford's column. Meanwhile Lord Edward Somerset's hussars were to move up the left of the Ers, while Vivian's cavalry moved up the right of that river, each destined to observe Berton's cavalry, which, having possession of the bridges of Bordes and Montaudran higher up, could pass from the right bank to the left, and destroying the bridge, fall upon the head of Beresford's troops while in march.

Battle of Toulouse.

The 10th of April, at two o'clock in the morning, the light division passed the Garonne by the bridge at Seilh, and about six o'clock the whole army moved forwards in the order assigned for the different columns. Picton and Alten, on the right, drove the French advanced posts behind the works at the bridge over the canal. Freyre's columns, marching along the Alby road, were cannonaded by St. Pol with two guns until they had passed a small stream by the help of some temporary bridges, when the French general retired to the horn-work on the Calvinet platform. The Spaniards were thus established on the Pugade, from whence the Portuguese guns under Major Arentschild opened a heavy cannonade against Calvinet. Meanwhile Beresford, preceded by the hussars, marched from Croix d'Orade in three columns abreast. Passing behind the Pugade, through the village of Montblanc, he entered the marshy ground between the Ers river and the Mont Rave; but he left his artillery at Montblanc, fearing to engage it in that deep and difficult country under the fire of the enemy. Beyond the Ers, on his left, Vivian's cavalry, now under Colonel Arentschild, drove Berton's horsemen back with loss, and nearly seized the bridge of Bordes, which the French general passed and destroyed with difficulty at the last moment. However, the German hussars succeeded in gaining the bridge of Montaudran higher up, though it was barricaded, and defended by a detachment of cavalry sent there by Berton, who remained himself in position near the bridge of Bordes, looking down the left of the Ers.

While these operations were in progress, General Freyre, who had asked as a favour to lead the battle at Calvinet, whether from error or impatience, assailed the horn-work on that platform about eleven o'clock, and while Beresford was still in march. The Spaniards, 9000 strong, moved in two lines and a reserve, and advanced with great resolution at first, throwing forwards their flanks so as to embrace the end of the Calvinet hill. The French musketry and great guns thinned the ranks at every step, yet closing upon their centre they still ascended the hill, the formidable fire they were exposed to increasing in violence until their right wing, which was also raked from the bridge of Matabiau, unable to endure the torment, wavered. The leading ranks, rushing madly onwards, jumped for shelter into a hollow road, twenty-five feet deep in parts, and covering this part of the French entrenchment; but the left wing and the second line ran back in great disorder, the Cantabrian fusiliers under Colonel Leon de Sicilia alone maintaining their ground under cover of a bank which protected them. Then the French came leaping out of their works with loud cries, and lining the edge of the hollow road, poured an incessant stream of shot upon the helpless crowds entangled in the gulf below, while the battery from the bridge of Matabiau, constructed to rake this opening, sent its bullets from flank to flank hissing through the quivering mass of flesh and bones.

The Spanish generals, rallying the troops who had fled, led them back again to the brink of the fatal hollow, but the frightful carnage below and the unmitigated fire in front filled them with horror. Again they fled, and again the French, bounding from their trenches, pursued, while several battalions sallying from the bridge of Matabiau and from behind the Calvinet followed hard after. The country was now covered with fugitives whose headlong flight could not be restrained, and with pursuers whose numbers and vehemence increased, until Lord Wellington, who was at that point, covered the panic-stricken troops with Ponsonby's cavalry and the reserve artillery, which opened with great vigour. Meanwhile the Portuguese guns on the Pugade never ceased firing, and a brigade of the light division, wheeling to its left, menaced the flank of the victorious French, who immediately retired to their entrenchments on Calvinet; but more than 1500 Spaniards had been killed or wounded, and their defeat was not the only misfortune.

General Picton, regardless of his orders, which, his temper on such occasions being known, were especially given, had turned his false attack into a real one against the bridge of Jumeaux, and the enemy, fighting from a work too high to be forced without ladders and approachable only along an open flat, repulsed him with a loss of nearly 400 men and officers: amongst the latter, Colonel Forbes of the 45th was killed, and General Brisbane, who commanded the brigade, was wounded. Thus from the hill of Pugade to the Garonne the French had completely vindicated their position, the allies had suffered enormously, and beyond the Garonne, although General Hill had now forced the first line of entrenchments covering St. Cyprien, and was menacing the second line, the latter, being much more contracted and very strongly fortified, could not be stormed. The musketry battle, therefore, subsided for a time, but a prodigious cannonade was kept up along the whole of the French line, and on the allies' side from St. Cyprien to Montblanc, where the artillery left by Beresford, acting in conjunction with the Portuguese guns on the Pugade, poured its shot incessantly against the works on the Calvinet platform.

It was now evident that the victory must be won or lost by Beresford, and yet, from Picton's error, Lord Wellington had no reserves to enforce the decision; for the light division and the heavy cavalry only remained in hand, and these troops were necessarily retained to cover the rallying of the Spaniards, and to protect the artillery employed to keep the enemy in check. The crisis, therefore, approached with all happy promise to the French general. The repulse of Picton, the utter dispersion of the Spaniards, and the strength of the second line of entrenchments at St. Cyprien enabled him to draw, first Taupin's whole division, and then one of Maransin's brigades from that quarter, to reinforce his battle on the Mont Rave. Thus three divisions and his cavalry, nearly 15,000 combatants, were disposable for an offensive movement without in any manner weakening the defence of his works on Mont Rave or on the canal. With this mass he might have fallen upon Beresford, whose force, originally less than 13,000 bayonets, was cruelly reduced as it made slow and difficult way for two miles through a deep marshy country crossed and tangled with water-courses; for, sometimes moving in mass, sometimes filing under the French musketry, and always under the fire of their artillery from the Mont Rave, without a gun to reply, the length of the column had augmented so much at every step from the difficulty of the way that frequent halts were necessary to close up the ranks.

The flat miry ground between the river and the heights became narrower and deeper as the troops advanced, Berton's cavalry was ahead, an impassable river was on the left, and three French divisions supported by artillery and horsemen overshadowed the right flank. Fortune came to their aid. Soult, always eyeing their march, had, when the Spaniards were defeated, carried Taupin's division to the platform of St. Sypiere, and supporting it with a brigade of D'Armagnac's division, disposed the whole about the redoubts. From thence, after a short exhortation to act vigorously, he ordered Taupin to fall on with the utmost fury, at the same time directing a regiment of Vial's cavalry to descend the heights and intercept the line of retreat, while Berton's horsemen assailed the other flank from the side of the bridge of Bordes. But this was not half of the force which the French general might have employed. Taupin's artillery, retarded in its march, was still in the streets of Toulouse, and that general, instead of attacking at once, took ground to his right, waiting until Beresford, having completed his flank march, had wheeled into lines at the foot of the heights.

Taupin's infantry, unskilfully arranged for action, at last poured down the hill, but some rockets discharged in good time ravaged the ranks, and with their noise and terrible appearance, unknown before, dismayed the French soldiers; then the British skirmishers running forwards plied them with a biting fire, and Lambert's brigade of the sixth division, aided by Anson's brigade and some provisional battalions of the fourth division, rushed forwards with a terrible shout, and the French turning, fled back to the upper ground. Vial's horsemen now charged on the right flank, but the second and third lines of the sixth division, being thrown into squares, repulsed them; and on the other flank General Cole had been so sudden in his advance up the heights that Berton's cavalry had no opportunity to charge. Lambert, following hard upon the beaten infantry in his front, killed Taupin, wounded a general of brigade, and without a check won the summit of the platform; his skirmishers even descended in pursuit on the reverse slope; and meanwhile, on his left, General Cole, meeting with less resistance, had still more rapidly gained the height at that side—so complete was the rout that the two redoubts were abandoned from panic, and the French, with the utmost disorder, sought shelter in the works of Sacarin and Cambon.

Soult, astonished at this weakness in troops from whom he had expected so much, and who had but just before given him assurances of their resolution and confidence, was in fear that Beresford, pushing his success, would seize the bridge of the Demoiselles on the canal. Wherefore, covering the flight as he could with the remainder of Vial's cavalry, he hastily led D'Armagnac's reserve brigade to the works of Sacarin, checked the foremost British skirmishers, and rallied the fugitives; Taupin's guns arrived from the town at the same moment, and the mischief being stayed, a part of the reserve immediately moved to defend the bridge of the Demoiselles. A fresh order of battle was thus organised, but the indomitable courage of the British soldiers, overcoming all obstacles and all opposition, had decided the first great crisis of the fight.

Lambert's brigade immediately wheeled to its right, menacing the flank of the French on the Calvinet platform, while Pack's Scotch brigade and Douglas's Portuguese were disposed on the right with a view to march against the Colombette redoubts on the original front of the enemy. Now also the 18th and German hussars, having forced the bridge of Montaudran on the Ers river, came round the south end of the Mont Rave, where, in conjunction with the skirmishers of the fourth division, they menaced the bridge of the Demoiselles, from whence and from the works of Cambon and Sacarin the enemy's guns played incessantly.

The aspect and form of the battle were thus entirely changed. The French, thrown entirely on the defensive, occupied three sides of a square. Their right, extending from the works of Sacarin to the redoubts of Calvinet and Colombette, was closely menaced by Lambert, who was solidly posted on the platform of St. Sypiere, while the redoubts themselves were menaced by Pack and Douglas. The French left, thrown back to the bridge-head of Matabiau, awaited the renewed attack of the Spaniards, and the whole position was very strong, not exceeding a thousand yards on each side, with the angles all defended by formidable works. The canal and city of Toulouse, its walls and entrenched suburbs, offered a sure refuge in case of disaster, while the Matabiau on one side, Sacarin and Cambon on the other, ensured the power of retreat. In this contracted space were concentrated Vial's cavalry, the whole of Villatte's division, one brigade of Maransin's, another of D'Armagnac's, and with the exception of the regiment driven from the St. Sypiere redoubt, the whole of Harispe's division. On the allies' side, therefore, defeat had been staved off, but victory was still to be contended for, and with apparently inadequate means; for Picton, being successfully opposed, was so far paralysed; the Spaniards, rallying slowly, were not to be depended upon for another attack; and there remained only the heavy cavalry and the light division, which Lord Wellington could not venture to thrust into the action under pain of being left without any reserve in the event of a repulse. The final stroke, therefore, was still to be made on the left, and with a very small force, seeing that Lambert's brigade and the fourth division were necessarily employed to keep in check the French troops at the bridge of the Demoiselles, Cambon, and Sacarin. This heavy mass was commanded by General Clausel, who disposed the greater part in advance of the entrenchments, as if to retake the offensive.

Such was the state of affairs about half-past two o'clock, when Beresford renewed the action with Pack's Scotch brigade and the Portuguese under Colonel Douglas. These troops, ensconced in the hollow road on Lambert's right, had been hitherto well protected from the fire of the French works, but now, scrambling up the steep banks of that road, they wheeled to their left by wings of regiments as they could get out, and ascending the heights by the slope facing the Ers, under a wasting fire of cannon and musketry, carried all the French breastworks, and the Colombette and Calvinet redoubts. It was a surprising action, when the loose, disorderly nature of the attack imposed by the difficulty of the ground is considered; but the French, although they yielded at first to the thronging rush of the British troops, soon rallied and came back with a reflux. Their cannonade was incessant, their reserves strong, and the struggle became terrible; for Harispe, who commanded in person at this part, and under whom the French seemed always to fight with redoubled vigour, brought up fresh men, and surrounded the two redoubts with a surging multitude, absolutely broke into the Colombette, killed or wounded four-fifths of the 42nd, and drove the rest out. The British troops were, however, supported by the 71st and 91st, and the whole, clinging to the brow of the hill, fought with a wonderful courage and firmness, until so many men had fallen that their order of battle was reduced to a thin line of skirmishers. Some of the British cavalry then rode up from the low ground and attempted a charge, but they were stopped by a deep hollow road, of which there were many, and some of the foremost troopers tumbling headlong in, perished. Meanwhile the combat about the redoubt continued fiercely. The French, from their numbers, had certainly the advantage, but they never retook the Calvinet fort, nor could they force their opponents down from the brow of the hill. At last, when the whole of the sixth division had rallied, and again assailed them, flank and front, when their generals, Harispe and Baurot, had fallen dangerously wounded, and the Colombette was retaken by the 79th, the battle turned, and the French finally abandoned the platform.

It was now about four o'clock. The Spaniards, during this contest, had once more partially attacked, but they were again put to flight, and the French thus remained masters of their entrenchments in that quarter; for the sixth division had been very hardly handled, and Beresford halted to re-form his order of battle and receive his artillery. It came to him, indeed, about this time, yet with great difficulty, and with little ammunition, in consequence of the heavy cannonade it had previously furnished from Montblanc. However, Soult, seeing that the Spaniards, supported by the light division, had rallied a fourth time, that Picton again menaced the bridge of Jumeaux and the Minime convent, while Beresford, master of three-fourths of Mont Rave, was now advancing along the summit, deemed further resistance useless, and relinquished the northern end of the Calvinet platform also. About five o'clock he withdrew his whole army behind the canal, still, however, holding the advanced works of Sacarin and Cambon. Lord Wellington then established the Spaniards in the abandoned works, and so became master of the Mont Rave in all its extent. Thus terminated the battle of Toulouse. The French had five generals and perhaps 3000 men killed or wounded, and they lost one piece of artillery. The allies lost four generals and 4659 men and officers, of which 2000 were Spaniards. A lamentable and useless spilling of blood, for before this period Napoleon had abdicated the throne of France, and a provisional government was constituted at Paris.

During the night the French general, defeated but undismayed, replaced the ammunition expended in the action, reorganised and augmented his field artillery from the arsenal of Toulouse, and made dispositions for fighting the next morning behind the canal. Yet, looking to the final necessity of a retreat, he wrote to Suchet to inform him of the result of the contest, and proposed a combined plan of operations illustrative of the firmness and pertinacity of his temper.

On the morning of the 11th April he was again ready to fight, but the English general was not. The French position, within musket-shot of the walls of Toulouse, was still inexpugnable on the northern and eastern fronts. The possession of Mont Rave was only a preliminary step to the passage of the canal at the bridge of the Demoiselles and other points above the works of Sacarin and Cambon, with the view of throwing the army, as originally designed, on to the south side of the town. But this was a great affair, requiring fresh dispositions and a fresh provision of ammunition, only to be obtained from the park on the other side of the Garonne. Hence to accelerate the preparations, to ascertain the state of General Hill's position, and to give that general further instructions, Lord Wellington repaired on the 11th to St. Cyprien; but the day was spent before the ammunition arrived and the final arrangements for the passage of the canal could be completed. The attack was therefore deferred until daylight on the 12th.

Meanwhile all the light cavalry were sent up the canal, to interrupt the communications with Suchet and menace Soult's retreat. The appearance of these horsemen, together with the preparations in his front, taught Soult that he could no longer delay if he would not be shut up in Toulouse. Wherefore, having terminated all his arrangements, he left eight pieces of heavy artillery, two generals, the gallant Harispe being one, and 1600 men, whose wounds were severe, to the humanity of the conquerors; then filing out of the city with surprising order and ability, he made a forced march of twenty-two miles, cut the bridges over the canal and the Upper Ers, and on the 12th established his army at Villefranche. On the same day General Hill's troops were pushed close in pursuit, and the light cavalry beat the French with the loss of twenty-five men, and cut off a like number of gens-d'armes on the side of Revel.

Lord Wellington now entered Toulouse in triumph. The white flag was displayed, and, as at Bordeaux, a great crowd of persons adopted the Bourbon colours; but the mayor, faithful to his sovereign, had retired with the French army. The British general, true to his line of policy, did not fail to warn the Bourbonists that their revolutionary movement must be at their own risk; but in the afternoon two officers, the English colonel, Cooke, and the French colonel, St. Simon, arrived from Paris. Charged to make known to the armies the abdication of Napoleon, they had been detained near Blois by the officiousness of the police attending the court of the Empress Louisa, and the blood of 8000 brave men had been shed on Mont Rave in consequence. Nor did their arrival immediately put a stop to the war. When St. Simon, in pursuance of his mission, reached Soult's quarters, that marshal, not without just cause, demurred to his authority, and proposed to suspend hostilities until authentic information could be obtained from the ministers of the emperor. Lord Wellington refused to accede to his proposal, and as General Loverdo, commanding at Montauban, acknowledged the authority of the provisional government and readily concluded an armistice, he judged that Soult designed to make a civil war, and therefore marched against him. On the 17th the outposts were on the point of engaging, when the Duke of Dalmatia, who had now received official information from the chief of the emperor's staff, notified his adhesion to the new state of affairs in France; with this honourable distinction, that he had faithfully sustained the cause of his monarch until the very last moment.

A convention, which included Suchet's army, was immediately agreed upon; but that marshal had previously adopted the white colours of his own motion, and Lord Wellington instantly transmitted the intelligence to General Clinton in Catalonia, and to the troops at Bayonne. Too late it came for both, and useless battles were fought. At Bayonne misfortune and suffering had fallen upon one of the brightest soldiers of the British army.

Sally from Bayonne.

During the progress of the main army in the interior, Sir John Hope conducted the investment of Bayonne with all the zeal, the intelligence, and unremitting vigilance and activity which the difficult nature of the operation required. He had gathered great stores of gabions and fascines and platforms, and was ready to attack the citadel, when rumours of the events at Paris reached him, yet indirectly, and without any official character to warrant a formal communication to the garrison without Lord Wellington's authority. These rumours were, however, made known at the outposts, and perhaps lulled the vigilance of the besiegers; but to such irregular communications, which might be intended to deceive, the governor naturally paid little attention.

The picquets and fortified posts at St. Etienne were at this time furnished by a brigade of the fifth division; but from thence to the extreme right the guards had charge of the line, and they had also one company in St. Etienne itself. General Hinuber's German brigade was encamped as a support to the left; the remainder of the first division was encamped in the rear. In this state, about one o'clock in the morning of the 14th, a deserter, coming over to General Hay, who commanded the outposts that night, gave an exact account of a projected sally. The general, not able to speak French, sent him to General Hinuber, who, immediately interpreting the man's story to General Hay, assembled his own troops under arms and transmitted the intelligence to Sir John Hope. It would appear that Hay, perhaps disbelieving the man's story, took no additional precautions; and it is probable that neither the German brigade nor the reserves of the guards would have been put under arms but for the activity of General Hinuber. However, at three o'clock, the French, commencing with a false attack on the left of the Adour as a blind, poured suddenly out of the citadel to the number of 3000 combatants. They surprised the picquets, and with loud shouts breaking through the chain of posts at various points, carried with one rush the whole of the village of St. Etienne, with the exception of a fortified house, which was defended by Captain Forster of the 38th regiment. Masters of every other part, and overthrowing all who stood before them, they drove the picquets and supports in heaps along the Peyrehorade road, killed General Hay, took Colonel Townsend of the guards prisoner, divided the wings of the investing troops, and, passing in rear of the right, threw the whole line into confusion. Then it was that Hinuber, having his Germans well in hand, moved up on the side of St. Etienne, rallied some of the fifth division, and being joined by a battalion of General Bradford's Portuguese, bravely gave the counter-stroke to the enemy, and regained the village.

The combat on the right was, at first, even more disastrous than in the centre; neither the picquets nor the reserves were able to sustain the fury of the assault, and the battle was most confused and terrible; for on both sides the troops, broken into small bodies by the enclosures and unable to recover their order, came dashing together in the darkness, fighting often with the bayonet, and sometimes friends encountered, sometimes foes—all was tumult and horror. The guns of the citadel, vaguely guided by the flashes of the musketry, sent their shot and shells, booming at random, through the lines of fight; and the gunboats, dropping down the river, opened their fire upon the flank of the supporting columns, which, being put in motion by Sir John Hope on the first alarm, were now coming up. Thus nearly a hundred pieces of artillery were in full play at once; and the shells having set fire to the fascine-depôts and to several houses, the flames cast a horrid glare over the striving masses.

Amidst this confusion Sir John Hope suddenly disappeared, none knew how, or wherefore, at the time; but it afterwards appeared that, having brought up the reserves on the right to stem the torrent in that quarter, he pushed for St. Etienne by a hollow road which led close behind the line of picquets. The French had, however, lined both banks, and when he endeavoured to return, a shot struck him in the arm, while his horse—a large one, as was necessary to sustain the gigantic warrior—received eight bullets and fell upon his leg. His followers had by this time escaped from the defile; but two of them, Captain Herries and Mr. Moore, a nephew of Sir John Moore, seeing his helpless state, turned back, and alighting, endeavoured amidst the heavy fire of the enemy to draw him from beneath the horse. While thus engaged they were both struck down with dangerous wounds; the French carried them all off, and Sir John Hope was again severely hurt in the foot by an English bullet before they gained the citadel.

The day was now beginning to break, and the allies were enabled to act with more unity and effect. The Germans were in possession of St. Etienne; and the reserve brigades of the guards, being properly disposed by General Howard, who had succeeded to the command, suddenly raised a loud shout, and running in upon the French, drove them back into the works with such slaughter, that their own writers admit a loss of one general and more than 900 men. But on the British side General Stopford was wounded, and the whole loss was 830 men and officers. Of these more than 200 were taken, besides the commander-in-chief; and it is generally acknowledged that Captain Forster's firm defence of the fortified house first, and next the readiness and gallantry with which General Hinuber and his Germans retook St. Etienne, saved the allies from a very terrible disaster.

A few days after this piteous event the convention made with Soult became known, and hostilities ceased.

All the French troops in the south were now reorganised in one body under the command of Suchet; but they were so little inclined to acquiesce in the revolution, that Prince Polignac, acting for the Duke of Angoulême, applied to the British commissary-general, Kennedy, for a sum of money to quiet them.

The Portuguese army returned to Portugal, the Spanish army to Spain; the generals being, it is said, inclined at first to declare for the Cortes against the king, but they were diverted from their purpose by the influence and authority of Lord Wellington.

The British infantry embarked at Bordeaux, some for America, some for England, and the cavalry, marching through France, took shipping at Boulogne.

Thus the war terminated, and with it all remembrance of the veteran's services.

Fortune always asserts her supremacy in war, and often from a slight mistake such disastrous consequences flow, that in every age and every nation the uncertainty of arms has been proverbial. Napoleon's march upon Madrid in 1808, before he knew the exact situation of the British army, is an example. By that march he lent his flank to his enemy. Sir John Moore seized the advantage, and though the French emperor repaired the error for the moment by his astonishing march from Madrid to Astorga, the fate of the Peninsula was then decided. If he had not been forced to turn against Moore, Lisbon would have fallen, Portugal could not have been organised for resistance, and the jealousy of the Spaniards would never have suffered Wellington to establish a solid base at Cadiz: that general's after successes would then have been with the things that are unborn. It was not so ordained. Wellington was victorious; the great conqueror was overthrown. England stood the most triumphant nation of the world. She rejoices in the glory of her arms! And it is a stirring sound! War is the condition of this world. From man to the smallest insect, all are at strife, and the glory of arms, which cannot be obtained without the exercise of honour, fortitude, courage, obedience, modesty, and temperance, excites the brave man's patriotism, and is a chastening corrective for the rich man's pride. It is yet no security for power. Napoleon, the greatest man of whom history makes mention; Napoleon, the most wonderful commander, the most sagacious politician, the most profound statesman, lost by arms Poland, Germany, Italy, Portugal, Spain, and France. Fortune, that name for the unknown combinations of infinite power, was wanting to him, and without her aid the designs of man are as bubbles on a troubled ocean.

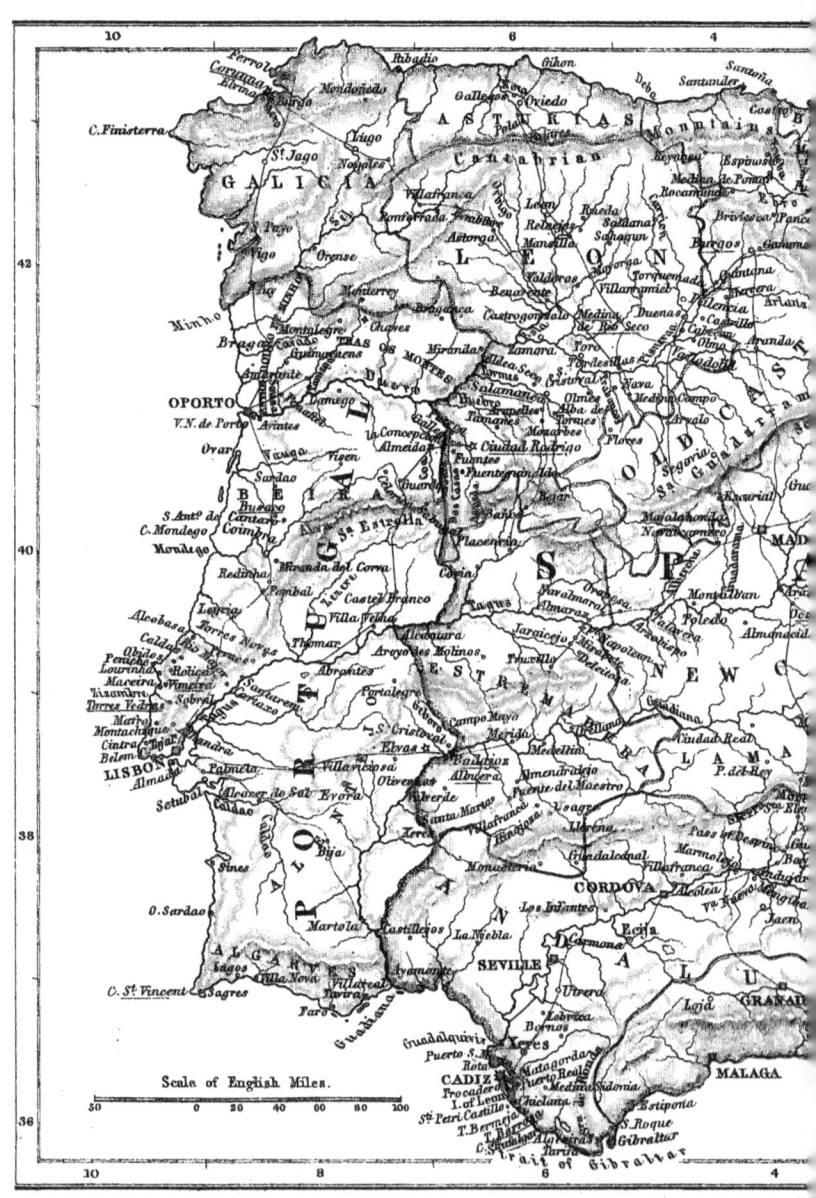

www.ingramcontent.com/pod-product-compliance
Lightning Source LLC
Chambersburg PA
CBHW020742100426
42735CB00037B/174